MW01145526

Llewellyn's 1996

Moon Sign Book

& Lunar Planting Guide

Copyright © 1995 Llewellyn Publications
All rights reserved
Printed in the United States of America
Typography property of Llewellyn Worldwide, Ltd.
ISBN 1-56718-912-1
Editor/Designer: Cynthia Ahlquist
Cover Design: Tom Grewe
Lunar Forecasts: Gloria Star
Special thanks to Leslie Nielsen for astrological proofreading.

LLEWELLYN PUBLICATIONS
P.O. Box 64383-912
St. Paul, MN 55164-0383 U.S.A.

1995

JANUARY
S	M	T	W	T	F	S
1	2	3	4	5	6	7
8	9	10	11	12	13	14
15	16	17	18	19	20	21
22	23	24	25	26	27	28
29	30	31				

FEBRUARY
S	M	T	W	T	F	S
			1	2	3	4
5	6	7	8	9	10	11
12	13	14	15	16	17	18
19	20	21	22	23	24	25
26	27	28				

MARCH
S	M	T	W	T	F	S
			1	2	3	4
5	6	7	8	9	10	11
12	13	14	15	16	17	18
19	20	21	22	23	24	25
26	27	28	29	30	31	

APRIL
S	M	T	W	T	F	S
						1
2	3	4	5	6	7	8
9	10	11	12	13	14	15
16	17	18	19	20	21	22
23	24	25	26	27	28	29
30						

MAY
S	M	T	W	T	F	S
	1	2	3	4	5	6
7	8	9	10	11	12	13
14	15	16	17	18	19	20
21	22	23	24	25	26	27
28	29	30	31			

JUNE
S	M	T	W	T	F	S
				1	2	3
4	5	6	7	8	9	10
11	12	13	14	15	16	17
18	19	20	21	22	23	24
25	26	27	28	29	30	

JULY
S	M	T	W	T	F	S
						1
2	3	4	5	6	7	8
9	10	11	12	13	14	15
16	17	18	19	20	21	22
23	24	25	26	27	28	29
30	31					

AUGUST
S	M	T	W	T	F	S
		1	2	3	4	5
6	7	8	9	10	11	12
13	14	15	16	17	18	19
20	21	22	23	24	25	26
27	28	29	30	31		

SEPTEMBER
S	M	T	W	T	F	S
					1	2
3	4	5	6	7	8	9
10	11	12	13	14	15	16
17	18	19	20	21	22	23
24	25	26	27	28	29	30

OCTOBER
S	M	T	W	T	F	S
1	2	3	4	5	6	7
8	9	10	11	12	13	14
15	16	17	18	19	20	21
22	23	24	25	26	27	28
29	30	31				

NOVEMBER
S	M	T	W	T	F	S
			1	2	3	4
5	6	7	8	9	10	11
12	13	14	15	16	17	18
19	20	21	22	23	24	25
26	27	28	29	30		

DECEMBER
S	M	T	W	T	F	S
					1	2
3	4	5	6	7	8	9
10	11	12	13	14	15	16
17	18	19	20	21	22	23
24	25	26	27	28	29	30
31						

1996

JANUARY
S	M	T	W	T	F	S
	1	2	3	4	5	6
7	8	9	10	11	12	13
14	15	16	17	18	19	20
21	22	23	24	25	26	27
28	29	30	31			

FEBRUARY
S	M	T	W	T	F	S
				1	2	3
4	5	6	7	8	9	10
11	12	13	14	15	16	17
18	19	20	21	22	23	24
25	26	27	28	29		

MARCH
S	M	T	W	T	F	S
					1	2
3	4	5	6	7	8	9
10	11	12	13	14	15	16
17	18	19	20	21	22	23
24	25	26	27	28	29	30
31						

APRIL
S	M	T	W	T	F	S
	1	2	3	4	5	6
7	8	9	10	11	12	13
14	15	16	17	18	19	20
21	22	23	24	25	26	27
28	29	30				

MAY
S	M	T	W	T	F	S
			1	2	3	4
5	6	7	8	9	10	11
12	13	14	15	16	17	18
19	20	21	22	23	24	25
26	27	28	29	30	31	

JUNE
S	M	T	W	T	F	S
						1
2	3	4	5	6	7	8
9	10	11	12	13	14	15
16	17	18	19	20	21	22
23	24	25	26	27	28	29
30						

JULY
S	M	T	W	T	F	S
	1	2	3	4	5	6
7	8	9	10	11	12	13
14	15	16	17	18	19	20
21	22	23	24	25	26	27
28	29	30	31			

AUGUST
S	M	T	W	T	F	S
				1	2	3
4	5	6	7	8	9	10
11	12	13	14	15	16	17
18	19	20	21	22	23	24
25	26	27	28	29	30	31

SEPTEMBER
S	M	T	W	T	F	S
1	2	3	4	5	6	7
8	9	10	11	12	13	14
15	16	17	18	19	20	21
22	23	24	25	26	27	28
29	30					

OCTOBER
S	M	T	W	T	F	S
		1	2	3	4	5
6	7	8	9	10	11	12
13	14	15	16	17	18	19
20	21	22	23	24	25	26
27	28	29	30	31		

NOVEMBER
S	M	T	W	T	F	S
					1	2
3	4	5	6	7	8	9
10	11	12	13	14	15	16
17	18	19	20	21	22	23
24	25	26	27	28	29	30

DECEMBER
S	M	T	W	T	F	S
1	2	3	4	5	6	7
8	9	10	11	12	13	14
15	16	17	18	19	20	21
22	23	24	25	26	27	28
29	30	31				

1997

JANUARY
S	M	T	W	T	F	S
			1	2	3	4
5	6	7	8	9	10	11
12	13	14	15	16	17	18
19	20	21	22	23	24	25
26	27	28	29	30	31	

FEBRUARY
S	M	T	W	T	F	S
						1
2	3	4	5	6	7	8
9	10	11	12	13	14	15
16	17	18	19	20	21	22
23	24	25	26	27	28	

MARCH
S	M	T	W	T	F	S
						1
2	3	4	5	6	7	8
9	10	11	12	13	14	15
16	17	18	19	20	21	22
23	24	25	26	27	28	29
30	31					

APRIL
S	M	T	W	T	F	S
		1	2	3	4	5
6	7	8	9	10	11	12
13	14	15	16	17	18	19
20	21	22	23	24	25	26
27	28	29	30			

MAY
S	M	T	W	T	F	S
				1	2	3
4	5	6	7	8	9	10
11	12	13	14	15	16	17
18	19	20	21	22	23	24
25	26	27	28	29	30	31

JUNE
S	M	T	W	T	F	S
1	2	3	4	5	6	7
8	9	10	11	12	13	14
15	16	17	18	19	20	21
22	23	24	25	26	27	28
29	30					

JULY
S	M	T	W	T	F	S
		1	2	3	4	5
6	7	8	9	10	11	12
13	14	15	16	17	18	19
20	21	22	23	24	25	26
27	28	29	30	31		

AUGUST
S	M	T	W	T	F	S
					1	2
3	4	5	6	7	8	9
10	11	12	13	14	15	16
17	18	19	20	21	22	23
24	25	26	27	28	29	30
31						

SEPTEMBER
S	M	T	W	T	F	S
	1	2	3	4	5	6
7	8	9	10	11	12	13
14	15	16	17	18	19	20
21	22	23	24	25	26	27
28	29	30				

OCTOBER
S	M	T	W	T	F	S
			1	2	3	4
5	6	7	8	9	10	11
12	13	14	15	16	17	18
19	20	21	22	23	24	25
26	27	28	29	30	31	

NOVEMBER
S	M	T	W	T	F	S
						1
2	3	4	5	6	7	8
9	10	11	12	13	14	15
16	17	18	19	20	21	22
23	24	25	26	27	28	29
30						

DECEMBER
S	M	T	W	T	F	S
	1	2	3	4	5	6
7	8	9	10	11	12	13
14	15	16	17	18	19	20
21	22	23	24	25	26	27
28	29	30	31			

Table of Contents

From the Editor

Welcome to the 1996 *Moon Sign Book*! The *Moon Sign Book* has gone through several big changes over the last year and I am proud to introduce the new *Moon Sign Book* to you.

As soon as the 1995 *Moon Sign Book* was finished and out the door, we began to discuss the 1996 edition. We agreed that it was time for some changes.

For inspiration, we pulled out all of the old records detailing the history of this book and its various transformations. We discovered letters from readers asking for a thinner book for easier reading, information on how individuals' Moon signs affect their personalities and their relationships, lunar data in table format, a more almanac-like look for the book (instead of a thick mass market paperback), and information on the activities ruled by the Moon and the best ways to accomplish these tasks. With these letters in mind, we decided to re-focus the articles on the Moon, make the design of the pages more "friendly," include new lunar-based horoscopes by Gloria Star, and update our lunar data with the newest technology.

Each of the articles in this year's edition details some activity or theme directly related to the influence of the lunar sphere. You will find such topics as the Moon and office relationships, the Moon and our moods, the Moon and biorhythms, the Moon and crime, and some great recipes for lunar vegetable wines and mushroom dishes—using fungi collected during the Full Moon, of course!

You will also find that the book design has moved toward a more whimsical, old-fashioned almanac, with larger, two-column pages and 19th century illustrations. We have also formatted all of the lunar dates in tables for easier reading. In so doing, we have been able to reduce the thickness of the book—thus making it easier to hold, open, and read—without losing any valuable information.

The horoscope section of the *Moon Sign Book* has also had an overhaul this year. Gloria Star has written Moon Sign horoscopes for 1996 to replace the Sun Sign horoscopes printed in previous editions. These insightful and inspiring horoscopes will tell you what role your Moon Sign will play in your life in the coming year. Gloria has also included a brief explanation detailing how the Moon Sign works in the horoscope, and what parts of your life it rules. If you are not sure what your Moon Sign is, please see the Mystic Moon section of this book for more information.

One of the most exciting changes that has happened this year is that we have taken advantage of new studies and updated information to refine the process for determining dates for the Moon Tables, Lunar Aspectarian, Astro-Almanac, gardening dates, egg setting dates, and fishing and hunting dates. We have done this to provide you with listings of the best days possible for all of your lunar activities.

As in the past three years, early in our production process for 1996 we received raw astrological data from Matrix Software. This data includes the daily aspects which we list in our *Daily Planetary Guide*, as well as ephemeris information. (For more information on Matrix Software and their many astrological products, please see the advertisement in the back of this book.) We then put the raw data through our own computer system, which determines which dates are best for which activity.

The difference between this year's data and that of years past is

that for 1996, Leslie Nielsen, our freelance astrological consultant, has taken the original *Moon Sign Book* date-determining criteria that we feed into our computer system and updated it. To do this she has used information she has gleaned from her years as an astrologer and gardener, in combination with data from *The Rulership Book* by Rex Bills, which is a trusted classic in the astrological field. Leslie has also used work by several other prominent astrologers, including E. Adams, E. Benjamine, F. Brunhubner, Dr. G. Carey, C. E. O. Carter, Dr. H. Cornell, H. Daath, R. Davidson, R. DeLuce, N. DeVore, D. Doane, R. Ebertin, L. George, J. Goodavage, P. Grell, M. P. Hall, H. Heindel, H. Hone, I. Goldstein-Jacobson, E. Johndro, M. E. Jones, D. Lee, A. Leo, C. Luntz, E. Lyndoe, M. MacNiece, J. Mayo, S. Omarr, A. Pearce, Raphael, Dr. W. Tucker, F. VanNorstrand, M. Weymuss, E. Whitman, J. Wilson and C. Zain. I think you will find that our refined program will give you the best dates possible for all of your Moon-centered activities.

I hope you enjoy your *1996 Moon Sign Book*. We welcome your comments and questions by mail at Llewellyn Publications, P.O. Box 64383-912, St. Paul, MN 55164-0383. May the Moon shine brightly upon you during 1996!

—Cynthia Ahlquist, Editor

How To Use This Book

We get a number of letters and phone calls every year from readers asking the same types of questions. Most of these have to do with how to find certain information in the *Moon Sign Book* and how to use this information.

The best advice we can give is to read the entire introduction, in particular the section on how to use the tables. We provide examples, using the current Moon and Aspect Tables, so that you can follow along and easily figure out the best dates for all of your important activities.

Working With The Moon

When working with the Moon's energies we consider two things—the inception, or beginning of an activity, and the desired outcome. We begin a project under a certain Moon sign and phase in order to achieve certain results. The results are influenced by the attributes of the sign and phase under which we started the project.

For example, a tomato plant which was planted in the fertile sign of Cancer during the first quarter of the Moon should have large fruits because of the increasing nature of the first quarter and the fertility of Cancer and its association with plants that produce their fruit above the ground. (Cancer is ruled by the Moon, which in turn rules round, water-filled objects such as fruit.) If the same tomato plant was planted under the sign of Scorpio in the first quarter, it would still have the increasing qualities of the first quarter and the benefits of being planted under a fertile water sign. However, more of the plant's energy could be channeled into the vines rather than the fruit, because Scorpio rules vines.

Please bear this important note in mind as you use the new lunar dates: **not everyone will have the same goal for each activity that they start.** Therefore, not everyone will want to start every activity at the same time. For example, let's say you decide to plant a flower garden. Which attributes would you like most in your flowers? Beauty? Then you may want to plant in Libra, because Libra is ruled by Venus, which in turn governs appearance. How about planting for quantity or abundance? Then you might try Cancer or Pisces, the two most fertile signs. What if you were going to be transporting the flowers somewhere, either in pots or as cut blooms? Then you might want to try Scorpio for sturdiness, or Taurus for hardiness.

For the reasons listed above, we encourage you not only to use the lunar dates that we provide, but to examine the chapter sections which describe *why* we choose those dates. You may have a different reason for starting an activity than the one for which we chose the dates. Perhaps you want to buy a new car. Do you want one that is inexpensive, gas-efficient, good looking, or reliable? Or do you just want to make sure you get a good deal? By reading up on the attributes of the phases and signs and then consulting the Moon tables to find out which days fall under those conditions, you can determine for yourself which days are best for your personal needs.

You can also use the book to chart which signs worked particularly well for certain projects, or which ones were not helpful. One *Moon Sign Book* reader wrote to tell us that he never tries to fix his car or have a picnic when the Moon was in a water sign, because where he lives a water sign Moon almost always means rain. Another reader wrote to say that he never goes shopping for groceries when the Moon is in Taurus, because this seems to make him so hungry that he ends up buying more food than he can eat! A third reader, who raises pedigree retrievers, noted that she always tries to teach her dogs the most difficult tricks for their field trials (contests where dogs can win awards for performing certain tasks correctly) during the sign of Taurus. It seems they are more obedient during this sign and that they remember the instructions better after these sessions.

Tailor the *Moon Sign Book* to your needs and empower yourself to use the Moon's energies in the best and most positive ways for you. You do not have to be a professional astrologer to harness the power of the Moon!

Moon Void of Course

It is important to note that the Moon Tables do **not** take into account the Moon void of course. Just before the Moon enters a new sign it will have one last aspect to a planet. From that point until it enters the next sign, it is void. It is said that decisions made while the Moon is void never come to fruition. Sometimes purchases made during a Moon void turn out to be poorly made or a bad investment. If you want to avoid making your decisions during a void of course Moon, please refer to the

"Moon Void of Course", section in this book. Many people do not pay attention to the voids, as it is virtually impossible to bypass all of them when making decisions. However, it may be helpful to consult the tables before making an especially large purchase or a particularly important decision.

Retrograde Planets

Although we have included a list of retrograde planets in this year's *Moon Sign Book*, the Astro-Almanac does **not** take into account planetary retrogrades. For more information on these see *Llewellyn's Astrological Calendar*.

Time Zones

All times given in the *Moon Sign Book* are set in **Eastern Standard Time**. You must adjust for your time zone and for daylight savings time. A chart and map are provided on pages 20-21 to assist you.

Sign Changes

A common misunderstanding among our readers has to do with the time the Moon enters or leaves a sign. Sometimes we will have a certain day listed as being good for an activity (let's use fishing as an example), but someone tries it out and doesn't even get a nibble. Often times the reason for this is that the Moon changed signs during the day at some point before the person went fishing. For example, let's say that at the beginning of the day the Moon was in Pisces (a good fishing sign), but at 4 AM it moved into Aries. The day would be listed as good for fishing because the first sign the Moon was in during that day was Pisces, but it wouldn't be beneficial to fish after 4 AM EST. Remember to check when the Moon changes signs, and also at what time. 4 AM EST would, of course, be 1 AM PST!

For astronomical calculations the Moon's place in almanacs is given as being in the constellation. For astrological purposes the Moon's place is figured in the zodiacal sign, which is its true place in the zodiac, and nearly one sign (30 degrees) different from the astronomical constellation.

To illustrate: If the common almanac gives the Moon's place in Taurus (constellation) on a certain date, its true place in the zodiac is in Gemini (zodiacal sign). Thus, it is readily seen that those who use the common almanac may be planting seeds, or engaging in other endeavors, when they think the Moon is in a fruitful sign, while in reality it would be in one of the most barren signs in the zodiac.

Common almanacs are worthless to follow for planting. Some almanacs even make a bad matter worse by inserting at the head of their columns "Moon's Sign" when they mean "Moon's Constellation," and this has brought much unmerited discredit to the value of planting by the Moon. The constellations form a belt outside the zodiac, but do not conform with the signs in position or time.

To obtain desired results, planting must be done according to the Moon's place in the signs of the zodiac.

Therefore, using Llewellyn's *Moon Sign Book* for all of your planting and planning purposes is the best thing to do!

Not All Almanacs Are the Same!

Phases & Signs of the Moon

New Moon

The time of new beginnings, beginnings of projects that favor growth, externalization of activities, the growth of ideas.

Full Moon

Illumination, fulfillment, culmination, completion, drawing inward, unrest, emotional expressions, hasty actions leading to failure.

First Quarter

Germination, emergence, beginnings, outwardly directed activity.

Second Quarter

Growth, development, articulation of things which already exist.

Third Quarter

Maturity, fruition, assumption of full form of expression.

Fourth Quarter

Disintegration, drawing back for reorganization, reflection.

Moon in Aries

Good for starting things, but lacking in staying power. Things occur rapidly, but also quickly pass.

Moon in Taurus

Things begun now last the longest and tend to increase in value. Things begun now become habitual and hard to alter.

Moon in Gemini

An inconsistent position for the Moon. Things begun now are easily changed by outside influence. A lot of talk.

Moon in Cancer

Stimulates emotional rapport between people. Pinpoints need, supports growth and nurturance.

Moon in Leo

Showmanship, favors being seen, drama, recreation, and happy pursuits. May be overly concerned with praise and subject to flattery.

Moon in Virgo

Favors accomplishment of details and commands from higher up while discouraging independent thinking.

Moon in Libra

Increases self-awareness, favors self-examination and interaction with others but discourages spontaneous initiative.

Moon in Scorpio

Increases awareness of psychic power. Precipitates psychic crises and ends connections thoroughly.

Moon in Sagittarius

Encourages expansionary flights of imagination and confidence in the flow of life.

Moon in Capricorn

Increases awareness of the need for structure, to be disciplined and a need for organization. Institutional activities are favored.

Moon in Aquarius

Favors activites that are unique and individualistic, concern for the humanitarian needs, society as a whole and improvements that can be made.

Moon in Pisces

Energy withdraws from the surface of life, hibernates within, secretly reorganizing and realigning for a new day.

Using the Moon Tables

Timing your activities is one of the most important things you can do to ensure success. In many Eastern countries, timing by the planets is so important that practically no event takes place without first setting up a chart for it. Weddings have occurred in the middle of the night because that was when the influences were the best. You may not want to take it that far, and you don't really need to set up a chart for each activity, but you can still make use of the influences of the Moon whenever possible. It's easy and it works!

In the *Moon Sign Book* you will find the information you need to plan just about any activity: weddings, fishing, buying a car or house, cutting your hair, traveling, and more. Not all of the things you do will fall on favorable days, but we provide the guidelines you need to pick the best day out of the several from which you have to choose.

Let's run through some examples. Say you need to make an appointment to have your hair cut. You have thin hair and would like it to look thicker. Look in the Home, Health, & Beauty section under

Hair Care. You see that you should cut hair during a Full Moon (marked FM in the Moon Tables or O under the Sun in the Lunar Aspectarian). You should, however, avoid the Moon in Virgo. We'll say that it is the month of June. Look up June in the Moon Tables. The Full Moon falls on June 1st at 3:48 pm. It is in the sign of Sagittarius, which is good for cutting hair. Since the Full Moon happens late in the day, the next day would be just as good. The times are fairly flexible; you do not have to use the exact time of the Moon change.

That was easy. Let's move on to a more difficult example that uses the phase and sign of the Moon. You want to buy a house for a permanent home. Look in the Home, Health, & Beauty section under House. It says that you should buy a home when the Moon is in Taurus, Leo, Scorpio, or Aquarius (fixed signs). You need to get a loan, so you should look in the Business, Finance & Legal section under Loans. Here it says that the third and fourth quarters favor the borrower (you). You are going to buy the house in July. Look up July in the Moon Tables. The Moon is in the 3rd quarter from July 1st to July 7th and in the 4th quarter from the 7th to the 14th. The best days for obtaining a loan would be the 8th from 3:44 pm to the 10th when in the Moon is in Taurus and sextile Mercury, trine Jupiter, sextile the Sun, and trine Neptune. After the 14th the Moon has entered Leo, Scorpio, and Aquarius, but is in the 1st and 2nd quarters. Just match up the best signs and phases (quarters) to come up with the best dates.

With all activities, be sure to check the Favorable and Unfavorable Days for your Sun sign in the table adjoining the Lunar Aspectarian. If there is a choice between several dates, pick the one most favorable for you (marked F).

Now let's look at an example that uses signs, phases, and aspects. You will find the aspects listed in the Lunar Aspectarian on the pages facing the Moon Tables. The letters listed under the planets stand for specific aspects: C=conjunction, X=sextile, Q=square, T=trine, and O=opposition. Try to avoid any squares (Q) to the Moon when electing the best time to begin any activity, as squares tend to hinder progress. Conjunctions with Mars, Saturn, or Neptune may also be challenging.

Our example this time is fixing your car. We will use June as the ex-

ample month. Look in the Home, Health, & Beauty section under automobile repair. It says that the Moon should be in a fixed sign (Taurus, Leo, Scorpio, or Aquarius) in the first or second quarter and well-aspected to the Sun. (Good aspects are sextiles and trines, marked S and T.) It also tells you to avoid negative aspects to Mars, Saturn, Uranus, Neptune, and Pluto. (Negative aspects are squares and oppositions, marked Q and O.) Look in the Moon Tables under June. You will see that the Moon is in the first and second quarters from June 16th to the 30th. The Moon is in Leo on the 18th from 6:23 pm to 7:08 am on the 21st.

Looking to the Lunar Aspectarian we see the best aspects on the 19th and 20th of July.

You have just gone through the entire process of choosing the best dates for a special event. With practice, you will be able to scan the information in the tables and do it very quickly. You will also begin to get a feel for what works best for you. Everyone has his or her own high and low cycles.

Gardening activities depend on many outside factors, weather being the most influential. Obviously, you can't go out and plant when there is still a foot of snow on the ground. You have to adjust to the conditions at hand. If the weather was bad or you were on vacation during the first quarter when it was best to plant, do it during the second quarter while the Moon is in a fruitful sign instead. If the Moon is not in a fruitful sign during the first or second quarter, choose a day when it is in a semi-fruitful sign. The best advice is to choose either the sign or phase that is most favorable when the two don't coincide.

To summarize, in order to make the most of your plans and activities, check with the *Moon Sign Book*. First, look up the activity in the corresponding section under the proper heading. Then, look for the information given in the tables (the Moon Tables, Lunar Aspectarian or Favorable and Unfavorable Days, or all three). Choose the best date according to the number of positive factors in effect. If most of the dates are favorable, then there is no problem choosing the one that will best fit your schedule. However, if there just don't seem to be any really good dates, pick the ones with the least number of negative influences. We guarantee that you will be very pleased with the results if you use nature's influences to your advantage.

For quick reference, use the Astro-Almanac. This is a general guide for planning certain activities.

How to Use the Tables

First, read the preceding section on how to use your *Moon Sign Book*.

You will be using the tables on the following pages in conjunction with the information given in the individual sections: Home & Family; Leisure & Recreation; Home, Health & Beauty; Business & Legal; and Farm & Garden.

The Moon Tables include the date, the sign the Moon is in, the element of that sign, the nature of the sign, the Moon's phase and the times that it changes sign or phase. The abbreviation FM signifies Full Moon and NM signifies New Moon. The times listed directly after the date are the times when the Moon changes sign. The times listed after the phase indicate the times when the Moon changes phase. All times are listed in Eastern Standard Time. You need to adjust them according to your own time zone.

On the pages opposite the Moon Tables you will find the Lunar Aspectarian and the Favorable and Unfavorable Days. To use the Lunar Aspectarian, find the planet that the activity lists and run down the column to the date desired. If you want to find a favorable aspect (sextile or trine) to Mercury, run your finger down the column under Mercury until you find an X or T; positive or good aspects are signified by these letters. Negative or adverse aspects (square or opposition) are signified by a Q or O. A conjunction, C, is sometimes good, sometimes bad, depending on the activity or planets involved. The Lunar Aspectarian gives the aspects of the Moon to the other planets.

The Favorable and Unfavorable Days table lists all of the Sun signs. To find out if a day is positive for you, find your sign and then look down the column. If it is marked F, it is very favorable. If it is marked f, it is slightly favorable. U means very unfavorable and u means slightly unfavorable.

Key of Abbreviations

X: sextile/positive

T: trine/positive

Q: square/negative

O: opposition/negative

C: conjunction/positive/negative/neutral

F: very favorable

f: slightly favorable

U: very unfavorable

u: slightly unfavorable

FM: Full Moon

NM: New Moon

Lunar Lore

Compiled by D. J. Conway

☽ In medieval Europe and England, "Moon's men" were thieves and highwaymen who plied their trade by night. The current term "moonlighting" is similar, meaning to hold down an additional night job.

☽ In certain parts of England, the term "Moonrakers" eventually came to mean simple-minded people. The factual story behind this, though, reveals some pretty fast thinking by local smugglers. The English excise men (a combination of border patrol, ATF, and IRS) were out at night, trying to catch the smugglers red handed. Hearing the excise men coming, the smugglers sank their loot in a lake and pretended to be fishing for the Moon reflected in the water. When the excise men asked what they were doing, the smugglers innocently replied that they were raking for the Moon. The excise men went away shaking their heads over the stupidity of the local folk, while the smugglers fished up their goods and went on with their business.

Retrogrades

When the planets cross the sky, they occasionally appear to move backward as seen from Earth. When a planet turns "backward" it is said to be *retrograde*. When it turns forward again, it is said to go *direct*. The point at which the movement changes from one direction to another is called a *station*.

When a planet is retrograde its expression is delayed or out of kilter with the normal progression of events. Generally, it can be said that whatever is planned during this period will be delayed, but usually it will come to fruition when the retrograde is over. Of course, this only applies to activities ruled by the planet which is retrograde. Mercury and Venus retrogrades are particularly easy to follow.

Mercury Retrograde

Mercury rules informal communications—reading, writing, speaking, and short errands. Whenever Mercury goes retrograde, personal communications get fouled up or misunderstood. The rule astrologers have developed is *when Mercury is retrograde, avoid informal means of communication*.

Venus Retrograde

This is the planet of love, affection, friendship, and marriage, so the retrograde is an unreliable time for these activities. Affectional misunderstandings and alienations are more common.

Planetary Stations for 1996 (EST)

Planet	Begin		End	
Mercury	01/09/96	4:46 PM	01/30/96	5:11 PM
Pluto	03/05/96	11:16 AM	08/10/96	3:11 AM
Neptune	04/29/96	2:37 AM	10/06/96	5:36 AM
Mercury	05/03/96	9:10 AM	05/27/96	1:56 PM
Jupiter	05/04/96	9:10 AM	09/03/96	8:37 AM
Uranus	05/08/96	10:35 AM	10/09/96	5:15 PM
Venus	05/20/96	12:59 AM	07/02/96	1:46 AM
Saturn	07/18/96	1:52 PM	12/03/96	5:54 AM
Mercury	09/04/96	12:42 AM	09/26/96	11:58 AM
Mercury	12/23/96	2:39 PM	01/12/97	3:37 PM

Lunar Activity Guide

Activity	Quarter	Sign
Buy Animals	New Moon, 1st	All except Scorpio or Pisces
Baking	1st or 2nd	Cancer
Hair Care	1st	Aquarius
Cut Hair—Growth	1st or 2nd	Cancer, Pisces, also at New Moon
Cut Hair—Thickness	Prior to Full Moon	Taurus, Cancer, Leo
Cut Hair—Less Growth	3rd or 4th	Gemini, Aries, Virgo
Start a Diet	3rd or 4th	Aries, Leo, Virgo, Sagittarius, Aquarius
Gain Weight	1st or 2nd	Cancer, Pisces
Buy Clothes		Taurus, Libra
Buy Antiques		Cancer, Scorpio, Capricorn
Borrow Money	3rd or 4th	Leo, Sagittarius, Aquarius, Pisces
Start Savings Account	1st or 2nd	Taurus
Join a Club		Gemini, Libra, Aquarius
Give a Party		Gemini, Leo, Libra, Aquarius
Travel for Pleasure	1st or 2nd	Gemini, Leo, Sagittarius
Begin Study	1st or 2nd	Gemini, Virgo, Sagittarius
Begin a New Job	1st or 2nd	Taurus, Virgo, Capricorn
Canning	3rd or 4th	Cancer, Virgo
Make Preserves	3rd or 4th	Taurus, Cancer, Virgo
Dry Produce	3rd	Aries, Leo, Sagittarius, Gemini
Remove Teeth	1st or 4th; not Full	Gemini, Virgo, Sagittarius
Fill Teeth	3rd or 4th	Taurus, Leo, Aquarius
Sewing		Taurus, Leo, Libra

Lunar Activity Guide

Activity	Quarter	Sign
Buy Health Foods		Virgo
Buy Medicine		Scorpio, Virgo
Buy a Home	New Moon	Taurus, Cancer, Leo
Send Mail		Gemini, Virgo, Sagittarius, Pisces
Beauty Treatments	1st or 2nd	Taurus, Cancer, Leo, Libra, Aquarius
Brewing	3rd or 4th	Cancer, Pisces
Start Building	New Moon	Taurus, Leo, Aquarius
Pour Cement	Full Moon	Leo, Taurus, Aquarius
Break Habits		Leo, Virgo
Fix Cars	1st or 2nd	Taurus, Leo, Aquarius
Weddings	Avoid Full Moon	Taurus, Cancer, Leo, Libra, Pisces
Move		Taurus, Leo, Scorpio, Aquarius
Paint		Taurus, Leo, Aquarius
Train a Pet	Best at New Moon	Taurus
Buy a Car		Gemini, Sagittarius, Virgo
Collect Debts		Aries, Cancer, Libra, Capricorn

Time Zone Conversions

World Time Zones

(Compared to Eastern Standard Time)

(R) EST—Used

(A) Add 6 hours

(S) CST—Subtract 1 hour

(T) MST—Subtract 2 hours

(U) PST—Subtract 3 hours

(V) Subtract 4 hours

(W) Subtract 5 hours

(X) Subtract 6 hours

(Y) Subtract 7 hours

(Q) Add 1 hour

(P) Add 2 hours

(O) Add 3 hours

(N) Add 4 hours

(Z) Add 5 hours

(B) Add 7 hours

(C) Add 8 hours

(D) Add 9 hours

(E) Add 10 hours

(F) Add 11 hours

(G) Add 12 hours

(H) Add 13 hours

(I) Add 14 hours

(K) Add 15 hours

(L) Add 16 hours

(M) Add 17 hours

WORLD MAP OF TIME ZONES

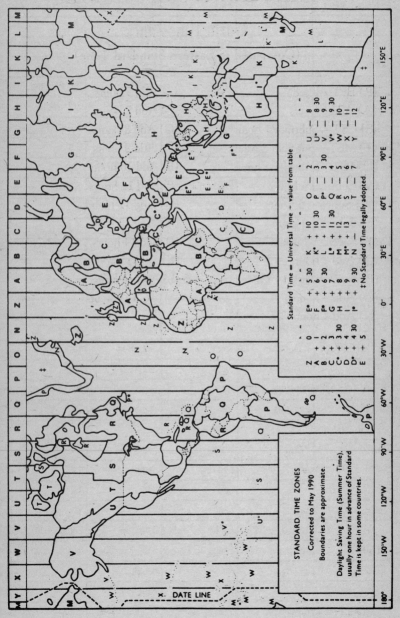

January Moon Table

Date	Sign	Element	Nature	Phase
1 MON 9:30 pm	Gemini	Air	Barren	2nd
2 TUE	Gemini	Air	Barren	2nd
3 WED	Gemini	Air	Barren	2nd
4 THU 9:56 am	Cancer	Water	Fruitful	2nd
5 FRI	Cancer	Water	Fruitful	Full 3:51 pm
6 SAT 10:31 pm	Leo	Fire	Barren	3rd
7 SUN	Leo	Fire	Barren	3rd
8 MON	Leo	Fire	Barren	3rd
9 TUE 10:29 am	Virgo	Earth	Barren	3rd
10 WED	Virgo	Earth	Barren	3rd
11 THU 8:55 pm	Libra	Air	Semi-fruit	3rd
12 FRI	Libra	Air	Semi-fruit	3rd
13 SAT	Libra	Air	Semi-fruit	4th 3:45 pm
14 SUN 4:30 am	Scorpio	Water	Fruitful	4th
15 MON	Scorpio	Water	Fruitful	4th
16 TUE 8:25 am	Sagittarius	Fire	Barren	4th
17 WED	Sagittarius	Fire	Barren	4th
18 THU 9:07 am	Capricorn	Earth	Semi-fruit	4th
19 FRI	Capricorn	Earth	Semi-fruit	4th
20 SAT 8:15 am	Aquarius	Air	Barren	New 7:51 am
21 SUN	Aquarius	Air	Barren	1st
22 MON 8:02 am	Pisces	Water	Fruitful	1st
23 TUE	Pisces	Water	Fruitful	1st
24 WED 10:37 am	Aries	Fire	Barren	1st
25 THU	Aries	Fire	Barren	1st
26 FRI 5:17 pm	Taurus	Earth	Semi-fruit	1st
27 SAT	Taurus	Earth	Semi-fruit	2nd 6:14 am
28 SUN	Taurus	Earth	Semi-fruit	2nd
29 MON 3:43 am	Gemini	Air	Barren	2nd
30 TUE	Gemini	Air	Barren	2nd
31 WED 4:11 pm	Cancer	Water	Fruitful	2nd

January

Lunar Aspectarian   Favorable and Unfavorable Days

Day	Sun	Mercury	Venus	Mars	Jupiter	Saturn	Uranus	Neptune	Pluto	Aries	Taurus	Gemini	Cancer	Leo	Virgo	Libra	Scorpio	Sagittarius	Capricorn	Aquarius	Pisces
1		T		T		X	T	T	0	f		F		f	u	f		U		f	u
2									0	f		F		f	u	f		U		f	u
3			T			Q				f		F		f	u	f		U		f	u
4					0					f		F		f	u	f		U		f	u
5	0					T				u	f		F		f	u	f		U		f
6				0		T	0	0	T	u	f		F		f	u	f		U		f
7		0							T	f	u	f		F		f	u	f		U	
8			0							f	u	f		F		f	u	f		U	
9				T					Q	f	u	f		F		f	u	f		U	
10											f	u	f		F		f	u	f		U
11	T				Q	0	T	T			f	u	f		F		f	u	f		U
12		T		T	Q				X	U		f	u	f		F		f	u	f	
13	Q							Q		U		f	u	f		F		f	u	f	
14		Q	T	Q	X		Q			U		f	u	f		F		f	u	f	
15						T		X			U		f	u	f		F		f	u	f
16	X	X	Q	X			X	X	C		U		f	u	f		F		f	u	f
17						Q				f		U		f	u	f		F		f	u
18			X		C					f		U		f	u	f		F		f	u
19						X				u	f		U		f	u	f		F		f
20	C	C		C		C	C		X	u	f		U		f	u	f		F		f
21				C						f	u	f		U		f	u	f		F	
22					X				Q	f	u	f		U		f	u	f		F	
23		X	C			C					f	u	f		U		f	u	f		F
24	X				Q		X	X	T		f	u	f		U		f	u	f		F
25		Q		X						F		f	u	f		U		f	u	f	
26						Q	Q			F		f	u	f		U		f	u	f	
27	Q		X	Q	T						F		f	u	f		U		f	u	f
28		T				X		T			F		f	u	f		U		f	u	f
29	T						T		0	f		F		f	u	f		U		f	u
30			Q	T		Q				f		F		f	u	f		U		f	u
31						Q				f		F		f	u	f		U		f	u

February Moon Table

Date	Sign	Element	Nature	Phase
1 THU	Cancer	Water	Fruitful	2nd
2 FRI	Cancer	Water	Fruitful	2nd
3 SAT 4:46 am	Leo	Fire	Barren	2nd
4 SUN	Leo	Fire	Barren	Full 10:58 am
5 MON 4:22 pm	Virgo	Earth	Barren	3rd
6 TUE	Virgo	Earth	Barren	3rd
7 WED	Virgo	Earth	Barren	3rd
8 THU 2:30 am	Libra	Air	Semi-fruit	3rd
9 FRI	Libra	Air	Semi-fruit	3rd
10 SAT 10:35 am	Scorpio	Water	Fruitful	3rd
11 SUN	Scorpio	Water	Fruitful	3rd
12 MON 3:59 pm	Sagittarius	Fire	Barren	4th 3:38 am
13 TUE	Sagittarius	Fire	Barren	4th
14 WED 6:30 pm	Capricorn	Earth	Semi-fruit	4th
15 THU	Capricorn	Earth	Semi-fruit	4th
16 FRI 7:00 pm	Aquarius	Air	Barren	4th
17 SAT	Aquarius	Air	Barren	4th
18 SUN 7:10 pm	Pisces	Water	Fruitful	New 6:31 pm
19 MON	Pisces	Water	Fruitful	1st
20 TUE 8:58 pm	Aries	Fire	Barren	1st
21 WED	Aries	Fire	Barren	1st
22 THU	Aries	Fire	Barren	1st
23 FRI 2:08 am	Taurus	Earth	Semi-fruit	1st
24 SAT	Taurus	Earth	Semi-fruit	1st
25 SUN 11:14 am	Gemini	Air	Barren	1st
26 MON	Gemini	Air	Barren	2nd 12:52 am
27 TUE 11:10 pm	Cancer	Water	Fruitful	2nd
28 WED	Cancer	Water	Fruitful	2nd
29 THU	Cancer	Water	Fruitful	2nd

February

Lunar Aspectarian   Favorable and Unfavorable Days

	Sun	Mercury	Venus	Mars	Jupiter	Saturn	Uranus	Neptune	Pluto	Aries	Taurus	Gemini	Cancer	Leo	Virgo	Libra	Scorpio	Sagittarius	Capricorn	Aquarius	Pisces
1					0					u	f		F		f	u	f		U		f
2		0	T			T		0		u	f		F		f	u	f		U		f
3							0		T	u	f		F		f	u	f		U		f
4	0									f	u	f		F		f	u	f		U	
5				0					Q	f	u	f		F		f	u	f		U	
6					T						f	u	f	F		f	u	f			U
7		T				0		T			f	u	f	F		f	u	f			U
8			0		Q		T		X		f	u	f	F		f	u	f			U
9	T									U		f	u	f	F		f	u	f		
10		Q		T			Q	Q		U		f	u	f	F		f	u	f		
11					X						U		f	u	f	F		f	u	f	
12	Q	X		Q		T	X	X	C		U		f	u	f	F		f	u	f	
13			T							f	U		f	u	f		F		f		u
14	X			X		Q				f	U		f	u	f		F		f		u
15			Q		C					u	f	U		f	u	f		f		F	f
16		C				X	C	C	X	u	f	U		f	u	f		f		F	f
17			X							f	u	f	U		f	u	f		f	F	
18	C			C						f	u	f	U		f	u	f		f	F	
19					X				Q		f	u	f	U		f	u	f			F
20						C	X				f	u	f	U		f	u	f			F
21		X	C		Q		X		T	F		f	u	f		U		f	u	f	
22								Q		F		f	u	f		U		f	u	f	
23	X	Q		X	T		Q				F		f	u	f		U		f	u	f
24											F		f	u	f		U		f	u	f
25						X	T	T	0		F		f	u	f		U		f	u	f
26	Q	T		Q						f		F		f	u	f		U		f	u
27			X			Q				f		F		f	u	f		U		f	u
28	T			T	0					u	f		F		f	u	f		U		f
29										u	f		F		f	u	f		U		f

March Moon Table

Date	Sign	Element	Nature	Phase
1 FRI 11:47 am	Leo	Fire	Barren	2nd
2 SAT	Leo	Fire	Barren	2nd
3 SUN 11:13 pm	Virgo	Earth	Barren	2nd
4 MON	Virgo	Earth	Barren	2nd
5 TUE	Virgo	Earth	Barren	Full 4:23 am
6 WED 8:41 am	Libra	Air	Semi-fruit	3rd
7 THU	Libra	Air	Semi-fruit	3rd
8 FRI 4:06 pm	Scorpio	Water	Fruitful	3rd
9 SAT	Scorpio	Water	Fruitful	3rd
10 SUN 9:33 pm	Sagittarius	Fire	Barren	3rd
11 MON	Sagittarius	Fire	Barren	3rd
12 TUE	Sagittarius	Fire	Barren	4th 12:15 pm
13 WED 1:08 am	Capricorn	Earth	Semi-fruit	4th
14 THU	Capricorn	Earth	Semi-fruit	4th
15 FRI 3:15 am	Aquarius	Air	Barren	4th
16 SAT	Aquarius	Air	Barren	4th
17 SUN 4:50 am	Pisces	Water	Fruitful	4th
18 MON	Pisces	Water	Fruitful	4th
19 TUE 7:15 am	Aries	Fire	Barren	New 5:45 am
20 WED	Aries	Fire	Barren	1st
21 THU 11:58 am	Taurus	Earth	Semi-fruit	1st
22 FRI	Taurus	Earth	Semi-fruit	1st
23 SAT 7:59 pm	Gemini	Air	Barren	1st
24 SUN	Gemini	Air	Barren	1st
25 MON	Gemini	Air	Barren	1st
26 TUE 7:06 am	Cancer	Water	Fruitful	2nd 8:31 pm
27 WED	Cancer	Water	Fruitful	2nd
28 THU 7:38 pm	Leo	Fire	Barren	2nd
29 FRI	Leo	Fire	Barren	2nd
30 SAT	Leo	Fire	Barren	2nd
31 SUN 7:15 am	Virgo	Earth	Barren	2nd

March

Lunar Aspectarian   **Favorable and Unfavorable Days**

	Sun	Mercury	Venus	Mars	Jupiter	Saturn	Uranus	Neptune	Pluto	Aries	Taurus	Gemini	Cancer	Leo	Virgo	Libra	Scorpio	Sagittarius	Capricorn	Aquarius	Pisces
1			Q			T	0	0	T	u	f		F		f	u	f		U		f
2										f	u	f		F		f	u	f		U	
3		0	T							f	u	f		F		f	u	f		U	
4					T				Q		f	u	f		F		f	u	f		U
5	0			0							f	u	f		F		f	u	f		U
6						0	T	T	X		f	u	f		F		f	u	f		U
7					Q					U		f	u	f		F		f	u	f	
8		T	0				Q	Q		U		f	u	f		F		f	u	f	
9				X							U		f	u	f		F		f	u	f
10	T			T		T		X			U		f	u	f		F		f	u	f
11		Q					X		C	f		U		f	u	f		F		f	u
12	Q			Q		Q				f		U		f	u	f		F		f	u
13		X	T							u	f		U		f	u	f		F		f
14	X			X	C	X		C		u	f		U		f	u	f		F		f
15			Q				C		X	u	f		U		f	u	f		F		f
16										f	u	f		U		f	u	f		F	
17									Q	f	u	f		U		f	u	f		F	
18		C	X		X						f	u	f		U		f	u	f		F
19	C			C		C	X	X	T		f	u	f		U		f	u	f		F
20					Q					F		f	u	f		U		f	u	f	
21							Q	Q		F		f	u	f		U		f	u	f	
22			C		T						F		f	u	f		U		f	u	f
23		X		X		X		T			F		f	u	f		U		f	u	f
24	X					T		0		f		F		f	u	f		U		f	u
25										f		F		f	u	f		U		f	u
26	Q	Q		Q		Q				f		F		f	u	f		U		f	u
27					0					u	f		F		f	u	f		U		f
28			X			T		0		u	f		F		f	u	f		U		f
29	T	T		T				0	T	f	u	f		F		f	u	f		U	
30										f	u	f		F		f	u	f		U	
31			Q						Q	f	u	f		F		f	u	f		U	

April Moon Table

Date	Sign	Element	Nature	Phase
1 MON	Virgo	Earth	Barren	2nd
2 TUE 4:27 pm	Libra	Air	Semi-fruit	2nd
3 WED	Libra	Air	Semi-fruit	Full 7:08 pm
4 THU 10:57 pm	Scorpio	Water	Fruitful	3rd
5 FRI	Scorpio	Water	Fruitful	3rd
6 SAT	Scorpio	Water	Fruitful	3rd
7 SUN 3:21 am	Sagittarius	Fire	Barren	3rd
8 MON	Sagittarius	Fire	Barren	3rd
9 TUE 6:30 am	Capricorn	Earth	Semi-fruit	3rd
10 WED	Capricorn	Earth	Semi-fruit	4th 6:36 pm
11 THU 9:09 am	Aquarius	Air	Barren	4th
12 FRI	Aquarius	Air	Barren	4th
13 SAT 11:59 am	Pisces	Water	Fruitful	4th
14 SUN	Pisces	Water	Fruitful	4th
15 MON 3:43 pm	Aries	Fire	Barren	4th
16 TUE	Aries	Fire	Barren	4th
17 WED 9:06 pm	Taurus	Earth	Semi-fruit	New 5:49 pm
18 THU	Taurus	Earth	Semi-fruit	1st
19 FRI	Taurus	Earth	Semi-fruit	1st
20 SAT 4:55 am	Gemini	Air	Barren	1st
21 SUN	Gemini	Air	Barren	1st
22 MON 3:25 pm	Cancer	Water	Fruitful	1st
23 TUE	Cancer	Water	Fruitful	1st
24 WED	Cancer	Water	Fruitful	1st
25 THU 3:45 am	Leo	Fire	Barren	2nd 3:41 pm
26 FRI	Leo	Fire	Barren	2nd
27 SAT 3:49 pm	Virgo	Earth	Barren	2nd
28 SUN	Virgo	Earth	Barren	2nd
29 MON	Libra	Air	Semi-fruit	2nd
30 TUE 1:27 am	Libra	Air	Semi-fruit	2nd

April

| Lunar Aspectarian | | | | | | | | | Favorable and Unfavorable Days | | | | | | | | | | | |

Day	Sun	Mercury	Venus	Mars	Jupiter	Saturn	Uranus	Neptune	Pluto	Aries	Taurus	Gemini	Cancer	Leo	Virgo	Libra	Scorpio	Sagittarius	Capricorn	Aquarius	Pisces
1					T						f	u	f		F		f	u	f		U
2			T			O	T	T	X		f	u	f		F		f	u	f		U
3	O				O	Q				U		f	u	f		F		f	u	f	
4		O						Q		U		f	u	f		F		f	u	f	
5						Q					U		f	u	f		F		f	u	f
6				X				X			U		f	u	f		F		f	u	f
7			O	T		T	X		C		U		f	u	f		F		f	u	f
8	T									f		U		f	u	f		F		f	u
9		T				Q				f		U		f	u	f		F		f	u
10	Q			Q	C					u	f		U		f	u	f		F		f
11		Q	T			X	C	C	X	u	f		U		f	u	f		F		f
12				X						f	u	f		U		f	u	f		F	
13	X								Q	f	u	f		U		f	u	f		F	
14		X	Q	X							f	u	f		U		f	u	f		F
15						C	X	X	T		f	u	f		U		f	u	f		F
16			X	C	Q					F		f	u	f		U		f	u	f	
17	C							Q		F		f	u	f		U		f	u	f	
18						Q					F		f	u	f		U		f	u	f
19		C			T						F		f	u	f		U		f	u	f
20						X	T	T	O		F		f	u	f		U		f	u	f
21			C	X						f		F		f	u	f		U		f	u
22	X					Q				f		F		f	u	f		U		f	u
23					O					u	f		F		f	u	f		U		f
24		X		Q	O			O		u	f		F		f	u	f		U		f
25	Q					T	O		T	u	f		F		f	u	f		U		f
26			X							f	u	f		F		f	u	f		U	
27		Q		T					Q	f	u	f		F		f	u	f		U	
28	T										f	u	f		F		f	u	f		U
29		T	Q	T				T			f	u	f		F		f	u	f		U
30						O	T		X	U		f	u	f		F		f	u	f	

May Moon Table

Date	Sign	Element	Nature	Phase
1 WED	Libra	Air	Semi-fruit	2nd
2 THU 7:43 am	Scorpio	Water	Fruitful	2nd
3 FRI	Scorpio	Water	Fruitful	Full 6:48 am
4 SAT 11:04 am	Sagittarius	Fire	Barren	3rd
5 SUN	Sagittarius	Fire	Barren	3rd
6 MON 12:54 pm	Capricorn	Earth	Semi-fruit	3rd
7 TUE	Capricorn	Earth	Semi-fruit	3rd
8 WED 2:39 pm	Aquarius	Air	Barren	3rd
9 THU	Aquarius	Air	Barren	3rd
10 FRI 5:29 pm	Pisces	Water	Fruitful	4th 12:04 am
11 SAT	Pisces	Water	Fruitful	4th
12 SUN 10:01 pm	Aries	Fire	Barren	4th
13 MON	Aries	Fire	Barren	4th
14 TUE	Aries	Fire	Barren	4th
15 WED 4:25 am	Taurus	Earth	Semi-fruit	4th
16 THU	Taurus	Earth	Semi-fruit	4th
17 FRI 12:48 pm	Gemini	Air	Barren	New 6:47 am
18 SAT	Gemini	Air	Barren	1st
19 SUN 11:17 pm	Cancer	Water	Fruitful	1st
20 MON	Cancer	Water	Fruitful	1st
21 TUE	Cancer	Water	Fruitful	1st
22 WED 11:28 am	Leo	Fire	Barren	1st
23 THU	Leo	Fire	Barren	1st
24 FRI 11:59 pm	Virgo	Earth	Barren	1st
25 SAT	Virgo	Earth	Barren	2nd 9:13 am
26 SUN	Virgo	Earth	Barren	2nd
27 MON 10:33 am	Libra	Air	Semi-fruit	2nd
28 TUE	Libra	Air	Semi-fruit	2nd
29 WED 5:30 pm	Scorpio	Water	Fruitful	2nd
30 THU	Scorpio	Water	Fruitful	2nd
31 FRI 8:43 pm	Sagittarius	Fire	Barren	2nd

May

Lunar Aspectarian   Favorable and Unfavorable Days

	Sun	Mercury	Venus	Mars	Jupiter	Saturn	Uranus	Neptune	Pluto	Aries	Taurus	Gemini	Cancer	Leo	Virgo	Libra	Scorpio	Sagittarius	Capricorn	Aquarius	Pisces
1			T		Q					U		f	u	f		F		f	u	f	
2				0			Q	Q		U		f	u	f		F		f	u	f	
3	0				X						U		f	u	f		F		f	u	f
4		0				T	X	X	C		U		f	u	f		F		f	u	f
5										f		U		f	u	f		F		f	u
6			0	T	Q					f		U		f	u	f		F		f	u
7	T				C					u	f		U		f	u	f		F		f
8		T		Q		X	C	C	X	u	f		U		f	u	f		F		f
9										f	u	f		U		f	u	f		F	
10	Q	Q	T						Q	f	u	f		U		f	u	f		F	
11				X							f	u	f		U		f	u	f		F
12	X	X	Q		X			X			f	u	f		U		f	u	f		F
13						C	X		T	F		f	u	f		U		f	u	f	
14					Q					F		f	u	f		U		f	u	f	
15			X	C				Q	Q	F		f	u	f		U		f	u	f	
16		C			T						F		f	u	f		U		f	u	f
17	C					X	T		0		F		f	u	f		U		f	u	f
18										f		F		f	u	f		U		f	u
19			C							f		F		f	u	f		U		f	u
20					Q					u	f		F		f	u	f		U		f
21		X		X	0					u	f		F		f	u	f		U		f
22	X					T	0	0	T	u	f		F		f	u	f		U		f
23				Q						f	u	f		F		f	u	f		U	
24		Q	X							f	u	f		F		f	u	f		U	
25	Q								Q		f	u	f		F		f	u	f		U
26		T		T	T						f	u	f		F		f	u	f		U
27			Q		0		T	T	X		f	u	f		F		f	u	f		U
28	T				Q					U		f	u	f		F		f	u	f	
29			T					Q		U		f	u	f		F		f	u	f	
30					X			Q			U		f	u	f		F		f	u	f
31		0		0				X	C		U		f	u	f		F		f	u	f

June Moon Table

Date	Sign	Element	Nature	Phase
1 SAT	Sagittarius	Fire	Barren	Full 3:47 pm
2 SUN 9:29 pm	Capricorn	Earth	Semi-fruit	3rd
3 MON	Capricorn	Earth	Semi-fruit	3rd
4 TUE 9:45 pm	Aquarius	Air	Barren	3rd
5 WED	Aquarius	Air	Barren	3rd
6 THU 11:20 pm	Pisces	Water	Fruitful	3rd
7 FRI	Pisces	Water	Fruitful	3rd
8 SAT	Pisces	Water	Fruitful	4th 6:06 am
9 SUN 3:24 am	Aries	Fire	Barren	4th
10 MON	Aries	Fire	Barren	4th
11 TUE 10:11 am	Taurus	Earth	Semi-fruit	4th
12 WED	Taurus	Earth	Semi-fruit	4th
13 THU 7:16 pm	Gemini	Air	Barren	4th
14 FRI	Gemini	Air	Barren	4th
15 SAT	Gemini	Air	Barren	New 8:36 pm
16 SUN 6:08 am	Cancer	Water	Fruitful	1st
17 MON	Cancer	Water	Fruitful	1st
18 TUE 6:21 pm	Leo	Fire	Barren	1st
19 WED	Leo	Fire	Barren	1st
20 THU	Leo	Fire	Barren	1st
21 FRI 7:07 am	Virgo	Earth	Barren	1st
22 SAT	Virgo	Earth	Barren	1st
23 SUN 6:38 pm	Libra	Air	Semi-fruit	1st
24 MON	Libra	Air	Semi-fruit	2nd 12:23 am
25 TUE	Libra	Air	Semi-fruit	2nd
26 WED 2:54 am	Scorpio	Water	Fruitful	2nd
27 THU	Scorpio	Water	Fruitful	2nd
28 FRI 7:02 am	Sagittarius	Fire	Barren	2nd
29 SAT	Sagittarius	Fire	Barren	2nd
30 SUN 7:48 am	Capricorn	Earth	Semi-fruit	Full 10:59 pm

June

Lunar Aspectarian   Favorable and Unfavorable Days

	Sun	Mercury	Venus	Mars	Jupiter	Saturn	Uranus	Neptune	Pluto	Aries	Taurus	Gemini	Cancer	Leo	Virgo	Libra	Scorpio	Sagittarius	Capricorn	Aquarius	Pisces
1	O					T	X			f		U		f	u	f		F		f	u
2			O							f		U		f	u	f		F		f	u
3					C	Q				u	f		U		f	u	f		F		f
4		T		T				C	X	u	f		U		f	u	f		F		f
5	T					X	C			f	u	f		U		f	u	f		F	
6		Q	T	Q						f	u	f		U		f	u	f		F	
7									Q		f	u	f		U		f	u	f		F
8	Q	X	Q	X	X			X			f	u	f		U		f	u	f		F
9						C	X		T		f	u	f		U		f	u	f		F
10	X		X		Q					F		f	u	f		U		f	u	f	
11							Q	Q		F		f	u	f		U		f	u	f	
12				T							F		f	u	f		U		f	u	f
13		C		C				T	O		F		f	u	f		U		f	u	f
14						X	T			f		F		f	u	f		U		f	u
15	C		C							f		F		f	u	f		U		f	u
16						Q				f		F		f	u	f		U		f	u
17					O					u	f		F		f	u	f		U		f
18							O	O	T	u	f		F		f	u	f		U		f
19		X		X		T	O			f	u	f		F		f	u	f		U	
20			X							f	u	f		F		f	u	f		U	
21	X			Q					Q	f	u	f		F		f	u	f		U	
22		Q	Q	T							f	u	f		F		f	u	f		U
23								T	X		f	u	f		F		f	u	f		U
24	Q		T	T	Q	O	T			U		f	u	f		F		f	u	f	
25		T						Q		U		f	u	f		F		f	u	f	
26	T							Q		U		f	u	f		F		f	u	f	
27				X							U		f	u	f		F		f	u	f
28			O	O		T	X	X	C		U		f	u	f		F		f	u	f
29			O	O						f		U		f	u	f		F		f	u
30	O	O				Q				f		U		f	u	f		F		f	u

July Moon Table

Date	Sign	Element	Nature	Phase
1 MON	Capricorn	Earth	Semi-fruit	3rd
2 TUE 7:06 am	Aquarius	Air	Barren	3rd
3 WED	Aquarius	Air	Barren	3rd
4 THU 7:07 am	Pisces	Water	Fruitful	3rd
5 FRI	Pisces	Water	Fruitful	3rd
6 SAT 9:42 am	Aries	Fire	Barren	3rd
7 SUN	Aries	Fire	Barren	4th 1:55 pm
8 MON 3:43 pm	Taurus	Earth	Semi-fruit	4th
9 TUE	Taurus	Earth	Semi-fruit	4th
10 WED	Taurus	Earth	Semi-fruit	4th
11 THU 12:52 am	Gemini	Air	Barren	4th
12 FRI	Gemini	Air	Barren	4th
13 SAT 12:08 pm	Cancer	Water	Fruitful	4th
14 SUN	Cancer	Water	Fruitful	4th
15 MON	Cancer	Water	Fruitful	New 11:15 am
16 TUE 12:31 am	Leo	Fire	Barren	1st
17 WED	Leo	Fire	Barren	1st
18 THU 1:17 pm	Virgo	Earth	Barren	1st
19 FRI	Virgo	Earth	Barren	1st
20 SAT	Virgo	Earth	Barren	1st
21 SUN 1:14 am	Libra	Air	Semi-fruit	1st
22 MON	Libra	Air	Semi-fruit	1st
23 TUE 10:43 am	Scorpio	Water	Fruitful	2nd 12:50 pm
24 WED	Scorpio	Water	Fruitful	2nd
25 THU 4:24 pm	Sagittarius	Fire	Barren	2nd
26 FRI	Sagittarius	Fire	Barren	2nd
27 SAT 6:18 pm	Capricorn	Earth	Semi-fruit	2nd
28 SUN	Capricorn	Earth	Semi-fruit	2nd
29 MON 5:48 pm	Aquarius	Air	Barren	2nd
30 TUE	Aquarius	Air	Barren	Full 5:36 am
31 WED 5:01 pm	Pisces	Water	Fruitful	3rd

July

Lunar Aspectarian | **Favorable and Unfavorable Days**

	Sun	Mercury	Venus	Mars	Jupiter	Saturn	Uranus	Neptune	Pluto	Aries	Taurus	Gemini	Cancer	Leo	Virgo	Libra	Scorpio	Sagittarius	Capricorn	Aquarius	Pisces
1					C					u	f		U		f	u	f		F		f
2						X	C	C	X	u	f		U		f	u	f		F		f
3			T	T						f	u	f		U		f	u	f		F	
4		T							Q	f	u	f		U		f	u	f		F	
5	T		Q	Q	X						f	u	f		U		f	u	f		F
6						C	X	X	T		f	u	f		U		f	u	f		F
7	Q	Q	X	X	Q					F		f	u	f		U		f	u	f	
8								Q	Q	F		f	u	f		U		f	u	f	
9		X		T							F		f	u	f		U		f	u	f
10	X							T			F		f	u	f		U		f	u	f
11						X	T		0	f		F		f	u	f		U		f	u
12			C	C						f		F		f	u	f		U		f	u
13										f		F		f	u	f		U		f	u
14					0	Q				u	f		F		f	u	f		U		f
15	C	C						0		u	f		F		f	u	f		U		f
16						T	0		T	f	u	f		F		f	u	f		U	
17			X							f	u	f		F		f	u	f		U	
18				X					Q	f	u	f		F		f	u	f		U	
19			Q	T							f	u	f		F		f	u	f		U
20	X			Q				T	X		f	u	f		F		f	u	f		U
21		X			Q	0	T		X	U		f	u	f		F		f	u	f	
22			T							U		f	u	f		F		f	u	f	
23	Q			T				Q	Q	U		f	u	f		F		f	u	f	
24		Q			X						U		f	u	f		F		f	u	f
25	T						X	X	C		U		f	u	f		F		f	u	f
26						T				f		U		f	u	f		F		f	u
27		T	0	0						f		U		f	u	f		F		f	u
28					C	Q				u	f		U		f	u	f		F		f
29							C	C	X	u	f		U		f	u	f		F		f
30	0					X				f	u	f		U		f	u	f		F	
31		0	T	T					Q	f	u	f		U		f	u	f		F	

August Moon Table

Date	Sign	Element	Nature	Phase
1 THU	Pisces	Water	Fruitful	3rd
2 FRI 6:05 pm	Aries	Fire	Barren	3rd
3 SAT	Aries	Fire	Barren	3rd
4 SUN 10:33 pm	Taurus	Earth	Semi-fruit	3rd
5 MON	Taurus	Earth	Semi-fruit	3rd
6 TUE	Taurus	Earth	Semi-fruit	4th 12:25 am
7 WED 6:49 am	Gemini	Air	Barren	4th
8 THU	Gemini	Air	Barren	4th
9 FRI 5:58 pm	Cancer	Water	Fruitful	4th
10 SAT	Cancer	Water	Fruitful	4th
11 SUN	Cancer	Water	Fruitful	4th
12 MON 6:29 am	Leo	Fire	Barren	4th
13 TUE	Leo	Fire	Barren	4th
14 WED 7:08 pm	Virgo	Earth	Barren	New 2:35 am
15 THU	Virgo	Earth	Barren	1st
16 FRI	Virgo	Earth	Barren	1st
17 SAT 6:56 am	Libra	Air	Semi-fruit	1st
18 SUN	Libra	Air	Semi-fruit	1st
19 MON 4:51 pm	Scorpio	Water	Fruitful	1st
20 TUE	Scorpio	Water	Fruitful	1st
21 WED 11:48 pm	Sagittarius	Fire	Barren	2nd 10:37 pm
22 THU	Sagittarius	Fire	Barren	2nd
23 FRI	Sagittarius	Fire	Barren	2nd
24 SAT 3:22 am	Capricorn	Earth	Semi-fruit	2nd
25 SUN	Capricorn	Earth	Semi-fruit	2nd
26 MON 4:10 am	Aquarius	Air	Barren	2nd
27 TUE	Aquarius	Air	Barren	2nd
28 WED 3:48 am	Pisces	Water	Fruitful	Full 12:52 pm
29 THU	Pisces	Water	Fruitful	3rd
30 FRI 4:15 am	Aries	Fire	Barren	3rd
31 SAT	Aries	Fire	Barren	3rd

August

Lunar Aspectarian   Favorable and Unfavorable Days

	Sun	Mercury	Venus	Mars	Jupiter	Saturn	Uranus	Neptune	Pluto	Aries	Taurus	Gemini	Cancer	Leo	Virgo	Libra	Scorpio	Sagittarius	Capricorn	Aquarius	Pisces
1					X						f	u	f		U		f	u	f		F
2			Q				X	X	T		f	u	f		U		f	u	f		F
3	T				Q	Q	C			F		f	u	f		U		f	u	f	
4			X					Q		F		f	u	f		U		f	u	f	
5		T		X	T		Q				F		f	u	f		U		f	u	f
6	Q							T			F		f	u	f		U		f	u	f
7		Q				X	T		0		F		f	u	f		U		f	u	f
8	X	Q								f		F		f	u	f		U		f	u
9			C							f		F		f	u	f		U		f	u
10		X		C	0	Q				u	f		F		f	u	f		U		f
11								0		u	f		F		f	u	f		U		f
12						T	0		T	u	f		F		f	u	f		U		f
13										f	u	f		F		f	u	f		U	
14	C							Q		f	u	f		F		f	u	f		U	
15			X	X	T						f	u	f		F		f	u	f		U
16		C						T			f	u	f		F		f	u	f		U
17					Q	0	T		X		f	u	f		F		f	u	f		U
18			Q	Q						U		f	u	f		F		f	u	f	
19	X						Q	Q		U		f	u	f		F		f	u	f	
20			T		X						U		f	u	f		F		f	u	f
21	Q	X		T				X			U		f	u	f		F		f	u	f
22						T	X		C	f		U		f	u	f		F		f	u
23										f		U		f	u	f		F		f	u
24	T	Q			C	Q				f		U		f	u	f		F		f	u
25			0	0					C	u	f		U		f	u	f		F		f
26		T				X	C		X	u	f		U		f	u	f		F		f
27										f	u	f		U		f	u	f		F	
28	0				X				Q	f	u	f		U		f	u	f		F	
29			T	T				X			f	u	f		U		f	u	f		F
30		0			Q	C	X		T		f	u	f		U		f	u	f		F
31			Q	Q				Q		F		f	u	f		U		f	u	f	

September Moon Table

Date	Sign	Element	Nature	Phase
1 SUN 7:20 am	Taurus	Earth	Semi-fruit	3rd
2 MON	Taurus	Earth	Semi-fruit	3rd
3 TUE 2:09 pm	Gemini	Air	Barren	3rd
4 WED	Gemini	Air	Barren	4th 2:07 pm
5 THU	Gemini	Air	Barren	4th
6 FRI 12:30 am	Cancer	Water	Fruitful	4th
7 SAT	Cancer	Water	Fruitful	4th
8 SUN 12:55 pm	Leo	Fire	Barren	4th
9 MON	Leo	Fire	Barren	4th
10 TUE	Leo	Fire	Barren	4th
11 WED 1:29 am	Virgo	Earth	Barren	4th
12 THU	Virgo	Earth	Barren	New 6:08 pm
13 FRI 12:51 pm	Libra	Air	Semi-fruit	1st
14 SAT	Libra	Air	Semi-fruit	1st
15 SUN 10:20 pm	Scorpio	Water	Fruitful	1st
16 MON	Scorpio	Water	Fruitful	1st
17 TUE	Scorpio	Water	Fruitful	1st
18 WED 5:30 am	Sagittarius	Fire	Barren	1st
19 THU	Sagittarius	Fire	Barren	1st
20 FRI 10:12 am	Capricorn	Earth	Semi-fruit	2nd 6:23 am
21 SAT	Capricorn	Earth	Semi-fruit	2nd
22 SUN 12:39 pm	Aquarius	Air	Barren	2nd
23 MON	Aquarius	Air	Barren	2nd
24 TUE 1:43 pm	Pisces	Water	Fruitful	2nd
25 WED	Pisces	Water	Fruitful	2nd
26 THU 2:46 pm	Aries	Fire	Barren	Full
27 FRI	Aries	Fire	Barren	3rd
28 SAT 5:24 pm	Taurus	Earth	Semi-fruit	3rd
29 SUN	Taurus	Earth	Semi-fruit	3rd
30 MON 11:02 pm	Gemini	Air	Barren	3rd

September

Lunar Aspectarian   Favorable and Unfavorable Days

	Sun	Mercury	Venus	Mars	Jupiter	Saturn	Uranus	Neptune	Pluto	Aries	Taurus	Gemini	Cancer	Leo	Virgo	Libra	Scorpio	Sagittarius	Capricorn	Aquarius	Pisces
1					T			Q		F		f	u	f		U		f	u	f	
2	T										F		f	u	f		U		f	u	f
3	.	T	X	X			T	T	0		F		f	u	f		U		f	u	f
4	Q					X				f		F		f	u	f		U		f	u
5										f		F		f	u	f		U		f	u
6		Q			0	Q				u	f		F		f	u	f		U		f
7	X									u	f		F		f	u	f		U		f
8		X	C	C		T	0	0	T	u	f		F		f	u	f		U		f
9										f	u	f		F		f	u	f		U	
10										f	u	f		F		f	u	f		U	
11					T				Q		f	u	f		F		f	u	f		U
12	C										f	u	f		F		f	u	f		U
13		C		X		0	T	T	X		f	u	f		F		f	u	f		U
14			X	Q						U		f	u	f		F		f	u	f	
15							Q	Q		U		f	u	f		F		f	u	f	
16			Q	Q	X						U		f	u	f		F		f	u	f
17	X	X						X			U		f	u	f		F		f	u	f
18				T		T	X		C		U		f	u	f		F		f	u	f
19		Q	T							f		U		f	u	f		F		f	u
20	Q					Q				f		U		f	u	f		F		f	u
21		T			C					u	f		U		f	u	f		F		f
22	T					X	C	C	X	u	f		U		f	u	f		F		f
23			0	0						f	u	f		U		f	u	f		F	
24									Q	f	u	f		U		f	u	f		F	
25		0			X						f	u	f		U		f	u	f		F
26	0					C	X	X	T		f	u	f		U		f	u	f		F
27			T		Q					F		f	u	f		U		f	u	f	
28		T					Q	Q		F		f	u	f		U		f	u	f	
29			Q	T							F		f	u	f		U		f	u	f
30		T	Q					T			F		f	u	f		U		f	u	f

October Moon Table

Date	Sign	Element	Nature	Phase
1 TUE	Gemini	Air	Barren	3rd
2 WED	Gemini	Air	Barren	3rd
3 THU 8:15 am	Cancer	Water	Fruitful	3rd
4 FRI	Cancer	Water	Fruitful	4th 7:05 am
5 SAT 8:12 pm	Leo	Fire	Barren	4th
6 SUN	Leo	Fire	Barren	4th
7 MON	Leo	Fire	Barren	4th
8 TUE 8:49 am	Virgo	Earth	Barren	4th
9 WED	Virgo	Earth	Barren	4th
10 THU 8:00 pm	Libra	Air	Semi-fruit	4th
11 FRI	Libra	Air	Semi-fruit	4th
12 SAT	Libra	Air	Semi-fruit	New 9:14 am
13 SUN 4:46 am	Scorpio	Water	Fruitful	1st
14 MON	Scorpio	Water	Fruitful	1st
15 TUE 11:07 am	Sagittarius	Fire	Barren	1st
16 WED	Sagittarius	Fire	Barren	1st
17 THU 3:38 pm	Capricorn	Earth	Semi-fruit	1st
18 FRI	Capricorn	Earth	Semi-fruit	1st
19 SAT 6:52 pm	Aquarius	Air	Barren	2nd 1:10 pm
20 SUN	Aquarius	Air	Barren	2nd
21 MON 9:23 pm	Pisces	Water	Fruitful	2nd
22 TUE	Pisces	Water	Fruitful	2nd
23 WED 11:51 pm	Aries	Fire	Barren	2nd
24 THU	Aries	Fire	Barren	2nd
25 FRI	Aries	Fire	Barren	2nd
26 SAT 3:12 am	Taurus	Earth	Semi-fruit	Full 9:12 am
27 SUN	Taurus	Earth	Semi-fruit	3rd
28 MON 8:35 am	Gemini	Air	Barren	3rd
29 TUE	Gemini	Air	Barren	3rd
30 WED 4:57 pm	Cancer	Water	Fruitful	3rd
31 THU	Cancer	Water	Fruitful	3rd

October

Lunar Aspectarian   Favorable and Unfavorable Days

	Sun	Mercury	Venus	Mars	Jupiter	Saturn	Uranus	Neptune	Pluto	Aries	Taurus	Gemini	Cancer	Leo	Virgo	Libra	Scorpio	Sagittarius	Capricorn	Aquarius	Pisces
1	T					X	T		O	f		F		f	u	f		U		f	u
2		Q		X						f		F		f	u	f		U		f	u
3			X		O	Q				f		F		f	u	f		U		f	u
4	Q				O					u	f		F		f	u	f		U		f
5		X					O	O	T	u	f		F		f	u	f		U		f
6						T				f	u	f		F		f	u	f		U	
7	X			C						f	u	f		F		f	u	f		U	
8			C						Q	f	u	f		F		f	u	f		U	
9					T						f	u	f		F		f	u	f		U
10							T	T	X		f	u	f		F		f	u	f		U
11		C			Q	O				U		f	u	f		F		f	u	f	
12	C			X				Q		U		f	u	f		F		f	u	f	
13				X		Q				U		f	u	f		F		f	u	f	
14			X	Q							U		f	u	f		F		f	u	f
15						T	X	X	C		U		f	u	f		F		f	u	f
16		X	Q							f	U			f	u	f		F		f	u
17	X			T		Q				f	U			f	u	f		F		f	u
18		Q	T		C					u	f		U		f	u	f		F		f
19	Q					X	C	C	X	u	f		U		f	u	f		F		f
20										f	u	f		U		f	u	f		F	
21	T	T		O						f	u	f		U		f	u	f		F	
22				X					Q	f	u	f		U		f	u	f			F
23			O					X		f	u	f		U		f	u	f			F
24					Q	C	X		T	F		f	u	f			U		f	u	f	
25				T				Q		F		f	u	f			U		f	u	f	
26	O	O						Q		F		f	u	f			U		f	u	f	
27					T			T			F		f	u	f			U		f	u	f
28		T	Q		X	T			O		F		f	u	f			U		f	u	f
29										f		F		f	u	f		U		f	u
30			Q	X		Q				f		F		f	u	f		U		f	u
31	T	T			O					u	f		F		f	u	f		U		f

November Moon Table

Date	Sign	Element	Nature	Phase
1 FRI	Cancer	Water	Fruitful	3rd
2 SAT 4:16 am	Leo	Fire	Barren	3rd
3 SUN	Leo	Fire	Barren	4th 2:50 am
4 MON 4:57 pm	Virgo	Earth	Barren	4th
5 TUE	Virgo	Earth	Barren	4th
6 WED	Virgo	Earth	Barren	4th
7 THU 4:29 am	Libra	Air	Semi-fruit	4th
8 FRI	Libra	Air	Semi-fruit	4th
9 SAT 1:02 pm	Scorpio	Water	Fruitful	4th
10 SUN	Scorpio	Water	Fruitful	New 11:17 pm
11 MON 6:27 pm	Sagittarius	Fire	Barren	1st
12 TUE	Sagittarius	Fire	Barren	1st
13 WED 9:44 pm	Capricorn	Earth	Semi-fruit	1st
14 THU	Capricorn	Earth	Semi-fruit	1st
15 FRI	Capricorn	Earth	Semi-fruit	1st
16 SAT 12:15 am	Aquarius	Air	Barren	1st
17 SUN	Aquarius	Air	Barren	2nd 8:10 pm
18 MON 3:00 am	Pisces	Water	Fruitful	2nd
19 TUE	Pisces	Water	Fruitful	2nd
20 WED 6:34 am	Aries	Fire	Barren	2nd
21 THU	Aries	Fire	Barren	2nd
22 FRI 11:12 am	Taurus	Earth	Semi-fruit	2nd
23 SAT	Taurus	Earth	Semi-fruit	2nd
24 SUN 5:19 pm	Gemini	Air	Barren	Full 11:10 pm
25 MON	Gemini	Air	Barren	3rd
26 TUE	Gemini	Air	Barren	3rd
27 WED 1:37 am	Cancer	Water	Fruitful	3rd
28 THU	Cancer	Water	Fruitful	3rd
29 FRI 12:30 pm	Leo	Fire	Barren	3rd
30 SAT	Leo	Fire	Barren	3rd

November

Lunar Aspectarian   Favorable and Unfavorable Days

	Sun	Mercury	Venus	Mars	Jupiter	Saturn	Uranus	Neptune	Pluto	Aries	Taurus	Gemini	Cancer	Leo	Virgo	Libra	Scorpio	Sagittarius	Capricorn	Aquarius	Pisces
1								0		u	f		F		f	u	f		U		f
2			X			T	0		T	u	f		F		f	u	f		U		f
3	Q	Q								f	u	f		F		f	u	f		U	
4				C					Q	f	u	f		F		f	u	f		U	
5	X				T						f	u	f		F		f	u	f		U
6		X						T			f	u	f		F		f	u	f		U
7						0	T		X		f	u	f		F		f	u	f		U
8			C		Q					U		f	u	f		F		f	u	f	
9				X			Q	Q		U		f	u	f		F		f	u	f	
10	C			X						U		f	u	f		F		f	u	f	
11		C				T	X	X	C	U		f	u	f		F		f	u	f	
12				Q						f		U		f	u	f		F		f	u
13			X		Q					f		U		f	u	f		F		f	u
14				T	C					u	f		U		f	u	f		F		f
15	X		Q					C		u	f		U		f	u	f		F		f
16		X				X	C		X	f	u	f		U		f	u	f		F	
17	Q		T							f	u	f		U		f	u	f		F	
18		Q		0					Q	f	u	f		U		f	u	f		F	
19					X			X			f	u	f		U		f	u	f		F
20	T					C	X		T		f	u	f		U		f	u	f		F
21		T			Q					F		f	u	f		U		f	u	f	
22			0				Q	Q		F		f	u	f		U		f	u	f	
23				T	T					F		f	u	f		U		f	u	f	
24	0					X	T	T	0	F		f	u	f		U		f	u	f	
25		0		Q						f		F		f	u	f		U		f	u
26		0			Q					f		F		f	u	f		U		f	u
27			T		Q					u	f		F		f	u	f		U		f
28				X	0					u	f		F		f	u	f		U		f
29						T	0	0	T	u	f		F		f	u	f		U		f
30	T		Q							f	u	f		F		f	u	f		U	

December Moon Table

Date	Sign	Element	Nature	Phase
1 SUN	Leo	Fire	Barren	3rd
2 MON 1:11 am	Virgo	Earth	Barren	3rd
3 TUE	Virgo	Earth	Barren	4th 12:06 am
4 WED 1:24 pm	Libra	Air	Semi-fruit	4th
5 THU	Libra	Air	Semi-fruit	4th
6 FRI 10:39 pm	Scorpio	Water	Fruitful	4th
7 SAT	Scorpio	Water	Fruitful	4th
8 SUN	Scorpio	Water	Fruitful	4th
9 MON 3:59 am	Sagittarius	Fire	Barren	4th
10 TUE	Sagittarius	Fire	Barren	New 11:57 am
11 WED 6:15 am	Capricorn	Earth	Semi-fruit	1st
12 THU	Capricorn	Earth	Semi-fruit	1st
13 FRI 7:14 am	Aquarius	Air	Barren	1st
14 SAT	Aquarius	Air	Barren	1st
15 SUN 8:44 am	Pisces	Water	Fruitful	1st
16 MON	Pisces	Water	Fruitful	1st
17 TUE 11:55 am	Aries	Fire	Barren	2nd 4:31 am
18 WED	Aries	Fire	Barren	2nd
19 THU 5:09 pm	Taurus	Earth	Semi-fruit	2nd
20 FRI	Taurus	Earth	Semi-fruit	2nd
21 SAT	Taurus	Earth	Semi-fruit	2nd
22 SUN 12:17 am	Gemini	Air	Barren	2nd
23 MON	Gemini	Air	Barren	2nd
24 TUE 9:14 am	Cancer	Water	Fruitful	Full 3:41 pm
25 WED	Cancer	Water	Fruitful	3rd
26 THU 8:09 pm	Leo	Fire	Barren	3rd
27 FRI	Leo	Fire	Barren	3rd
28 SAT	Leo	Fire	Barren	3rd
29 SUN 8:46 am	Virgo	Earth	Barren	3rd
30 MON	Virgo	Earth	Barren	3rd
31 TUE 9:33 pm	Libra	Air	Semi-fruit	3rd

December

Lunar Aspectarian   Favorable and Unfavorable Days

	Sun	Mercury	Venus	Mars	Jupiter	Saturn	Uranus	Neptune	Pluto	Aries	Taurus	Gemini	Cancer	Leo	Virgo	Libra	Scorpio	Sagittarius	Capricorn	Aquarius	Pisces
1		T								f	u	f		F		f	u	f		U	
2									Q	f	u	f		F		f	u	f		U	
3	Q		X	C	T						f	u	f		F		f	u	f		U
4		Q				0	T	T	X		f	u	f		F		f	u	f		U
5	X									U		f	u	f		F		f	u	f	
6						Q		Q		U		f	u	f		F		f	u	f	
7		X					Q				U		f	u	f		F		f	u	f
8			C	X	X			X			U		f	u	f		F		f	u	f
9						T	X		C		U		f	u	f		F		f	u	f
10	C			Q						f		U		f	u	f		F		f	u
11		C			Q					f		U		f	u	f		F		f	u
12			X	T	C					u	f		U		f	u	f		F		f
13						X	C	C	X	u	f		U		f	u	f		F		f
14	X									f	u	f		U		f	u	f		F	
15			Q						Q	f	u	f		U		f	u	f		F	
16		X			X						f	u	f		U		f	u	f		F
17	Q		T	0		C	X	X	T		f	u	f		U		f	u	f		F
18		Q								F		f	u	f		U		f	u	f	
19	T				Q		Q	Q		F		f	u	f		U		f	u	f	
20											F		f	u	f		U		f	u	f
21		T		T	T			T			F		f	u	f		U		f	u	f
22			0			X	T		0	f		F		f	u	f		U		f	u
23										f		F		f	u	f		U		f	u
24	0			Q	Q					f		F		f	u	f		U		f	u
25		0								u	f		F		f	u	f		U		f
26				X	0	T			0	u	f		F		f	u	f		U		f
27			T				0		T	f	u	f		F		f	u	f		U	
28										f	u	f		F		f	u	f		U	
29									Q	f	u	f		F		f	u	f		U	
30	T	T	Q								f	u	f		F		f	u	f		U
31				C	T	0		T			f	u	f		F		f	u	f		U

Moon Void of Course

Last Aspect		Moon Enters New Phase		
Date	**Time**	**Date**	**Sign**	**Time**
January				
1	8:19 pm	1	Gemini	9:30 pm
3	12:54 pm	4	Cancer	9:56 am
6	9:54 pm	6	Leo	10:31 pm
8	7:33 pm	9	Virgo	10:29 am
14	2:36 am	14	Scorpio	4:30 am
16	12:38 am	16	Sagittarius	8:25 am
17	6:21 pm	18	Capricorn	9:08am
20	7:51 am	20	Aquarius	8:15 am
21	12:02 am	22	Pisces	8:03 am
24	2:54 am	24	Aries	10:38 am
26	9:05 am	26	Taurus	5:17 pm
28	7:14 pm	29	Gemini	3:43 am
31	12:01 am	31	Cancer	4:12 pm
February				
2	8:34 pm	3	Leo	4:46 am
5	12:23 am	5	Virgo	4:23 pm
8	12:32 am	8	Libra	2:31 am
10	3:35 am	10	Scorpio	10:35 am
12	12:10 pm	12	Sagittarius	3:59 pm
14	5:48 pm	14	Capricorn	6:30 pm
16	1:15 pm	16	Aquarius	7:00 pm
18	6:31 pm	18	Pisces	7:10 pm
20	3:05 pm	20	Aries	8:58 pm
22	7:56 pm	23	Taurus	2:08 am
25	4:44 am	25	Gemini	11:14 am
March				
1	5:25 am	1	Leo	11:47 am
3	6:38 pm	3	Virgo	11:13 pm
6	2:59 am	6	Libra	8:41 am

Moon Void of Course

Last Aspect		Moon Enters New Phase		
Date	Time	Date	Sign	Time
8	10:43 am	8	Scorpio	4:06 pm
10	4:28 pm	10	Sagittarius	9:33 pm
12	7:51 pm	13	Capricorn	1:08 am
14	10:37 pm	15	Aquarius	3:15 am
15	9:25 pm	17	Pisces	4:50 am
19	5:45 am	19	Aries	7:15 am
21	7:11 am	21	Taurus	11:58 am
23	7:03 pm	23	Gemini	7:59 pm
26	4:10 am	26	Cancer	7:06 am
28	5:19 pm	28	Leo	7:38 pm
31	12:45 am	31	Virgo	7:15 am
		April		
2	3:26 pm	2	Libra	4:27 pm
4	6:40 pm	4	Scorpio	10:57 pm
7	11:15 pm	7	Sagittarius	3:22 am
8	12:05 pm	9	Capricorn	6:30 am
11	5:13 am	11	Aquarius	9:09 am
13	1:06 am	13	Pisces	11:59 am
15	11:42 am	15	Aries	3:43 pm
17	5:49 pm	17	Taurus	9:06 pm
20	12:36 am	20	Gemini	4:55 am
21	11:35 pm	22	Cancer	3:25 pm
24	11:12 pm	25	Leo	3:45 am
27	9:33 am	27	Virgo	3:49 pm
29	9:41 pm	30	Libra	1:27 am
		May		
2	7:23 am	2	Scorpio	7:43 am
4	8:46 am	4	Sagittarius	11:04 am
6	4:29 am	6	Capricorn	12:54 pm
8	10:53 am	8	Aquarius	2:39 pm

Moon Vold of Course

Last Aspect		Moon Enters New Phase		
Date	**Time**	**Date**	**Sign**	**Time**
10	12:07 pm	10	Pisces	5:29 pm
12	5:56 pm	12	Aries	10:01 pm
15	12:24 am	15	Taurus	4:25 am
17	8:21 am	17	Gemini	12:48 pm
19	7:54 pm	19	Cancer	11:17 pm
22	6:39 am	22	Leo	11:28 am
24	7:40 pm	24	Virgo	11:59 pm
27	5:53 am	27	Libra	10:33 am
29	1:06 pm	29	Scorpio	5:30 pm
31	4:32 pm	31	Sagittarius	8:43 pm
		June		
2	12:59 pm	2	Capricorn	9:29 pm
4	5:34 pm	4	Aquarius	9:45 pm
6	4:24 pm	6	Pisces	11:20 pm
8	10:59 pm	9	Aries	3:24 am
11	5:08 am	11	Taurus	10:11 am
13	1:56 pm	13	Gemini	7:16 pm
15	8:36 pm	16	Cancer	6:08 am
18	12:33 pm	18	Leo	6:21 pm
20	12:00 am	21	Virgo	7:07 am
23	12:49 pm	23	Libra	6:38 pm
25	9:23 pm	26	Scorpio	2:54 am
28	1:50 am	28	Sagittarius	7:02 am
30	1:12 am	30	Capricorn	7:48 am
		July		
2	2:04 am	2	Aquarius	7:06 am
3	6:27 am	4	Pisces	7:07 am
6	3:58 am	6	Aries	9:42 am
8	9:30 am	8	Taurus	3:43 pm
10	6:13 pm	11	Gemini	12:52 am

Moon Void of Course

Last Aspect		Moon Enters New Phase		
Date	**Time**	**Date**	**Sign**	**Time**
12	6:47 pm	13	Cancer	12:08 pm
15	11:35 pm	16	Leo	12:31 am
18	3:05 am	18	Virgo	1:17 pm
20	10:36 pm	21	Libra	1:14 am
23	7:55 am	23	Scorpio	10:43 am
25	9:48 am	25	Sagittarius	4:24 pm
27	4:43 am	27	Capricorn	6:18 pm
29	11:38 am	29	Aquarius	5:48 pm
31	2:48 pm	31	Pisces	5:01 pm
		August		
2	11:51 am	2	Aries	6:05 pm
4	7:11 pm	4	Taurus	10:33 pm
6	10:50 pm	7	Gemini	6:49 am
8	3:08 pm	9	Cancer	5:58 pm
11	9:50 pm	12	Leo	6:29 am
14	2:35 am	14	Virgo	7:08 am
16	10:16 pm	17	Libra	6:56 am
19	11:03 am	19	Scorpio	4:51 pm
21	10:37 pm	21	Sagittarius	11:48 pm
24	12:49 am	24	Capricorn	3:22 am
25	8:50 pm	26	Aquarius	4:10 am
26	2:01 pm	28	Pisces	3:48 am
29	8:36 pm	30	Aries	4:15 am
31	11:06 pm	1	Taurus	7:20 am
		September		
3	6:45 am	3	Gemini	2:09 pm
4	2:07 pm	6	Cancer	12:30 am
8	11:27 am	8	Leo	12:55 pm
8	11:39 pm	11	Virgo	1:29 am
13	10:40 am	13	Libra	12:51 pm

Moon Void of Course

Last Aspect		Moon Enters New Phase		
Date	Time	Date	Sign	Time
15	1:05 pm	15	Scorpio	10:20 pm
17	9:18 pm	18	Sagittarius	5:30 am
20	6:23 am	20	Capricorn	10:12 am
22	12:38 pm	22	Aquarius	12:39 pm
23	6:52 pm	24	Pisces	1:43 pm
26	6:32 am	26	Aries	2:46 pm
28	8:47 am	28	Taurus	5:24 pm
30	4:08 pm	30	Gemini	11:02 pm
		October		
3	6:47 am	3	Cancer	8:15 am
5	10:23 am	5	Leo	8:12 pm
7	6:22 am	8	Virgo	8:49 am
10	10:15 am	10	Libra	8:00 pm
12	7:27 pm	13	Scorpio	4:46 am
15	2:12 am	15	Sagittarius	11:07 am
17	5:51 am	17	Capricorn	3:38 pm
19	1:10 pm	19	Aquarius	6:52 pm
21	7:31 pm	21	Pisces	9:23 pm
23	3:30 pm	23	Aries	11:51 pm
26	12:52 am	26	Taurus	3:12 am
28	6:44 am	28	Gemini	8:35 am
28	12:08 pm	30	Cancer	4:57 pm
		November		
1	6:33 pm	2	Leo	4:16 am
3	4:47 am	4	Virgo	4:57 pm
6	7:13 pm	7	Libra	4:29 am
9	4:23 am	9	Scorpio	1:02 pm
11	10:19 am	11	Sagittarius	6:27 pm
13	1:18 am	13	Capricorn	9:44 pm
15	4:33 pm	16	Aquarius	12:15 am

Moon Void of Course

Last Aspect		Moon Enters New Phase		
Date	**Time**	**Date**	**Sign**	**Time**
17	8:10 pm	18	Pisces	3:00 am
20	3:38 am	20	Aries	6:34 am
22	10:16 am	22	Taurus	11:12 am
24	9:19 am	24	Gemini	5:19 pm
26	2:22 am	27	Cancer	1:37 am
29	4:01 am	29	Leo	12:30pm
December				
1	5:22 pm	2	Virgo	1:11 am
4	5:18 am	4	Libra	1:24 pm
6	3:12 pm	6	Scorpio	10:39 pm
8	9:10 pm	9	Sagittarius	3:59 am
10	3:21 pm	11	Capricorn	6:15 am
13	12:59 am	13	Aquarius	7:14 am
15	4:57 am	15	Pisces	8:44 am
17	5:31 am	17	Aries	11:55 am
19	1:51 pm	19	Taurus	5:09 pm
21	5:42 pm	22	Gemini	12:17 am
24	2:29 am	24	Cancer	9:14 am
26	3:02 pm	26	Leo	8:09 pm
27	11:39 pm	29	Virgo	8:46 am
31	8:03 pm	31	Libra	9:33 pm

Best Days for Activities

When you wish to choose a favorable day for something other than matters governed by your own ruling planet, read the following list and note the planet which rules the matter in question. Turn to the list of Favorable and Unfavorable Days in the Moon Tables section. Choose a date for the activity listed below that is both marked favorable (F or f) for your Sun sign and one that is marked with an X or T in the Lunar Aspectarian under the planet described. Never choose a date for any of these activities which is marked with an O or Q under Saturn, Mars, or Uranus, as these are negative aspects. They tend to counteract good results.

The more good aspects in operation on the date you choose, the better the outlook for your affairs. The better the day, the better the deed. To review: Choose a date from the proper lists of dates marked X or T under the planet ruling the activity and also marked F or f in your own sign, but never a date marked O or Q in the Lunar Aspectarian to Mars, Saturn, or Uranus.

Moon

For housecleaning or baking, putting up preserves, washing, using liquids, matters connected with babies or small children, and to deal with the public in general, choose the good aspects of the Moon.

Sun

To gain favors of persons of high rank or prominent social standing, or those in government office, to make a change or try for promotion, choose the good dates of the Sun.

Mercury

For writing or signing an important document, seeking news or information, shopping, or studying, choose the good dates of Mercury.

Venus

To give a successful party, to marry, for matters of courtship, art, beauty, adornment, to cultivate the friendship of a woman, choose the good dates of Venus.

Mars

For dealing with surgeons, dentists, hair stylists, assayers, contractors, mechanics, lumber workers, police officers, army or navy personnel, choose the good dates of Mars.

Jupiter

To deal with physicians, educators, sportspeople, bankers, brokers, philanthropists, to collect money or make important changes, choose the good dates of Jupiter.

Saturn

For dealing with plumbers, excavators, or miners, for starting a new building, leasing a house or dealing in land, choose the good dates of Saturn.

Uranus

For successful work on an invention, for dealing with inventors, metaphysicians or astrologers, for new methods, or starting a journey, choose the good dates of Uranus.

Neptune

For affairs connected with the deep sea or liquids in general, for practicing psychometry or developing mediumship, photography, tobacco and drugs, choose the good dates of Neptune.

Pluto

For uncovering errors, overcoming habits, healing, fumigation, pasteurizing, pest control, also for matters related to the affairs of the dead, taxes, inheritance, etc., choose the good dates of Pluto.

Astro Almanac 1996

	Jan	Feb	Mar	Apr	May	Jun	July	Aug	Sep	Oct	Nov	Dec
Advertise	18		13	9			27	24	20	16		11
Advertise new venture	18	26	13	9			27	24	20	16		11
Buy animals	21-22, 25-27	21-26	20-25	18-25	18-25	17-23	16-23	15-16, 18-19	14-15, 19	13,16, 18-19	12, 14-17	12-15
Neuturing animals	2-4, 6-9, 19-22, 30-31	1-3, 5,15-18, 26-29	1-3, 14-17, 24-31	10-13, 21-27	7-10, 18-24	3-6, 14-21	1-4, 12-18, 28, 29, 31	8-14, 25-27	4-11, 21-24	1-8, 18-21, 29-31	1-4, 14-18, 25-30	1-2, 12 15, 22-25-29
Dock animals	13-22	11-18	12-17, 24-26	10-13, 20-24	17-24	14-22	12-22	8-21	5-19	5-19	3-17	3-15
Permanent wave	1, 7-9, 27-29	4-5, 23-25	2-3, 22-23, 29-31	18-20, 26-27	16-17, 23-24	12-13, 19-21	9-11, 17-18	5-7, 13-14	2-3,9-11, 29-30	6-8, 27-28	3-4, 23-24, 30	1-2, 20 21, 27-
Cut hair for thickness	4,5	2,3,4	3								22,23,24	21
Cut hair to slow growth	10-11	6-8	6	16-17	13-14	10-11, 14-15	7-8, 12-13	3-4, 8-9, 31	1, 4-6, 12, 27-28	1-3, 9-10, 29-30	5-7, 25-26	3-4, 31
Cut hair for growth	5, 23-24	1-3, 19-20, 28-29	1, 27-28	23-25	20-22	17-8	16		25-26	22-23	19-20	16-17
Start a diet	7-11, 17-18	5-8, 13-14, 17-18	6, 11-13, 16-17	8-9, 12-13, 16-17	5-6, 9-10, 13-14	2, 5-6, 10-11	3-4, 7-8, 31	3-4, 13-14, 31	1, 9-12, 27-28	6-10	3-7, 30	1-4, 1? 27-31
Apply for a job	10-11, 20, 27, 29	6, 15, 23	4, 14, 22	1, 10, 19, 28-29	7, 16-17, 26-27	3, 12, 22	1, 9-10, 19-20, 28	5, 15	2, 12, 21-22, 29	9, 18, 27	5, 14-15, 23	3, 12, 21, 30 31
Ask for a raise	1, 9, 12-13, 16, 18-19, 22, 28	6, 10-11, 13, 15-17, 19	8-9, 13-14, 22-23, 28-29	6, 11, 14, 19, 21, 26, 28-29	7, 11-12, 16, 19, 21, 24, 26, 29-30	4, 7-8, 10, 12, 15, 19-20, 22, 25	1-4, 7, 9, 15, 17, 19, 22, 24, 31	1, 4-5, 9, 15-16, 20-21, 29	1, 3, 11, 14, 17, 19, 21, 28, 30	5, 8-9, 13, 16, 18, 22, 27, 31	2, 5, 6, 8, 10-11, 14, 16-17, 19, 21, 23	1, 2, 7 8, 12, 27, 30
Entertain	2-4, 7-9, 12-14, 21-22, 30-31	4-5, 9-10, 17-18, 26-27	2-3, 7-8, 16-17, 24-26, 29-31	3-4, 12-13, 21-22, 26-27	1-2, 9-10, 18-19, 23-24, 28-29	5-6, 14-16, 19-21, 24-26	3-4, 12-13, 17-18, 22-23, 30-31	8-9, 13-14, 18-19, 27-28	4-6, 9-11, 14-15, 23-24	1-3, 6-8, 11-13, 20-21, 29-30	3-4, 8-9, 17-18, 25-26, 30	1-2, 5 14-15, 22-24, 27-29
Canning	6, 10, 11	6-8	6				14-15	10-12	7-8, 12	4,-5, 9-10, 31	1-2, 5-6, 7, 27-29	3-4, 2 26, 30 31
Brewing	5		18-19	14-15	11-12	9	14-15	10-12, 28	7-8, 26	5		
Buy a home	27	23-25	22-23	18-20, 23-25	20-24	17-21	16-18					

Astro Almanac 1996

	Jan	Feb	Mar	Apr	May	Jun	July	Aug	Sep	Oct	Nov	Dec
...y real estate appreciation	13-14	2, 10, 21	28	16	1, 14, 29	10, 24	7, 22	4	1, 8, 14, 28	13, 26	2, 8, 27	
...tart house ...onstruction	1, 20, 28	18, 24-25	19, 23	17, 20	17	5, 15, 19	11, 15, 30	7, 14	3, 12	6, 12, 28	10, 24	10, 21
...ur concrete	1, 5, 6, 15, 19, 28	2, 12, 16, 24-25, 29	1, 10, 14, 23, 28	7, 11, 20, 25	4, 8, 17, 22	1, 5, 14, 19, 28	2, 11, 16, 26, 30	7, 12, 22, 26	3, 4, 8, 18, 22	1, 5-6, 15, 19, 28	2, 11, 15-16, 24, 29	9, 13, 21-22, 26
...model house	1	12, 25	10, 23	7, 20	4, 17	28	11	7, 22	3, 18	15, 28	11, 24	9
...aint house	3, 13-4, 18, 22-23, 27	2, 12-3, 17, 21, 27	3, 13, 18, 22, 28	2, 11, 16, 21, 26	1, 10, 14, 19, 24, 29	6, 10, 15, 19-20, 24	2-3, 7, 12, 17, 22, 31	4, 9, 15, 20, 29	3, 8, 14, 19, 28	3, 8, 13, 14, 18, 28	2, 8, 12-13, 17, 27	2-3, 8, 12, 17, 27
Roofing	7-9	5, 17-18	16-17	12-13	9-10, 16-17	5-6, 12-13	3-4, 9-11, 31	5-7, 13-14	2,-3, 9-11, 29-30	6-8, 27-28	3-4, 30	1-2, 27-29
Set posts	1, 5-6, 15, 19, 28	2, 12, 16, 24-25, 29	1, 10, 14, 23, 28	7, 11, 20, 25	4, 8, 17, 22	1, 5, 14, 19, 28	2, 11, 16, 26, 30	7, 12, 22, 26	3, 4, 8, 18, 22	1, 5-6, 15, 19, 28	2, 11, 15-16, 24, 29	9, 13, 21-22, 26
...ow to slow growth	7-20	5-18	6-17	4-17	4-17	2-6, 10-15	1-4, 7-13, 31	3,-9, 13-14, 31	1-6, 9-12, 27-30	1, -3, 6-12, 27-30	3-10, 25-26, 30	1-10, 27-31
...ut timber	7-14, 17-20	5-10, 13-18	6-8, 11-17	4, 8-13, 16-17	5-10, 13-14, 16-17	2-6, 10-15	1-4, 7-13, 31	3-9, 13-14, 31	1-6, 9-12, 27-30	1-3, 6-12, 27-30	3-9, 25-26, 30	1-6, 10, 27-31
...gal matters	9, 14, 18, 22, 27	6, 10, 15, 19, 23	4, 13, 14, 18, 22	1, 10, 14, 19, 28-29	7, 11-12, 16, 26	3, 7-8, 12, 22	1, 5, 9, 19, 28	1, 5, 15, 24, 28	1, 11, 20-21, 25, 29	9, 13, 18, 22, 26-27	5, 14, 19, 23	3, 12, 16, 21, 31
...n contracts	1, 9, 22, 27-28	23	22-23, 29	19	16	12-13, 19	4, 9	5, 28	3, 11, 29-30	21, 27	23	1, 21
...the dentist	1, 28	24, 25	23	20	17	5, 19	11, 30	7	3	6, 28	24	21
...tract teeth	17-18	13-14, 26	13, 24-25, 26	21-22	18-19, 25	14-16, 22-23	12-13, 19-21	8-9, 15-17	5-6, 12-13, 19-20	9-10, 16-17	5-7, 12-13	4, 10-11
Consult a ...hysician			4, 5	1, 2, 28-30	25, 26-27	22-23	19-21	15-17	13			
...ect money	13	2, 10, 15, 21	14, 28	11	1, 7, 29	10	1, 2, 7, 22	4	1, 14, 21, 28	13, 18, 26	2, 8, 14	12
...ek credit	9, 18, 22-24	13-14, 17-19	3, 13, 18-19, 29	8, 12-14, 26	10-12, 24	5-8, 19-21	3, 5, 17, 31	1, 13-14, 24, 28-29	11, 19-20, 25	6-8, 17, 21-22	12-13, 17, 19-20, 30	2, 10, 14, 16-17, 27, 29

Astro Almanac 1996

	Jan	Feb	Mar	Apr	May	Jun	July	Aug	Sep	Oct	Nov	Dec
Stop a habit	11	7	5, 6	2, 29	27	23	20	16	13	10	6	4, 31
Write letters	2-4, 10-11, 17-18, 23-24, 30-31	6-8, 13-14, 19-20, 26-27	4-6, 11-13, 18-19, 24-26	1, 2, 8-9, 14-15, 21-22, 28-30	5-6, 11-12, 18-19, 25-27	1-2, 7-9, 14-16, 22-23, 29-30	5-6, 12-13, 19-21, 26-27	1-2, 8-9, 15-17, 22-24, 29-30	4-6, 12-13, 19-20, 25-26	1-3, 9-10, 16-17, 22-23, 29-30	5,-7, 12-13, 19-20, 25-26	3-4, 11, 18, 22-24, 30-31
Buy appliances	1, 6, 11, 14, 16, 20, 24, 26, 29	3, 8, 10, 12, 16, 20, 21, 23, 25	1, 6, 8, 11, 15, 19, 21, 24, 29	2, 5, 7, 11, 15, 18, 20, 25, 30	2, 4, 8, 13, 14, 17, 22, 27, 29, 30	1, 5, 9, 11, 14,18, 19, 23, 24, 26, 28	2, 6, 8, 11, 16, 21, 23, 25, 29	2, 4, 5, 7, 12, 17, 19, 21, 22, 26, 30	1, 3, 8, 13, 15, 18, 22, 26, 28, 30	1, 5, 10, 15, 19, 23, 24, 26, 28	2, 7, 9, 11, 15, 16, 20, 22, 24, 29	4, 6, 13, 17, 19, 22, 26, 27
Buy antiques	5-6, 15-16, 19-20	1-3, 11-12, 15-16, 28-29	1, 9-10, 14-15, 27-28	5-7, 10-11, 23-25	3-4, 7-8, 20-22, 30-31	3-4, 17-18, 27-28	1-2, 14-16, 24-25, 28-29	10-12, 20-21, 25-26	7-8, 16-18, 21-22	4-5, 14-15, 18-19, 31	1-2, 10-11, 14,-16, 27-29	7-9, 25-28
Buy cameras	1, 11, 15-16, 23-24, 28	7, 12, 20, 25	5-6, 10, 18-19, 23	2, 6, 15, 19, 20, 29	4, 12, 27, 31	8, 13, 23, 27-28	6, 10, 20, 25	2, 6, 16, 21, 29	3, 13, 17, 26, 30	10, 14, 15, 23, 27	6, 11, 19, 24	4, 8, 21, 3
Buy a car		26	11, 13, 24	9		1, 14	27	22		1, 16		11, 2
Buy TVs or computers	1, 6, 11, 14, 16, 20, 24, 26, 29	3, 8, 10, 12, 16, 20, 21, 23, 25	1, 6, 8, 11, 15, 19, 21, 24, 29	2, 5, 7, 11, 15, 18, 20, 25, 30	2, 4, 8, 13, 14, 17, 22, 27, 29, 30	1, 5, 9, 11, 14,18-19, 23-24, 26, 28	2, 6, 8, 11, 16, 21, 23-25, 29	2, 4, 5, 7, 12, 17, 19, 21-22, 26, 30	1, 3, 8, 13, 15, 18, 22, 26, 28	1, 5, 10, 15, 19, 23-24, 26, 28	2, 7, 9, 11, 15-16, 20, 22, 24, 29	4, 6, 13, 1 19, 2 26, 2
Marriage	3, 10-11, 13-16, 18, 20, 22-23, 24, 27, 29	2, 9, 12-14, 17-18, 21, 23, 27-28	3, 10, 13-14, 18-19, 22, 24, 28-29	2, 8, 11-13, 16-17, 21-22, 28	1, 7, 10, 12, 14, 17, 19, 22, 24, 27, 28-29	5-6, 10, 15, 19-21, 24, 26	2-3, 5, 7, 9-10, 12, 15, 17, 20, 22, 25, 31	3-4, 8-9, 13-14, 15, 19-20, 24, 29	1-3, 7-8, 12, 14, 17, 19, 22, 28	1, 3, 6, 8, 12-14, 17-18, 21, 28, 31	2, 5, 8, 10-13, 15, 17, 20, 27, 30	2, 3, 10, 12, 17, 1 20, 27, 2
Marry for happiness	9, 13, 29	2, 9, 10, 23, 28	3, 22, 28, 29	19, 26	1, 16, 17, 22, 24, 28, 29	12, 19-20, 24, 26	9-10, 15, 17, 22	5, 13-14, 19	2, 3, 7, 11, 14	6, 8, 12-13, 27, 31	2, 8, 23, 27, 30	2, 5, 27, 2
Marry for longevity		23	22	19								
Divorce	6-20	5-18	6-19	4-17	4-17	2-15	1-15, 31	1-14, 29-31	1-12, 27-30	1-12, 27-31	1-10, 25-30	1-10 25-3
Repair a car	1, 29	23, 25	29	18, 20	17	5, 19	11	5, 7	3, 30	28	24	27
Sell real estate	5-6	2, 29	1, 28	25	22		16	12	1, 8	5, 26	2, 29	26
Sell possessions	3, 13-14, 18, 22-23, 27	2, 12-13, 17, 21, 27	3, 13, 18, 22, 28	2, 11, 16, 21, 26	1, 10, 14, 19, 24, 29	6, 10, 15, 19-20, 24	2-3, 7, 12, 17, 22, 31	4, 9, 15, 20, 29	3, 8, 14, 19, 28	3, 8, 13, 14, 18, 28	2,-8, 12, 13, 17, 27	2, 3, 12, 17, 27
Sporting activities	9, 18, 25	14	13, 29	27	6	19	7, 18	24	1, 11, 20, 27	16-17, 25, 26		
Travel			11, 13, 24, 29	9		1, 14, 19		22		1, 16		1, 1 22,

Home, Health, & Beauty

Do You Wear Your Sign?

Venus rules beauty and clothes in general. Days when the Moon is in Taurus or Libra are good times to work on your wardrobe. Buying clothes is particularly good in Taurus. Good times to buy particular articles of clothing depend on the astrological rulerships of those items. Refer to the following list and plan your purchases to correspond with the Moon in those signs. First and second quarters work best.

Clothing, Colors, and Beauty Aids

Aries (Mars): hats, earrings, eyeglasses, makeup. Flaming hues, red, scarlet.

Taurus (Venus): collars, jewelry, purses, perfumes, scarves. Pastels, pink, turquoise.

Gemini (Mercury): breath fresheners, nail polish, bracelets. Monochromatic shades; silver.

Cancer (Moon): coats, shirts, blouses, vests, swimsuits. Iridescent hues; gray, silver, brown.

Leo (Sun): permanents, flamboyant hats. Full spectral tones; gold, scarlet.

Virgo (Mercury): clothing in general, health care. Dark, indefinite colors; navy, gray, silver.

Libra (Venus): belts, costumes, visits to beauty parlors, wigs, cosmetics. Cloudy tints; blue-green.

Scorpio (Pluto): gloves, underwear. Murky, luminous shades; blood red.

Sagittarius (Jupiter): skirts, sports clothes, suits. Rich, full hues; dark blue, purple, green.

Capricorn (Saturn): hair, leather goods, furs, watches, underwear. Flat, dark values, black, dark brown, gray.

Aquarius (Uranus): anklets. Electric, mixed, changeable colors; checks and stripes.

Pisces (Neptune): boots, shoes, socks, pajamas, suspenders. White, lilac, mauve, sea green.

Home, Health, & Beauty

Automobile Purchase

The Moon is helpful when in favorable aspect to Mercury and Uranus and in the signs of Gemini or Sagittarius.

Automobile Repair

The Moon should be in favorable aspect to Uranus and in the signs of Taurus, Leo, Aquarius, or Virgo. Avoid any unfavorable aspects between the Moon and Mars, Saturn, Uranus, Neptune, or Pluto.

Baking

Baking should be done when the Moon is in Cancer. Bakers who have experimented say that dough rises higher and bread is lighter during the increase of the Moon (first or second quarter).

Beauty Care

For beauty treatments, skin care, and massage, the Moon should be in Taurus, Cancer, Leo, Libra, or Aquarius and sextile, trine, or conjunct Venus and/or Jupiter.

Fingernails should be cut when the Moon is not in any aspect with Mercury or Jupiter. Saturn and Mars must not be marked Q or O because this makes the nails grow slowly or thin and weak. The Moon should be in Aries, Taurus, Cancer, or Leo. For toenails, the Moon should not be in Gemini or Pisces. Corns are best cut when the Moon is in the third or fourth quarter.

Brewing

It is best to brew during the Full Moon and the fourth quarter. Plan to have the Moon in Cancer or Pisces.

Building

Turning the first sod for the foundation of a home or laying the cornerstone for a public building marks the beginning of the building. Excavate, lay foundations, and pour cement when the Moon is full and in a fixed sign (Taurus, Leo, Aquarius). Saturn should be aspected, but not Mars, for Mars aspects may indicate accidents.

Canning

Can fruits and vegetables when the Moon is in either the third or fourth quarter, and when it is in Cancer or Pisces. For preserves and jellies, use the same quarters but see that the Moon is in Cancer, Pisces, or Taurus.

Cement and Concrete

Pour cement and concrete during the Full Moon. It is best, too, for the Moon to be in one of the fixed signs (Taurus, Leo, Aquarius).

Dental Work

Pick a day that is marked favorable for your Sun sign. Mars should be marked X, T, or C and Saturn, Uranus, and Jupiter should not be marked Q or O.

Teeth are best removed during the increase of the Moon in the first or second quarter in Gemini, Virgo or Sagittarius. Avoid the Full Moon! The day should be favorable for your lunar cycle, and Mars and Saturn should be marked C, T, or X.

Fillings should be done in the 3rd or 4th quarters in the signs of Taurus, Leo, or Aquarius. The same applies for making plates.

Dieting

Weight gain occurs more readily when the Moon is in a water sign (Cancer, Scorpio, Pisces). Experience has shown that weight may be lost if a diet is started when the Moon is decreasing in light (third or fourth quarter) and when it is in Aries, Leo, Virgo, Sagittarius, or Aquarius.

Dressmaking

Design, cut, repair, or make clothes in Taurus, Leo, or Libra on a day marked favorable for your Sun sign. Venus, Jupiter, and Mercury should be aspected, but avoid Mars or Saturn aspects.

Eyeglasses

Eyes should be tested and glasses fitted on a day marked favorable for your Sun sign and on a day which falls during your favorable lunar cycle. Mars should not be in aspect with the Moon. The same applies for any treatment of the eyes, which should also be started during the increase of the Moon (first or second quarter).

Habits

To end any habit, start on a day when the Moon is in the third or fourth quarter and in a barren sign. Gemini, Leo, or Virgo are the best times. Make sure your lunar cycle is favorable. Avoid lunar aspects to Mars or Jupiter. Aspects to Neptune or Saturn are helpful. These rules apply to smoking and will produce a good start.

Hair Care

For faster growth, the Moon should be in Cancer or Pisces. To make hair grow thicker, cut it when the Moon is full or in opposition to the Sun (marked O in the Lunar Aspectarian) in the signs of Taurus,

Cancer, or Leo. However, if you want your hair to grow more slowly, the Moon should be in Aries, Gemini, or Virgo in the third or fourth quarter with Saturn square or opposite the Moon.

Permanents, straightening, and hair coloring will take well if the Moon is in Taurus or Leo and Venus is marked T or X. You should avoid doing your hair if Mars is marked Q or O, especially if heat is to be used. For permanents, a trine to Jupiter is helpful. The Moon also should be in the first quarter and at the same time check the lunar cycle for a favorable day in relation to your Sun sign.

Health

Diagnosis is more likely to be successful when the Moon is in a cardinal sign (Aries, Cancer, Libra, Capricorn), and less so when in a mutable sign. Begin a program for recuperation when the Moon is in a cardinal or fixed sign and the day is favorable to your sign. Enter hospitals at these times. For surgery, see Surgical Procedures. Buy medicines when the Moon is in Virgo or Scorpio.

House Furnishings

Follow the same rules for buying clothing, avoiding days when Mars is aspected. Days when Saturn is aspected make things wear longer and tend to a more conservative purchase. Saturn days are good for buying, and Jupiter days are good for selling.

House Purchasing

If you desire a permanent home, buy when the Moon is in Taurus, Leo, or Cancer, preferably when the Moon is New. If you're buying for speculation and a quick turnover, be certain that the Moon is not in a fixed sign, but in Aries, Cancer, or Libra.

Lost Articles

Search for lost articles during the first quarter and when your Sun sign is marked favorable. Also check to see that the planet ruling the lost item is trine, sextile, or conjunct the Moon. The Moon governs household utensils, Mercury letters and books, and Venus clothing, jewelry, and money.

Marriage

As a general rule, the best time for marriage to take place is during the increase of the Moon, just past the first quarter, but not under the Full Moon. Such marriages will bear a higher tendency towards optimism. Good signs for the Moon to be in are Taurus, Cancer, Leo, and Libra. The Moon in Taurus produces the most steadfast marriages, but if the partners later want to separate they may have a very difficult time. Avoid Aries, Gemini, Virgo, Scorpio, and Aquarius. Make sure that the Moon is well-aspected (X or T), especially to Venus or Jupiter. Avoid aspects to Mars, Uranus, or Pluto.

Moving into a House or Office

Make sure that Mars is not aspected to the Moon. Try to move on a day which is favorable to your Sun sign, or when the Moon is conjunct, sextile, or trine the Sun.

Mowing the Lawn

Mow the lawn in the first or second quarter to increase growth. If you wish to retard growth, mow in the third or fourth quarter.

Painting

The best time to paint buildings is during the decrease of the Moon (third and fourth quarter).

If the weather is hot, do the painting while the Moon is in Taurus; if the weather is cold, paint while the Moon is in Leo. Another good sign for painting is Aquarius. By painting in the fourth quarter, the wood is drier and the paint will penetrate; when painting around the New Moon the wood is damp and the paint is subject to scalding when hot weather hits it. It is not advisable to paint while the Moon is in a water sign if the temperature is below 70 degrees, as it is apt to creep, check, or run.

Pets

Take home new pets when the date is favorable to your Sun sign, or the Moon is well-aspected by the Sun, Venus, Jupiter, Uranus, or Neptune. Avoid days when the Moon is afflicted by the Sun, Mars, Saturn, Uranus, Neptune, or Pluto.

When selecting a new pet it is good to have the Moon well-aspected by the planet which rules the animal. Cats are ruled by the Sun, dogs by Mercury, birds by Venus, horses by Jupiter, and fish by Neptune.

Train pets starting when the Moon is in Taurus. Neuter them in Gemini, Cancer, Leo, Capricorn, or Aquarius. Avoid the week before and after the Full Moon. Declaw cats in the dark of the Moon. Avoid the week before and after the Full Moon and the sign of Pisces.

Predetermining Sex

Count from the last day of menstruation to the day next beginning, and divide the interval between the two dates into halves. Pregnancy occurring in the first half produces females, but copulation should take place when the Moon is in a feminine sign.

Pregnancy occurring in the later half, up to within three days of the beginning of menstruation, produces males, but copulation should take place when the Moon is in a masculine sign. This three-day period to the end of the first half of the next period again produces females.

Romance

The same principles hold true for starting a relationship as for marriage. However, since there is less control over when a romance starts, it is sometimes necessary to study it after the fact. Romances begun under an increasing Moon are more likely to be permanent, or at least satisfying. Those started on the waning Moon will more readily transform the participants. The general tone of the relationship can be guessed from the sign the Moon is in. For instance, those begun when the Moon is in Aries may be impulsive and quick to burn out. Good aspects between the Moon and Venus are excellent influences. Avoid Mars, Uranus, and Pluto aspects. Ending relationships is facilitated by a decreasing Moon, particularly in the fourth quarter.

Surgical Procedures

The flow of blood appears to be related to the Moon's phases. *Time* magazine reported on 1,000 tonsillectomy case histories analyzed by Dr. Edson J. Andrews—only 18 percent of associated hemorrhaging occurred in the fourth and first quarters. Thus, an astrological rule: To reduce the hazard of hemorrhage after a surgical procedure, plan to have the surgery within one week before or after the New Moon. Also select a date when the Moon is not in the sign governing the part of the body involved in the operation. The farther removed the Moon sign from the sign ruling the afflicted part of the body, the better for healing. There should be no lunar aspects to Mars, and favorable aspects to Venus and Jupiter should be present.

Cosmetic surgery should be done in the increase of the Moon, when the Moon is not in square or opposition to Mars. Avoid days when the Moon is square or opposite Saturn or the Sun.

Weaning Children

This should be done when the Moon is in Sagittarius, Capricorn, Aquarius, or Pisces. The child should nurse the last time in a fruitful sign. Venus should then be trine, sextile, or conjunct the Moon.

Wine and Drinks Other Than Beer

It is best to start when the Moon is in Pisces or Taurus. Good aspects (X or T) with Venus are favorable. Avoid aspects with Mars or Saturn.

Anatomy & the Zodiac

By K.D. Spitzer

It was Nicholas Culpeper who said unequivocally that a physician without astrology is like a lamp without oil. Indeed, until the 18th century, medicine and astrology were inextricably mixed. Medical astrology looks at the emotional and mental symptoms of an illness, as well as the ailing part of the body. A chart is cast for the moment a patient takes sick and outlines the course of the illness and the medicines to cure it. The birthchart itself indicates the types of food to eat to maintain good health, the possible areas of disease, and the herbs to serve as preventative measures.

Traditionally, the particular sign that the Sun rules in a birth chart indicates the part of the body undergoing the most stress during one's lifetime. More recent research indicates that zodiacal polarity, or opposites, may show the underlying cause of illness. For example, the headache of Aries may be caused by Libran-ruled kidneys.

The rulerships of the various parts of the body are as old as astrology and range from head (Aries) to toe (Pisces). The position of your natal Sun will indicate the area of strongest stress on your body; however, in order to look for other areas of weakness, you might want to read about the sign of your Ascendant as well.

Aries rules the head. Arians often suffer headaches from overwork or rushing head first into things. Look for a scar on the head or face of someone with Aries strong in their chart. Aries rules the subrenals, which produce adrenaline, the fight or flight juice.

Taurus rules the throat and neck. Knit your Taurus a muffler, for here you'll find colds, chills, and larygitis. The thyroid gland is in the throat, and its malfunction affects metabolism and weight, which is often a problem with this sign.

Gemini rules lungs, nerves, arms, shoulders, hands, and fingers. Here are broken arms and collar bones, bronchial conditions, and nervous complaints. Geminis are restless and move so quickly they often injure their fingers. Look for band-aids on their dancing digits!

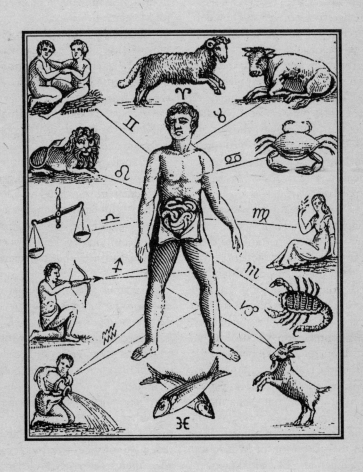

Zodiac Signs &
Their Corresponding Body Parts

Cancer rules the breast, chest, stomach, and alimentary canal. Prone to worry and internalizing their upsets, they often have ulcers or digestive problems. They definitely need to eat several small meals each day. Cancers are the nurturers of the zodiac, and their sign rules the mammary glands.

Leo rules the heart, spine, and back. The big-hearted lion often eats the wrong foods, thus paving the way for his middle-aged spread and heart attacks. Look for many of them to suffer with bad backs and slipped discs.

Virgo rules the nervous system and intestines. Their stomach and bowel disorders are similar to those of Cancer, but stem more from nervous tension than worry. Many are vegetarians, but quite often their food peculiarities stand in the way of a nutritionally balanced diet, thus setting up their ill health.

Libra rules the kidneys and the part of the body surrounding them. This Venus-ruled sign seeks perfection, and when out of harmony, due to arguments or accidents, will suffer kidney disfunctions. These can take the form of headaches, which can also be caused by overdosing on sugar, a comfort food when the Scales are out of balance.

Scorpio rules the reproductive and excretory organs. Here is energy in its most basic and hard-driving form. When it's frustrated, it can take any one of several outlets, from unpleasant behavior to a need for Metamucil.

Sagittarius rules the thighs, hips, and liver. This Sun sign needs physical exercise to avoid putting weight on the hips and thighs. At the first sign of unpleasantness, you can get a good look at those thighs walking right on out of the room. This sign needs to travel!

Capricorn rules the knees, bones, and teeth. The sea goat generally doesn't like to bend his knees on the trip to the mountain top, but sometimes his joints stiffen up from the arduous journey. Here's where you'll find arthritis and often dental decay.

Aquarius rules the circulatory system, as well as shins and ankles. This sign opposing Leo develops hardening of the arteries and varicose veins. If exercise doesn't cause shinsplints, then a slip could break an ankle.

Pisces rules the feet. This most mutable of water signs maintains such a delicate personal balance that a pair of shoes that pinch can affect their sense of self. Avoidance of drugs and alcohol and care in administering proper amounts of medicines is crucial to this sign.

Soothsayers Stuffed Chicken
By K.D. Spitzer

Babylonian astrologers were undoubtedly often paid in food by farmers looking for some special intercession with the mighty planets for their crops. A chicken and a few bags of rice might buy peace of mind for six months, or at least until the next eclipse. The following recipe is very similar to dishes once eaten in ancient Babylonia.

Chicken

Whole chicken, about 3–4 pounds
Clarified butter or olive oil
Freshly minced garlic, salt, and freshly ground pepper to season
½ cup water or chicken stock

Rice Stuffing

¼ cup butter
1 small onion, finely chopped
¼ cup pine nuts or slivered almonds
½ cup white or brown basmati rice
¼ cup chopped walnuts
¼ cup sultanas or California raisins
1 cup water
½ teaspoon ground allspice
Salt and freshly ground pepper

To make the stuffing: Heat the butter and sauté the onion until transparent. Stir in the nuts and rice and sauté for 5 minutes, stirring several times. Stir in the sultanas, water, and seasoning. Cover and simmer on low heat until the water is absorbed, about 10 minutes. Remove from heat.

Clean the chicken and wipe dry. Sprinkle salt in the cavity, and fill with rice mixture, and truss. Rub the outside with butter or oil and sprinkle with freshly minced garlic, salt, and pepper. Add water or stock to dish and roast 2½ hours in a 350°F oven. Baste often with pan juices. When done, remove from pan. Add a little more stock to pan juices and bring to boil. The pan juices can be served separately or drizzled over the chicken. Serve the carved chicken on a bed of the rice stuffing.

The Moon: A Mirror of our Moods

By Leslie Nielsen

As most of us truly enjoy seeing a radiant sunset so, too, do we view with wonderment the rising of a Full Moon as evening settles in. Our two great lights have always held our fascination as we attempted to better understand them; the Sun in its radiant light and the Moon as reflector, or mirror, of the Sun. Civilizations past have tried to unravel the mysteries of the Moon, even as we did in 1969 by landing a man on the Moon, planting a flag on the Moon and checking the Moon's gravity by playing golf on its surface.

In the past, nomadic tribes traveled by the seasons and phases of the Moon, which acted as a celestial signpost to give them direction. The Moon was their helpmate to determine weather (particularly precipitation) and, using the Moon, they were better able to plant their seeds, grow and harvest food, work with their livestock and, thus, support life. Now we do much the same thing. We plant by the Moon, harvest by the Moon, care for our animals by the Moon, and get a very good weather forecast using the Moon. The difference today, though, is that we have very reliable printed Moon tables which can quickly give us our needed information rather than gazing into the evening sky ... although, that can be a great deal of fun, too!

The Moon has been labeled female from the time of Olympian mythology and she has been used to describe our characteristic of change. The ancient Greeks symbolized her as a cup, being first empty, slowly filling up and, then, slowly pouring out. She was representative of our own changes, our moods and our needs. She signaled the ups and downs of our own responses.

As we do our own viewing, we find some nights quite dark. This is the time when the Moon is in its new phase. It has just been born. It affords us a time to begin new projects. Throughout the week following the New Moon we see a thin sliver of light starting to appear. Then, about 7 days later, the Moon has reached its first quarter stage and we may think about changing our original plans slightly; modifying them to make them work better. Another 7 days later, our Moon is at full stage, bright in the sky and illuminating the night. At this point of great illumination we, too, seem to see things most clearly. It's the great "ah-ha" time. Slowly the Moon is starting to lose its light, and 21 days after her birth she is at third quarter phase and we are given the opportunity, again, to correct or put to rest some project which we began at New Moon. Then, finally, approximately 28 days from the start of the New Moon, we again experience the

As we look into the evening sky we see the Moon and we know she is working for us

darkened night and the beginning of another New Moon. There is a definite ebb and flow, a rising and a falling of energies showing the Moon as representative of our own emotions.

In 1977, I read a book in which the author had outlined just why we experience emotional changes by the phases of the Moon. It seems that at the time of the New Moon (which is when the Sun and Moon are together in the heavens) negatized ions are released, which enter our atmosphere. We inhale this and oxygenate our blood, and our blood temperature remains normal. At the time of the Full Moon stage (that is, when the Sun and Moon are opposite each other, or 180 degrees apart, with the Earth in the middle) positized ions are being released into our atmosphere. We inhale these, oxygenating our blood, and our blood temperature is actually warmer, which gives meaning to the phrase "being hot-headed."

In 1965 in Dade County, Florida, a study was done on postoperative hemorrhaging and it was found that surgeries done 2-3 days prior to a Full Moon had significantly more blood flow than surgeries performed at other times. Those of us who have worked in the police and fire department can support the increase in activities during this time.

Eclipses

Just briefly moving aside from the New Moon/Full Moon information, I would like to insert something else for consideration. That is, a short paragraph about eclipses. An eclipse is when the light of either the Sun or the Moon is being blocked from our viewing stand here on Earth. At the time of my writing we have just witnessed what I refer to as a 10-day "public instability cycle." On November 3, 1994 we experienced an eclipse of the Sun. That meant that the Sun and the Moon were together in the sky and the Moon was blocking out some of the solar rays from the earth. Okay, now, the Sun and the Moon were both at between 10 and 11 degrees in the sign of Scorpio. Ninety days from that time the sun reached a square (90 degrees) from that point and was setting off the energy from that eclipse. Also, I like to allow 5 degrees plus or minus from that point. So, if the exact days of the square to the eclipse point were January 30th and 31st, the 5 days before and after would make the "public instability cycle" from January 25, 1995 to February 4, 1995, or the Sun by position at 5 degrees to 15 degrees Aquarius. It is said that it is not that worse things happen during these times, but just that we as human beings are less able to cope and, in some instances, make things more serious by our inability to rationally act. You may wish to use this tool for getting a reading on mundane events. It's particularly useful for those astrologers who like to do political research as well as those interested in economics and major news events.

Moon Void of Course

Another factor to consider is when the Moon is considered "void of course." That is, when the Moon is in no major angular relationship (aspect) with another planet before changing sign. This is when the Moon is in the latest degree of any planet in any sign before going into the next sign. This time period can be a matter of a few minutes to a few days. These appear to be poor times to conduct business but are remarkably good times to do some inner work; i.e., dream therapy or inner psychology. Averaging out the times when the Moon is void-of-course during the year and when business is normally conducted (the hours of 8:00 am to 5:00 pm) it is "void" about 5% of the time. These would be the times when promises made may be forgotten, commitments fail and, in general, things fall apart. My suggestion is that if you plan to start out on a trip or make an appointment during one of these times that you confirm it later to be sure everyone has the right information. It saves a lot of trouble!

The Natal Moon

The Moon in our birth (natal) charts gives us some clue as to what our basic security needs are and how we go about getting them met. It's also our familial imprint; it's our history. It particularly defines our mother, how we were nurtured, how we go about nurturing others and how we nurture ourselves and, in general, how we respond to our everyday environment. Certainly our Moon is necessary to find out "how" we respond, but also, "where" (house position) we go to have our emotional needs met. The speed the Moon traveled on the day we were born is a factor. The Moon can travel from 11 degrees 30 minutes to 15 degrees 15 minutes in a 24-hour period. While not always true, generally the faster Moon occurs right around the time of a New Moon, and when the Sun and Moon are opposite each other at the time of the Full Moon, the rate of travel appears to slow down. This rate of travel is indicative of how quickly we grasp and process information and how we make our decisions. Yes, I know, in our society fast is considered wonderful, but think of how many times we have suffered bumps on our noses by acting too quickly. Knowing Moon speed can be most helpful as well as "how" we respond and ultimately act.

Those folks who have their Moons in one of the water signs—Cancer, Scorpio, or Pisces—as well as those with their ascendants in one of these water signs, respond significantly to their environments. They are concerned with being protected and sometimes the world gets a little bit much for them. They are given to greater displays of emotion than some of the other signs. As the Moon is representative of our familial patterns, most particularly our mothers, why, then, is it that not all children in the same family have the same Moon sign? Because the children view mother differently.

We can use our Moon to sense and feel what is about us. We can use our Moon to get us out of tough scrapes (if we're willing to listen to it) and to express ourselves in a more loving manner. Through the phases of the Moon we can work with change, help things grow and better work with the rhythms in our own lives. Through knowledge we can be released from the bondage of ignorance which keeps us in a state of victimization. The phases of the Moon give us opportunities for daily betterment in our lives. As we look into the evening sky we see the Moon and we know she is working for us.

The Zodiac Houses

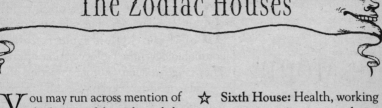

You may run across mention of the houses of the zodiac while reading the Moon Sign Book. These houses are the 12 divisions of the horoscope wheel. Each house has a specific meaning assigned to it. Below are the descriptions normally attributed to each house.

☆ **First House:** Self-interest, physical appearance, basic character.

☆ **Second House:** Personal values, monies earned and spent, moveable possessions, self-worth and esteem, resources for fulfilling security needs.

☆ **Third House:** Neighborhood, communications, siblings, schooling, buying and selling, busy activities, short trips.

☆ **Fourth House:** Home, family, real estate, parent(s), one's private sector of life, childhood years, old age.

☆ **Fifth House:** Creative endeavors, hobbies, pleasures, entertainments, children, speculative ventures, loved ones.

☆ **Sixth House:** Health, working environment, co-workers, small pets, service to others, food, armed forces.

☆ **Seventh House:** One-on-one encounters, business and personal partners, significant others, legal matters.

☆ **Eighth House:** Values of others, joint finances, other people's money, death and rebirth, surgery, psychotherapy.

☆ **Ninth House:** Higher education, religion, long trips, spirituality, languages, publishing.

☆ **Tenth House:** Social status, reputation, career, public honors, parents, the limelight.

☆ **Eleventh House:** Friends, social work, community work, causes, surprises, luck, rewards from career, circumstances beyond your control.

☆ **Twelfth House:** Hidden weaknesses and strengths, behind-the-scenes activity, institutions, confinement, psychic attunement, government.

The Moon and Biorhythms

By Donald Tyson

Biorhythms are cyclical changes inside the human body. The scientific study of these rhythm cycle is called chronobiology—the biology of time effects. They range in duration from a fraction of a second to months or even years, and are too numerous to count. The alpha rhythm of brain waves is a short duration biorhythm. Seasonal stress disorder, which causes some residents in northern climes to suffer severe depression during the winter months, is a long duration biorhythm tied to the cycle of the year.

The best understood cycle and the easiest to recognize is the circadian rhythm, the rhythm of human biology linked to the cycle of day and night. We all know that we tend to get hungry at the same times of day, to wake up at the same time, to get sleepy at the same time. More subtly, we experience heightened alertness at a specific stage in this cycle, usually the afternoon, and suffer a drop in body temperature at a certain time of night, usually around three or four o'clock in the morning. These subtle changes are less easy to detect but are quite real. Our body temperature drops once a day whether we are asleep or awake. That is why, when we disrupt our sleep cycle, we sometimes find ourselves shivering for no apparent reason—our body clock thinks we are asleep in bed under the blankets and lowers our temperature.

Modern biorhythms are based on three cycles of 23, 28, and 33 days. The 23 day physical cycle indicates the rise and fall of vitality and the level of health in the body. The 28 day emotional cycle relates to cyclic changes in feelings and attitudes. The 33 day intellectual cycle charts fluctuations in the ability to learn, remember and reason.

All three rhythms begin at the moment of birth and ascend in energy levels before returning to the same level, called the baseline, held at birth. The rhythms cross the baseline and descend in energy below the line before turning back upward. Each rhythm spends half of each cycle above the line and the other half below the line. For example, the emotional rhythm with a period of 28 days begins on the basal line at birth, ascends for seven days, descends back to the baseline for another seven, then descends below the baseline for seven before finally rising back up to the baseline over the final seven days of the cycle.

It is a simple matter to plot these three biorhythms on a graph by making the vertical axis stand for rise and fall of energy levels above and below the baseline, and the horizontal axis stand for duration in days.

Although the three rhythms begin together, they do not stay together. Because each has its own cycle, they constantly tug and push against each other, sometimes combining their energies for the same effect, at other times warring against each other so that their effects

Even in our contemporary folklore, the Full Moon is supposed to bring the crazies out

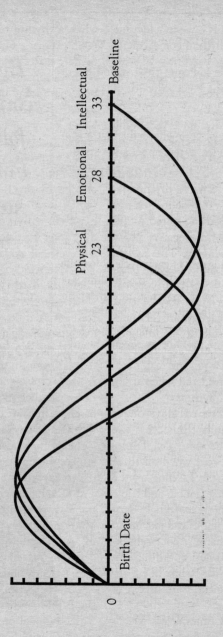

The Three Major Biorhythms

cancel out. Only once in a lifetime do the three rhythms come exactly together on the baseline—58 years and 66 or 67 days after the day of birth. This period is called a biorhythmic life-span.

When a rhythm is ascending above the baseline, energy is being expended at an accelerated rate. This is a positive phase of heightened vitality. When a rhythm descends below the baseline, energy is being gathered and stored for future use. This is a negative phase of decreased energy. The day on which a rhythm crosses the baseline, and its polarity inverts, is called the critical day of that rhythm. Critical days are the times of greatest instability and danger, when mistakes are most likely to be made. These are the major factors to be considered when using predictive biorhythms.

Double-critical days occur when two biorhythms cross the baseline on the same day. Triple-critical days occur when all three rhythms cross the baseline on the same day. These double and triple critical days are exceedingly dangerous, and result in bad judgment, frustration, quarrels, poor self-expression, awkward coordination, and depression. It has been observed that suicides are linked to these days.

In recent times a less serious danger point has been identified, when a rhythm reaches its maximum extent of travel either above or below the baseline and then changes direction relative to the baseline. Going up, it pauses and inverts its direction of energy flow before going down, or going down, it pauses and invents its energy flow before returning up, to the baseline. These apparent hesitations and changes of direction are known as mini-critical days. On the 28 day emotional rhythm, mini-critical days occur on day 7 and day 21 of the cycle, for example.

Attention has also recently been given to the direction in which the rhythms move relative to each other. Two or more rhythms moving in the same direction are thought to reinforce the effects of one another, while two rhythms crossing in opposite directions, whether above or below the baseline, indicate conflict.

The 28 day emotional rhythm is the most obvious and most powerful of the three supradian (longer than a day) rhythms. It is common, and reasonable, to link the emotional rhythm with the cycle of the Moon, which also completes itself in approximately 28 days, but the details of this relationship are by no means clearly understood.

For centuries, even millennia, the Full Moon has been associated with irrational or unstable behavior. The word lunatic comes from the Latin *luna*, meaning Moon. The legend of the werewolf, whose shape-changes are tied to the lunar cycle, is one aspect of this belief. Even in our contemporary folklore, the Full Moon is supposed to bring the crazies out onto the street and fill up the emergency wards of hospitals. Modern statistical studies showing no link between the Full Moon and increases in criminal behavior have done little to dispel this notion, which is deeply ingrained in our culture.

The sole link that seems indisputable is that between the cycle of the Moon and the menstrual cycle in women. It has been observed that shortly before menstruation heightened levels of hormones cause emotional behavior. It was probably this emotional phase of the menstrual cycle that gave rise to the idea of biorhythms in the first place. It is the one long-period rhythm that is undeniable.

Although men do not menstruate, a study done by an industrial psychologist named Rexford B. Hersey in the 30s suggests that they may experience emotional mood swings with a period of approximately 28 days. Hersey found that men become cheerful and energetic during the high phase of their cycle, then withdraw emotionally and grow moody during the low phase.

It might seem strange that men would exhibit menstrual symptoms without menstruation. However, we have only to reflect that men have nipples even though they are never required to breast feed to understand how this can be so. There are many female characteristics in male physiology. Genetically, the difference between men and women is slight. It may well be that the Moon acts on the hormones in the male body to produce emotional variations, just as it acts on the hormones in women.

Modern experts on biorhythms have tried to relate the emotional rhythm of 28 days to the cycle of the Moon by focusing on the lunar phase at the time of birth. A study done by Sandia Laboratories in 1971 found the possibility of a heightened susceptibility to accidents during the phase of the Moon corresponding with the lunar phase at birth, and a similarly high accident rate during the lunar phase 180 degrees away from the birth phase. The birth phase indicates the first of the two critical days of each complete cycle in the emotional rhythm, while the second critical day is marked by the phase of the Moon 180 degrees away from the birth phase For example, if you are born when the Moon is exactly in its third quarter, every third quarter of the Moon will be your critical day on the emotional rhythm, along with every first quarter day.

The problem with this theory is that the period between Full Moons, called the synodic month or lunation cycle, is not 28 days but 29½ days. Since traditional biorhythm doctrine maintains that the three major rhythms never vary their periods, the phase of the Moon at birth would soon get badly out of sync with the fixed 28 day cycle of the emotional rhythm. After the first 28 days. the birth phase of the Moon would be 1½ days ahead of the emotional cycle, after 56 days the lunar phase would be 3 days ahead, and so on.

The debate boils down to whether biorhythms are fixed and invariable, or whether they are cued by changes in the environment. Thanks to modern research into such things as jet lag and prolonged light deprivation experiments, where subjects have isolated themselves for months in deep caves away from the circadian cycle of day and night, it has become impossible to deny that some biorhythms are influenced by environmental clues after desynchronization, from 4 to 11 days are required to re-synchronize the biological clock. Whether the three great supradian rhythms are influenced in this way is a moot point (since science has not even agreed on their existence), but it seems very probable.

Two possibilities present themselves. The emotional rhythm is fixed at birth to a 28 day cycle which never varies regardless of changes in the environment or the state of the body. Or, the emotional rhythm is tied to the 29½ day cycle of the Moon. In this latter scenario, the Moon cues and regulates the emotional cycle through its gravitational pull, or possibly through the effect of its light. There is some scientific evidence that light can be used to make the menstrual cycle in women more regular, which tends to support the view that moonlight is a regulating factor.

Even if the second scenario is true and the Moon does regulate the emotional rhythm in men and women, we should not assume that the period of this rhythm is always 29½ days, or even that it is the same for everyone. The menstrual cycle refutes this view. Its period varies over roughly the full range of the three main rhythms, from 23 to 33 days, and in some cases ranges even more widely. Wilhelm Fliess, an early researcher into biorhythms, accounted for this disturbing anomaly with the explanation that the menstrual period is determined by the interaction of the 23 day physical and 28 day emotional rhythms, presumably reasoning that since menstruation is accompanied by obvious physical as well as emotional effects, it must involve both rhythms.

If the emotional rhythm varied as widely as the menstrual cycle it would be very difficult to have a system for charting biorhythms. Each individual would need to study their own emotional responses over a span of months, or even years, to subjectively arrive at their individual emotional period. The same would be true of their physical and intellectual rhythms, because if the emotional rhythm varied from person to person, we might suppose that the physical and mental rhythms varied as well. Proponents of biorhythms have gotten around this awkward problem by mandating that all three rhythms are fixed from the date of birth and invariable through life. Whether or not this is true, it certainly simplified the calculation of biorhythms.

You can determine your own critical days on the emotional rhythm simply by knowing what day of the week you were born. If you were born on a Wednesday, every second Wednesday after your birth is a critical day. On these days you should avoid confrontations and dangerous situations, and put off making important decisions. Every Wednesday between these critical days, when your emotional rhythm is at its peak above or below the baseline and is in the process of changing direction, is your mini-critical day, when you may expect some minor emotional flare-ups

and outbursts. These will be fairly easy to control provided you catch them before they gain momentum.

On the week following your birth and every fourth week following that week, your emotions will be expansive and high. You will feel confident, outgoing, and cheerful. It will be easy for you to meet new friends and seek fresh experiences.

On the second week following your birth and every fourth week after your emotions will be more settled and controlled. You will feel comfortable rather than enthusiastic. Your responses to new situations will be quiet and considered and you will not seek out challenges

On the third week following your birth and every fourth week after, you will feel empty and become easily depressed, you will have little desire to do anything that requires an investment in personal feelings, and you will have to force yourself to keep up your half of relationships with friends and family.

On the fourth week following your birth and every fourth week after, you will feel confidence gradually return and building of optimism. New hopes and dreams will arise in your heart. You will be ready to accept challenges, although still a bit hesitantly, like a young bird ready to fly but afraid to leap out of the nest.

These general effects of the various phases of the emotional

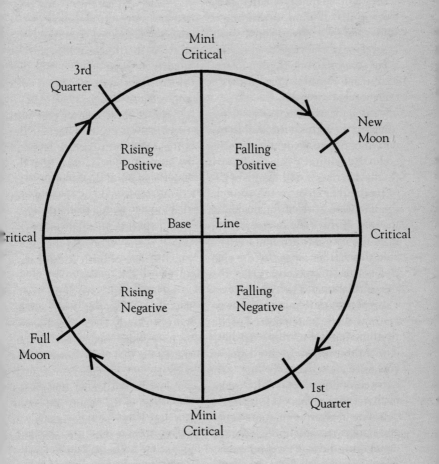

Emotional Rhythm of the Lunation Cycle

rhythm will be greatly modified by the other two great supradian rhythms. By turns the other rhythms will hinder or enhance the emotional rhythm, depending on whether they move against or with the flow of the emotional rhythm. For an accurate biorhythm forecast all three rhythms must always be considered together.

People who feel a special closeness to the soil and the seasons may be inclined to favor the view that the emotional cycle is directly linked to the synodic month of 29 ½ days, rather than to the artificial human measure of four calendar weeks. If this view is adopted, it is an easy matter to determine critical days and other aspects of the emotional cycle by observing the phases of the Moon. The exact phase of the Moon on the day of birth determines the start point. The following quarter of the lunar cycle traces the rise above the baseline, which culminates in the first of the two mini-critical days. The second quarter of the lunar cycle traces the decline in positive emotional energy back to the baseline and the second critical day. The third quarter of the lunar cycle indicates the descent below the baseline, culminating in the second of the two mini-critical days. The final quarter of the lunar cycle marks the rise of negative emotional energies back up to the baseline, culminating in the first critical day of the next emotional period.

Only very rarely will the critical and mini-critical days of the emotional rhythm correspond exactly with the New Moon, first quarter, second quarter, and Full Moon. More often, the day of birth will occur several days before or after one of these quarter points in the lunation cycle. Then all the critical and mini-critical days will be similarly a few days off from the exact quarters of the Moon.

We can make a circle graph that displays the phases of the emotional rhythm in relation to the phases of the Moon. On the example, the date of birth is three days after the full Moon.

There will be around seven days in each quarter of the circle, but not exactly seven days because we have chosen here to assume that the emotional cycle corresponds with the 29 ½ day lunation cycle. If you look at a calendar that shows the phases of the Moon and count the days between the phases, you will find seven days between most phases, but sometimes six and sometimes eight. Therefore this chart is intended only as a rough guide to your emotional rhythm. To be absolutely certain concerning your critical and mini-critical days, it is necessary to consult the calendar.

Leisure &
Recreation

Rosh Chodesh

By Tina Finneyfrock

Many Jewish women keep the monthly advent of the New Moon as a holy day called Rosh Chodesh (pronounced ko-desh). Each month, women are given this day to rest from all work and responsibilities in return for their ancestral mother's noncompliance with the worship of the Golden Calf during the Exodus from Egypt.

As the Jewish calendar is reckoned upon the Moon cycle, the New Moon portends the beginning of the month. One person in every village was appointed to watch for the new crescent and to announce its arrival by ligh ing a fire atop a hill and by offering special prayers.

Women celebrate this day in many ways, often gathering in small groups to share festive foods, songs, dancing, and stories. Rosh Chodesh can be a symbolic time to establish new cycles in our lives. If it is unrealistic to have the whole day to yourself, arrange for an evening gathering or simply pause to light a candle and contemplate changes you wish for the coming month, along with thanks for the gifts of the passing month. Keep this holy day as a way of staying in touch with the many forces in your life.

Leisure & Recreation

The best time to perform an activity is when its ruling planet is in favorable aspect to the Moon or when the Moon is in its ruling sign—that is, when its ruling planet is trine, sextile, or conjunct the Moon (marked T, X, or C in the Lunar Aspectarian or when its ruling sign is marked F in the Favorable and Unfavorable Days tables).

Animals and Hunting

Animals in general: Mercury, Jupiter, Virgo, Pisces

Animal training: Taurus, Venus

Cats: Leo, Sun, Virgo, Venus

Dogs: Mercury, Virgo

Fish: Neptune, Pisces, Moon, Cancer

Birds: Mercury, Venus

Game animals: Sagittarius

Horses, trainers, riders: Jupiter, Sagittarius

Hunters: Jupiter, Sagittarius

Arts

Acting, actors: Neptune, Pisces, Sun, Leo

Art in general: Venus, Libra

Ballet: Neptune, Venus

Ceramics: Saturn

Crafts: Mercury, Venus

Dancing: Venus, Taurus, Neptune, Pisces

Drama: Venus, Neptune

Embroidery: Venus

Etching: Mars

Films, filmmaking: Neptune, Leo, Uranus, Aquarius

Literature: Mercury, Gemini

Music: Venus, Libra, Taurus

Painting: Venus, Libra

Photography: Neptune, Pisces, Uranus, Aquarius

Printing: Mercury, Gemini

Theaters: Sun, Leo, Venus

Fishing

During the summer months the best time of the day for fishing is from sunrise to three hours after, and from about two hours before sunset until one hour after. In cooler months, the fish are not biting until the air is warm. At this time the best hours are from noon to 3 pm. Warm and cloudy days are good. The most favorable winds are from the south and southwest. Easterly winds are unfavorable.

The best days of the month for fishing are those on which the Moon changes quarters, especially if the change occurs on a day when the Moon is in a watery sign (Cancer, Scorpio, Pisces). The best period in any month is the day after the Full Moon.

Friends

The need for friendship is greater when Uranus aspects the Moon, or the Moon is in Aquarius. Friendship prospers when Venus or Uranus is trine, sextile, or conjunct the Moon. The chance meeting of acquaintances and friends is facilitated by the Moon in Gemini.

Parties

The best time for parties is when the Moon is in Gemini, Leo, Libra, or Aquarius with good aspects to Venus and Jupiter. There should be no aspects to Mars or Saturn.

Sports

Acrobatics: Mars, Aries

Archery: Jupiter, Sagittarius

Ball games in general: Venus

Baseball: Mars

Bicycling: Uranus, Mercury, Gemini

Boxing: Mars

Calisthenics: Mars, Neptune

Chess: Mercury, Mars

Competitive sports: Mars

Coordination: Mars

Deep-sea diving: Neptune, Pisces

Exercising: Sun

Football: Mars

Horse racing: Jupiter, Sagittarius

Jogging: Mercury, Gemini

Physical vitality: Sun

Polo: Uranus, Jupiter, Venus, Saturn

Racing (other than horse): Sun, Uranus

Ice skating: Neptune

Roller skating: Mercury

Sporting equipment: Jupiter, Sagittarius

Sports in general: Sun, Leo

Strategy: Saturn

Swimming: Neptune, Pisces, Moon, Cancer

Tennis: Mercury, Venus, Uranus, Mars

Wrestling: Mars

Travel

Air travel: Mercury, Sagittarius, Uranus

Automobile travel: Mercury, Gemini

Boating: Moon, Cancer, Neptune

Camping: Leo

Helicopters: Uranus

Hotels: Cancer, Venus

Journeys in general: Sun

Long journeys: Jupiter, Sagittarius

Parks: Sun, Leo

Picnics: Venus, Leo

Rail travel: Uranus, Mercury, Gemini

Restaurants: Moon, Cancer, Virgo, Jupiter

Short journeys: Mercury, Gemini

Vacations, holidays: Venus, Neptune

Long trips are best begun when the Sun is well-aspected to the Moon and the date is favorable for the traveler. If traveling with others, good aspects from Venus are desirable. For enjoyment, aspects to Jupiter are preferable; for visiting, aspects to Mercury. To prevent accidents, avoid squares or oppositions to Mars, Saturn, Uranus, or Pluto.

For air travel, choose a day when the Moon is in Gemini or Libra, and well-aspected by Mercury and/or Jupiter. Avoid adverse aspects of Mars, Saturn or Uranus.

Writing

Write for pleasure or publication when the Moon is in Gemini. Mercury should be direct. Favorable aspects to Mercury, Uranus, and Neptune promote ingenuity.

Other Entertainments

Barbecues: Moon, Mars

Casinos: Venus, Sun, Jupiter

Festivals: Venus

Parades: Jupiter, Venus

Hunting & Fishing Dates

From/To	Qtr	Sign
January 4, 9:56 am - January 6, 10:31 pm	2nd	Cancer
January 14, 4:30 am - January 16, 8:25 am	4th	Scorpio
January 22, 8:02 am - January 24, 10:37 am	1st	Pisces
January 31 4:11 pm - February 3, 4:46 am	2nd	Cancer
February 4, 10:58 am	Full Moon	
February 10, 10:35 am - February 12, 3:59 pm	3rd	Scorpio
February 18, 7:10 pm - February 20, 8:58 pm	1st	Pisces
February 27, 11:10 pm - March 1, 11:47 am	2nd	Cancer
March 5, 4:23 am	Full Moon	
March 8, 4:06 pm - March 10, 9:33 pm	3rd	Scorpio
March 17, 4:50 am - March 19, 7:15 am	4th	Pisces
March 26, 7:06 am - March 28, 7:38 pm	1st	Cancer
April 3, 7:08 pm	Full Moon	
April 4, 10:57 pm - April 7, 3:21 am	3rd	Scorpio
April 13, 11:59 am - April 15, 3:43 pm	4th	Pisces
April 22, 3:25 pm - April 25, 3:45 am	1st	Cancer
May 2, 7:43 am - May 4, 11:04 am	2nd	Scorpio
May 3, 6:48 am	Full Moon	
May 10, 5:29 pm - May 12, 10:01 pm	4th	Pisces
May 19, 11:17 pm - May 22, 11:28 am	1st	Cancer
May 29, 5:30 pm - May 31, 8:43 pm	2nd	Scorpio
June 1, 3:47 pm	Full Moon	
June 6, 11:20 pm - June 9, 3:24 am	3rd	Pisces
June 16, 6:08 am - June 18, 6:21 pm	1st	Cancer
June 26, 2:54 am - June 28, 7:02 am	2nd	Scorpio
June 30, 10:59 pm	Full Moon	
July 4, 7:07 am - July 6, 9:42 am	3rd	Pisces
July 13, 12:08 pm - July 16, 12:31 am	4th	Cancer
July 23, 10:43 am - July 25, 4:24 pm	1st	Scorpio
July 30, 5:36 am	Full Moon	
July 31, 5:01 pm - August 2, 6:05 pm	3rd	Pisces

Hunting & Fishing Dates

From/To	Qtr	Sign
August 9, 5:58 pm - August 12, 6:29 am	4th	Cancer
August 19, 4:51 pm - August 21, 11:48 pm	1st	Scorpio
August 28, 3:48 am - August 30, 4:15 am	2nd	Pisces
September 6, 12:30 am - September 8, 12:55 pm	4th	Cancer
September 15, 10:20 pm - September 18, 5:30 am	1st	Scorpio
September 24, 1:43 pm - September 26, 2:46 pm	2nd	Pisces
September 26, 9:51 pm	Full Moon	
October 3, 8:15 am - October 5, 8:12 pm	3rd	Cancer
October 13, 4:46 am - October 15, 11:07 am	1st	Scorpio
October 21, 9:23 pm - October 23, 11:51 pm	2nd	Pisces
October 26, 9:12 am	Full Moon	
October 30, 4:57 pm - November 2, 4:16 am	3rd	Cancer
November 9, 1:02 pm - November 11, 6:27 pm	4th	Scorpio
November 18, 3:00 am - November 20, 6:34 am	2nd	Pisces
November 24, 11:10 pm	Full Moon	
November 27, 1:37 am - November 29, 12:30 pm	3rd	Cancer
December 6, 10:39 pm - December 9, 3:59 am	4th	Scorpio
December 15, 8:44 am - December 17, 11:55 am	1st	Pisces
December 24, 9:14 am - December 26, 8:09 pm	3rd	Cancer

Country Root Wines

By K.D. Spitzer

Country folk have always been careful food management. When winter sta ed sloshing to a close, the need arose sort through the fruits and vegetables in c storage, getting rid of any that develop mold and setting aside the ones that we dried and shriveled. The ones that were t tired to revive for dinner were earmarked homemade root wines, because the ol and drier the potatoes, beets, parsnips, carrots, the more flavorful the wine.

The end of February and beginning March was the usual time for making r wines. It wasn't just coincidence that ma country people thought that wine beg when the Sun was in Pisces was the best surance for success. While it is beneficial utilize the energies of the Sun, it is actua the Moon in Pisces in the first or seco quarter that offers the best energy to e pand wine yeast, fruits, and water into a m low, dulcet liquid. White wines and coun wines are ruled by the Moon, and so tho days when the Moon is in Cancer (which its natural home) can offer another id open window of time for starting a n batch, especially if peak harvesting isn't c operating with your astrological agenda

In spring and summer almost a flower blossom can be used to ma wine. Dandelion is the most famo while delicate elderflower is one of t most popular. If you don't strip all t flowers from your bushes in June, y can make wine from the resulti luscious ripe berries in August. Of cour any berries in the garden, strawberries, ra berries, blackberries, or even rose hips make fine country wines. In Victorian kitchens what fruit was left in the drip bag from jelly-making was never thrown out, but reused to make fruit wines. Any edible berries from wild shrubs were gathered and used for jelly or winemaking: winterberries, rowan berries, partridge, juniper, buffalo and tea berries.

Rhubarb used to be called pie plant in recognition of its considerable use in pies, but by far, more people recognized it by its name of wine plant. Seventy-five years ago every kitchen had at least one recipe for rhubarb wine.

Herbs also are used to make wines and bring the same therapeutic value to an aged wine as they do to dinner entrees or nonalcoholic medicinals. Parsley and sage wines are great favorites. Other leaves that have been used to make flavorful wines are oak leaves and birch leaves. Even pea shucks enjoy a reputation as a flavorful wine, although with the availability of so many other really wonderful ingredients, it would seem that pea shucks would be better used on the compost pile.

Mead was one of the earliest fermented beverages; it was used ritually (and prayerfully) to increase fertility, and especially to increase the odds for male children. A beverage based on honey, mead includes a whole range of forms. Mead with less than 8% alcohol is called mead ale; with between 12% and 15% alcohol, it is sweet mead or sack mead. If fruit has been added to it, it is called melomel; with herbs like rosemary or sage, or spices like

It is actually the Moon in Pisces in the first or second quarter that offers the best energy to expand wine yeast, fruits, and water into a mellow, dulcet liquid

cinnamon, nutmeg, cloves, and ginger, it becomes metheglin. If you add honey to sweeten fermented grapes, it is called pyment, while spiced pyment is called hypocras.

This diversity is due to the fact that for many centuries, honey was the major sweetener available in Europe. Until such time as sugar was available in large quantities, most wines were based on honey or grapes, which provided on their own much of the sugar needed for fermentation.

Country wines are incredibly simple to make. You don't need to live in the country to obtain ingredients; certainly many of them can be found in any grocery store. Homemade wines can offer flavor and sometimes quality that can't be found commercially.

For sure, the alcohol content is higher than "store-bought"; those thimblefuls of wine that our grandmothers served owed much to their high proof content. Also many of them are medicinal and thus should be imbibed only in therapeutic amounts. More than a couple delightful ounces of rhubarb wine will amply demonstrate that plant's other common name: piss plant.

After you've followed all the simple directions, the magic that turns shriveled carrots into a fine, delicate beverage is simply time. It requires nothing but patience—anywhere from six months to as

long as a year—but the wait is usually worth it. Naturally you're tasting as you go along!

There are a few simple rules to observe to obtain consistent success. Keep a journal to record everything you do; you'll never remember the next year how you did it. Don't use hand-me-down recipes without modern adaptations. Use wine yeast instead of baker's yeast. Wine yeast is bottom-fermenting, and unlike baker's yeast, won't be killed by the developing alcohol.

Always use the best and freshest of opened blossoms for your flower wines, free of any pesticides. Dandelion blossoms especially need to have the green sepals peeled away to avoid bitterness. If using commercially bottled fruit juice, choose one without preservatives.

The most important consideration for success is to keep everything you use scrupulously clean. There are molds and spores in the air today that can spoil your labors if you do not take steps to protect them. Some inexpensive equipment is a worthwhile investment toward this end.

Wine and metals do not mix, but if necessary, stainless steel can be used. Other metals can turn the wine. Fermentation pails can be obtained that are made of a food-grade plastic. Traditionally wood and crockery were used, but they are both porous and can't be sterilized well. Smaller wooden items like wooden spoons are fine. Campden tablets added to the wine must will help with sterilizing and also contribute to a superior product, as you do not need to boil the must to kill the "bad" bacteria.

Glass bottles with screw caps are fine for non-grape wines; ask your favorite restaurant to save theirs for you to recycle with your own vintages. Champagne bottles and plastic corks can be collected and recycled on weekends from a place that specializes in wedding receptions.

A hydrometer is a neat gadget which tests the sugar present in the wine and helps to calculate the amount of alcohol it will convert to. It can tell you if you need to add more sugar. It is inexpensive, but still an optional tool.

The last important consideration is to keep out air and vinegar flies while the wine must is fermenting. Either will spoil the batch. Inexpensive airlocks will serve both purposes.

Some vintners have luck placing plastic wrap loosely on the opening of the fermentation vessel and securing it with a loose rubber band. This allows the wine to "burp" without exploding or letting in the vinegar flies, which, by the way, are aptly named. If they are drowned in your wine, discard it, for you have lost the batch.

The recipe procedures are applicable regardless of the main ingredient. Stick to the recipe amounts; changing them is not going to make the wine more potent or flavorful. The ingredients need to be washed. Fruit needs to be stoned and then crushed; place in cheesecloth or a jelly bag to obtain juice and allow to drip. Keeping the pulp in the bag, place juice, pulp, and any other ingredients except yeast into the fermentation jug. After 24 hours, add the yeast. Stir daily and keep covered. Don't store in a cool place at this point; it needs to be kept warm at 65°-70°. When the yeast stops frothing, siphon the wine off into sterilized glass jugs, without disturbing the bottom sediment.

Attach air locks. When fermentation is complete (after about 3 weeks) then siphon off again into clean sterilized jugs. You may need to do this every couple of months until the wine is perfectly clear. Try not to disturb the bottom sediment. Do not place in individual bottles unless the wine is clear, as it could explode into an exciting but distressing mess.

A gallon recipe can be multiplied to increase your yield. Just double or triple all ingredients but the yeast. One packet of yeast will feed up to 5 gallons and does not need to be increased unless your ambition or harvest exceeds that.

Don't Mind if I Do
Fruit Wine

8 pounds of plums OR 4½ pounds blackberries

4 pounds sugar

Juice of 1 lemon

1 packet wine yeast

1 gallon water brought to a boil

1 crushed Campden tablet

Any sweet, ripe plum will do the job here. Wash the fruit, stone, and chop. Place in cheesecloth bag and crush fruit so that its juices pour into the sterilized fermenting container. Toss in the tied up bag of pulp and then stir in everything but the yeast. Secure cover.

After 24 hours, or when it has cooled to room temperature, check with hydrometer for specific gravity of 1.095. If the hydrometer reads less than 1.095, stir in more sugar to bring it up to this mark; if it is over, then add enough water to bring it back down. Then, sprinkle the yeast on the surface of the liquid.

Once the fermentation starts, stir with a wooden spoon twice a day. Keep the wine securely covered. If you have a hydrometer, you need to monitor for specific gravity. When it reaches 1.030, it's time to rack it off into secondary fermentation jugs. (Otherwise it will take about 14 to 21 days for the wine to stop frothing.) Sterilized, 1 gallon glass jugs are fine for this intermediary step. Don't use soap, but baking soda to ensure cleanliness. Squeeze the bag of fruit as dry as possible and discard. Stir up the wine and then siphon off into the jugs. Seal the jugs with an air lock or plastic wrap. Turn a brown paper bag over each jug and store in the coolest place in the house.

After 3 weeks you'll need to rack the wine off again. Then once more in 2 to 3 months. The wine should be clear enough by then to bottle. (The hydrometer should read under 1.000.) Be sure the bottles are absolutely clean. You can purchase ametabisulphite or chlorine cleaner at a wine-making supply houseto kill all bacteria.

At this point the wine is drinkable, but if you can stand the wait, store it for another 2-3 months for a smoother taste that is less astringent on the tongue.

Carrot Wine

3 pounds carrots, parsnips, potatoes, turnips, or mixed root veggies

1 gallon water

1 pound raisins

2½ pounds sugar

Juice of 1 lemon and 1 orange

1 knob of bruised ginger

1 crushed Campden tablet

1 packet wine yeast

Scrub vegetables and cut off root ends and tops. Cup up vegetables and cover with 1 gallon water. Bring to boil and simmer just until tender. Do not overcook. In the mean time, cover raisins with a small amount of boiling water and let sit several minutes to plump. Drain and tie up along with the ginger in a cheesecloth bag. Strain the carrot water into a sterilized fermentation jug; toss in the raisins and add the sugar, lemon, and orange juices and Campden tablet. When liquid is cool, check with hydrometer if you have one; add wine yeast and proceed as described. Carrot wine is a gorgeous golden color, with a delicious flavor. Omit the ginger knob if you make a pure potato wine, which has a surprisingly straightforward flavor that's perfect with a cold summer supper.

Flower Wine

1   gallon of pesticide-free flower petals: dandelions, carnations, elderflowers, roses
1   gallon water
    Juice of 1 orange and 1 lemon
3   pounds sugar
1   Campden tablet, crushed
1   packet wine yeast

Flowers need to be freshly picked; in the morning right after the dew has burned off is the best time. Opened blossoms will ensure that you have not added protein in the form of bugs! Dandelions especially should have no sepals or stems attached; they will add a bitterness that cannot be rectified and will waste a winter's work.

Bring water to a boil and pour over the flower petals. Cover well and allow to steep for 3 days. Strain off and warm the liquid enough to help the sugar dissolve. Add sugar, Campden tablet, and fruit juices. Use a sterilized fermentation vessel. Let cool and measure with hydrometer. When satisfactory, add yeast and let ferment for at least 2 weeks. Check again and proceed as directed. in previous recipe.

Spiced Mead or Metheglin

This requires a little bigger investment than the price of fruit, as honey is rather expensive. It is important to use a light, pure, clover honey in making mead to order to achieve a good product. If you can't obtain the best, wait until such time as you can find it. The following has been known as an aphrodisiac.

7   pounds clover honey
2   teaspoons whole cloves
1   (3" stick) cinnamon
    Grated ½ whole nutmeg
½   pound sugar
1   gallon water
1   Campden tablet, crushed
1   packet wine yeast

Bring water to a boil; add honey, spices, Campden tablet, and sugar. Stir to dissolve honey and sugar. Cover. When cool, add yeast and cover. Stir every day. After about 5 days, check with hydrometer and syphon off into glass gallon jugs. Proceed as directed for winemaking. It is extremely critical in successfully making mead that everything be sterilized, from the pot you initially boil the water in, to the spoon you stir it with daily. Otherwise you may end up with an incurable off-flavor or a ruined batch of honeyed vinegar.

Country winemaking is not just a craft but an art, which will offer many rewards from the initial step of gathering materials from woods, meadows or gardens. Take a picnic, enjoy the sunshine, make a day of it. In another year, you will have the pleasure of packing a bottle of your best to accompany your luncheon as you prepare for the following year. Once you've made a couple batches and seen how simple it really is, you'll be ready to experiment with fruits and flavors. Keep good notes and start looking now for some special wine glasses just suited for your own special vintages. Salut!

Recommended Reading:

Vargas, Pattie. *Country Wines* (1992, Garden Way Publishing; ISBN: 0-88266-749-1)

Mail Order Sources:

Stout Billy's
61 Market Street
Portsmouth, NH 03801
603-436-1792

Home Sweet Homebrew
2008 Sanson Street
Philadelphia, PA
215-569-9469

Business & Legal

A Scottish New Moon Tradition

By Tina Finneyfrock

In the Scottish Highlands it is considered ill fortune to view the New Moon through a window. One must, upon seeing the new crescent for the first time each month, turn a coin over in his or her pocket and bow three times.

In trying to uncover the hidden meaning in this ritual, it is obvious that the advent of the New Moon was considered important enough to treat it with great reverence. To see the crescent from a window meant that you were not properly prepared to pay your respects or display humility.

It seems to be a custom worth keeping today as it draws us outside to gaze at the stars, reminds us of the renewal we can experience each month, and keeps us in humble awe of the natural world.

Business & Legal

When starting a new business or any type of new venture, check to make sure that the Moon is in the first or second quarter. You should also check the aspects of the Moon to the type of venture with which you are becoming involved. Look for positive aspects to the planet that rules the activity and avoid any dates marked Q or O, as you are sure to have trouble with the client or deal. Listed below are business activities and their ruling planets:

Sun

Advertising, executive positions, acting, finance, government, jewelry, law, public relations.

Mercury

Accounting, brokerage, clerical, disc jockey, doctor, editor, inspector, librarian, linguist, medical technician, scientist, teacher, writer, publishing, communication, mass media.

Venus

Architect, art and artist, beautician, dancer, designer, fashion and marketing, musician, poet, and chiropractor.

Mars

Barber, butcher, carpenter, chemist, construction, dentist, metal worker, surgeon, and the soldier.

Jupiter

Counseling, horse training, judge, lawyer, legislator, minister, pharmacist, psychologist, public analyst, social clubs, research, and self-improvement.

Saturn

Agronomy, math, mining, plumbing, real estate, repairperson, printer, paper-making, and working with older people.

Uranus

Aeronautics, broadcasting, electrician, inventing, lecturing, radiology, and computers.

Neptune

Photography, investigator, institutions, shipping, pets, movies, wine merchant, health foods, resorts, travel by water, and welfare.

Pluto

Acrobatics, athletic manager, atomic energy, research, speculation, sports, stockbroker, and any purely personal endeavors.

The Folly of Crime

The Moon & Crime

By Edna Rowland

The Moon's influence on the Earth has been acknowledged, and researchers generally agree that its influence is greatest when the Moon is New or Full, or nearest the Earth (perigee). The Moon's influence on the tides has also been accepted and recognized.

But for many years scientists denied the possibility of the Moon's influence on humans. In 1966 during the International Geophysical Year, however, it was shown that the Moon, like the Sun, can modify the Earth's magnetic state or atmosphere. In his little-known book called *How Atmospheric Conditions Affect Your Health*, Michel Gauquelin explores how the four phases of the Moon may affect the weather, and the possibility that abrupt or disruptive changes in cosmic energies may also affect those already predisposed to violent behavior. In his book, Gauquelin covers his tracks by adding that "no clear explanation for this phenomenon which seems to justify ancient beliefs, has yet been given. But it does appear that the Moon exerts an influence on meterological phenomena."

Since the beginning of humanity, the Moon has been credited with having an effect on mental instability. The word "lunatic" used to be in vogue. Now, "mentally ill" is the preferred term. But is there any truth to ancient legends and folklore surrounding the Moon? Crime, murder and psychiatric admissions to hospitals—do they really increase around the Full Moon? Is there such a thing as a "Full-Moon murderer?"

Some believe that violent crimes by mentally unbalanced people may coincide with the Moon's phases, and cases such as New York's Son of Sam have been cited as examples. David Berkowitz killed on eight different nights—five of them during New or Full Moons. Other similar cases include the Zodiac Killer, Jack the Ripper, and Albert DeSalvo, the Boston Strangler. Doris Gloss, murderer from Menlo Park, California and John Edward Allen, the Vampire of Lancashire, have also been frequently mentioned.

Just how much credence can we place in legends and myths

about blood-thirsty vampires and/or werewolves that prey on human beings around the Full Moon? We can, of course, discard the myth about humans turning into vampires or werewolves as nothing more than pure superstition. But let's not throw out the baby with the bath water, so to speak. The myth or legend probably exists because it contains a kernel of truth which isn't always so obvious to our logical (solar), linear, left-oriented brains. As every Stephen King or horror movie fan knows, our subconscious fears are more easily stimulated by pictures, not words.

From this perspective, werewolves depict the hidden or secret anger and aggressiveness that tends to erupt when we least expect it, or when we're under duress, turning us momentarily into literal monsters. The analogy of a human being becoming a werewolf can also symbolize the startling and sometimes sudden biological changes and psychological transformations that occur during adolescence, when a child is reaching puberty. The process of watching one's child transform into an adult can prompt some parents to testify that their children have "become little monsters," and that they don't really know or understand them any longer. That is understandable. So, is it possible that this mythical analogy about werewolves may refer to a "regression" to an earlier or stunted stage of growth? Analogies like this have often been used to illustrate or refer to an earlier or more primitive state of civilization—the hunting stage, for instance.

It's often been said that we hear so much more about crime or homicide these days mainly because the media (which is always competing with itself for first place) tends to favor these types of sensational events. Is murder really a random event, or does it occur in cycles?

If it is random, of course, it cannot be predicted.

According to recently reported statistics in the *Data Press News*, the murder rate is rising. "In 1991, there were 10.9 homicides for every 100,000 Americans, more than twice the 1960 rate of 5.2 per 100,000." On the other hand, violent crime—rape, robbery, and aggravated assault (attempted murder where the victim survives)—is now reportedly lower than it was 20 years ago. So, just what is going on? What, if anything, can we believe about these conflicting data reports and/or statistics?

In his book titled *Whoever Fights Monsters: My Twenty Years Tracking Serial Killers*, Robert K. Ressler, an FBI veteran, states that violent crimes against strangers are the most difficult of all crimes to solve, and these types of crimes are actually on the increase. He states that by 1980, some 25 percent of murders were "stranger murders." As a member of the BSU (Behavioral Sciences Unit), Ressler has personally interviewed murderers, rapists, and serial killers, and compiled thousands of personality profiles or case histories. Stating that he is against the death penalty, Ressler believes that murderers should be studied rather than eliminated. During Ressler's professional career as a lawyer and respected forensic scientist, he established an international computer database and network called the VICAP program to aid police and speed up the capture of dangerous criminals. He was interested in the motivations behind the crimes, and a true-to-life assessment of the murderer's basic personality and background. Needless to say, he had an uphill battle to overcome some of his colleagues' objections to his rather unique and pioneering approach to law enforcement.

In *Destined for Murder*, my book with co-author Sandra Young published by Llewellyn Publications, I astrologically analyze the birth charts of seven serial killers, such as Jeffrey Dahmer, John Wayne Gacy, the Boston Strangler, and Angelo Buono and Kenneth Bianchi—the Hillside Stranglers. None of these killers were born at the Full Moon, but Albert DeSalvo, the Boston Strangler, killed a majority of his victims at or near the New Moon and the Full Moon.

Here's an interesting case of a killer who was born on the date of a Solar Eclipse and died on the date of a Solar Eclipse. In my book I devote an entire chapter to the mass murderer of over 33 young boys, John Wayne Gacy, who was born March 17, 1942, exactly on the date of a New Moon (Solar Eclipse) at 26° Pisces. Strangely enough, after several failed appeals, this notorious convicted killer was executed and died on May 10, 1994, the date of another New Moon at 19º Taurus.

In examining my research files, I note that Ted Bundy, a rather well-known serial killer who stalked and preyed on women, was executed by lethal injection in Florida on January 24, 1989. Bundy was born the day after a Solar Eclipse, on November 24, 1946. (Incidentally, Solar Eclipses can only occur during a New Moon at a time when the nodes are also being activated.) A Solar Eclipse occurred at 0º Sagittarius on November 23, 1946.

Another serial killer, who killed prostitutes in Manhattan's red light district, Richard Cottingham, was born only one day after Ted Bundy, on November 25, 1946, in the Bronx, New York. Cottingham was convicted of three murders in 1980. According to Lois Rodden's *Profiles of Crime, Astro*

Data V, he was a computer operator, married, but leading a double life. Both he and Ted Bundy had natal Sun and Moon in Sagittarius, but different Ascendants. They both pursued a professional career, and killed only members of the opposite sex.

The only Full Moon murderer I could find in my files was the case of Jeffrey MacDonald, the Green Beret killer who was convicted of murdering his pregnant wife and two children in 1979. MacDonald was born October 12, 1943—just one day before a Full Moon at 19° Aries. His natal Moon is rising and occupies a plus "Gauquelin key sector."

As astrologers, most of us are fully aware of planetary cycles, but unlike astronomers, we believe there is an affect or corresponding influence on human beings and on human behavior. However, it's not entirely accurate to declare that the Moon causes violence or crime. Rather, it's the "repression" of the Moon's influence and what it symbolizes that brings about disharmony, or social stress and tension which often results in unexpected violence and disruption. Our repressed emotions often cause fluid or water retention in our bodies. Or to put it another way, the balance or harmony between the male and female principles—symbolized by the Sun and Moon—creates a nat-

ural harmony, but when this is disrupted, it in turn causes considerable stress and disharmony, especially in those who are more susceptible.

There is still another factor that we tend to forget. None of us are born at exactly the same time and place, so we're all at different stages of development and experiencing a different cycle due to age, environmental influences, heredity, etc.

From the astrological viewpoint, the "imprint" from our natal birth chart has its own individual effect upon how and when we are most receptive to planetary energies, as well as how we tend to interpret these influences.

Most social workers, psychiatrists, and criminologists tend to agree that the first seven years of a child's life are probably the most important in molding a child's future character and behavior as an adult, and astrologers, too, are fully aware of these psychological principles. According to natal astrological tenets, the first formative seven years of a child's life are ruled by the Moon and symbolized by the first quadrant (the first three houses) of the birth chart, regardless of where the Moon may actually be located by sign or house position. In traditional Western astrology, the Moon always symbolizes the nurturing or biological mother, and is also associated with the psychological aspects of the feminine mystique as described in Jungian analysis of a chart, for example.

When interpreting a chart, most astrologers refer to the Sun and Moon as the primary symbols depicting the parents. The Moon represents our feelings and emotions, our psychic nature or astral body; it also stands for our childhood conditioning and parental heritage. Unfortunately, our predominantly solar-oriented Western astrology tends to either ignore the Moon or refer to its influence as secondary. In other words, we've walked all over the Moon both literally and figuratively!

The Moon is not alone in the universe. She is the Earth's faithful, loyal satellite and only companion. The Moon's tides and her monthly phases are affected by the reciprocal action of the Earth and the Sun. Astrologically, the Moon actually connects us to ALL the planetary energies because it is the fastest-moving luminary. Being (Yin, or feminine) in contrast to the Sun's influence (Yang, or masculine), we don't usually connect the Moon with human aggression or violent behavior. Yet, there have been many reports indicating that the Moon's phases (and the Sun-Moon's synodic cycle) may have a definite relationship to human behavior. These reports at least deserve to be examined, since many of them are from people accredited in their fields or careers, and not from cranks, so let's just take a closer look at a few of them.

A respected psychiatrist, Donald Lunde, at the Stanford University Medical School, has written a book entitled *Murder and Madness* which remains a classic in its field. Although he isn't an astrologer, Dr. Lunde mentions two lunar cycles which correlate with murder—the Full Moon and a second peak just after the New Moon. He also mentions an 11-year Sunspot cycle of solar eruptions and magnetic fluctuations associated with murder and violence in recent years.

Another academic, Vernon Fox, a professor of criminology at Florida University, states that in his classes, police officers indicate their belief that crime rates go up during the Full Moon.

A report published by Inspector Wilfred Faust of the Philadelphia Police Department called *Effects of Full Moon on Human Behavior*, states "The seventy police officers who deal with telephone complaints claim that they have much more work when the Full Moon draws near." The report then goes on to say that arsonists, kleptomanics, careless drivers, and homicidal alcoholics go on rampages more often when the Moon is waxing (increasing in light or going toward the Full Moon) than when the Moon is waning.

Dr. Arnold L. Lieber, a psychiatrist with a private practice in Miami, Florida, decided to set up a statistical experiment that would either tend to confirm or deny these type of reports once and for all. Dr. Lieber is not an astrologer, but he has written a book entitled *The Lunar Effect: Biological Tides and Human Emotions*, which was first published by Doubleday in 1978 and is still on the market. In his book, Dr. Lieber describes his theory of "biological tides" and devotes an entire chapter to the subject of the Moon and murder. Dr. Lieber coined the term "biological tides" to refer to supposed fluctuations in the distribution of body fluids caused by the Moon.

The doctor was also interested in the gravitational effects, if any, of the Moon on human violent behavior, so he collected over 1,887 cases of homicides from Dade county, Florida spanning a 15-year period. The number of homicides was compared to the number expected by pure chance. Results showed a definite relation to the 29½ day lunar-synodical cycle (Sun-Moon phase cycle) since homicides peaked at the Full Moon, and there was a secondary peak immediately after the New Moon. Dr. Lieber and his team researcher, Dr. Carolyn Sherin, used

the "time of injury or assault" rather than the time of death, and referred to a lunar synodical calendar. His initial research data and findings were published in the July 1972 issue of the *American Journal of Psychiatry*.

Later on, in order to confirm and replicate his data, Dr. Lieber collected an additional 2,008 homicide cases in another location from Cuyahoga County, Cleveland, Ohio, covering 13 years, for a second sample of homicide victims. The peaks from the resulting graph showed a lag of about three days after both New Moon and Full Moon. According to Dr. Lieber, the "lag," or shift to the right as seen on the graph can be attributed to the difference in latitude between the two samples.

Two years later, in 1974, Alex D. Pokomy, M.D. and Joseph Jachimczyk, M.D., using statistics from Houston, Texas, attempted to replicate the results of Dr. Lieber's original data on the Moon's influence but failed to do so. Dr. Lieber attributes this failure to find significant lunar periodicity in their data to the fact that the researchers used the "time of death" rather than the time of injury and did not use latitude. However, an independent study in 1976 by Drs. Jodi Tasso and Elizabeth Miller of Edgecliff College in Cincinnati, Ohio finally corroborated the relationship between the cycle of the Moon and crime.

Now let's turn to another diligent researcher. In his book entitled *Murderers and Psychotics*, Michel Gauquelin, a Sorbonne trained psychologist and statistician, mentions a statistical study of the timed birth charts of 623 murderers, showing a slightly higher distribution of the natal Moon in the zodiacal signs of Virgo and Gemini.

Except for an excess of the Moon after its rise and culmination in "Gauquelin key sectors" of the murderer's birth charts, he found the study largely negative. The actual results showed 124 murderers (the expected frequency was 103.8) born with the Moon in the two key sectors mentioned above, but Gauquelin considered this only an intriguing observation which needs to be replicated on a much larger sample. Perhaps some aspiring astrology researcher with a knack for mathematics and statistics will take on this unfinished project now that Michel Gauquelin is no longer with us. He passed away several years ago.

Bibliography

Gauquelin, Michel. *How Atmospheric Conditions Affect Your Health*. New York, NY: ASI Publishers, 1980.

Murderers and Psychotics. Paris, France: Laboratoire D'Etude Des Relations Entre Rythmes Cosmiques et Psychophysiologiques, 1981.

Laurence, E.A. *The Cosmic Bonds*. New York, NY: Warner Books, 1981.

Lieber, Arnold L. M.D. *The Lunar Effect: Biological Tides and Human Emotions*. Garden City, NY: Doubleday/AnchorPress, 1978.

Lunde, Donald T. *Murder and Madness*. Stanford, CA: Stanford Alumni Association, 1975.

Ressler, Robert K. & Tom Schatman. *Whoever Fights Monsters*. New York, NY: St. Martin's Paperbacks, 1992.

Rodden, Lois M. *Profiles of Crime*, Astro Data V.

Data News Press, Hollywood, CA: 1991.

The Tides of Human Affairs

By Barbara Koval,
D.F. Astrol. S.

The Moon rules the tides of the o
and the tides of human aff
Whether it is the popularity of a p
dent or the readiness with which the m
ity of people will pay a high or low pric
a stock or a house, we know that our ne
heavenly body pulls and tugs at our co
tive emotions and desires. The secrets o
human psychology at any point in this
mentous year of 1996 reveal themselv
the charts of the waxing and wa
strength of the Moon.

We all know the Moon's power inc
es to Full Moon and wanes toward the
Moon. We know the ocean tides
stronger at Lunation time. Up to now
has been no measure of why some tides
to be stronger than others, why the Do
es higher at one Full Moon and ha
makes a blip at another, why crime
bloodshed reach troubling peaks at ce
times of the year and decline at ot
While the Moon is not the sole cause o
broad activity's annual rise and fall, it i
prime determinant of the monthly pres
The Moon is the consort of the Sun. L
consort, her power is far stronger than
pears.

Not only does the Moon wax and
relative to the Sun, she waxes and w
with respect to every other planet. W
planets fill one small sector of the sk
they do in 1996, we get layer upon lay
pressure pounding in the same direc
The Graph for January of 1996 (see
110) reveals an extraordinary buildup o
creasing and declining pressure.

In the above and in subsequent charts the light shading indicates increasing pressure, and the dark shading reflects decreasing pressure. Vertical shading indicates stress points and reversals. No shading indicates a weekend or neutral pressure. Lunar Tide charts are excellent prognosticators for stock market averages. Prices tend to rise where there is light shading and fall where there is dark. A predominance of shading in a given column, which represents a single day, indicates the dominant price pressure (all other things being equal) for the day. Of course, other factors, often stronger, support or neutralize Lunar pressures, but the Moon intensity is remarkably potent in gauging human psychology in economic, political, and personal terms.

1996 is unique in that the winter months have a tight configuration of planets and the summer months spread the pressure to create a better balance.

> *The Moon is the consort of the Sun. Like a consort, her power is far stronger than it appears*

January

The year starts with the most unbalanced month to date. Unusually high and low tides are likely. In January of 1995, which had a similar but slightly less severe imbalance, we saw the Kobe earthquake. In January of 1994 we saw the Northridge earthquake. Because of the extreme pressures on the Earth it would not be unthinkable to have another quake at this time.

Financial

Although the January Stock Market usually peaks at the Sun, Uranus, Neptune conjunctions, between the 16th and the 21st,

Figure 1:

January 1996 Lunar Tides

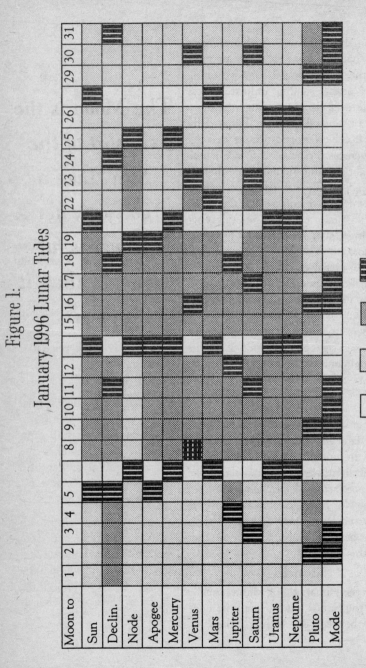

we see the highest intensity of downward pressure on the Lunar Graph on the 15th. This suggests a relatively lackluster rise, immediately followed by a steep drop on the 17th.

Politics

The year starts off with Pluto on the Ascendant of the U.S. Chart. The voters are angry and ready to throw everyone out. Debts, deficits, and taxes remain the concern. People lose confidence mid-month.

Personal

Bargain hunters find the lowest prices mid-month on everything from houses to clothes. Sell early on. If you live by the ocean, watch the weather reports, especially at New, Full, and Quarter Moons. A number of damage indicators are in play.

February

Although February eases somewhat, there are still heavy ups and downs for lunar tides. The most intense pressures are the 9th through 15th and the 21st through 22nd. In the case of weather, it does not matter whether the trend is waxing or waning, only the lopsidedness itself. Heed weather warnings.

Financial

Market low between the 9th and 12th. Market high 22,23.

Politics

The public mood eases, but the mudslinging for the presidential campaign gets ugly mid-month.

Personal

People are more likely to be depressed between the 9th and 16th and optimistic from the 21st to the 29th. If you have any unpleasantness to communicate, wait until the end of the month.

March

The dark days narrow to the period from the 8th to the 12th. The lightest days are from the 21st to 26th.

Financial

The Lunar low for the stock market is the 11th. The high is between the 19th and 22nd. Gold prices rise after the 21st.

Politics

People coalesce into their special interest groups. The opposition to the president swells. A third party emerges. The secrets hatched the first half of the month are revealed the last week.

Personal

Do your shopping between the 7th and the 14th. Avoid the mall from the 20th to the 27th. Unfortunately, you'll find nothing you like the first period. You'll love everything the last. Delay the actual purchase until next month.

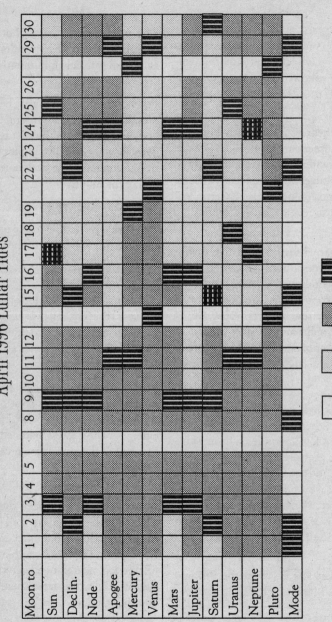

Figure 2
April 1996 Lunar Tides

April

Two important lunar pressures develop this month. Not only does the period of total dark intensify, but the shift indicators group together on single days. The latter are especially prominent on the 2nd, 3rd, 9th, and 24th. Shift indicators can turn the market fast. Other factors make April a critical month. The Lunar Eclipse falls across the United States Saturn, just as it did in the market crash of 1987.

Financial

In addition to the severe lunar down pressures and disruptions from the 3rd to the 9th, we also see several market crash indicators. While this presages a severe downturn, the United States almost inevitably has its market crashes in October, a stronger timing on the relevant charts. However, in 1987 Japan experienced a severe correction in April. It would be wise to avoid Pacific Rim stocks at this time.

Politics

Expect a contender for the presidential nomination to be bumped out of the running. He's probably a member of Congress. The Solar Eclipse could expose a scandal.

Personal

Lock your doors on the darkest days. You might want to stay off the roads on the 9th and 24th. These are bad collision days.

May

We get some breathing space in May as the Lunar Tides shift into a more counterbalancing mode. The high energy positive days are somewhat better than the dark ones, especially the 17th through 22nd.

Financial

Markets may trade in a narrower range. Low on the 3rd. High on the 22nd.

Politics

As convention time grows near, everyone is looking for the middle ground. Secrecy abounds. The passionate convictions emerge only on the high and low days. Look to these for what candidates really mean.

Personal

Ask the boss for a raise as the Sun enters Gemini. Everyone will be more confident of positive changes from that point on.

June

No solid columns appear in the June Lunar Tide Chart, but weekends and abutting days accumulate shift indicators. This does not look positive for good weather on the weekends.

Financial

The lack of intense buildup in lunar pressures and the predominance of change on the weekends could make for some jumpy Fridays. The market is likely to trade in a relatively narrow range. Probable high the 21st.

Politics

Words of inspiration are lacking. People are looking and hoping for someone or something to make sense. In short, nobody is excited by the current crop of candidates, chosen or about to be. Bill Clinton loses the incredible protection the United States chart affords him at this time. It could be all over but the voting.

Personal

Make alternate plans for your weekend excursions. Lots of interference is indicated.

July

The 8th to the 12th is the most positive week. The 22nd to the 26th is the most negative. Neither are unusually strong. The weekends and Fridays are still the most critical. If the weather stays good, the roads will be clogged. If the weather is bad, there goes the mini-vacation.

Financial

As the Lunar pressures even out, we may be witnessing a subtle shift from a speculation strategy in the markets to an investment strategy. People will be inclined to buy and hold, not buy and sell. But, keep your eye on those Fridays. The

market could stay elevated between the 5th and 15th. Other factors could sustain and upward momentum to the 26th.

Politics

The polls show voters are fickle and/or disinterested. The electorate is looking to be electrified. It could happen the 1st or 2nd. The president may make an important announcement on the 15th.

Personal

Fasten your safety belts and zip your lips on the weekends. Confrontation mounts.

August

The August Tide Chart is a good illustration of counterbalancing pressures. After looking at that conflagration of shift indicators the end of the month, we may all vote to eliminate weekends from the calendar.

Financial

August tends to be a high month for stocks and gold. With mostly counterbalancing pressures, we have some good movement up midmonth. Stocks and gold could top between the 16th and 19th. Markets traditionally start the fall downturn when the Sun enters Virgo. The monthly tides regain strength toward another peak on the 27th or 28th. The market is poised for a significant shift the final Friday.

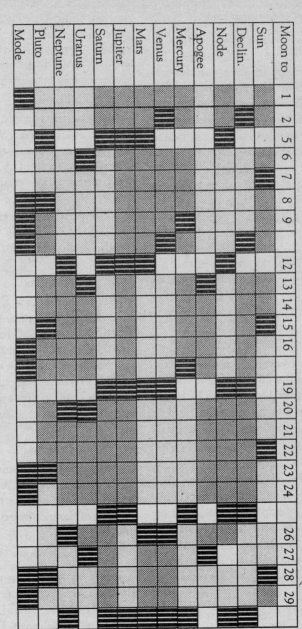

Figure 3
August 1996 Lunar Tides

Politics

Neptune and Mars sit on the U.S. Mercury, ruler of the president. Together they are argumentative and deceptive. The Full Moon on the 28th is right across the 4th and 10th Houses on the U.S. chart. The people are definitely on the side of the challenger.

Personal

Consider the 27th and the 28th the last chance to capture good will. Ask your boss for a raise.

September

With September comes the increasing tendency for the tides to "take sides." The first week is strong on the upside. The third week is strong on the downside.

Financial

Mercury retrograde adds down pressure mid month. Look for a stock market low between the 17th and 19th, a high the 5th.

Politics

Dark pressures are for change and light pressures are for the status quo. A third party candidate is most likely to capture the black. Expect an important announcement about or by the president on the 26th. It is the last favorable day for incumbents. The next day is an eclipse, possible bad news for the economy.

Personal

Do your bargain hunting between the 12th and the 18th.

October

The 7th to the 18th have the heaviest of downturning Lunar Tides. Weekends lose some of their sting.

Financial

October is often a crash month for the U.S. Stock Market. While we can expect a jolt with the Solar Eclipse close to the U.S. Saturn, many of the normal crash indicators are not present. The most intense days are the 7th (probable low) and the 14th (about the same level). Conditions improve after the 18th.

Politics

While the Lunar Tide chart still has a degree of balance, the U.S. Chart, relocated to D.C., has Pluto exactly conjunct the Ascendant with Saturn in the radix U.S. Ascendant degree. No question that the public is fed up with everything and will demand change at any price.

Personal

Try to get plenty of sunlight between the 7th and the 18th. The shortening days and the negative pressures of the month tend to depress.

November

Election time! One of the most intense down days on the Lunar Tide graph is November 5th. Maybe we should call it bad news Tuesday.

The most intense high points hit between the 20th and 22nd.

Financial

Expect the low the 5th or 6th. The high should hit between the 20th and 22nd. It appears the election news will be bearish for the stock market.

Politics

In addition to the anti-incumbent mood suggested by the Lunar Tides on election day, the U.S. Chart has Saturn, Uranus, and Pluto affecting its Ascendant. If there is a chance for a third party win, this will be the year. A third party victory could explain a jittery stock market.

Personal

The negative energies are very strong between the 4th and 8th. Be sure to get plenty of rest.

December

We move back into lunar manic depression this month: strongly negative to the 10th; strongly positive between the 13th and 24th. While it does not approach the intensity of January, it is close.

Financial

Market low the 6th or 9th. Market high 23rd, 24th. Confidence briefly returns.

Politics

The mood definitely lightens as people look forward to a new regime. Expect lots of happy talk. Nothing of substance.

Personal

Shop early for the lowest prices. Open your presents by the 24th. The 25th is disappointing.

Although 1996 is less prosperous than 1995, we still have money in our pockets. The Lunar Tide graphs tell us our fears and joys will be exaggerated. Keep cool. Get your personal budget in balance and elect those who will do the same for the country. What we don't mend in 1996 will haunt us in 2002.

Workplace Dynamics & the Moon: A User's Guide

By Kim Rogers-Gallagher

Our Moon is the Queen of the Night, lovely lady in silver who circles our planet protectively in her monthly—or should I say "moonthly"—orbit. She's the Head of the Department of Feelings, the bringer of "moods"—another great Moon word—and the keeper of the finance. We feel her influence ebb and flow through the ever-changing moods we experience, both en masse and individually, as she appears and disappears, winding her way around the Earth.

Cooperating with the emotional "tone" of the moment is important—it's working with the Moon, and it can make or break any day. To get an idea of what that current "tone" is, we look to the sign the Moon is currently passing through. Since we spend so very much of our time on the job, it's especially important to understand the Moon's influence on ourselves and our coworkers. Take a peek at the following guide, then, intended to make your life—and the lives of those you work with—ever so much easier. On an emotional level, at least...

Aries

Imagine, if you will, an Aries personality being told what to do. Since celebrity examples are so easy to work with, think of David Letterman, Bette Davis, or Eddie Murphy on the receiving end of an order that's just been barked out by a supervisor. What's wrong with that picture? Well, first of all, it wouldn't work. We know that. Not one of those personalities would ever allow anyone to tell them what to do, not for one single second. Aries is ruled by Mars, and Mars is the plan et that's in charge of taking action—a real let's-do-somethin'-even-if-it's-wrong kind of guy. That means that his sign is The Giver of the Orders, not The Taker. So the first thing you need to know about an Aries Moon is that it's going to make your co-workers kind of antsy, especially if they're bored or unhappy with their job. It will also make everyone at work want to be in charge of everyone else at work. Everyone. Yes, that includes you.

This doesn't mean that everyone is going to set out to scoop the boss' job when the Moon is in Aries—not necessarily, anyway. They'll just be acting as if they were. Pointing their fingers in each others' faces. Tapping the desk with a #2 until it breaks. Most importantly, they'll all want to make their own decisions about whatever comes up during the course of the day, thank you—so if you're already a supervisor or manager of some kind, don't be surprised at the attitudes you run across when you give someone instructions right about now. Regardless of what it is they're doing under this Moon sign, it's good to keep in mind that folks will work better on it if they're allowed to do it alone.

Now, let's talk about the dare-devil stuff, shall we? I mean, Aries has an impetuous streak that's nothing short of amazing. It's the sign that takes corners on two wheels, and never thinks about the consequences. When the Moon is in this action-packed sign, we crave adrenalin, all of us—and we'll do just about anything to get our pulse-rates up. Anything. Now, if you hap-

> *Cooperating with the emotional "tone" of the moment is important—it's working with the Moon, and it can make or break any day*

pen to have a job that involves working with fire or metal or any other "dangerous" material, you've already got a built-in outlet for all that fire. Since you're used to having your adrenalin level cranked, you may be a little less feisty than others, and you'll certainly be "in your element" during this two-day period. Careers that involve "enforcement" also go along quite well now, since wearing a uniform allows you to be in charge. Mars rules muscles, too, so professions involving the muscular system are especially favored now, too occupational therapies, for example, or sports-trainers.

Aries has the same "kindred spirit" feeling with automobiles that some folks have with power animals—so Aries energy is also deliriously happy when it's tinkering around, in—or under—a car. Regardless of your gender, then, if you're drawn to cars, if they're "fun" for you, you'll be in the mood to be working on one now.

Taurus

It's true what you've heard—Taurus is absolutely the hardest working sign around. No doubt about it. So when the Moon is in this sign, no matter what type of job they're doing, folks will work, literally, from sunrise to sundown, to get it done. You'll notice that your coworkers will become much more concerned

with the quality of their job, too, with doing it right the first time—as will you. We all tend to take our time with any project under a Taurus Moon—even the fire signs—and we pay attention to every step in the process of a task, too.

We're also a lot more stubborn, personality-wise, when the Moon is here, and a lot more positive that our way is the right way. Unfortunately, since the Moon affects everyone, that means we're all positive we're right, and all unwilling to budge an inch, which makes for truly "interesting" times on the job. Good thing the Moon only spends two and half days in a sign, hmmm?

So much for how you and others will work when the Moon is in this sign—now let's talk about what you'll enjoy doing for work. Since Taurus is ruled by the planet Venus, you'll be naturally pulled toward situations where it will be possible to create beauty. For example, you may want to work with some type of interior design, or you may be drawn toward doing something artistic. Any facet of your occupation that will allow you to interpret or mold earthly goods into pleasing shapes or sounds will do just fine. Of course, Taurus is famous for its love of food, too, so it's not surprising that when the Moon is in this sign, we're all more inclined toward becoming chefs. If there's a kitchen at the office, in other words, now's the time when you'll run into each other at the microwave.

Whatever you do under a Taurus Moon, if you're not absolutely sure that it's profitable, right from the start, you won't want to bother doing it at all. This sign understands that time certainly does mean money, and you won't want to waste either. Taurus' ruling planet is Venus, and she's in charge of money—so you may even find yourself suddenly struck with a knack for creating it during this two-day period. Needless to say, this is the time to make investments that will show a profit. Remember, one of Taurus's key-words is "appreciation," which also means that an item has increased in value.

Taurus's connection with the earth will often bring you into dealings with real estate under this Moon sign, too. If this is the case, keep your standards high and your morals about you, and you'll be naturally successful at whatever you channel that considerable fixed energy into.

Gemini

Storytelling—weaving words in some way. That's what we all love best when the Moon is in fun, chatty Gemini. Whether we write them down or say them out loud doesn't really matter, as long as we get to exercise our brains. When the Moon is in this mutable air sign, you and your co-workers will definitely be happiest, and most productive, too, in jobs that require you to communicate—with a capital "C". Now, storytelling—literally, to both adults and children—is the very best "job" to do under a Gemini Moon, since it's fun, it allows you to put your imagination to work, and it frees you up to be a kid again—to re-live what will always be the most carefree years of your life. If you can, then, when the Moon is in Gemini, allow yourself to fabricate a tale or two. Play a word game, or solve a puzzle. You won't feel much like doing anything that requires too much concentration, anyway.

If your occupation tends toward something a little more "professional," well, then, step aside for a bit, take pen in hand, and jot down your impressions of the people and places around you. Air Moons bring along intellectual understanding, an ability to really see what makes someone or something "tick." That's the stuff good novels are built of—and we've all got at least one novel lurking around inside of us.

Now, regardless of whether you're a reporter or a cosmetician, under a Gemini Moon, you've got to be able to move, to get there fast—wherever "there" is—make your point skillfully, and go on to the next project. Needless to say, jobs like telemarketing, where we're virtually attached to a phone, are a dream come true at this time. Phones, after all, are the most Geminiian tool around. No matter what your occupation, you'll be amazed at how easily you "know" how to turn a phrase just right when the Moon is in Mercury's sign. If you're in sales, now's definitely the time to go out prospecting. Others will be in the mood to play word games, and that's a Gemini Moon's favorite sport. You'll walk in, grab the owner's attention immediately with a clever opening line, state your purpose quickly, which all business-owners appreciate—and have a perfectly logical answer ready for every question, a remedy for every objection. There's no contest.

Any job that will allow you to move around and do various and sundry tasks will keep you and your coworkers happy when the Moon is in Gemini. Remember, air signs can't be contained—if you feel restless, move on to a new task.

Cancer

Cancer is the Moon's sign of rulership. In other words, it's the outfit she performs best in—her favorite work clothes. Makes sense, too—it's a cardinal water sign. Cardinal energy is what we use to begin, to create—to start something. Water is emotional.

When you combine those two characteristics, you're literally creating emotional bonds—and that's what families are made of. Yes, like no other sign, Cancer understands the importance of family—and when the Moon is in Cancer, so do we. We're in a family frame of mind wherever we go—work included. Besides, since you spend the majority of your day with them, your coworkers are already a type of "family" to you. So if you find yourself in the mood to bring goodies to the office on Friday, or have the whole gang over for an impromptu dinner party, don't be surprised.

Now, don't be surprised if your coworkers are also a lot more emotional over this two-day period than they usually are. Since Cancer is so in tune with the Moon, it's important to realize that this Moon sign brings out the "baby" in all of us—which means we also want to be babied. That goes for the boss, too, by the way, who may secretly want to climb on someone's lap if he or she is having a bad day. Fortunately, at this time, we all have a magical way of tapping into the Moon's nurturing nature and "fixing" each other, just by smiling and nodding and saying "Shhhh, it'll be all right."

Since your maternal instinct is so strong at this time (and this applies to both sexes), if you have options when it comes to job selection, you may find yourself preferring to work with children. If you're already a grade-school teacher or a child-care professional, you'll be doing what comes naturally to you—even better. Kids don't fight caretaking like adults do—so when you tie their mittens to their sleeves and wipe their noses, they just stand there and enjoy it. Kids are also little bundles of personal emotions, and whether they're giggling and bubbling over with joy or stomping their feet because they can't have what they want right now, when there's a Cancer Moon in the neighborhood, you'll know how to handle it.

Course, there are other professions that will appeal to you at this time—cooking, for example. You may find yourself wanting work as a chef, in a school kitchen, or for a catering service. The caretaking profession will appeal to you, or counseling. Under this Moon's influence, you'll be more in the mood to work out of your home than to go anywhere at all. Needless to say, if you do any traveling for work, try to schedule it for any Moon sign other than this one.

Leo

Well, if all the world's a stage, when the Moon is in Leo, we're all actors and actresses. Now, the spotlight is only so big, and each of us is positive it belongs to us, personally, when the Moon is in this sign. That goes for you and your coworkers, by the way, so remember to share the air time, no matter how much you want to take center stage and run with it—and you will. Now, anyone can perform anywhere, for anyone, so if you don't have a job in the entertainment field, per se, you'll still be able to use the energy of a Leo Moon to the fullest. We each carry our tools with us wherever we go—all we need is a stage and an audience. When we're at work, the audience part is easy. We automatically attract attention while we're doing our job, no matter what that job might be—sometimes even when we don't want it.

The stage isn't too hard to come by, either. Ever watch a hotel staff set up a dance floor? They wheel a cart with 20 or 30 squares on it into a perfectly empty room, snap those squares together, and in no time flat—tadaaaa—a dance floor is born. That's how we operate when the Moon is in Leo and we're "on the job." We walk in, scan the room for the most visible spot, and quickly assemble imaginary tiles into a stage. Before long, we've got the perimeter mapped out, our boundaries drawn, and all the best spots memorized. Of course, although the size and shape of our stage varies, no matter what occupation we're in, we've all got one. Bartenders use their bar for a "stage," and aerobic instructors use their classrooms. When we're at work under a Leo Moon, any ordinary space automatically transforms into living theater because we're feeling so darned "showy" and proud of ourselves.

Now, remember, the Moon's sign affects everyone. So when a Leo Moon is on stage, expect your coworkers to suddenly turn into an Entertainment Committee, equal parts stand-up comics and storytellers. Although performing on a real stage is what we'd all really, really love to do when the Moon is in Leo—whether or not we'll admit it—no matter where we are or where we work, there's a Star on our dressing-room door. We go out of our way to "perform" when the Moon in in the sign of the entertainer. No one minds working under this Moon sign—as long as they're appreciated. As long as their audience says "Thanks" —and means it. Keep in mind that it's just as important to applaud another's efforts as it is to be recognized for your own.

Virgo

No sign is better at seeing imperfections than Virgo. So when the Moon is here, it's natural that we've all got our automatic faultfinders on high. As far as work relationships go, this means that it's going to be darned near impossible to resist the urge to pick lint off a coworker's lapel, or to not mention the run in her stockings to the girl at the desk next door, who's tearfully explaining what happened with her boyfriend last night. But try. This sign also rules the caretaking occupations so if you can manage to offer some help or advice rather than criticism, you'll both be better off when the Moon goes into Libra, later in the week.

Now, since this sign is Head of the Health R Us Department of the zodiac, we're all quite naturally involved with the state of our health at this time. Since Virgo is soooo good at spotting details, and since assembling enough teeny, tiny symptoms can produce a malady where there may not really be one, this combination can also rapidly turn into hypochondriac tendencies. We've all got one of those "Physician's Desk References" hidden away somewhere, with certain pages dogeared because we're secretly sure that's what we've got, but the doctors just can't find it. At any rate, under Virgo Moons we may find ourselves thumbing through it a little more often. Which means there can be more absenteeism than usual at work, visits to health practitioners, and more folks leaving early.

If you're in the health-care field, by the way, this will be a time when you'll feel especially good at your job. You've already got a sincere desire to help, to fix, and to mend, and now's the time when you'll be able to put those talents to good, constructive use on others. You'll be able to spot the problem with your patient a mile away, and you'll know what to prescribe, too.

Under Virgo Moons, we may also be drawn to professions that help others in different ways. Service professions, for example, like restaurant work, cleaning, or personal care is ideal for this Moon sign, since the natural humility we feel at this time makes us a most accomodating employee. No matter what the job, the secret to getting the most out of a Virgo Moon is to prioritize, to learn to trouble-shoot, and to spend time wisely. You may find yourself staying on a bit later than you're scheduled—or paid for—to finish up a project, or just to straighten up your desk. Regardless of what you do, however, you'll do it well—or you won't do it.

Libra

Smile when you say that—and you will, too. During Libra Moons, everyone is just a little bit nicer, a little more tolerant, and a lot more sociable. Even if our manners are ordinarily impeccable, we make a special effort to be nice when the Moon is in this sign. Even the fire signs don't barge through the door first, no matter how much of a hurry they're in. We nod at all the right places, listen politely to each other's stories, and are much more prone to absolutely agree with everyone—no matter what they're saying. Everyone goes along when someone suggests dinner or happy hour at the place around the corner, and even before 5 o'clock rolls around, we're all huddled together around a coworker's desk, patting each other on the backs and laughing. It's called "comeraderie," and you'll feel an awful lot of it around the workplace when the Moon is in this other-oriented sign. That's the high side of it, at least.

There's a bit more to the situation than meets the eye, however. Mainly because some folks are in the middle of crises which demand their attention. So, contrary to popular opinion, Libra Moons do not necessarily mean that we will all drift peacefully from one balanced situation to the next—and we're not even supposed to. If we did, we'd never get to do our real job at this time, which, in a nutshell, is to learn to restore balance. See, Libra isn't the sign that is balanced, it's just born with a knack for fixing the scales when they're out of balance. So when the Moon is in this sign, we may be called upon to mediate, or to allow someone to mediate a situation for us. That can range from a simple one-on-one all the way to a major union grievance.

Now, if things at work are going along well at this time, chances are we'll experience this Moon-sign peacefully like we saw in the first paragraph. If things aren't okay, however, remember that keeping the peace in any situation is tough, exhausting even. Still, at this time, there's nothing that will please you more than witnessing a compromise you engineered.

Now, if your job involves mediating, being a go-between, smoothing over social situations, or bringing peace between warring factions, this will be a most productive two and a half days. You'll be able to do all that because the Moon in Libra brings along a gift for seeing both sides of an issue, if we take the time to look. We know what to say at this time that will get both sides to understand what the other is going through—and that's a rare and wonderful talent.

Scorpio

Ever watch a spider build a web? Well, that's how we work when we've got a project to do, and the Moon's in Scorpio. We set ourselves up in a corner, size up what's needed, and start spinning. If the web gets knocked down, we start again. We fixate. We work without breaks. In short, we become relentless. So don't start a project if you can't stay with it, because no matter what you start under a Scorpio

Moon, once you're involved, you can't even force yourself to stop. Not until there's absolutely no stone left unturned.

Now, speaking of turning over stones, you're going to be able to watch folks at work digging, both literally and figuratively, when the Moon is here. No sign loves "unearthing" like Scorpio does, probably because there's no telling what you'll find, and Scorpio just loves secret stuff. Anything that no one else has ever seen is irresistible to Scorpio.

Needless to say, if you're involved in research, you're going to get an awful lot done right around now. You'll be in the mood to sit in a corner and work, literally, for hours without realizing it. Naturally, the "hidden professions" will appeal to you, those vocations that require operation behind the scenes, in a spider-like corner. You may even find yourself taking on a Scorpionic occupation informally—by "playing detective" at work. If you've been wondering about someone or something for some time, and if you'd have to dig secretly to get your information, now's the time when you'll get into the office early—or stay late—and dig.

You'll also find, at this time, that folks will pay very special attention to the issue of power, and even more attention to powerful people. So you may find yourself sitting up late into the night, mentally reviewing the day, sifting through for details, for the subtle clues that will tell you what the boss really meant by that. Of course, you may also be spending sleepless hours thinking about how to send those signals back out into the world, at how you might imperceptibly alter or transform circumstances around you with just the right phrase or just the right gesture. In a nutshell, when the Moon is in Scorpio, everyone has a bit more of an idea of how to work the crowd.

Desire is Scorpio's middle name. When the Moon is here, we all become experts at the delicate art of strategy—which means that if we need to plan something, now's the time to begin work on the project. To plan and plot. Waiting is no problem—you'll wait forever for what you start under a Scorpio Moon. You won't quit until you've won, either—no matter what it takes, no matter how long.

Sagittarius

Well, first off, think about this: Sagittarius is the only sign out there that's got a legitimate nickname. I mean, nobody ever calls Scorpio "Scorp," do they? (Not for long, anyway...) And it certainly wouldn't be cool to refer to formal Capricorn as "Cap." "Sag," however, adores nicknames, and that tells us a lot about how folks feel when the Moon is in this sign. Sag is an expert at being very, um ... "casual," let's say, at making everyone feel comfortable enough to be exactly what they are—no pretenses required. Sag has everything to do with letting it all hang out—and that includes your shirttail. So you'll find folks at work in the mood to be a lot less "professional" than they might ordinarily be— laughing too loud, taking extra-long lunch breaks, and, in general, pushing their luck to the limit, in typical Sag style. That goes for the boss, too.

Now, Sag is not a sign that's particularly noted for its neatness and attention to detail. When the Moon is in Sag, you'll want to be outdoors, to live in your blue jeans, and cruise around in your pick-up truck. Needless to say, this is not conducive to getting a lot of work done. So here lies the rub. If your supervisor isn't in the same frame of mind, you might find yourself out of a job at this time. Fortunately, you may not mind. Sag is a sign that loves freedom. It has perpetual grass is greener syndrome and sometimes the grass is greener. So if a difficult or stifling job becomes too much for you at this time, or if you see a coworker on their way out, opportunity may have beckoned and the Sag Moon may have provided just the right oomph to go.

In general, under a Sag Moon, others tend to see the lighter side of things. That's what Sag is famous for. But let's not forget about the serious side of Sagittarius, the philosopher that's interested in everything. Sag is mutable fire, and mutable means changeable, so you'll need to be involved in an occupation that will keep you interested. At this time you'll also notice that your attention span—and that of your coworkers—will tend to flare up and die down, more like a series of little bonfires than one roaring blaze.

Now, as a rule, occupations that place you outdoors or on the move—preferably long-distance—will hold your attention well at these times, as will people-oriented jobs. Jobs that allow you to "preach," will also go quite well—like journalism, or teaching, or lecturing. Above all, try to give yourself some freedom when the Moon is in this sign—and don't stay in any job if you're dreadfully unhappy there. Remember Sag's philosophy—that work involves trading hours of your life for money. Now's the time to be sure it's a trade you can live with.

Capricorn

One of the things superiors love best about Capricorn Moons—whether or not they're aware of it—is that, for once, folks have no problem separating their private lives from their jobs. No matter what's happening at home, everyone arrives at the usual time in the usual mood—it seems. They may discuss the problem calmly or not even mention that they've just initiated a divorce. Folks tend to see what needs to be done and to carry it out methodically under the influence of a Capricorn Moon—and that's what productive work-days are made of.

You'll never, ever allow a customer to see any change in your manner when the Moon is in this sign. All in all, everyone is a much more ideal employee—even rebellious Aquarians. The customer is always right, and work is separate from other things.

However, all that self-discipline and executive ability as standard equipment make each of us an apprentice authority figure when the Moon is in this sign, so we all act like we're in training for the boss's job—it's similar to the Moon in Aries, except under Capricorn, folks are more bossy than pushy. Everyone becomes very, very good at taking charge. Even you. Just go ahead and admit it. It's okay. See, when there's a Capricorn Moon around, folks can sense the need for a natural order to things, the need for organizing people, and the need to size up all situations realistically. You're perfectly willing to do your job under this Moon's influence, and it's at this time that someone up in the office will probably notice that. Do things the way they're supposed to be done when the Moon is here, and you'll get your cookie. Perform above and beyond the call of duty, instead of just following the rules, and you'll be drafted into a position of authority. Really. If you're pushing for a promotion, these two and half days are when you ought to be really pushing. Especially if you're involved in big business, where a clear, realistic mind, unaffected by emotions, is your best asset.

Aquarius

If it were possible to make a career of organizing the take-over of the Dean's office, and if, right now, the Moon were in Aquarius and you'd just received the job offer—you'd think about it. Yes, even if you're a nice, sedate, Capricorn, or a rock-solid Taurus. See, when the Moon is in Aquarius, we all get radical. Rebellious, too. We get right into causes when the Moon is here regardless of what that cause is. If it happens to be our favorite cause, well, God help whoever comes between us and it, because Aquarius is a Fixed sign, and when the Moon is in Aquarius, we all get surprisingly fixed in our belief systems.

How does this apply to work? Well, first of all, if you've got the type of job that means you work for someone else, and if the job doesn't mesh with what you believe, now's the time when you'll want everyone to know how wrong the whole situation really is. If you happen to like where you're working, don't be surprised if one of your coworkers starts acting like this.

Now, to the average employer, this two-day period can represent some rather shocking revelations, and, as with the Moon in Sag, all the freedom this sign requires doesn't always make for the most productive of times. Of course, if you work for yourself, drumming up business as you tour through the day, free and clear of restrictions on your time—well, then, this will be a productive stretch for you. When the Moon is here, we understand the beauty of being able to do what we're in the mood to do, without the restrictions of a schedule.

Now, whether or not your job involves actually being on the payroll of your favorite environmental organization, you'll definitely be in the mood to put in full-time hours for it right around now. So what is your cause? Is it Greenpeace? Or an anti-nuke group? Maybe you just campaign like a crazy person for Amnesty International. Doesn't matter—whatever it is, you'll put it first when the Moon is here, before anything. And you'll have the urge to plaster bumper stickers all over your car to prove it. In a nutshell, you'll find that under this two and a half day Moon influence, when you're taken by an idea, that idea becomes all. Everything else will pale in the face of it. That includes work. The cause is everything. That is, until you get hit with a lightning bolt, courtesy of your ruling planet, Uranus the Unpredictable, and do a complete turnaround, switch over to a new cause, and pursue it every bit as emphatically as the last.

Regardless of what you do for work, when the Moon is in Aquarius, don't lock yourself into situations that rob you of your space.

Pisces

When the Moon is in Pisces, we all walk around feeling everything everybody else feels. Everything. That can be simultaneously good and bad, on the job. When we're at work with kindred spirits, it's a big plus. Nobody can merge, blend, and help us to fit right in like a Pisces Moon can. We're open to our environments, so it's easy to just soak up the good vibes, unobstructed— to let ourselves go. Being this sensitive isn't so great when there's tension in the air, however. So if we're involved in a high-stress occupation of some kind, a Pisces Moon can make us feel as if we're walking across battlefields without a shield, dodging hidden landmines, and

ducking from invisible slings and arrows we can't ordinarily feel. It's draining—and downright exhausting—when there's an argument in the vicinity. Doesn't matter whether we're involved, or whether the anger is spoken or unspoken. Our antennae are turned up to high, so we can feel what's "generated" on all levels.

Now, when the Moon is in Pisces, we also have a strong urge to shelter the homeless. This will definitely come out, one way or the other, but the perfect way to feed this side of you—and keep yourself feeling good about yourself, when the Moon is in this sign, is by really helping to shelter the homeless. Volunteer fund-raising for the SPCA, or spending the weekend doing telemarketing for The League of Conservation Voters. Whatever it takes to fulfill your need to help.

Of course, you can also take up a job that allows the play pretend side of you a chance to fantasize all day—at work. There's a special place in the heart of a Pisces Moon for disguises and costumes, so theatre work would be fun at this time, too. Pulling a veil over someone's eyes is her specialty, so the fields of cosmetics and beauty are pretty appealing, too. She's in charge of modern-day spellcasting which isn't anything you won't already be in the mood to do, anyway.

Farm, Garden, & Weather

The Zodiac Garden

Although the plants below are ruled by the signs listed, they should not necessarily be planted while the Moon is in that sign. For planting information, please read the "Gardening by the Moon" section of this book.

Aries (Mars): aloe, arum, bayberry, cayenne, cowslip, crowfoot, garlic, hemp, holly, hops, juniper, leeks, marjoram, mustard, onions, peppermint, thistle.

Taurus (Venus): alder, asparagus, beans, coltsfoot, lovage, mint, poppy, sage, spearmint, tansy, thyme, yarrow.

Gemini (Mercury): anise, bittersweet, cabbage, caraway, celery, fern, lily of the valley, parsley, valerian.

Cancer (Moon): chickweed, cucumbers, flax, geraniums, honeysuckle, hyssop, jasmine, lemon balm, lettuce, melons, mushrooms, pumpkins, turnips, wintergreen.

Leo (Sun) almond, angelica, bay, borage, bugloss, celandine, chamomile, citrus, cowslip, heliotrope, marigold, mistletoe, olive, peony, poppy, rue, saffron, St. John's wort, sunflower.

Virgo (Mercury): artemisia, cabbage, caraway, carrots, celery, cornflower, fennel, hazelnut, lavender, myrtle.

Libra (Venus): asparagus, beans, cloves, daisies, feverfew, orchids, pennyroyal, thyme, violets.

Scorpio (Pluto): basil, blackberry, heather, horehound, horseradish, witch hazel, wormwood.

Sagittarius (Jupiter): agrimony, balm, borage, carnations, clover, dandelions, dock, pinks, sage, tomatoes, wallflowers.

Capricorn (Saturn): aconite, beets, comfrey, flaxseed, heartsease, horsetail grass, ivy, pansies, plantain, shepherd's purse, spinach, wintergreen.

Aquarius (Uranus): coltsfoot, grapes, marigold, marsh mallow, pears, primrose, snakeroot, sorrel, southernwood, valerian.

Pisces (Neptune): chamomile, Irish moss, liverwort, mint, sea mosses and other water plants, verbena, wormwood.

Farm, Garden, & Weather

Gardening by the Moon

Today, we still find those who reject the notion of Moon gardening—the usual non-believer is not the scientist, but the city dweller who has never had any real contact with nature and no conscious experience of natural rhythms.

Cato wrote that "fig, apple, olive, and pear trees, as well as vines, should be planted in the dark of the Moon in the afternoon, when there is no south wind blowing."

Camille Flammarian, the French astronomer, also testifies to Moon planting. "Cucumbers increase at Full Moon, as well as radishes, turnips, leeks, lilies, horseradish, saffron; onions, on the contrary, are much larger and better nourished during the decline and old age of the Moon than at its increase, during its youth and fullness, which is the reason the Egyptians abstained from onions, on account of their antipathy to the Moon. Herbs gathered while the Moon increases are of great efficiency. If the vines are trimmed at night when the Moon is in the sign of the Lion, Sagittarius, the Scorpion, or the Bull, it will save them from field-rats, moles, snails, flies, and other animals."

Dr. Clark Timmins is one of the few modern scientists to have conducted tests in Moon planting. The following is a summary of some of his experiments:

Beets: When sown with the Moon in Scorpio, the germination rate was 71%; when sown in Sagittarius, the germination rate was 58%.

Scotch marigold: When sown with the Moon in Cancer, the germination rate was 90%; when sown in Leo, the germination rate was 32%.

Carrots: When sown with the Moon in Scorpio, the germination rate was 64%; when sown in Sagittarius, the germination rate was 47%.

Tomatoes: When sown with the Moon in Cancer, the germination rate was 90%; when sown in Leo, the germination rate was 58%.

Two things should be emphasized. First, remember that this is only a summary of the results of the experiments; the experiments themselves were conducted in a scientific manner to eliminate any variation in soil, temperature, moisture, etc., so that only the Moon's sign used in planting varied. Second, note that these astonishing results were obtained without regard to the phase of the Moon—the other factor we use in Moon planting, and which presumably would have increased the differential in germination rates.

Further experiments by Dr. Timmins involved transplanting Cancer and Leo-planted tomato seedlings while the Moon was increasing and in Cancer. The result was 100% survival. When the transplanting was done with the Moon decreasing and in Sagittarius, there was 0% survival.

The results of Dr. Timmins' tests show that the Cancer-planted tomatoes had first blossoms 12 days earlier than those planted under Leo; the Cancer-planted tomatoes had an average height of 20 inches at the same age when the Leo plants were only 15 inches high; the first ripe tomatoes were gathered from the Cancer plantings 11 days ahead of the Leo plantings; and finally, a count of the hanging fruit and comparison of size and weight shows an advantage to the Cancer plants over the Leo plants of 45%.

Dr. Timmins also observed that there have been similar tests that did not indicate results favorable to the Moon planting theory. As a scientist, he asked why one set of experiments indicated a positive verification of Moon planting, and others did not. He checked these other tests and found that the experimenters had not followed the geocentric system for determining the Moon sign positions, but the heliocentric. When the times used in these other tests were converted to the geocentric system, the dates chosen often were found to be in barren rather than fertile signs. Without going into the technical explanations, it is sufficient to point out that geocentric and heliocentric positions often vary by as much as four days. This is a large enough differential to place the Moon in Cancer, for example, in the heliocentric system, and at the same time in Leo by the geocentric system.

Most almanacs and calendars show the Moon's signs heliocentrically—and thus incorrectly for Moon planting—while the *Moon Sign Book* is calculated correctly for planting purposes, using the geocentric system.

Some readers are also confused because the *Moon Sign Book* talks of first, second, third, and fourth quarters, while some almanacs refer to these same divisions as New Moon, first quarter, Full Moon, and last quarter. Thus, the almanac says first quarter when the *Moon Sign Book* says second quarter. (Refer to the introductory material in this book for more information.)

There is nothing complicated about using astrology in agriculture and horticulture in order to increase both pleasure and profit, but there is one very important rule that is often neglected—use common sense! Of course this is one rule that should be remembered in every activity we undertake, but in the case of gardening and farming by the Moon it is not always possible to use the best dates for planting or harvesting, and we must select the next best and just try to do the best we can.

This brings up the matter of the other factors to consider in your gardening work. The dates we give as best for a certain activity apply to the entire country (with slight time correction), but in your section of the country you may be buried under three feet of snow on a date we say is a good day to plant your flowers. So we have factors of weather, season, temperature and moisture variations, soil conditions, your own available time and opportunity, and so forth. And don't forget the matter of the "green thumb." Some astrologers like to think it is all a matter of science, but gardening is also an art. In art you develop an instinctive identification with your work so that you influence it with your feelings and visualization of what you want to accomplish.

The *Moon Sign Book* gives you the place of the Moon for every day

of the year so that you can select the best times once you have become familiar with the rules and practices of lunar agriculture. We try to give you specific, easy-to-follow directions so that you can get right down to work.

We give you the best dates for planting, and also for various related activities, including cultivation, fertilizing, harvesting, irrigation, and getting rid of weeds and pests. But we cannot just tell you when it's good to plant at the time. Many of these rules were learned by observation and experience, but as our body of experience grew, we could see various patterns emerging which allowed us to make judgments about new things. Then we tested the new possible applications and learned still more. That's what you should do, too. After you have worked with lunar agriculture for a while and have gained a working background of knowledge, you will probably begin to try new things—and we hope you will share your experiments and findings with us. That's how the science grows.

Here's an example of what we mean. Years ago, Llewellyn George suggested that we try to combine our bits of knowledge about what to expect in planting under each of the Moon signs in order to benefit with several such lunar factors in one plant. From this came our rule for developing "thoroughbred seed." To develop thoroughbred seed, save the seed for three successive years from plants grown by the correct Moon sign and phase. You can plant in the first quarter phase and in the sign of Cancer for fruitfulness; the second year, plant seeds from the first year plants in Libra for beauty; and in the third year, plant the seeds from the second year plants in Taurus to produce hardiness. In a similar manner you can combine the fruitfulness of Cancer, the good root growth of Pisces, and the sturdiness and good vine growth of Scorpio. And don't forget the characteristics of Capricorn: hardy like Taurus, but drier and perhaps more resistant to drought and disease.

Unlike common almanacs, we consider both the Moon's phase and the Moon's sign in making our calculations for the proper timing of our work within nature's rhythm. It is perhaps a little easier to understand this if we remind you that we are all living in the center of a vast electromagnetic field that is the Earth and its environment in space. Everything that occurs within this electromagnetic field has an effect on everything else within the same field, but since we are living on the Earth we must relate these happenings and effects to our own health and happiness. The Moon and the Sun are the most important and dynamic of the rhythmically changing factors affecting the life of the Earth, and it is their relative positions to the Earth that we project for each day of the coming year.

Many people claim that not only do they achieve larger crops gardening by the Moon, but that their fruits and vegetables are much tastier and more healthful.

A number of organic gardeners have also become lunar gardeners using the natural growing methods within the natural rhythm of life forces that we experience through the relative movements of the Sun and Moon.

We provide a few basic rules and then give you month-by-month and day-by-day guidance for your farming and gardening work. You will be able to choose the best dates to meet your own needs and opportunities.

Planting by the Moon's Phases

During the increasing light (from New Moon to Full Moon), plant annuals that produce their yield above the ground. (An annual is a plant that completes its entire life cycle within one growing season and has to be seeded anew each year.)

During the decreasing light (from Full Moon to New Moon), plant biennials, perennials, bulb and root plants. (Biennials include crops that are planted one season to winter over and produce crops the next, such as winter wheat. Perennials and bulb and root plants include all plants that grow from the same root year after year.)

A simple, though less accurate, rule is to plant crops that produce above the ground during the increase of the Moon, and to plant crops that produce below the ground during the decrease of the Moon. This is the source of the old adage, "Plant potatoes during the dark of the Moon."

Llewellyn George went a step further and divided the lunar month into quarters. He called the first two from New Moon to Full Moon the first and second quarters, and the last two from Full Moon to New Moon the third and fourth quarters. Using these divisions, we can increase our accuracy in timing our efforts to coincide with natural forces.

First Quarter (Increasing)

Plant annuals producing their yield above the ground, which are generally of the leafy kind that produce their seed outside the fruit. Examples are asparagus, broccoli, Brussels sprouts, cabbage, cauliflower, celery, cress, endive, kohlrabi, lettuce, parsley, spinach, etc. Cucumbers are an exception, as they do best in the first quarter rather than the second, even though the seeds are inside the fruit. Also in the first quarter, plant cereals and grains.

Second Quarter (Increasing)

Plant annuals producing their yield above the ground, which are generally of the viney kind that produce their seed inside the fruit. Examples include beans, eggplant, melons, peas, peppers, pumpkins, squash, tomatoes, etc. These are not hard and fast divisions. If you can't plant during the first quarter, plant during the second, and vice versa. There are many plants that seem to do equally well planted in either quarter, such as watermelon, garlic, hay, and cereals and grains.

Third Quarter (Decreasing)

Plant biennials, perennials, and bulb and root plants. Also plant trees, shrubs, berries, beets, carrots, onions, parsnips, peanuts, potatoes, radishes, rhubarb, rutabagas, strawberries, turnips, winter wheat, grapes, etc.

Fourth Quarter (Decreasing)

This is the best time to cultivate, turn sod, pull weeds and destroy pests of all kinds, especially when the Moon is in the barren signs of Aries, Leo, Virgo, Gemini, Aquarius and Sagittarius.

Planting by Moon Sign

Moon in Aries

Barren and dry, fiery and masculine. Used for destroying noxious growths, weeds, pests, etc., and for cultivating.

Moon in Taurus

Productive and moist, earthy and feminine. Used for planting many crops, particularly potatoes and root crops, and when hardiness is important. Also used for lettuce, cabbage, and similar leafy vegetables.

Moon in Gemini

Barren and dry, airy and masculine. Used for destroying noxious growths, weeds and pests, and for cultivation.

Moon in Cancer

Very fruitful and moist, watery and feminine. This is the most productive sign, used extensively for planting and irrigation.

Moon in Leo

Barren and dry, fiery and masculine. This is the most barren sign, used only for killing weeds and for cultivation.

Moon in Virgo

Barren and moist, earthy and feminine. Good for cultivation and destroying weeds and pests.

Moon in Libra

Semi-fruitful and moist, airy and masculine. Used for planting many crops and producing good pulp growth and roots. A very good sign for flowers and vines. Also used for seeding hay, corn fodder, etc.

Moon in Scorpio

Very fruitful and moist, watery and feminine. Nearly as productive as Cancer; used for the same purposes. Especially good for vine growth and sturdiness.

Moon in Sagittarius

Barren and dry, fiery and masculine. Used for planting onions, seeding hay, and for cultivation.

Moon in Capricorn

Productive and dry, earthy and feminine. Used for planting potatoes, tubers, etc.

Moon in Aquarius

Barren and dry, airy and masculine. Used for cultivation and destroying noxious growths, weeds, and pests.

Moon in Pisces

Very fruitful and moist, watery and feminine. Used along with Cancer and Scorpio, especially good for root growth.

A Guide to Planting
Using Phase & Sign Rulerships

Plant	Phase	Sign
Annuals	1st or 2nd	
Apple trees	1st or 2nd	Cancer, Pisces, Taurus
Artichokes	1st	Cancer, Pisces,
Asparagus	1st	Cancer, Scorpio, Pisces
Asters	1st or 2nd	Virgo, Libra
Barley	1st or 2nd	Cancer, Pisces, Libra, Capricorn, Virgo
Beans (bush & pole)	2nd	Cancer, Taurus Pisces, Libra
Beans (kidney, white, & navy)	1st or 2nd	Cancer, Pisces
Beech Trees	1st or 2nd	Virgo, Taurus
Beets	1st or 2nd	Cancer, Capricorn, Pisces, Libra,
Biennials	3rd or 4th	
Broccoli	1st	Cancer, Pisces, Libra
Brussels Sprouts	1st	Cancer, Scorpio, Pisces, Libra
Buckwheat	1st or 2nd	Capricorn
Bulbs	3rd	Cancer, Scorpio, Pisces
Bulbs for Seed	2nd or 3rd	
Cabbage	1st	Cancer, Scorpio, Pisces, Libra, Taurus

Plant	Phase	Sign
Cactus		Taurus, Capricorn
Canes (raspberries, black-berries, and gooseberries)	2nd	Cancer, Scorpio, Pisces
Cantaloupes	1st or 2nd	Cancer, Scorpio, Pisces, Libra, Taurus
Carrots	3rd	Taurus
Cauliflower	1st	Cancer, Scorpio, Pisces, Libra
Celeriac	3rd	Cancer, Scorpio, Pisces
Celery	1st or 2nd	Cancer, Scorpio, Pisces
Cereals	1st or 2nd	Cancer, Scorpio, Pisces, Libra
Chard	1st or 2nd	Cancer, Scorpio, Pisces
Chicory	3rd	Cancer, Scorpio, Pisces
Chrysanthemums	1st or 2nd	Virgo
Clover	1st or 2nd	Cancer, Scorpio, Pisces
Corn	1st	Cancer, Scorpio, Pisces
Corn for Fodder	1st or 2nd	Libra
Coryopsis	2nd or 3rd	Libra
Cosmos	2nd or 3rd	Libra
Cress	1st	Cancer, Scorpio, Pisces
Crocus	1st or 2nd	Virgo
Cucumbers	1st	Cancer, Scorpio, Pisces

Plant	Phase	Sign
Daffodils	1st or 2nd	Libra, Virgo
Dahlias	1st or 2nd	Libra, Virgo
Deciduous Trees	1st or 2nd	Cancer, Scorpio, Pisces, Virgo
Eggplant	2nd	Cancer, Scorpio, Pisces, Libra
Endive	1st	Cancer, Scorpio, Pisces, Libra
Flowers	1st	Libra, Cancer, Pisces, Virgo, Scorpio, Taurus
Garlic	1st or 2nd	Cancer, Pisces
Gladiola	1st or 2nd	Libra, Virgo
Gourds	1st or 2nd	Cancer, Scorpio, Pisces, Libra
Grapes	2nd or 3rd	Cancer, Scorpio, Pisces, Virgo
Hay	1st or 2nd	Cancer, Scorpio, Pisces, Libra, Taurus
Herbs	1st or 2nd	Cancer, Scorpio, Pisces
Honeysuckle	1st or 2nd	Scorpio, Virgo
Hops	1st or 2nd	Scorpio, Libra
Horseradish	1st or 2nd	Cancer, Scorpio, Pisces
House Plants	1st	Libra, Cancer, Scorpio, Pisces
Hyacinths	3rd	Cancer, Scorpio, Pisces
Iris	1st or 2nd	Cancer, Virgo
Kohlrabi	1st or 2nd	Cancer, Scorpio, Pisces, Libra

Plant	Phase	Sign
Leeks	1st or 2nd	Cancer, Pisces
Lettuce	1st	Cancer, Scorpio, Pisces, Libra, Taurus
Lilies	1st or 2nd	Cancer, Scorpio, Pisces
Maple Trees	1st or 2nd	Virgo
Plant	Phase	Sign
Melons	1st or 2nd	Cancer, Scorpio, Pisces
Moon Vine	1st or 2nd	Virgo
Morning-glory	1st or 2nd	Cancer, Scorpio, Pisces, Virgo
Oak Trees	3rd	Virgo
Oats	1st or 2nd	Cancer, Scorpio, Pisces, Libra
Okra	1st	Cancer, Scorpio, Pisces, Libra
Onion Seeds	2nd	Scorpio, Cancer
Onion Sets	3rd or 4th	Libra, Taurus, Pisces
Pansies	1st or 2nd	Cancer, Scorpio, Pisces
Parsley	1st	Cancer, Scorpio, Pisces, Libra
Parsnips	3rd	Taurus, Capricorn, Cancer, Scorpio
Peach trees	3rd	Taurus, Libra
Peanuts	3rd	Cancer, Scorpio, Pisces
Pear trees	3rd	Taurus, Libra

Plant	Phase	Sign
Peas	2nd or 3rd	Cancer, Scorpio, Pisces, Libra
Peonies	1st or 2nd	Virgo
Peppers	1st or 2nd	Cancer, Pisces
Perennials	3rd	
Petunias	1st or 2nd	Libra, Virgo
Plum Trees	1st or 2nd	Taurus, Virgo
Poppies	1st or 2nd	Virgo
Portulaca	1st or 2nd	Virgo
Potatoes	3rd	Cancer, Scorpio, Taurus, Libra, Capricorn
Privet	1st or 2nd	Taurus, Libra
Pumpkins	2nd	Cancer, Scorpio, Pisces, Libra
Quinces	1st or 2nd	Capricorn
Radishes	1st or 2nd	Cancer, Libra, Taurus, Pisces, Capricorn
Rhubarb	1st or 2nd	Cancer, Pisces
Rice	1st or 2nd	Scorpio
Roses	1st or 2nd	Cancer, Virgo
Rutabagas	3rd	Cancer, Scorpio, Pisces, Taurus
Saffron	1st or 2nd	Cancer, Scorpio, Pisces
Sage	3rd	Cancer, Scorpio, Pisces

Plant	Phase	Sign
Salsify	1st or 2nd	Cancer, Scorpio, Pisces
Shallots	2nd	Scorpio
Spinach	1st	Cancer, Scorpio, Pisces
Squash	2nd	Cancer, Scorpio, Pisces, Libra
Strawberries	3rd	Cancer, Scorpio, Pisces
String beans	1st or 2nd	Taurus
Sunflowers	3rd or 4th	Libra
Sweet peas	1st or 2nd	Cancer, Scorpio, Pisces
Tomatoes	2nd, transplant in 3rd	Cancer, Scorpio, Pisces, Capricorn
Shade Trees	3rd	Taurus, Capricorn
Ornamental Trees	2nd	Libra, Taurus
Trumpet Vines	1st or 2nd	Cancer, Scorpio, Pisces
Tubers for Seed	3rd	Cancer, Scorpio, Pisces, Libra
Tulips	1st or 2nd	Libra, Virgo
Turnips	3rd	Cancer, Scorpio, Pisces, Taurus, Capricorn, Libra
Valerian	1st or 2nd	Virgo, Gemini
Watermelons	1st or 2nd	Cancer, Scorpio, Pisces, Libra
Wheat	1st or 2nd	Cancer, Scorpio, Pisces, Libra

Gardening Dates

Dates	Qtr	Sign	Activity
Jan. 4, 9:56 am - Jan. 5, 3:51 pm	2nd	Cancer	Plant grains, leafy annuals. Fertilize. Graft or bud plants. Irrigate. Trim to increase growth.
Jan. 5, 3:51 pm - Jan. 6, 10:31 pm	3rd	Cancer	Plant biennials, perennials, bulbs and roots. Prune. Irrigate. Fertilize (organic).
Jan. 6, 10:31 pm - Jan. 9, 10:29 am	3rd	Leo	Cultivate. Destroy weeds and pests.
Jan. 9, 10:29 am - Jan. 11, 8:55 pm	3rd	Virgo	Cultivate, especially medicinal plants. Destroy weeds and pests. Trim to retard growth.
Jan. 14, 4:30 am - Jan. 16, 8:25 am	4th	Scorpio	Plant biennials, perennials, bulbs and roots. Prune. Irrigate. Fertilize (organic).
Jan. 16, 8:25 am - Jan. 18, 9:07 am	4th	Sagittarius	Cultivate. Destroy weeds and pests. Harvest fruits and root crops. Trim to retard growth.
Jan. 18, 9:07 am - Jan. 20, 7:51 am	4th	Capricorn	Plant potatos and tubers. Trim to retard growth.
Jan. 20, 7:51 am - Jan. 20, 8:15 am	1st	Capricorn	Graft or bud plants. Trim to increase growth.
Jan. 22, 8:02 am - Jan. 24, 10:37 am	1st	Pisces	Plant grains, leafy annuals. Fertilize. Graft or bud plants. Irrigate. Trim to increase growth.
Jan. 26, 5:17 pm - Jan. 27, 6:14 am	1st	Taurus	Plant annuals for hardiness. Trim to increase growth.
Jan. 27, 6:14 am - Jan. 29, 3:43 am	2nd	Taurus	Plant annuals for hardiness. Trim to increase growth.
Jan. 31, 4:11 pm - Feb. 3, 4:46 am	2nd	Cancer	Plant grains, leafy annuals. Fertilize. Graft or bud plants. Irrigate. Trim to increase growth.
Feb. 4, 10:58 am - Feb. 5, 4:22 pm	3rd	Leo	Cultivate. Destroy weeds and pests. Harvest fruits and root crops. Trim to retard growth.
Feb. 5, 4:22 pm - Feb. 8, 2:30 am	3rd	Virgo	Cultivate, especially medicinal plants. Destroy weeds and pests. Trim to retard growth.
Feb. 10, 10:35 am - Feb. 12, 3:38 am	3rd	Scorpio	Plant biennials, perennials, bulbs and roots. Prune. Irrigate. Fertilize (organic).
Feb. 12, 3:38 am - Feb. 12, 3:59 pm	4th	Scorpio	Plant biennials, perennials, bulbs and roots. Prune. Irrigate. Fertilize (organic).
Feb. 12, 3:59 pm - Feb. 14, 6:30 pm	4th	Sagittarius	Cultivate. Destroy weeds and pests. Harvest fruits and root crops. Trim to retard growth.
Feb. 14, 6:30 pm - Feb. 16, 7:00 pm	4th	Capricorn	Plant potatos and tubers. Trim to retard growth.
Feb. 16, 7:00 pm - Feb. 18, 6:31 pm	4th	Aquarius	Cultivate. Destroy weeds and pests. Harvest fruits and root crops. Trim to retard growth.

Gardening Dates

Dates	Qtr	Sign	Activity
Feb. 18, 7:10 pm - Feb. 20, 8:58 pm	1st	Pisces	Plant grains, leafy annuals. Fertilize (chemical). Graft orbud plants. Irrigate. Trim to increase growth.
Feb. 23, 2:08 am - Feb. 25, 11:14 am	1st	Taurus	Plant annuals for hardiness. Trim to increase growth.
Feb. 27, 11:10 pm - Mar. 1, 11:47 am	2nd	Cancer	Plant grains, leafy annuals. Fertilize. Graft or bud plants. Irrigate. Trim to increase growth.
Mar. 5, 4:23 am - Mar. 6, 8:41 am	3rd	Virgo	Cultivate, especially medicinal plants. Destroy weeds and pests. Trim to retard growth.
Mar. 8, 4:06 pm - Mar. 10, 9:33 pm	3rd	Scorpio	Plant biennials, perennials, bulbs and roots. Prune. Irrigate. Fertilize (organic).
Mar. 10, 9:33 pm - Mar. 12, 12:15 pm	3rd	Sagittarius	Cultivate. Destroy weeds and pests. Harvest fruits and root crops. Trim to retard growth.
Mar. 12, 12:15 pm - Mar. 13, 1:08 am	4th	Sagittarius	Cultivate. Destroy weeds and pests. Harvest fruits and root crops. Trim to retard growth.
Mar. 13, 1:08 am - Mar. 15, 3:15 am	4th	Capricorn	Plant potatos and tubers. Trim to retard growth.
Mar. 15, 3:15 am - Mar. 17, 4:50 am	4th	Aquarius	Cultivate. Destroy weeds and pests. Harvest fruits and root crops. Trim to retard growth.
Mar. 17, 4:50 am - Mar. 19, 5:45 am	4th	Pisces	Plant biennials, perennials, bulbs and roots. Prune. Irrigate. Fertilize (organic).
Mar. 19, 5:45 am - Mar. 19, 7:15 am	1st	Pisces	Plant grains, leafy annuals. Fertilize. Graft or bud plants. Irrigate. Trim to increase growth.
Mar. 21, 11:58 am - Mar. 23, 7:59 pm	1st	Taurus	Plant annuals for hardiness. Trim to increase growth.
Mar. 26, 7:06 am - Mar. 26, 8:31 am	1st	Cancer	Plant grains, leafy annuals. Fertilize. Graft or bud plants. Irrigate. Trim to increase growth.
Mar. 26, 8:31 am - Mar. 28, 7:38 pm	2nd	Cancer	Plant grains, leafy annuals. Fertilize. Graft or bud plants. Irrigate. Trim to increase growth.
Apr. 2, 4:27 pm - Apr. 3, 7:08 pm	2nd	Libra	Plant annuals for fragrance and beauty. Trim to increase growth.
Apr. 4, 10:57 pm - Apr. 7, 3:21 am	3rd	Scorpio	Plant biennials, perennials, bulbs and roots. Prune. Irrigate. Fertilize (organic).
Apr. 7, 3:21 am - Apr. 9, 6:30.am	3rd	Sagittarius	Cultivate. Destroy weeds and pests. Harvest fruits and root crops. Trim to retard growth.
Apr. 9, 6:30 am - Apr. 10, 6:36 pm	3rd	Capricorn	Plant potatos and tubers. Trim to retard growth.
Apr. 10, 6:36 pm - Apr. 11, 9:09 am	4th	Capricorn'	Plant potatos and tubers. Trim to retard growth.

Gardening Dates

Dates	Qtr	Sign	Activity
Apr. 11, 9:09 am - Apr. 13, 11:59 am	4th	Aquarius	Cultivate. Destroy weeds and pests. Harvest fruits and root crops. Trim to retard growth.
Apr. 13, 11:59 am - Apr. 15, 3:43 pm	4th	Pisces	Plant biennials, perennials, bulbs and roots. Prune. Irrigate. Fertilize (organic).
Apr. 15, 3:43 pm - Apr. 17, 5:49 pm	4th	Aries	Cultivate. Destroy weeds and pests. Harvest fruits and root crops. Trim to retard growth.
Apr. 17, 9:06 pm - Apr. 20, 4:55 am	1st	Taurus	Plant annuals for hardiness. Trim to increase growth.
Apr. 22, 3:25 pm - Apr. 25, 3:45 am	1st	Cancer	Plant grains, leafy annuals. Fertilize). Graft or bud plants. Irrigate. Trim to increase growth.
Apr. 30, 1:27 am - May 2, 7:43 am	2nd	Libra	Plant annuals for fragrance and beauty. Trim to increase growth.
May 2, 7:43 am - May 3, 6:48 am	2nd	Scorpio	Plant grains, leafy annuals. Fertilize. Graft or bud plants. Irrigate. Trim to increase growth.
May 3, 6:48 am - May 4, 11:04 am	3rd	Scorpio	Plant biennials, perennials, bulbs and roots. Prune. Irrigate. Fertilize (organic).
May 4, 11:04 am - May 6, 12:54 pm	3rd	Sagittarius	Cultivate. Destroy weeds and pests. Harvest fruits and root crops. Trim to retard growth.
May 6, 12:54 pm - May 8, 2:39 pm	3rd	Capricorn	Plant potatos and tubers. Trim to retard growth.
May 8, 2:39 pm - May 10, 12:04 am	3rd	Aquarius	Cultivate. Destroy weeds and pests. Harvest fruits and root crops. Trim to retard growth.
May 10, 12:04 am - May 10, 5:29 pm	4th	Aquarius	Cultivate. Destroy weeds and pests. Harvest fruits and root crops. Trim to retard growth.
May 10, 5:29 pm - May 12, 10:01 pm	4th	Pisces	Plant biennials, perennials, bulbs and roots. Prune. Irrigate. Fertilize (organic).
May 12, 10:01 pm - May 15, 4:25 am	4th	Aries	Cultivate. Destroy weeds and pests. Harvest fruits and root crops. Trim to retard growth.
May 15, 4:25 am - May 17, 6:47 am	4th	Taurus	Plant potatos and tubers. Trim to retard growth.
May 17, 6:47 am - May 17, 12:48 pm	1st	Taurus	Plant annuals for hardiness. Trim to increase growth.
May 19, 11:17 pm - May 22, 11:28 am	1st	Cancer	Plant grains, leafy annuals. Fertilize. Graft or bud plants. Irrigate. Trim to increase growth.
May 27, 10:33 am - May 29, 5:30 pm	2nd	Libra	Plant annuals for fragrance and beauty. Trim to increase growth.
May 29, 5:30 pm - May 31, 8:43 pm	2nd	Scorpio	Plant grains, leafy annuals. Fertilize. Graft or bud plants. Irrigate. Trim to increase growth.

Gardening Dates

Dates	Qtr	Sign	Activity
Jun. 1, 3:47 pm - Jun. 2, 9:29 pm	3rd	Sagittarius	Cultivate. Destroy weeds and pests. Harvest fruits and root crops. Trim to retard growth.
Jun. 2, 9:29 pm - Jun. 4, 9:45 pm	3rd	Capricorn	Plant potatoes and tubers. Trim to retard growth.
Jun. 4, 9:45 pm - Jun. 6, 11:20 pm	3rd	Aquarius	Cultivate. Destroy weeds and pests. Harvest fruits and root crops. Trim to retard growth.
Jun. 6, 11:20 pm - Jun. 8, 6:06 am	3rd	Pisces	Plant biennials, perennials, bulbs and roots. Prune. Irrigate. Fertilize (organic).
Jun. 8, 6:06 am - Jun. 9, 3:24 am	4th	Pisces	Plant biennials, perennials, bulbs and roots. Prune. Irrigate. Fertilize (organic).
Jun. 9, 3:24 am - Jun. 11, 10:11 am	4th	Aries	Cultivate. Destroy weeds and pests. Harvest fruits and root crops. Trim to retard growth.
Jun. 11, 10:11 am - Jun. 13, 7:16 pm	4th	Taurus	Plant potatoes and tubers. Trim to retard growth.
Jun. 16, 6:08 am - Jun. 18, 6:21 pm	1st	Cancer	Plant grains, leafy annuals. Fertilize. Graft or bud plants. Irrigate. Trim to increase growth.
Jun. 23, 6:38 pm - Jun. 24, 12:23 am	1st	Libra	Plant annuals for fragrance and beauty. Trim to increase growth.
Jun. 24, 12:23 am - Jun. 26, 2:54 am	2nd	Libra	Plant annuals for fragrance and beauty. Trim to increase growth.
Jun. 26, 2:54 am - Jun. 28, 7:02 am	2nd	Scorpio	Plant grains, leafy annuals. Fertilize. Graft or bud plants. Irrigate. Trim to increase growth.
Jun. 30, 7:48 am - Jun. 30, 10:59 pm	2nd	Capricorn	Graft or bud plants. Trim to increase growth.
Jun. 30, 10:59 pm - Jul. 2, 7:06 am	3rd	Capricorn	Plant potatoes and tubers. Trim to retard growth.
Jul. 2, 7:06 am - Jul. 4, 7:07 am	3rd	Aquarius	Cultivate. Destroy weeds and pests. Harvest fruits and root crops. Trim to retard growth.
Jul. 4, 7:07 am - Jul. 6, 9:42 am	3rd	Pisces	Plant biennials, perennials, bulbs and roots. Prune. Irrigate. Fertilize (organic).
Jul. 6, 9:42 am - Jul. 7, 1:55 pm	3rd	Aries	Cultivate. Destroy weeds and pests. Harvest fruits and root crops . Trim to retard growth.
Jul. 7, 1:55 pm - Jul. 8, 3:43 pm	4th	Aries	Cultivate. Destroy weeds and pests. Harvest fruits and root crops. Trim to retard growth.
Jul. 8, 3:43 pm - Jul. 11, 12:52 am	4th	Taurus	Plant potatoes and tubers. Trim to retard growth.
Jul. 13, 12:08 pm - Jul. 15, 11:15 am	4th	Cancer	Plant biennials, perennials, bulbs and roots. Prune. Irrigate. Fertilize (organic).

Gardening Dates

Dates	Qtr	Sign	Activity
Jul. 15, 11:15 am - Jul. 16, 12:31 am	1st	Cancer	Plant grains, leafy annuals. Fertilize). Graft or bud plants. Irrigate. Trim to increase growth.
Jul. 21, 1:14 am - Jul. 23, 10:43 am	1st	Libra	Plant annuals for fragrance and beauty. Trim to increase growth.
Jul. 23, 10:43 am - Jul. 23, 12:50 pm	1st	Scorpio	Plant grains, leafy annuals. Fertilize. Graft or bud plants. Irrigate. Trim to increase growth.
Jul. 23, 12:50 pm - Jul. 25, 4:24 pm	2nd	Scorpio	Plant grains, leafy annuals. Fertilize). Graft or bud plants. Irrigate. Trim to increase growth.
Jul. 27, 6:18 pm - Jul. 29, 5:48 pm	2nd	Capricorn	Graft or bud plants. Trim to increase growth.
Jul. 30, 5:36 am - Jul. 31, 5:01 pm	3rd	Aquarius	Cultivate. Destroy weeds and pests. Harvest fruits and root crops. Trim to retard growth.
Jul. 31, 5:01 pm - Aug 2, 6:05 pm	3rd	Pisces	Plant biennials, perennials, bulbs and roots. Prune. Irrigate. Fertilize (organic).
Aug 2, 6:05 pm - Aug 4, 10:33 pm	3rd	Aries	Cultivate. Destroy weeds and pests. Harvest fruits and root crops. Trim to retard growth.
Aug 4, 10:33 pm - Aug 6, 12:25 am	3rd	Taurus	Plant potatoes and tubers. Trim to retard growth.
Aug 6, 12:25 am - Aug 7, 6:49 am	4th	Taurus	Plant potatoes and tubers. Trim to retard growth.
Aug 9, 5:58 pm - Aug 12, 6:29 am	4th	Cancer	Plant biennials, perennials, bulbs and roots. Prune. Irrigate. Fertilize (organic).
Aug 12, 6:29 am - Aug 14, 2:35 am	4th	Leo	Cultivate. Destroy weeds and pests. Harvest fruits and root crops. Trim to retard growth.
Aug 17, 6:56 am - Aug 19, 4:51 pm	1st	Libra	Plant annuals for fragrance and beauty. Trim to increase growth.
Aug 19, 4:51 pm - Aug 21, 10:37 pm	1st	Scorpio	Plant grains, leafy annuals. Fertilize. Graft or bud plants. Irrigate. Trim to increase growth.
Aug 21, 10:37 pm - Aug 21, 11:48 pm	2nd	Scorpio	Plant grains, leafy annuals. Fertilize. Graft or bud plants. Irrigate. Trim to increase growth.
Aug 24, 3:22 am - Aug 26, 4:10 am	2nd	Capricorn	Graft or bud plants. Trim to increase growth.
Aug 28, 3:48 am - Aug 28, 12:52 pm	2nd	Pisces	Plant grains, leafy annuals. Fertilize. Graft or bud plants. Irrigate. Trim to increase growth.
Aug 28, 12:52 pm - Aug 30, 4:15 am	3rd	Pisces	Plant biennials, perennials, bulbs and roots. Prune. Irrigate. Fertilize (organic).
Aug. 30, 4:15 am - Sept. 1, 7:20 am	3rd	Aries	Cultivate. Destroy weeds and pests. Harvest fruits and root crops. Trim to retard growth.

Gardening Dates

Dates	Qtr	Sign	Activity
Sept. 1, 7:20 am - Sept. 3, 2:09 pm	3rd	Taurus	Plant potatos and tubers. Trim to retard growth.
Sept. 6, 12:30 am - Sept. 8, 12:55 pm	4th	Cancer	Plant biennials, perennials, bulbs and roots. Prune. Irrigate. Fertilize (organic).
Sept. 8, 12:55 pm - Sept. 11, 1:29 am	4th	Leo	Cultivate. Destroy weeds and pests. Harvest fruits and root crops. Trim to retard growth.
Sept. 11, 1:29 am - Sept. 12, 6:08 pm	4th	Virgo	Cultivate, especially medicinal plants. Destroy weeds and pests. Trim to retard growth.
Sept. 13, 12:51 pm - Sept. 15, 10:20 pm	1st	Libra	Plant annuals for fragrance and beauty. Trim to increase growth.
Sept. 15, 10:20 pm - Sept. 18, 5:30 am	1st	Scorpio	Plant grains, leafy annuals. Fertilize. Graft or bud plants. Irrigate. Trim to increase growth.
Sept. 20, 10:12 am - Sept. 22, 12:39 pm	2nd	Capricorn	Graft or bud plants. Trim to increase growth.
Sept. 24, 1:43 pm - Sept. 26, 2:46 pm	2nd	Pisces	Plant grains, leafy annuals. Fertilize. Graft or bud plants. Irrigate. Trim to increase growth.
Sept. 26, 9:51 pm - Sept. 28, 5:24 pm	3rd	Aries	Cultivate. Destroy weeds and pests. Harvest fruits and root crops. Trim to retard growth.
Sept. 28, 5:24 pm - Sept. 30, 11:02 pm	3rd	Taurus	Plant potatos and tubers. Trim to retard growth.
Oct. 3, 8:15 am - Oct. 4, 7:05 am	3rd	Cancer	Plant biennials, perennials, bulbs and roots. Prune. Irrigate. Fertilize (organic).
Oct. 4, 7:05 am - Oct. 5, 8:12 pm	4th	Cancer	Plant biennials, perennials, bulbs and roots. Prune. Irrigate. Fertilize (organic).
Oct. 5, 8:12 pm - Oct. 8, 8:49 am	4th	Leo	Cultivate. Destroy weeds and pests. Harvest fruits and root crops. Trim to retard growth.
Oct. 8, 8:49 am - Oct. 10, 8:00 pm	4th	Virgo	Cultivate, especially medicinal plants. Destroy weeds and pests. Trim to retard growth.
Oct. 12, 9:14 am - Oct. 13, 4:46 am	1st	Libra	Plant annuals for fragrance and beauty. Trim to increase growth.
Oct. 13, 4:46 am - Oct. 15, 11:07 am	1st	Scorpio	Plant grains, leafy annuals. Fertilize. Graft or bud plants. Irrigate. Trim to increase growth.
Oct. 17, 3:38 pm - Oct. 19, 1:10 pm	1st	Capricorn	Graft or bud plants. Trim to increase growth.
Oct. 19, 1:10 pm - Oct. 19, 6:52 pm	2nd	Capricorn	Graft or bud plants. Trim to increase growth.
Oct. 21, 9:23 pm - Oct. 23, 11:51 pm	2nd	Pisces	Plant grains, leafy annuals. Fertilize. Graft or bud plants. Irrigate. Trim to increase growth.

Gardening Dates

Dates	Qtr	Sign	Activity
Oct. 26, 3:12 am - Oct. 26, 9:12 am	2nd	Taurus	Plant annuals for hardiness. Trim to increase growth.
Oct. 26, 9:12 am - Oct. 28, 8:35 am	3rd	Taurus	Plant potatos and tubers. Trim to retard growth
Oct. 30, 4:57 pm - Nov. 2, 4:16 am	3rd	Cancer	Plant biennials, perennials, bulbs and roots. Prune. Irrigate. Fertilize (organic).
Nov. 2, 4:16 am - Nov. 3, 2:50 am	3rd	Leo	Cultivate. Destroy weeds and pests. Harvest fruits and root crops. Trim to retard growth.
Nov. 3, 2:50 am - Nov. 4, 4:57 pm	4th	Leo	Cultivate. Destroy weeds and pests. Harvest fruits and root crops. Trim to retard growth.
Nov. 4, 4:57 pm - Nov. 7, 4:29	4th	Virgo	Cultivate, especially medicinal plants. Destroy weeds and pests. Trim to retard growth.
Nov. 9, 1:02 pm - Nov. 10, 11:17 pm	4th	Scorpio	Plant biennials, perennials, bulbs and roots. Prune. Irrigate. Fertilize (organic).
Nov. 10, 11:17 pm - Nov. 11, 6:27 pm	1st	Scorpio	Plant grains, leafy annuals. Fertilize. Graft or bud plants. Irrigate. Trim to increase growth.
Nov. 13, 9:44 pm - Nov. 16, 12:15 am	1st	Capricorn	Graft or bud plants. Trim to increase growth.
Nov. 18, 3:00 am - Nov. 20, 6:34 am	2nd	Pisces	Plant grains, leafy annuals. Fertilize. Graft or bud plants. Irrigate. Trim to increase growth.
Nov. 22, 11:12 am - Nov. 24, 5:19 pm	2nd	Taurus	Plant annuals for hardiness. Trim to increase growth.
Nov. 27, 1:37 am - Nov. 29, 12:30 pm	3rd	Cancer	Plant biennials, perennials, bulbs and roots. Prune. Irrigate. Fertilize (organic).
Nov. 29, 12:30 pm - Dec. 2, 1:11 am	3rd	Leo	Cultivate. Destroy weeds and pests. Harvest fruits and root crops. Trim to retard growth.
Dec. 2, 1:11 am - Dec. 3, 12:06 am	3rd	Virgo	Cultivate, especially medicinal plants. Destroy weeds and pests. Trim to retard growth.
Dec. 3, 12:06 am - Dec. 4, 1:24 pm	4th	Virgo	Cultivate, especially medicinal plants. Destroy weeds and pests. Trim to retard growth.
Dec. 6, 10:39 pm - Dec. 9, 3:59 am	4th	Scorpio	Plant biennials, perennials, bulbs and roots. Prune. Irrigate. Fertilize (organic).
Dec. 9, 3:59 am - Dec. 10, 11:57 am	4th	Sagittarius	Cultivate. Destroy weeds and pests. Harvest fruits and root crops. Trim to retard growth.
Dec. 11, 6:15 am - Dec. 13, 7:14 am	1st	Capricorn	Graft or bud plants. Trim to increase growth.
Dec. 15, 8:44 am - Dec. 17, 4:31 am	1st	Pisces	Plant grains, leafy annuals. Fertilize. Graft or bud plants. Irrigate. Trim to increase growth.

Gardening Dates

Dates	Qtr	Sign	Activity
Dec. 17, 4:31 am - Dec. 17, 11:55 am	2nd	Pisces	Plant grains, leafy annuals. Fertilize. Graft or bud plants. Irrigate. Trim to increase growth.
Dec. 19, 5:09 pm - Dec. 22, 12:17 am	2nd	Taurus	Plant annuals for hardiness. Trim to increase growth.
Dec. 24, 9:14 am - Dec. 26, 8:09 pm	3rd	Cancer	Plant biennials, perennials, bulbs and roots. Prune. Irrigate. Fertilize (organic).
Dec. 26, 8:09 pm - Dec. 29, 8:46 am	3rd	Leo	Cultivate. Destroy weeds and pests. Harvest fruits and root crops. Trim to retard growth.
Dec. 29, 8:46 am - Dec. 31, 9:33 pm	3rd	Virgo	Cultivate, especially medicinal plants. Destroy weeds and pests. Trim to retard growth.

Other Garden Activities

Animals

Animals are easiest to handle when the Moon is in Taurus, Cancer, Libra, or Pisces. Avoid the Full Moon. Buy animals during the first quarter or New Moon in all signs except Scorpio or Pisces. Castrate animals in Gemini, Cancer, Leo, Capricorn, or Aquarius. Slaughter for food in the first three days after the Full Moon in any sign except Leo.

Animals, Breeding

Eggs should be set and animals mated so that the young will be born when the Moon is increasing and in Taurus, Cancer, Pisces, or Libra. Young born in these signs are generally healthier, mature faster and make better breeding stock. Those born during a semi-fruitful sign (Taurus and Capricorn) will generally mature quickly, but will produce leaner meat. The sign of Libra yields beautiful, graceful animals for showing and racing.

To determine the best date to mate animals or set eggs, subtract the number of days given for incubation or gestation from the fruitful dates given in the following tables. (Tables on page 155-157) For example, cats and dogs are mated 63 days previous to the desired birth date; chicken eggs are set 21 days previous.

Composting

Start compost when the Moon is in the fourth quarter in a water sign, especially Scorpio.

Cultivating

Cultivate when the Moon is in a barren sign and waning, ideally the fourth quarter in Aries, Gemini, Leo, Virgo, or Aquarius. Sagittarius also works.

Cutting Timber

Cut timber during the third and fourth quarters while the Moon is not in a water sign.

Drying Crops

Dry crops in the third quarter when the Moon is in a fire sign.

Fertilizing

Fertilize when the Moon is in a fruitful sign (Cancer, Scorpio, Pisces). Organic fertilizers are best used when the Moon is in the third or fourth quarter. Chemical fertilizers are best used in the first or second quarter.

Grafting

Graft during first or second quarter Capricorn, Cancer or Scorpio.

Harvesting

Harvest root crops when the Moon is in a dry sign (Aries, Leo, Sagittarius, Gemini, Aquarius) and in the third or fourth quarter. Harvest root crops intended for seed during the Full Moon. Harvest grain which will be stored just after the Full Moon, avoiding the water signs (Cancer, Scorpio, Pisces). Fire signs are best for cutting down on water content. Harvest fruits in the third and fourth quarters in the dry signs.

Irrigation

Irrigate when the Moon is in a water sign.

Pruning

Prune during the third and fourth quarters in Scorpio to retard growth and to promote better fruit, and in Capricorn to promote better healing.

Spraying

Destroy pests and weeds during the fourth quarter when the Moon is in Aries, Gemini, Leo, Virgo, Sagittarius, or Aquarius.

Transplanting

Transplant when the Moon is increasing and preferably in Cancer, Scorpio, or Pisces.

Gestation Table

Animal	Young/Eggs	Gestation/Incubation
Horse	1	346 days
Cow	1	283 days
Monkey	1	164 days
Goat	1-2	151 days
Sheep	1-2	150 days
Pig	10	112 days
Chinchilla	2	110 days
Fox	5-8	63 days
Dog	6-8	63 days
Cat	4-6	63 days
Guinea Pig	2-6	62 days
Ferret	6-9	40 days
Rabbit	4-8	30 days
Rat	10	22 days
Mouse	10	22 days
Turkey	12-15	26-30 days
Guinea	15-18	25-26 days
Pea Hen	10	28-30 days
Duck	9-12	25-32 days
Goose	15-18	27-33 days
Hen	12-15	19-24 days
Pigeon	2	16-20 days
Canary	3-4	13-14 days

Egg Setting Dates

Dates to be Born	Qtr	Sign	Set Eggs
JAN 4 9:56 am - JAN 5 3:51 pm	Cancer	2nd	Dec. 14, 15, 1995
JAN 22 8:02 am - JAN 24 10:37 am	Pisces	1st	Jan. 1, 3
JAN 26 5:17 pm - JAN 27 6:14 am	Taurus	1st	Jan. 5, 6
JAN 27 6:14 am - JAN 29 3:43 am	Taurus	2nd	Jan. 6, 8
JAN 31 4:11 pm - FEB 3 4:46 am	Cancer	2nd	Jan. 10, 13
FEB 18 7:10 pm - FEB 20 8:58 pm	Pisces	1st	Jan. 28, 30
FEB 23 2:08 am - FEB 25 11:14 am	Taurus	1st	Feb. 2, 4
FEB 27 11:10 pm - MAR 1 11:47 am	Cancer	2nd	Feb. 6, 9
MAR 19 5:45 am - MAR 19 7:15 am	Pisces	1st	Feb. 27
MAR 21 11:58 am - MAR 23 7:59 pm	Taurus	1st	Feb. 29, Mar. 2
MAR 26 7:06 am - MAR 26 8:31 pm	Cancer	1st	Mar. 5
MAR 26 8:31 pm - MAR 28 7:38 pm	Cancer	2nd	Mar. 5, 7
APR 2 4:27 pm - APR 3 7:08 pm	Libra	2nd	Mar. 12, 13
APR 17 9:06 pm - APR 20 4:55 am	Taurus	1st	Mar. 27, 30
APR 22 3:25 pm - APR 25 3:45 am	Cancer	1st	Apr. 1, 4
APR 30 1:27 am - MAY 2 7:43 am	Libra	2nd	Apr. 9, 11
MAY 17 6:47 am - MAY 17 12:48 pm	Taurus	1st	Apr. 26
MAY 19 11:17 pm - MAY 22 11:28 am	Cancer	1st	Apr. 28, May 1
MAY 27 10:33 am - MAY 29 5:30 pm	Libra	2nd	May 6, 8
JUN 16 6:08 am - JUN 18 6:21 pm	Cancer	1st	May 26, 28
JUN 23 6:38 pm - JUN 24 12:23 am	Libra	1st	Jun. 2, 3
JUN 24 12:23 am - JUN 26 2:54 am	Libra	2nd	Jun. 3, 5
JUL 15 11:15 am - JUL 16 12:31 am	Cancer	1st	Jun. 24, 25
JUL 21 1:14 am - JUL 23 10:43 am	Libra	1st	Jun. 30, Jul. 2
AUG 17 6:56 am - AUG 19 4:51 pm	Libra	1st	Jul. 27, 29
AUG 28 3:48 am - AUG 28 12:52 pm	Pisces	2nd	Aug. 7
SEP 13 12:51 pm - SEP 15 10:20 pm	Libra	1st	Aug. 23, 25
SEP 24 1:43 pm - SEP 26 2:46 pm	Pisces	2nd	Sep. 3, 5
OCT 12 9:14 am - OCT 13 4:46 am	Libra	1st	Sep. 21, 22
OCT 21 9:23 pm - OCT 23 11:51 pm	Pisces	2nd	Sep. 30, Oct. 2

Egg Setting Dates

Dates to be Born	Qtr	Sign	Set Eggs
OCT 26 3:12 am - OCT 26 9:12 am	Taurus	2nd	Oct. 5
NOV 18 3:00 am - NOV 20 6:34 am	Pisces	2nd	Oct. 28, 30
NOV 22 11:12 am - NOV 24 5:19 pm	Taurus	2nd	Nov. 1, 3
DEC 15 8:44 am - DEC 17 4:31 am	Pisces	1st	Nov. 24, 26
DEC 17 4:31 am - DEC 17 11:55 am	Pisces	2nd	Nov. 26
DEC 19 5:09 pm - DEC 22 12:17 am	Taurus	2nd	Nov. 28, Dec. 1

Dates to Destroy Weeds and Pests

From		To		Sign	Phase
JAN 6	10:31 pm	JAN 9	10:29 am	Leo	3rd
JAN 9	10:29 am	JAN 11	8:55 pm	Virgo	3rd
JAN 16	8:25 am	JAN 18	9:07 am	Sagittarius	4th
FEB 4	10:58 am	FEB 5	4:22 pm	Leo	3rd
FEB 5	4:22 pm	FEB 8	2:30 am	Virgo	3rd
FEB 12	3:59 pm	FEB 14	6:30 pm	Sagittarius	4th
FEB 16	7:00 pm	FEB 18	6:31 pm	Aquarius	4th
MAR 5	4:23 am	MAR 6	8:41 am	Virgo	3rd
MAR 10	9:33 pm	MAR 12	12:15 pm	Sagittarius	3rd
MAR 12	12:15 pm	MAR 13	1:08 am	Sagittarius	4th
MAR 15	3:15 am	MAR 17	4:50 am	Aquarius	4th
APR 7	3:21 am	APR 9	6:30 am	Sagittarius	3rd
APR 11	9:09 am	APR 13	11:59 am	Aquarius	4th
APR 15	3:43 pm	APR 17	5:49 pm	Aries	4th
MAY 4	11:04 am	MAY 6	12:54 pm	Sagittarius	3rd
MAY 8	2:39 pm	MAY 10	12:04 am	Aquarius	3rd
MAY 10	12:04 am	MAY 10	5:29 pm	Aquarius	4th
MAY 12	10:01 pm	MAY 15	4:25 am	Aries	4th
JUN 1	3:47 pm	JUN 2	9:29 pm	Sagittarius	3rd
JUN 4	9:45 pm	JUN 6	11:20 pm	Aquarius	3rd
JUN 9	3:24 am	JUN 11	10:11 am	Aries	4th
JUN 13	7:16 pm	JUN 15	8:36 pm	Gemini	4th
JUL 2	7:06 am	JUL 4	7:07 am	Aquarius	3rd
JUL 6	9:42 am	JUL 7	1:55 pm	Aries	3rd
JUL 7	1:55 pm	JUL 8	3:43 pm	Aries	4th
JUL 11	12:52 am	JUL 13	12:08 pm	Gemini	4th
JUL 30	5:36 am	JUL 31	5:01 pm	Aquarius	3rd
AUG 2	6:05 pm	AUG 4	10:33 pm	Aries	3rd

Dates to Destroy Weeds and Pests

From		To		Sign	Phase
AUG 7	6:49 am	AUG 9	5:58 pm	Gemini	4th
AUG 12	6:29 am	AUG 14	2:35 am	Leo	4th
AUG 30	4:15 am	SEP 1	7:20 am	Aries	3rd
SEP 3	2:09 pm	SEP 4	2:07 pm	Gemini	3rd
SEP 4	2:07 pm	SEP 6	12:30 am	Gemini	4th
SEP 8	12:55 pm	SEP 11	1:29 am	Leo	4th
SEP 11	1:29 am	SEP 12	6:08 pm	Virgo	4th
SEP 26	9:51 pm	SEP 28	5:24 pm	Aries	3rd
SEP 30	11:02 pm	OCT 3	8:15 am	Gemini	3rd
OCT 5	8:12 pm	OCT 8	8:49 am	Leo	4th
OCT 8	8:49 am	OCT 10	8:00 pm	Virgo	4th
OCT 28	8:35 am	OCT 30	4:57 pm	Gemini	3rd
NOV 2	4:16 am	NOV 3	2:50 am	Leo	3rd
NOV 3	2:50 am	NOV 4	4:57 pm	Leo	4th
NOV 4	4:57 pm	NOV 7	4:29	Virgo	4th
NOV 24	11:10 pm	NOV 27	1:37 am	Gemini	3rd
NOV 29	12:30 pm	DEC 2	1:11 am	Leo	3rd
DEC 2	1:11 am	DEC 3	12.06 am	Virgo	3rd
DEC 3	12:06 am	DEC 4	1:24 pm	Virgo	4th
DEC 9	3:59 am	DEC 10	11:57 am	Sagittarius	4th
DEC 24	3:41 pm	DEC 24	9:14 am	Gemini	3rd
DEC 26	8:09 pm	DEC 29	8:46 am	Leo	3rd
DEC 29	8:46 am	DEC 31	9:33 pm	Virgo	3rd

1996 Weather Predictions

By Nancy Soller

Normal precipitation and normal temperatures are predicted for the East Coast in the winter of 1996. Normal weather should extend west, but the Mississippi River Valley should see an unusually great amount of precipitation. Temperatures there will be normal. The heavy precipitation may be noted as far east as Cincinnati and extend west well into the plains. Really dry weather will be noted in the Rockies and seasonable weather with normal amounts of precipitation and normal temperatures will be noted on the West Coast. Much of Alaska will see less precipitation than usual and temperatures in the central part of the state will be above normal. Hawaiian weather will be seasonable.

Spring will bring unusually wet weather to the East Coast, but temperatures there should be normal. The Midwest may also see more precipitation than normal and, again, normal temperatures are predicted. Near the Rockies and in the Rockies it will be dry and temperatures may be slightly above normal. Warm, dry weather is forecast for the West Coast with Alaska weather drier and warmer than usual. Hawaiian weather will be normal .

Dry weather is forecast for the northeast in the summer of 1996; temperatures there will be above normal. To the south and west there will be seasonable weather, but wet weather is forecast for the Mississippi River Valley and areas west of the river. Weather that is warmer and drier than usual is forecast for the Rockies. Some areas on and near the West Coast may see some unusually wet, cool weather, but hot, dry weather is forecast for most of this area. Much of Alaska will have dry weather with temperatures above normal and this extends to Hawaii.

The fall of 1996 will see dry weather and above-normal temperatures on the East Coast. Much of the Midwest, however, will have a wet, chill season. The western plains will be dry, chill, and windy, and this weather will extend west to the eastern Rockies. Dry weather with above-normal temperatures is forecast for the West Coast and dry weather is forecast for much of Alaska. Hawaiian weather may be wetter than usual.

Zone 6 Alaska & Hawaii

United States Weather Zones

December 1995

Zone 1: Dry, bitterly chill weather north and more seasonable temperatures south are forecast for this zone in December. Precipitation south is likely to be unseasonably heavy.

Watch for snowfall December 4th, December 8th and the 10th, 15th and 16th; watch also the 20th, 22nd, 25th and 27th. Winds north will be strong, and snowfall coming Christmas Day may be heavy.

Zone 2: Cold, dry weather is forecast for the eastern portions of this zone this month. Areas near this Mississippi, however, should have an unusually great amount of snowfall. Watch for snowfall December 4th and 8th, the 10th, the 15th-16th; also December 20th, 22nd, 24th and 25th. December 27th could also result in a storm. Snow on the 24th and 25th could interfere with holiday travel.

Zone 3: Heavy precipitation is forecast for this zone in December. Areas east should have mild temperatures, but western portions of this zone should be bitterly chill. Watch for snowfall December 4th and 12th, December 15th, 16th and 22nd, December 24th in all areas and December 28th west. Snowfall north on the 24th may be so heavy that it interferes with holiday travel. Winds are predicted on this date also.

Zone 4: Chilly, wet weather east and mild temperatures west are forecast for this zone in December. Areas west are likely to see little snowfall. Dates most likely to result in snow are the 4th and 12th, the 15th and 22nd; also December 26th and 28th. Snow on the 24th will involve winds, so drifting is likely and holiday traffic may be impeded. A white Christmas is forecast for most of this zone.

Zone 5: Mild temperatures, unusually blue skies and relatively dry weather will mark this zone this month. Dates most likely to result in precipitation include the 12th and 15th, 16th and 22nd, 24th and 28th. Snowfall north on Christmas Eve will involve winds, making drifting likely. Not only is a white Christmas predicted north, but a temperature drop is due also. Rain south on the 24th promises a soggy Christmas there.

Zone 6: A month with dry weather and unseasonably warm temperatures is forecast for most of the state of Alaska. Snowfall will be most likely December 4th, 7th and 8th, December 10th and 12th, December 16th and also the 20th, 22nd, 24th and 25th. The 27th and 28th could also result in snowfall. Snow will be scant and short-lived on many snow dates. Hawaii will have a pleasant month.

Dates to Watch:

Watch for snow December 4th, 7th, 8th, 10th, 12th, 15th, 16th, 20th, 22nd and 24th-28th.

Watch for winds December 3rd, 4th, 8th, 20th, 22nd-25th and 27th-29th.

January 1996

Zone 1: Seasonable temperatures and normal amounts of precipitation are forecast for this zone in January. Watch for snow north January 3rd, 10th, 13th, 17th and 18th; also January 20th, 24th, 25th and 30th. These dates could result in other precipitation south. Winds will be prominent this month. Watch for winds January 1st, 3rd, 7th, 11th, 13th and 15th; also January 16th, 18th, 24th and 30th.

Zone 2: The very easternmost portions of this zone will see normal precipitation, but much of this zone will have an unusually wet month. Temperatures throughout this zone will be seasonable. Watch for snow north and rain south January 3rd, 10th, 11th, 13th and 15th; watch also January 17th, 18th, 20th, 24th and the 30th east. Winds are likely January 1st, 3rd, 7th, 11th, 13th and the 15th east; also January 18th and 24th, 26th and 30th.

Zone 3: Very wet weather and seasonable temperatures are predicted for this zone in January. Especially wet weather is predicted for the Mississippi River Valley. Watch for snowfall north and rain south January 3rd, 10th, 11th, 17th and 18th; watch also January 20th and 27th. Winds are likely January 3rd, 11th, 13th east, 15th, 18th, 20th west; also January 23rd and 26th.

Zone 4: Snowfall may be generous in eastern portions of this zone, but most locations west and central will have chill, dry and windy weather. Snowfall is likely north January 5th; in the west watch for precipitation also January 11th, 17th, 18th, 20th, 25th and 27th. Winds are most likely January 3rd, 11th, 15th, 18th, 20th and 21st. January 26th may also result in strong winds.

Zone 5: Seasonable temperatures and amounts of precipitation are forecast for this zone in January. Watch for snowfall north and rain south January 5th, 11th, 16th, 18th, 20th, 25th and 31st. Winds are likely January 1st, 11th, 16th, 21st and 25th. Weather patterns in effect this month will continue into February and throughout the winter. Spring will bring dry weather.

Zone 6: Dry weather and mild temperatures are forecast for most of Alaska this month, but western portions of the state will have more normal precipitation patterns. Weather in Hawaii will be seasonable. Dates most likely to result in precipitation include January 3rd, 5th, 10th, 13th, 16th-18th, 20th, 24th, 25th, 30th and 31st. Winds will be strong in most locations throughout the entire month.

Dates to Watch:

Watch for snow January 1st, 3rd, 6th, 11th, 13th, 16th, 17th, 18th, 20th, 24th, 25th, 27th, 30th and 31st.

Watch for winds January 1st, 3rd, 8th, 11th, 13th, 15th, 17th, 18th, 20th, 21st, 23rd, 24th, 25th, 26th and 30th.

February 1996

Zone 1: Temperatures will be seasonable this month in this zone; precipitation will be generous the first part of the month, but sparse later. Watch for snow north and rain south February 4th, 5th and 7th; more precipitation is due February 9th, 10th and 11th. February 26th promises precipitation also. Watch for winds on the 7th, 8th, 10th, 11th and 13th; also February 22nd.

Zone 2: Precipitation will be very generous in this zone the first part of the month; temperatures will be seasonable. Later in the month it will be drier. Watch for very generous snowfall north and rain south February 4th, 5th and 7th; other precipitation dates include the 9th-11th and the 26th. Winds are likely February 7th-8th, 10th, 11th, 13th and 22nd.

Zone 3: Generous snowfall north and generous rainfall south is the forecast for this zone in February, especially the first three weeks of the month. Watch for precipitation Groundhog's Day; also February 4th, 7th, 9th, 11th, 16th and 18th; February 26th should see precipitation also. Winds are likely the 7th, 9th, 11th, 16th, 17th and 29th.

Zone 4: Chill, dry and windy is the forecast for this zone in February. Watch for snow in widespread areas of this zone February 2nd; also the

11th, 16th, 17th and 29th. Winds are likely February 9th, 11th, 16th, 17th, 21st and 29th. Chill weather in this zone this month will continue into the month of March. Dry weather will continue throughout the spring.

Zone 5: Seasonable temperatures and normal amounts of precipitation are forecast for this zone in February. Watch for snow north February 2nd, watch also February 11th east, February 12th, the 16th and the 17th which should result in precipitation. Winds are likely February 10th, 11th, 17th, 19th, 21st and 29th. Weather patterns in effect this month should continue into the month of March.

Zone 6: A dry month, with relatively mild temperatures is forecast for most of Alaska. Snow is possible February 4th, 5th, 7th, 9th and 10th; also February 11th, 12th and 26th. Winds are likely on the 7th, 8th, 10th and 11th; also the 13th, 19th and 22nd. Hawaii should have a pleasant, normal month. Mild temperatures this month should continue into the months of March and April.

Dates to Watch:

Watch for snow February 2nd, 5th, 7th, 10th, 11th, 12th, 17th, 18th and 26th.

Watch for winds February 7th, 8th, 10th, 11th, 14th, 16th, 17th, 19th, 21st, 22nd and 29th.

March 1996

Zone 1: Normal temperatures and normal amounts of precipitation are forecast for this zone in March. Precipitation is most likely March 3rd, 6th, 10th, 12th and 15th; also March 17th, 19th, 20th, 22nd and 23rd. Watch for wind March 1st, 10th, 16th, 17th and 19th; also March 20th, 22nd, 23rd, 25th, 26th and 29th. Next month should bring very wet weather, but temperatures should be mild.

Zone 2: Much precipitation and seasonable temperatures are predicted for this zone in March. Watch for heavy precipitation March 3rd; precipitation is also likely March 6th, 10th, 12th, 15th and 17th. March 19th, 20th, 22nd and 23rd should also result in precipitation. Watch for winds March 1st, 10th, 16th, 17th, 20th, 22nd, 23rd, 25th, 26th and 29th. Wet weather should continue into April.

Zone 3: Generous amounts of precipitation and seasonable temperatures are predicted for this zone in March. The last week of the month may be dry west. Watch for precipitation March 3rd; March 8th, 12th, 15th, 17th, 19th and 20th should result in snow or rain. Rain is due March 22nd and 26th. Watch for winds March 9th, 15th, 22nd, 23rd, 26th and 28th. Dry weather the last week of the month west should continue into April.

Zone 4: Wet weather is forecast east, but most of this zone will be dry with variable temperatures in March. Watch for precipitation March 8th, March 12th east, March 17th and March 22nd. Winds are likely March 9th, 15th, 23rd, 26th and 28th. Dry weather in this zone this month should continue into the summer. Eastern portions of this zone, however, may be wet then.

Zone 5: Seasonable temperatures and normal precipitation are forecast for this zone this month, although the last week of the month may be dry. Watch for precipitation March 8th, 9th, 16th and 21st; also March 22nd. Winds are likely March 1st, 4th, 8th, 9th, 16th and 21st; also March 22nd, 23rd, 28th, 29th and 30th. Dry weather late in the month should continue throughout the spring.

Zone 6: Dry weather is forecast for Alaska this month; Hawaii will have normal precipitation. Temperatures in Alaska will be a little above normal. Watch for precipitation March 3rd, 6th, 8th and 10th; also March 12th, 15th, 17th, 19th and 20th. Precipitation is also due March 22nd and 23rd. Winds are likely March 1st, 10th, 16th and 19th; also March 22nd, 25th, 26th and 29th.

Dates to Watch:

Watch for snow March 3rd, 6th, 8th, 10th and 12th.

Watch for rain March 15th, 17th-19th, 21st-23rd and 27th.

Watch for winds March 1st, 2nd, 3rd, 8th, 9th, 10th, 15th, 16th, 18th, 21st, 22nd-25th, 26th, 28th, 29th and 30th.

April 1996

Zone 1: Wet weather is predicted for the first two weeks of this zone in April. Temperatures will be seasonable. Watch for precipitation April 2nd; also April 6th, 7th, 10th and 17th. Watch for winds April 1st, 6th and 7th. The end of the month should be dry, but wet weather will return later in the spring. Wet weather should extend west to the Mississippi. April weather should continue into May.

Zone 2: The first two weeks of this month will be very wet; dry weather should come the second half of the month. Temperatures should be seasonable. Rain is due the 2nd, 6th, 7th, 10th and 17th of the month. Winds are likely April 1st, 6th, 7th and 24th. The end of the month may be dry but normal precipitation patterns should return later in the season. Temperatures should continue in the normal range.

Zone 3: The first two weeks of the month will be wet east; dry weather will arrive there the last two weeks of the month. Dry weather, however, is forecast west all month.

Temperatures will likely be seasonable. Rain is likely April 1st and 3rd, April 10th, April 17th, April 28th and April 29th. Winds are likely April 1st, 7th and 10th; also April 17th, 24th, 28th and 29th. May weather patterns should be similar.

Zone 4: Warmer-than-usual temperatures and beautiful, blue skies are predicted for this zone in April. Rainfall will likely be sparse. Precipitation is most likely April 1st and 3rd, April 10th, 28th and 29th. Winds are likely April 1st and 7th; also April 15th and 29th. Dry weather will continue through the summer except in the extreme east where wet weather will be likely.

Zone 5: April will be a warm, dry month for most areas in this zone. Precipitation will be most likely April 1st, April 6th and 7th, April 10th and April 29th. Winds are due April 6th, 7th, 10th, 15th and 29th. Warm, dry weather this month should continue throughout the spring season. Areas south may see some weather that could best be described as hot rather than warm. April and May weather will be similar.

Zone 6: Seasonable temperatures and normal amounts of precipitation are forecast for the Alaskan Panhandle; central parts of the state should be warm and dry. Precipitation is most likely the 1st,

2nd, 6th and 7th; also the 10th, 17th, 25th and 29th. Winds are due April 1st, 6th, 7th and 10th; also April 15th and 29th. Hawaii will have a pleasant, normal month. April weather should continue into May.

Dates to Watch:

Watch for rain April 1st, 3rd, 5th, 6th, 8th, 10th, 17th, 25th, 28th and 29th.

Watch for winds April 1st, 6th, 8th, 10th, 15th, 18th, 24th, 28th and 29th.

May 1996

Zone 1: Seasonable temperatures and generous precipitation are predicted for this zone. Watch for rain May 8th; watch also May 10th, May 18th and May 25th. Rainfall may come on other dates, but the above dates will see the heaviest rain. Winds are likely May 8th, 21st, 22nd and 25th. Weather patterns in effect this month will continue into the month of June. The heaviest precipitation in May should come south.

Zone 2: Temperatures that are seasonable are predicted for this zone in May. Rainfall, when it comes, should be generous. Watch for precipitation May 8th, 10th, 18th and 25th. Winds are likely May 8th, 21st, 22nd and 25th. May weather patterns should continue into June. Dry weather may follow east at this time, but generous rainfall is forecast for the rest of this zone. Infrequent, but heavy describes May precipitation.

Zone 3: Eastern portions of this zone will be wet in May, but it will be dry in the western portions of this zone. Temperatures should be seasonable both places. Days most likely to result in rain include May 8th, May 10th, May 19th and May 25th. Winds are most likely May 8th, May 14th, May 25th and May 29th. May weather patterns should continue into the month of June.

Zone 4: Dry weather and seasonable temperatures are forecast for this zone in May. Precipitation may come May 3rd, May 8th, May 17th, May 19th and May 25th. Winds are likely May 8th, May 14th, May 19th, May 25th and May 29th. Dry weather this month should continue into the month of June, but more precipitation is likely later in the summer. Temperatures should stay seasonable until July.

Zone 5: Unusually hot weather and very little precipitation are forecast for this month in this zone. Watch for rainfall May 3rd, also May 17th and 19th and May 25th. Winds are likely May 13th and 29th. Weather patterns set this month are likely to continue into the summer, but there will a very small area north that may have abnormally low temperatures and much precipitation.

Zone 6th: The Alaskan Panhandle will have a relatively normal month weatherwise, but central portions of the state will have dry weather with temperatures markedly above normal. Watch for precipitation May 3rd, May 10th, May 18th and 19th and May 25th. Winds are likely May 8th, May 13th, May 19th, May 21st and 22nd, May 25th and May 29th. Hawaii may have a month that is drier than usual.

Dates to Watch:

Watch for rain May 4th, 8th, 10th, 17th, 18th, 25th and 26th.

Watch for winds May 8th, 14th, 15th, 19th, 21st, 22nd, 25th and 29th.

June 1996

Zone 1: A wet month is predicted for this zone in June. Temperatures will be seasonable. The very end of the month will be dry and hot north establishing a weather pattern that should continue all summer. Watch for rainfall June 8th and 9th, 16th and 20th, June 21st, 24th and 30th. Winds are likely June 8th, 14th, 16th, 17th, 20th, 21st, 26th and 29th. Dry weather will come later in the summer.

Zone 2: Precipitation should be generous in this zone this month; temperatures will be seasonable. Dates which will most likely result in rain include June 8th and 9th,

June 16th and 20th, June 21st, 24th and 30th. Winds are due June 8th, 9th and 14th, June 16th, 17th and 20th, June 21st, 26th and 30th. June's weather patterns should continue throughout the summer.

Zone 3: Eastern portions of this zone will be wet, but the rest of this zone should have a dry month. Temperatures will be seasonable. Rainfall is most likely June 8th and 9th, June 11th and 16th, June 20th east, June 21st and 23rd; also the 24th east. Winds are likely June 8th and 11th, June 16th east, June 17th, 21st and 23rd. Next month should be wet in widespread portions of this zone.

Zone 4: Dry weather is forecast for this zone this month. Temperatures should be within the normal range. The last week of the month may be hotter west starting a trend that should last through the summer. Rainfall is most likely June 8th and 9th, June 11th and 21st, June 23rd and June 28th. Winds are likely June 8th, 11th, 17th, 21st and 23rd. July may see more rainfall here.

Zone 5: Hot, dry weather is predicted for this zone in June. Rainfall is most likely June 1st and 8th, June 11th and 15th and June 18th and 28th. Winds are likely June 11th and 14th, June 15th and 17th and June 18th and 24th. Temperatures are likely to come down a bit

at the end of the month, but hot, dry weather should continue into the month of July. If temperatures are cool, they will be very cool.

Zone 6: Warm, dry weather is predicted for much of Alaska this month; but the panhandle of the state will have normal precipitation. Best chances for rain come on the 1st, 8th, 15th, 16th and 18th; also the 20th, 21st, 29th and 30th. Winds are due June 8th, 14th, 15th, 16th and 18th; also June 20th, 21st, 26th and 29th. Weather in Hawaii will be seasonable.

Dates to Watch:

Watch for rain June 2nd, 8th, 10th, 11th, 16th, 17th, 19th, 20th, 22nd, 23rd, 24th, 28th and 29th.

Watch for winds June 8th, 11th, 14th, 15th, 17th, 18th, 19th, 20th, 22nd, 23rd, 26th, 29th and 30th.

July 1996

Zone 1: Dry, hot weather is forecast north; southern portions of this zone will have normal temperatures. The first two weeks of the month, however, are likely to be dry south. Rainfall is most likely July 14th, 15th, 19th, 23rd north, 28th and 29th. Watch for winds July 4th, 11th, 16th, 19th, 22nd and 23rd. Weather patterns in effect in this zone this month will continue into August.

Zone 2: Normal temperatures are forecast for this zone this month, but the first two weeks of the month will be dry. The only exception may be some areas near the Mississippi River where there may be more precipitation than normal. Watch for rain July 14th, 15th, 18th, 19th, 23rd and the 27th-30th. Winds are likely July 4th, 11th, 14th, 19th and 22nd.

Zone 3: Temperatures will be seasonable in this zone this month; precipitation may be generous east and sparse in the westernmost portions of this zone. Dates most likely to result in rain include July 5th, 7th and 14th; also July 15th, 19th, 23rd, 28th, the 29th east and the 30th. Winds are likely July 4th, 5th and 11th, also July 14th, 17th, 19th, 23rd and 27th. August should be hot.

Zone 4: Dry weather is predicted for this zone in July. Temperatures will vary. Dates most likely to result in precipitation include July 5th and 7th, July 14th and 18th, July 19th and 23rd; also July 28th and 30th. Winds are likely July 5th, 11th, 17th, 19th, 23rd and 27th. Weather patterns in effect this month should continue throughout the entire summer. Fall will likely be dry west and wet east.

Zone 5: Dry weather and temperatures markedly above normal are forecast for this zone in July. Dates most likely to result in precipitation include July 5th, 7th, 18th and

19th, the 23rd east, the 22nd and 27th. Winds are likely July 5th, 11th, 17th and 19th; also July 22nd and 27th. Weather patterns in effect this month should continue into August and September.

Zone 6: The Alaskan Panhandle will have seasonable temperatures and normal rainfall, but July in the central part of the state will be unusually dry and unusually warm. Precipitation will be most likely July 14th and 15th, 18th and 19th, 23rd and 28th. Winds are likely July 4th, 7th, 11th, 14th, 16th and 19th; also July 22nd, 25th and 27th. Hawaii is likely to be warmer and drier than usual.

Dates to Watch:

Watch for rain July 2nd, 5th, 6th, 14th, 15th, 18th, 20th, 23rd, 27th, 29th, 30th and 31st.

Watch for winds July 4th, 5th, 8th, 11th, 14th, 16th, 17th, 18th, 20th, 23rd, 25th and 27th.

August 1996

Zone 1: August will be unusually hot and dry in New England; seasonable temperatures and normal precipitation patterns will prevail in other portions of this zone. Rainfall will be most likely the last two weeks of the month, especially on the 20th and 21st. Winds will be likely August 6th, 7th, 20th and 29th. Hot, dry weather in this zone should continue into September.

Zone 2: Dry weather should prevail in this zone for most of this month. Temperatures will be in the normal range. Rainfall will be most likely on the 6th, 20th, 21st and 28th. Winds will be most likely on the 6th, 7th, 20th and 29th. Hot, dry weather in this zone this month should continue well into the month of September. Fall may bring some wet weather to the Mississippi River Valley.

Zone 3: Wet weather is forecast for this zone in August, but precipitation is likely to be heavy rather than frequent. Temperatures will be within the normal range of temperatures for this month. Watch for rainfall August 5th, 6th, 16th and 20th; also August 21st and 29th. Winds are likely August 5th, 7th, 20th and 23rd. Weather patterns in effect this month should continue into September.

Zone 4: The most eastern portions of this zone may see wetter weather than usual, but most of this zone will be dry with seasonable temperatures. Rainfall will be most likely August 5th and 6th; also August 16th and 20th. Winds will be likely August 5th, 7th, 20th and 23rd. August weather patterns will continue well into the month of September. Fall will be chill and dry east.

Zone 5: Dry weather with seasonable temperatures is forecast for this zone in August. Rainfall will be most likely August 5th and 6th; also August 14th, 16th and 20th.

Winds are likely August 5th, 20th and 23rd. Dry weather in this zone this month is likely to continue well into the month of September. Temperature patterns will continue into September also.

Zone 6: The Alaskan Panhandle will have seasonable weather, but central parts of the state will be dry with temperatures well above normal. Watch for precipitation August 14th, 16th 20th, 21st and 29th. Winds are likely August 1st, 6th, 7th and 20th; also August 23rd, 26th and 28th. Weather patterns in effect in Alaska this month will continue into the fall. Hawaii will have seasonable weather.

Dates to Watch:

Watch for rain August 5th, 6th, 14th, 16th, 20th, 22nd and 29th.

Watch for winds August, 1st, 5th, 6th, 7th, 8th, 20th, 23rd, 26th and 28th.

September 1996

Zone 1: A hot, dry month is predicted north; seasonable temperatures and normal amounts of precipitation are forecast elsewhere in this zone. Watch for rainfall September 7th, 9th, 11th and 12th; also September 17th, 19th and 24th. Winds are due September 7th, 9th, 10th and 11th; also September 17th, 19th, 20th and 23rd. Dry, warm weather should prevail north the entire fall season.

Zone 2: Seasonable temperatures and normal to generous amounts of precipitation are forecast for this zone in September. Watch for rainfall September 3rd, 7th, 9th, 11th and 12th; also September 17th and 24th. Winds are likely September 7th, 9th, 10th and 11th; also September 17th, 19th, 20th and 23rd. Unusually wet, chill weather may prevail near the Mississippi later in the fall.

Zone 3: Generous amounts of precipitation are due this month; temperatures will be seasonable. Watch for rainfall September 4th, 7th and 9th; also September 11th, 12th, 17th and 24th. Winds are due September 7th, 9th, 10th and 11th; also September 17th, 19th, 20th and 23rd. The last week for the month will likely be chill; temperatures during the rest of the fall season may be low, too.

Zone 4: Seasonable temperatures and dry weather are predicted for this zone this month. The very easternmost portions of this zone, however, may be wet. Dates most likely to result in rain include September 4th, 7th and 9th; also the 12th east and September 17th and 19th. Seasonable temperatures should continue throughout the entire fall, but October may be a little drier.

Zone 5: Normal weather patterns should prevail in this zone this season. There will not be much fluctuation noted from the norm where temperatures or precipitation are concerned. Watch for rainfall September 4th, 7th, 11th and 17th; also September 20th. Winds are likely September 7th, 10th, 17th and 23rd. Unusually dry weather is forecast for the last week of the month.

Zone 6: The Alaskan Panhandle will have normal weather patterns in September, but the central part of the state will be dry with temperatures well above normal. Watch for precipitation September 2nd, 7th, 9th and 11th; also September 17th, 20th, 24th and 26th. Winds are due September 2nd, 7th, 9th, 10th and 11th; also September 17th, 19th, 20th and 23rd. Hawaiian weather will be warm and dry.

Dates to Watch:

Watch for rain September 2nd-4th, 7th-9th, 11th, 12th, 17th, 18th, 20th, 24th, 26th and 28th.

Watch for winds September 2nd, 3rd, 7th, 8th, 9th, 10th, 11th, 17th, 18th, 20th and 23rd.

October 1996

Zone 1: Mild temperatures and beautiful, blue skies are forecast for this zone in October. Dates most likely to result in precipitation include October 5th, 12th and 17th;

also October 23rd, 25th and 30th. Winds are likely October 5th, 9th, 13th and 15th; also October 23rd, 25th and 30th. October weather patterns should continue into November making the fall an especially pleasant season.

Zone 2: Unusual weather patterns are forecast for this zone in October. Some extremely nice days with mild temperatures are likely to alternate with chill, damp weather. Dates most likely to result in rain include October 4th, 5th, 12th and 17th; also October 23rd, 25th and 30th. Winds will be likely October 4th, 5th, 9th and 13th; also October 15th, 23rd, 25th and 30th.

Zone 3: Chill, damp weather is likely in the Upper Mississippi River Valley, but chill, dry and windy weather is forecast for the rest of this zone. Best chances for precipitation include October 4th, 5th, the 10th west, the 12th and 25th; also October 29th. Winds are likely October 4th, 5th, 9th and 13th; also the 23rd, 25th and 27th. Look for October weather patterns to continue into November.

Zone 4: Chill, dry and windy weather is forecast east in this zone, but most areas here will have seasonable temperatures and normal amounts of precipitation. Dates most likely to result in rain include October 4th, 5th and 10th; also October 25th and 29th. Winds are

likely October 4th and 5th, October 9th and 10th; also October 13th, 27th and 30th. Watch for November to echo these weather patterns.

Zone 5: This zone should have a dry month with temperatures well above normal. Dates most likely to result in rain include October 4th and 5th, October 10th and 12th, the 13th and also October 25th, 26th and 30th. Winds are likely October 4th, 5th, 9th and 10th; also October 13th, 23rd 27th, 29th and 30th. This month's weather patterns should continue into November.

Zone 6: The Alaskan Panhandle will have seasonable weather, but much of the central part of the state will have unusually cold and windy weather with very little precipitation. Best chances for precipitation will come on the 10th, 12th, 13th 17th and 23rd; also watch October 25th, 26th and 30th. Hawaii may have a wet month with temperatures that are in the normal range.

Dates to Watch:

Watch for rain October 4th, 5th, 10th, 12th, 14th, 18th, 19th, 24th, 25th, 27th, 30th and 31st.

Watch for winds October 5th, 9th, 10th, 13th, 14th, 15th, 23rd, 25th, 27th, 30th and 31st.

November 1996

Zone 1: New England may be wet this month, but most other portions of this zone will be dry. Temperatures will be unseasonably warm. Dates most likely to result in precipitation include November 5th, 10th, 11th and 13th; also November 15th, 20th, 22nd, 23rd and 25th. Winds will be likely November 3rd, 10th, 11th, 12th and 13th; also November 15th, 18th, 20th, 23rd and 24th.

Zone 2: Areas near the Mississippi may be unusually wet, but other portions of this zone will be normal to dry with seasonable temperatures. Watch for rainfall November 5th, 10th and 11th and snow November 15th, 20th, 22nd and 23rd. Winds are likely November 3rd, 10th, 11th, 12th and 13th; also November 15th, 18th, 20th, 23rd and 25th. The 17th and 19th could see precipitation west.

Zone 3: Generous amounts of rainfall are predicted for this zone in November. Temperatures will be normal. Watch for rain November 10th and 11th; watch for snow November 15th, 17th, 19th 22nd and 25th. Winds are due November 3rd, 11th, 13th and 15th; also November 18th, 22nd, 23rd and 24th. November's weather patterns should continue into December.

Zone 4: Wet weather is forecast east; dry, chill and windy weather is forecast for most locations in this zone this month. Watch for precipitation November 10th east, November 11th, 13th 15th and 17th;

also November 19th, 23rd and 25th. Winds are due November 1st, 3rd, 11th, 13th, 15th and 24th. Dry, chill weather should continue into the month of December.

Zone 5: Dry weather is forecast for this zone in November. Temperatures should be well above normal. Best chances for precipitation are on the 10th, 11th, 13th and 15th; also November 17th, 19th and 23rd. Winds are likely November 1st, 3rd, 13th and 15th; also November 24th. Dry weather with above-average temperatures should continue into December.

Zone 6: Wet weather and mild temperatures are forecast for the Alaskan Panhandle, but central portions of this state will have dry, chill and windy weather. Best chances for precipitation come November 3rd, 5th and 10th; also November 11th, 13th, 15th, 17th and 19th. Snow is due November 22nd and 24th. Winds will be frequent and strong. Hawaii will have a wet month with seasonable temperatures.

Dates to Watch:

Watch for rain November 3rd, 5th, 10th, 11th, 13th and 15th.

Watch for snow November 17th-19th, 22nd, 24th and 26th.

Watch for winds November 1st, 3rd, 4th, 10th, 11th, 13th, 15th, 16th, 18th, 20th, 22nd, and 23rd-25th.

December 1996

Zone 1: New England may be wet, but most areas in this zone will be slightly dry with temperatures that are normal or a little above normal. Precipitation will be likely December 3rd and 4th, December 9th and 17th, December 19th and 20th, December 21st and 22nd. Winds will be likely December 4th, 8th, 13th and 19th; also December 20th and 21st. Christmas should be clear and cold.

Zone 2: Areas near the Mississippi may be wet and cold, but most portions of this zone will be fairly dry with seasonable temperatures. Dates most likely to result in precipitation include December 3rd and 4th, December 9th and 17th east; also December 19th, 20th, 21st and 22nd. Dates that may result in wind include December 4th, 8th, 13th, 19th, 20th and the 21st.

Zone 3: Areas near the Mississippi will likely be wet, but most portions of this zone will be dry, chill and windy. Dates that could result in precipitation include December 3rd, 4th, 9th and 13th; watch also December 17th, 19th and 20th, the 22nd, the 24th and that 28th. Winds are likely the 4th, 8th, 9th, 19th, 24th and 27th. Snow is likely in many areas Christmas Eve.

Zone 4: Eastern portions of this zone will be unusually chill with little snowfall and much wind; other portions of this zone will have more seasonable weather. Snow is likely December 3rd east. Watch for snow also December 4th, 9th, 13th, 17th and 19th and again on the 22nd, 24th, 27th and 28th. Watch for winds December 4th, 9th, 19th, 24th and 27th. Snow is likely Christmas Eve.

Zone 5: Temperatures markedly above normal are forecast for this zone in December; snow and rain may be scant. Dates most likely to result in precipitation include December 3rd and 4th, December 9th and 13th, December 17th, 19th and 20th; also December 22nd, 27th and 28th. Winds are likely on the 9th of December; also the 24th, 25th and 27th of the month.

Zone 6: The Alaskan Panhandle will be wet, but most other portions of the state will be dry with warmer-than-normal temperatures east and unusually chill temperatures in the central portions of the state. Winds will be strong there. Watch for snowfall December 3rd, 4th, 9th, 13th, 17th and 19th; also December 20th, 22nd, 25th, 27th and 28th. Hawaii may have a wet month.

Dates to Watch:

Watch for snow December 3rd, 5th, 9th, 10th, 14th, 17th, 21st-25th, 27th and 28th.

Watch for winds December 5th, 8th, 9th, 14th, 19th-21st, 24th, 26th and 27th.

1996 Earthquake Predictions

By Nancy Soller

Ann E. Parker of Skokie, Illinois is revolutionizing the prediction of large, destructive earthquakes. Ann starts her predictions by studying solar and lunar eclipses. She uses geodetic equivalents to determine the likely location of large, disastrous quakes and the motions of Mars in relation to the eclipse-points to determine timing. Ann also notes that locations with Pluto, Mars and Uranus angular at the time of an eclipse are likely to see earthquake activity.

The geodetic system starts with 0° of Aries at Greenwich, England and counts to the east, 1° of the Zodiac for every degree east of Greenwich. 30° east of Greenwich is 0° of Taurus, 60° east of Greenwich is zero degrees of Gemini, 90° east of Greenwich is zero degrees of Cancer, etc.

Geodetic equivalents, valid since the prime meridian was located at Greenwich, England, place the midheaven of San Francisco at 28° of Scorpio, the midheaven of Los Angeles at 2° of Sagittarius, the midheaven of New Madrid at 1° of Capricorn and the midheaven of New York City at 16° of Capricorn.

Besides working with geodetic mid-heavens, Ann uses geodetic ascendants and geodetic vertices. She notes that 1996 is a likely year of a large quake in the Midwest because the geodetic ascent of New Madrid (2° of Aries) will be activated by the September 27th, 1996 lunar eclipse.

Besides using recent eclipses to determine where large, destructive quakes are going to occur, Ann also uses the eclipse-points of eclipses coming in the near future. Ann uses an one degree, fifteen minute orb when working with Mars as a trigger. She uses both geocentric (earth-centered) and heliocentric (sun-centered) hard angles of Mars to the eclipse-points as a trigger for the quakes. These include the conjunction, square, opposition, semi-square, and sesquiquadrate.

Possible dates for a Midwest quake using Ann's methods include these dates: March 29-April 8, 1996 when Mars will first geocentrically and then heliocentrically conjunct the geodetic ascendant; other danger dates for this area include January 23rd-27th,

February 1st-4th, May 28th-31st, June 18th-23rd, July 31st-August 3rd, September 13th-18th, October 10th-14th and December 20th-25th. Mars will form hard angles to the September 27th, 1996 eclipse-point on all these dates.

Strengthening the testimony for a large, destructive quake in the Midwest in 1996 is the fact that Pluto, Mars, and Uranus will all be angular to Midwest locations at the time of the eclipse.

Could other areas of the United States have large, destructive quakes in 1996? In her book on earthquakes Ann picks out dates of danger for Los Angeles (January 1st-4th, May 8th-17th, June 12th-20th, October 4th-19th and October 30th-November 2nd) and New York City (January 4th-10th, February 8th-18th, March 1st-8th, April 12th-15th, April 22nd-May 5th, May 12th-21st, June 12th-20th, June 30th-July 16th, August 2nd-8th, August 16th-20th, September 6th-12th, October 4thth-9, October 30th-November 8th and November 23rd-December 5th.) Ann's book, *Earthquakes*, may be ordered from her for $38.00 post paid. Write Ann E. Parker, 8836 La Vergne Avenue, #2B, Skokie, IL 60077.

Every year there are many, many sizeable quakes that don't make the news media. These are quakes that strike in remote, un-populated areas and/or in foreign countries. They aren't super-disastrous and we may not hear about them. A little study of quakes of about 6.0 or more on the Richter scale for one year, in this case 1987, reveals some interesting facts about these quakes.

There were 107 earthquakes of a magnitude of about 6.0 or more on the Richter scale in the year 1987. As many as three occurred on one day, January third, and as many as two occurred on eighteen other different dates throughout the year. These quakes appeared to be occurring when certain planets formed either geocentric or heliocentric hard angles to certain earthquake-sensitive degrees. These degrees include solar and lunar eclipse-points, the heliocentric planetary nodes and the solstice and equinox points. Recent eclipse-points for this study went back five years. Hard angles used in this study include the conjunction (0°), the square (90°) and the opposition (one hundred and eighty degrees). The semi-square (45°) and the octile (22.5°) were used when studying solstice and equinox points.

The planets that appeared to be triggering earthquake activity appeared to be Venus, Mars, and occasionally Jupiter. In addition, many quakes appeared to be coming on days when the sun formed a geocentric hard angle to an earthquake-sensitive degree as the earth formed a hard heliocentric hard angle to the same degree. Mercury did not appear to be a trigger and neither did the planets that orbit beyond Jupiter. The orb of influence used in studying these hard angles was one and one-half degrees rather than eight degrees. As in Ann Parker's study, multiple planets forming multiple critical angles appeared to be the rule rather than the exception.

Reviewing the 1987 quakes by using Ann Parker's discoveries found Mars in conjunction, square, opposition, semi-square or sesquiquadrate to eclipse-points that occurred within two and a half years before or after the quake in most cases.

Dates and magnitudes for 1987 earthquakes come from the Department of the Interior's Geologic Survey.

Dates in 1996 when earthquake-sensitive degrees will be aspected three or more ways and good-sized quakes could occur include:

January 1st, 3rd, 7th, 10th, 16th, 21st, 27th and 30th.

February 1st, 4th 10th, 18th, 23rd, 26th and 27th.

March 4th, 5th, 7th, 8th, 11th, 17th, 23rd, 24th and 25th.

April 12th, 21st and 30th.

May 3rd, 5th, 11th and 28th.

June 7th, 19th, 22nd and 23rd.

July 2nd, 12th, 14th, 15th, 18th, 24th and 31st.

August 3rd, 7th, 10th, 14th and 30th.

September 6th, 7th, 8th, 13th, 24th, 25th, 27th and 28th.

October 4th, 11th, 13th, 14th, 16th, 18th, 20th, 22nd, 25th and 29th.

November 1st, 2nd, 5th, 10th, 11th, 18th, 23rd, 26th and 29th.

December 2nd, 4th, 5th, 6th, 9th, 15th, 22nd, 28th and 29th.

Weather Lore

By Verna Gates

Even with all their fancy equipment, meteorologists still cannot predict rain any better than a robin, a pig or an old man's bunion. A treasury of folklore has emerged from centuries of observation to continuously challenge the accuracy of science and radar screens. Much of the folklore has been proven correct, some proven false, some may find redemption as science seduces more of the sky's secrets. In the meantime, we can share the wisdom of those who are weatherwise, and not otherwise, according to the standards of the venerable Benjamin Franklin:

Robins in the bush, rain's on the rush.

When pigs carry sticks, the clouds will play tricks;

When they lie in the mud, no fears of a flood.

And according to Samuel Butler:

As old sinners have all points o' the compass in their bones and joints—can by their pangs and aches find all turns and changes of the wind.

In fact, even better than robins, pigs and sinners, is the jackass (referring to the animal, of course). He may be the best rain predictor of all. Abraham Lincoln enjoyed telling this tale: his home town was ready to replace their weathercaster with a young boy whose predictions of rain were unfailing. However, the honest young fellow admitted his jackass was the real weathercaster, braying up a storm in order to predict one. So, the town bypassed the boy and appointed the jackass to the official capacity of town weathercaster. (Lincoln felt this was a mistake, as jackasses have been seeking public office ever since.)

> When the ass begins to bray,
>> we'll have rain that day.

The insect world is also sensitive to the onslaught of rain. Bees head for home, cockroaches scurry around more than usual, and gnats bite even more eagerly. Some also say rain is coming when ants walk in a straight line, or stay home to increase the pile of dirt around the ant bed.

> If ants build high, look for rain in the sky.
>
> A fly on your nose, you swat and it goes.
>
> If it comes back again, it will bring a good rain.
>
> When snails on the road you see, rain tomorrow it will be.
>
> A bee's wings never get wet.
>
> A little bug knows more about rain than all the almanacs.
>
> —Benjamin Franklin

Many old-timers swear by the trusty spider. Sensing high humidity, spiders will work overtime to build up their webs to catch other fleeing insects. Then, in a natural display of just-in-time delivery, the spider will snatch down the web before the storm comes. In this way, the spider keeps the rain from stealing the haul of food.

> Spiders do their webs expand when rainy weather is at hand.

Even with all their fancy equipment, meteorologists still cannot predict rain any better than a robin, a pig or an old man's bunion

> *If spiders their webs forsake, then*
> *it's certain the weather it will*
> *break.*
>
> *When spiders take in their net,*
>
> *Look for the ground to soon be wet.*

The plant kingdom can also alert a farmer as to whether or not his crops will be watered. For all the curses directed at the friendly little dandelion, gardeners still grudgingly admit its worth as a rain indicator: it closes its flower before rain. Chickweed, that delicate star lady, will also close her blossoms, shielding them from a storm. Since a low pressure system allows scent to travel more easily, many say they can smell rain by the strong scent of the flowers. Maple and oak trees will also lift their leaves to greet the rain, showing a silver lining long before the clouds reveal theirs.

> *When ditch and pond offend the*
> *nose, go straight home and win-*
> *dows close.*
>
> *When the chickweed blossoms open*
> *wide and free, then rain can't*
> *come before hours three.*
>
> *"The marigold that goes to bed with*
> *the sun, and with him rises,*
> *weeping."*
>
> —Shakespeare, *Winter's Tale*

Although humans are the creatures least sensitive to signs of weather, still, a few of us can read our own personal set of signs. My grandmother predicts storms by feeling the stickiness in the air. To confirm bad weather, she may try to boil up a burnt sugar cake—a sure test since the caramel that results from burning sugar won't harden in humidity. Others can also notice a marked improvement in their sight—low pressure clears the air. Still others can call on a "bad hair day" to confirm the moistness of the air, or a gloomy attitude may be some folk's sure sign. Warning: when clear weather is coming, watch out for your diet!

> *The farther the sight, the nearer the*
> *rain.*
>
> *Sound traveling far and wide, a*
> *stormy day will decide.*
>
> *The minds of men do in the weath-*
> *er share, dark or serene as the*
> *day's foul or fair.*
>
> —Cicero
>
> *Curls that kink, straight hair links,*
> *look for rain in a blink.*
>
> *When no food from the table is*
> *spared, clear skies are ahead.*

The ancient art of angling has built up its own special brand of rain lore. The importance of catching fish is the primary motive of these fishermen, getting drenched is merely a secondary concern.

> *Near the surface quick to bite;*
> *Catch your fish when rain's in*
> *sight.*
>
> *When the wind is in the north,*
> *The skillful fisher goes not forth.*
>
> *When the wind is in the east,*

> 'Tis good for neither man nor
> beast.
> When the wind is in the south,
> It blows the flies in the fish's
> mouth.
> But when the wind is in the west,
> There it is the very best.
> When trout refuse bait or fly,
> be sure to look for storm nearby.

On that rare occasion when the rain persists in falling, in spite of a Sun beaming through, don't worry. It's just the devil beating his wife. She'll overtake him soon, and the rain will stop. Watch for the devil's hand in the sunrise; even the Bible warns against a red sky in morning.

> Sunshine shower won't last half an
> hour.
> Rain long foretold, long last,
> Short notice soon will pass.
> Red sky in morning, sailor take
> warning,
> Red sky at night, sailor's delight.

Many a child and hopeful weekend athlete wishes for a rainy day to cease. One sure way to chase away the clouds is to offer the rain god a few water lilies to cry into. If that fails, prick him with a cactus.

> Rain, rain, go away, come again
> another day.
> Rain, rain, go to Spain, fair weather come again.
> The rain in Spain falls mainly on
> the plain.

Thunder, however, is a different animal. We all know not to challenge God as a witness and then proceed to tell a lie, since lightning might strike. One time, I drove past the theme park of a famous TV evangelist and his wife, then in the throes of charges of fraud, and noticed a huge storm cloud sitting only above that little corner of the earth. Everywhere else was clear and blue. I just couldn't help but wonder ... (They were discredited by the courts later, but seemingly the weather already knew.)

Thunder also offers good luck ramifications. If thunder and lightning occur to your left, good luck will come right to you, as long as you never point at the lightning itself. Lightning hates to be pointed at. If a tree is struck by lightning, it should be mined for splinters—these electrically sealed toothpicks can be applied to sore gums to cure the toothache.

> Point a finger, there lightning will
> linger.
> Winter's thunder is summer's
> wonder.
> When cocks crow and take a drink,
> Lightning and thunder are on the
> brink.

Often the problem isn't preparing for rain to come, but wishing for that ultimate "lady rain," the kind that gently and steadily descends to water gardens and crops. Rainmaker techniques have included hanging a snake on a bush belly up, an old Southern tradition among African-Americans. In China, rainmakers light firecrackers and toss them to the sky. The Native Americans used dances to call the clouds. In old England, rainmen used to sprinkle salt on two crossed matches. (If you try this one, be careful not to spill any extra salt. If you do spill it, throw a pinch over your left shoulder to break bad luck.)

To break a drought, dig up a mandrake root and place it in a miniature coffin. If all else fails, don protective clothing and attempt to bathe a cat in sulphur water—the cat will resist this procedure. Beware, though, because if you can take a sprig of broom and sprinkle water in the air, and you cause a storm, you are surely a witch and your neighbors will know you—a hazardous knowledge in past days.

These ancient techniques will work. However, my experience recommends more modern methods. To guarantee rain, wash your car, plan a picnic, or invite 10 preschoolers over for a birthday party. A friend also says to plan an outdoor wedding in May is a sure way to get your garden watered by the heavens.

Another concern extending even to our lives in heated homes, is the strength of winter's blast. The ancients, who had even more reason to dread a cold winter, explored a variety of signs to indicate the cold months ahead. My great, great Aunt Sis, who was so old, she'd seen the Yankees come through, stood hard by the groundhog. Every groundhog's day, she checked precisely at noon to see if a shadow was cast. If the groundhog sees his shadow, he goes back into his den for six more weeks of bad weather. If he doesn't see his shadow, spring is at hand. She also checked the fall corn husks—thick husks indicate a long winter ahead. A big crop of acorns also provide a clue, the oak ensured species survival by preparing lots of seed in the face of a long, cold season.

> Onion skins very thin, mild winter coming in.
>
> Onion skins hard and tough, winter's coming cold and rough.
>
> Year of snow, fruit will grow.
>
> A bad winter is betide, if hair grows thick on the bear's hide.
>
> When the buffalo hide is thick, the winter will be very cold.
>
> If on the trees the leaves still hold, the coming winter will be cold.

All of our senses alert us to the signs of spring: bird song, warm sun, the fresh scent in the air, the sight of plants pushing up through the ground. However, it is unwise to do your spring planting until after the Liverwort (*Hepatica americana*) blooms. According to great, great Aunt Sis, never plant until after the Blackberry Winter—the last frost that comes to ripen the blackberries, urging their white flowers to bloom.

> Spring has come when you can put your foot on three daisies.
>
> A warm Christmas, a cold Easter.
>
> When March roars in like a lion, it goes out like a lamb.
>
> April showers bring May flowers.

After April weather showers you with gentle rains, it will be time to treat the rainbow with proper respect. If you refrain from pointing at it, and cross it out by putting two matches or sticks in the form of the cross, you can qualify for a treasure search. The rainbow's riches will greatly reward the one who finds them.

As for the rest of us, we can use our treasury of weather lore to enhance our lives with a rich inheritance of wisdom. Look for the signs all around you. You'll learn more than just how to read the weather, you'll learn about all living things, including yourself.

The Healer of Red Lion Street:

The Life & Times of Nicholas Culpeper

By Jackie Slevin

To the modern medical world, the medicine practiced in the seventeenth century seems laughable in comparison to the technological sophistication of today, but this comparison is a fallacy. A certain humane yet irascible astrologer who plied the apothecary trade turned the medical profession of this bygone era on its ear. His legacy was an herbal compendium of natural healing methods that became the standard text for over three centuries. As we turn back the clock and peer through the shop window to observe this wiry wizard prepare his herbal distillations, infusions, decoctions, and poultices, we possess the uncanny feeling that we know this man. We do. His spirit is alive and well in the last decade of the twentieth century. Too bad he was hundreds of years ahead of his time, for everything old is new again.

Nicholas Culpeper was born on October 18, 1616, in the Julian calendar, at Ockley in Surrey, England, where a Culpeper was in residence as Lord of the Manor. His paternal family was wealthy and titled, owning Castles and Manor houses in Kent and Sussex. The family rose to high social position during the reign of King John in the twelfth century. Subsequently, the Culpeper men made it their business to marry titled heiresses and use their dowries to purchase land, so much so that, according to British historian William Camden, "they spread out over the whole face of the County of Kent."[1]

Culpeper was named after his father, the Reverend Nicholas Culpeper, who had been presented only a few months before

Nicholas' birth with the possession of Ockley Manor by his family. Reverend Culpeper died suddenly thirteen days before the birth of his son. For some unknown reason, Ockley Manor passed into other hands immediately upon his death. His widow took her infant son and promptly moved to the village of Isfield, where her father, the Reverend William Attersole, presided over a Puritan congregation. Attersole was renowned for his erudition and was the author of a famous commentary on the Biblical Book of Numbers.

Young Nicholas was raised by his mother. Grandfather Attersole, who recognized the boy's prodigious ability at an early age, provided him with an excellent education in preparation for University and a career in the ministry. Culpeper showed himself to be a quick study and wholeheartedly embraced the Puritan philosophy within his environment. In addition to overall academic excellence, he was especially well versed in Latin and Greek, the knowledge of which served him exceedingly well in his later medical studies. At the age of ten he became interested in the study of astrology and showed a particular aptitude for it. This too was an area of study that would be dusted off in later years and shine brightly.

Culpeper's adolescent years were spent cultivating his piercing intelligence and scathing tongue. He possessed the mind of a brilliant, humane scholar with a flair for languages coupled with the temperament of a hot-headed revolutionary. This combination of extremes produced a personality

He's nodding sagely from above as fully one third of the current American population, outraged at the Industry of Illness, are seeking more natural methods of healing

who would leave no stone unturned in helping those in need with no strings attached, coupled with an penchant to viciously slander and libel anyone, particularly those in authority, who dared to cross him. This intensity did not win him any popularity contests; he was a strong and loyal ally but a dangerous adversary.

In 1634, at the age of 18, Culpeper entered Cambridge University, where he distinguished himself in the Classics. It was during his salad days at Cambridge that he squandered his entire fortune left to him from his father's estate. True to family tradition, Culpeper then fell deeply in love with a beautiful heiress and wooed her into eloping with him. The time and meeting place were set and thus began a chain of events that served to transform young Nicholas Culpeper from bon-vivant scholar to gifted healer.

Culpeper set out at nightfall to meet his bride at the village of Lewes where the clandestine wedding was to take place. Weather conditions were treacherous that night due to a severe thunderstorm. The young woman, whose name has never been recorded, was arriving by coach from the opposite direction. As fate would have it, the woman's coach was struck by lightning and she died instantly. Sir Nicholas Astey, a Cambridge friend of Culpeper's and most likely to be his best man at the ceremony, was an eyewitness to this tragedy. He broke the news and escorted an grief-stricken and incoherent Culpeper home to his mother's cottage in Isfield.

This catastrophe exerted such a profound shock in Culpeper that, upon recovery after months of his mother's careful nursing, he emerged from his trauma a changed man, and thus changed his course of direction. He adamantly refused to return to his academic studies at Cambridge and, worse still, refused to enter the ministry for which he had been groomed since boyhood. The ramifications of these decisions cost Culpeper dearly; he was to lose his inheritance from his mother's family, and sever ties with his grandfather. His mother was the cornerstone of his life and he truly did not wish to hurt her, nevertheless she was devastated by his decisions. Despite her pleading, Culpeper remained undaunted. He had already suffered enough from his shattered love affair and could no longer play the role of dutiful son. The loss of another family fortune phased him not a whit as he had already shown his complete incompetence in financial matters. "It is most true, that he was always subject to a Consumption of the Purse, notwithstanding the many ways he had to assist him." [2]

The final blow came when Mrs. Culpeper's health deteriorated as a result of stress and crushing disappointment. Already exhausted from nursing her son through acute nervous collapse, she could not bear Culpeper's decision to fly in the face of his grandfather by refusing to complete his university education, and of herself by not following in his late father's footsteps as a Puritan minister. She then suffered her own nervous collapse and the tables became turned; Culpeper nursed his mother through her travail. Despite his tireless efforts to bring her through her crisis, she remained inconsolable. She died shortly thereafter, leaving Culpeper completely alone, financially destitute, emotionally bankrupt, and cut off from both sides of his titled family. The year was 1639. He was twenty-three years old. (Who needs Masterpiece Theatre?)

Culpeper never fully recovered from these traumatic events. The after-effect of these shock waves left him with episodes of depression which were to plague him for the rest of his days. "I remember to have heard him confess that melancholy was an extraordinary enemy unto him; so great at sometimes, that wanting company he would seem like a dead man..."[3]

A year after his mother's death, Culpeper turned his back on his past and traveled to London to seek his fortune, armed with nothing but a classical education and the clothes on his back. He promptly married fifteen-year-old Alice Field who was (you guessed it) an heiress with a considerable fortune. Finally realizing that it was not always feasible to live on inherited money all of the time, Culpeper apprenticed himself to an apothecary at St. Helen's, Bishopsgate, to obtain an income. He displayed an outstanding aptitude to be a "Student of Physick" and applied his proficient ability in classical languages to study and master the *Materia Medica* in Latin. Many of the medical lexicons of this time linked herbs with astrology, a childhood interest that Culpeper rekindled and mastered. He was to discover that a "Student of Physick" and a "Student of Astrologie" were often two sides of the same coin, but more on this later. He took over his employer's practice after his death and then used Alice's dowry to set up his own apothecary shop on Red Lion Street, Spitalfields, in London's East End. Alice's dowry also purchased their very comfortable home where, by all accounts, they enjoyed a happy marriage.

It was at his shop on Red Lion Street that Culpeper practiced the Art of Physick with astonishing skill. Possessing no business sense whatsoever, he preferred to treat the poor and charged them little or nothing at all. He regarded medicine as a science as well as an art, and it was especially not a business to be perpetrated upon an unassuming and largely uneducated population, a practice in which his contemporaries delighted. "Indeed he had a spirit so far above the Vulgar, that he condemned and scorned riches any other way other was then to make them serviceable to him"[4.]

The year 1642 marked the beginning of the English Civil War, when the Puritans, lead by Lord Protector Oliver Cromwell, took up arms against the Royalists, those who maintained loyalty to the Crown. Driven by his strong Puritan background and revolutionary personality, Culpeper went for a soldier and found himself in the Battle of Edgehill on October 23 of the same year. He was wounded in the torso by gunshot and the wound never healed completely.

Culpeper's radical nature and zealous convictions pitted him against an adversary in a duel in 1643. He was again wounded in the chest, and took refuge in France for several months. The combined effects of these two chest wounds depleted his health and left him tubercular. Upon his return to England, he did what he did best; he flew in the face of authority and took it upon himself to strip the shrouds of mystery from the medical profession as it was practiced at the time. This feat was achieved by translating the complete texts of *Materia Medica*, from Latin into English. Culpeper pored over every known medical text from the time of Galen and Hippocrates right through and including the seventeenth century. This Herculean task took six years in total, and was accomplished in the evening hours after his apothecary shop closed for the day. The publication of his *Pharmaconoeia* in 1649 brought him into bitter conflict with the College of Surgeons; he was severely and unfairly attacked and held up to public ridicule. Anyone with a working knowledge of English could now purchase a copy of the *Pharmaconoeia* and obtain information as to how to heal themselves in their own language. One no longer required the advantage of a University education, with its insistence of fluency in Latin, to study the *Materia Medica*. That such arcane information was made so accessible to the public was unheard of at that time. The College of Surgeons knew only too well that a little knowledge was a dangerous thing and, if the general population could heal themselves, they need not seek their "professional" services. Needless to say, Culpeper held his contemporary physicians in very low esteem, if not downright contempt. He warns his readers in his usual, hypocrisy-hating style, "Chirugians, in order to make slaves of you make fools of themselves." [5]

Culpeper had the last laugh, for all this so-called bad press only made his practice thrive even more. He lectured privately on medicine and linked horoscopes with health to an unusual and unprecedented degree. Illness was to be treated with respect and its cures to be revered with awe, as all cures hail from Dame Nature, whom Culpeper curiously refers to as his mother. "If you follow her you shall not want; she treads upon the world and looks upward. She always weeps, and yet I never saw her laugh We must know that there is a sympathy between Celestial and Terrestrial bodies; which will easily appear, if we consider that the whole of creation is one entire and united body, composed by the power of an All-wise God, of a composition of discords."[6] Culpeper held that Dame Nature is the paintbrush of all creation and that her two sons, Dr. Reason and Dr. Experience, will lead a student of medicine on the road to truth. One can deduce from his writings that the human body is an imitation of nature, and nature, like the body, can only be compartmentalized with his microcosmic philosophy in mind. Above all, "a physitian (sic) without astrology is like a pudding without fat."[7]

The cornerstone of Culpeper's medical trade was the decumbiture, of which the literal definition is "the point of time of invasion of disease." To define this more clearly, the actual time of decumbiture occurs when one takes to his/her bed, The exact time is noted and a horoscope is cast. This is the decumbiture, or chart of the illness. The cause, diagnosis, prognosis, and cure, or lack thereof, is present in this chart and thereby most cautiously judged.

This invaluable diagnostic tool proved life-saving on more than one occasion. Most notably was a case of a young woman who was misdiagnosed with the plague, when actually her disease was the small pox. According to her decumbiture, the woman was not only misdiagnosed but also given grossly inappropriate medical treatment. "...now her Doctor (If I may call him so without a Solecism) begins to play the antique, I had almost said, the mad man. Now he exerciseth his purging faculty, and left his wits abed with his last night's mistress. Doctor Dunce only judged she should die now, as indeed he did, he might have been pardoned, although he had fail'd; but also, he, poor man, had little skill in times and seasons; his skill was employed to know a woman from a man, when he got her into bed."[8] Thanks to Culpeper's mastery of astrology and arsenal of herbal remedies, the woman survived. During this time period he wrote his masterpiece, *The Compleat Herbal and English Physician*, the standard herbal in the Western world for over 30 years. This last served to make him a legend in his own time. It was subsequently plagiarized and went into many editions.

The aphorism "Physician, heal thyself" proved cruel irony in Culpeper's personal life. One cannot face illness and death on a continual basis and easily maintain a cheerful nature. Culpeper's bouts of depression were deepened from continual illness within his own family. Alice bore him seven children and only one, a daughter, survived him. His own health was ruined by tuberculosis, which finally wasted him down to a skeleton. He died on January 10, 1654, at the age of 38. His unpublished manuscripts and lectures were left in the care of Alice, who was then only then 29. She later married John Heydon, another Student of Physick with an interest in astrology and possibly a student of her late husband's. Some of Culpeper's books were published after his death, the most notable being *Culpeper's Astrological Judgment of Diseases*. The balance of his manuscripts were most likely destroyed in the Great Fire of London in 1666. An incalculable loss.

After studying Culpeper one can't help wondering to what heights he would climb if he had access to blood tests, CAT scans, or any of the accouterments of a modern medical laboratory. His so-called radical beliefs that individuals can take full responsibility of their own health, if they so choose, without slavishly following "Doctor's orders," is echoed in the present time. His altruism shines forth in the following passage, "I wish from my heart my present state would take this matter into consideration, and take a little care for the lives of the poor commonalty, that a poor man that wants money to buy his wife and children bread, may not perish for want of an Angel to see a proud insulting domineering Physitian (sic) to give him a visit. I think it is a duty belonging to the Keepers of the Liberty of England."[9] His plea is just as topical today as it was in 1654.

For all his bitter criticism and stinging sarcasm, consider the words of the dying man as he handed his manuscripts over: "Thus have you what I have done, and you know for whose sake I did it. What now remains, but that you labor with might and main for your own good, and the increase of your own knowledge to make experience of them? For as the diligent hand maketh rich, so the diligent mind encreaseth knowledge; and for my own particular, never fear, but during the time I am amongst the living, I shall never cease to do you good in what way I may or can"[10]

He's nodding sagely from above as fully one third of the current American population, outraged at the Industry of Illness (capitals mine), are seeking more natural methods of healing. Culpeper smiles on them, for those who cannot remember the past are condemned to repeat it. The medical profession is once again overturning and our Pied Piper of natural healing is in his element. He's coming closer to us all through the results of our improved health every time we turn full circle to our mother for advice, for Dame Nature is indeed the highest order and she never looked better. As he peers through the window of our corner pharmacy (the modern apothecary shop) and sees his mother's precious herbs on the shelves, we hear a knock on the door. Welcome back, Nicholas. You've come just in time.

End Notes

1   Culpeper, Nicholas. *Nicholas Culpeper's Herbal Remedies.* Wilshire Book Company, Hollywood, California, 1971. p.9.

2   Gadbury, John. *A Collection of Nativities.* London, 1661. Ballantrae Reprint, Universe Books, Ontario, Canada, p. 141.

3   Ibid., p. 140.

4   Op. Cit.

5   Culpeper, Nicholas. *Astrological Judgment of Disease.* London, 1655. Ballantrae Reprint, Universe Books, Ontario, Canada, p. 68.

6   Ibid. p. 16.

7   Ibid., p. 48.

8   Ibid., pp. 38-39.

9   Ibid.. p. 136.

10 Ibid., p. iii.

Mushroom Madness

By Carly Wall

It is night. Traveling along a mossy bank, we edge along the path through the wood. The pale lunar glow filters down upon us, creating a hushed and mysterious landscape, but we are on a mission, and we can't let the surreal beauty of the Moonbeams stop us. Our flashlights trace our steps, moving to and fro. Searching, in among the moss, and leaf-strewn ground. A warm spring breeze blows, caressing our cheeks. Still no sight of what we search for. We decide to bed down for the night under the big oak. We stretch out our sleeping bags, bid good night to each other and find some rest.

In the morning, we awake to the sounds of birds singing and the warmth of the Sun shining. Before us, where it wasn't just a few short hours before, is a patch of morels, fifteen or twenty of them; the tastiest mushrooms I've ever had the luck to eat. But we have been foiled again. We still haven't observed a mushroom in the making. Is it the kiss of moonlight that paves the way for their arrival? It almost seems as if the moonlight nourishes them, for mushrooms do not need the Sun. They appear instantly, and vanish almost as quickly, some in only 24 hours or a few days. What exactly are these mysterious night visitors of the forest floor? And why do we hunger for them?

The Mushroom Hunter

They say once you become a mushroom hunter, you forever have the madness burned into your soul. And whether you search for spring or fall mushrooms, you'll be seen wandering the wild landscape with a

Place
First Class
Stamp Here

Llewellyn Publications
P.O. Box 64383-K912RC
St. Paul, MN 55164-0383

bag in one hand, a walking stick in the other. But mushroom hunters must beware if it is edible mushrooms they are in search of. Often, an unsuspecting newcomer will confuse an edible mushroom for one that is deadly. Therefore, to become an experienced "living" hunter, one must either find an old-time mushroom hunter to learn from, or buy a color guidebook, and take any finds directly to the local agricultural department mycologist (mushroom expert) at the local university. When you become familiar with the edible mushrooms, then you are free to hunt and eat to your heart's content. You might say mushroom enthusiasts are like midnight farmers of a sort.

Today many of the wild mushrooms can be commercially grown, and you can sometimes find them in specialty grocery stores. Some include cepes, chanterelles, horn of plenty, oyster mushrooms, and even truffles. These are all exciting and tasty and fun to experiment with in your cooking, but there is still something basic, something thrilling, when you hunt them yourself. Some people may shudder at the thought of eating fungi, but perhaps they have only tasted those rubbery white buttons most groceries carry.

Let them taste the Morel. Although they aren't beautiful, with fat, flesh-colored stems, caps that look like an old sponge, and their spores developing in the wrinkles of these cone-shaped caps, they are the tastiest of all the wild mushrooms. You never know where they will turn up; some say they congregate around stands of may apples, others say they like dead trees, and still others swear they love to spring up near pine groves. Of-

What exactly are these mysterious night visitors of the forest floor? And why do we hunger for them?

ten, they've appeared on burned-over ground. In times past, the love of the taste of the morel was so great that in the west, people used to burn down whole forests to encourage them to grow. We know better than to do that today, of course.

It isn't so hard to find morels. Being a nature-lover doesn't hurt. If you are, then you are naturally led to them, perhaps spiritually, perhaps by smell (it's an earthy, warm, moist smell). If you want to try your luck, (after you have observed what the morel looks like and are sufficiently prepared), in April or May simply take an early morning walk. If you don't live in the country, visit a wooded city park. The mushrooms aren't fussy. Peer at the ground, brush aside old leaves. Investigate under trees. Of course, these instructions depend upon the area of the country you live in. The fruiting season will be longer in the Southeast, extending into the whole of winter in the South. In California, you must wait for the first rains. In the West, July and August are good hunting times. A field guide for your particular area will help you here. However, once you have found your mushroom, you may find the fever will grab you, too.

Fungi History

Primitive people decorated caves with the things important in their lives. Although paintings depicting mushrooms were rare, they were among some of the plant drawings found. Egyptian tombs held murals of mushrooms, specifically in the resting place of pharaoh Amen-emhep, which was painted around 1450 BC.

The Greek physician, Hippocrates, called the Father of Medicine, used mushrooms for food and medicine. Another Greek physician wrote a book on plants which proclaimed mushrooms a part of the plant world. Roman culture didn't ignore mushrooms, either. Pliny the Elder, of the 1st century AD, stated that mushrooms grew after a rainstorm, and many Romans were so fond of mushrooms that there were specially trained collectors who gathered them for the population to enjoy.

As time passed, a great deal of knowledge accumulated around fungi, along with superstition. Native North Americans also had their beliefs about the fungi growing around them. Among the Tewas, it was believed a stick must be laid across the top of the kettle containing the cooked mushrooms or the person eating them would have a poor memory. The Papagos in past times did not eat mushrooms and claimed they made one old.

But it is the Giant Puffball (sometimes nicknamed the Devil's Snuffbox), and commonly seen late spring through fall, which is the easiest of the edible mushrooms to hunt, and the Indians didn't miss out on this tasty fungi. You cannot mistake them. They resemble white balls nestled along a hillside or field. Some can reach enormous sizes (up to 28 inches or larger). At first they are white, but gradually they fade to dirty yellow, then brown, then the leathery skin will split and any touch will send a cloud of spores like an explosion out into the air. In the days before matches were invented, the threads inside these balls were used as tinder. None of the puffballs are poisonous (whether it is the giant or small varieties), but sometimes the small may be mistaken for the immature button stage of the dangerous Amanita. One good way of checking to see if it is indeed a puffball you have is to slice the mushroom from the base to top. If you see the slightest indication of an outline of a gilled mushroom, discard it. The puffball will be firm and creamy white, resembling a marshmallow inside. If it is powdery or slimy, it means the mushroom is past its prime and beginning to produce spores and therefore not a good specimen.

There are many instances where the Indians used puffballs. Native tribes used the spores of old puffballs to stop the flow of blood from wounds. The Zunis, a South-western tribe from New Mexico, gathered puffballs in great numbers, eating them fresh and drying the rest for winter use in soups and stews. In fact, the Zunis believed plants were sacred as they were given to them by the Star people, who dropped them to Earth. As such, plants (mushrooms included) were believed to be filled with spirit.

A Mystic Journey

Perhaps the most interesting history of mushroom use is that of the connection of mushrooms and religion. Robert Graves, English poet and novelist, considered the Amanita mushroom "ambrosia of the Greek Gods," though today we consider this fungus dangerous. Sacred mushrooms were in fact used in Siberia, Mexico, and Borneo. It was in Mexico and Central America that primitive people carved stone sculptures known as mushroom stones to be used in religious ceremonies. These stones are estimated to have been made between 200 BC and 300 AD, but some have been dated 2000 BC. Many cultures used hallucinatory mushrooms in religious ceremonies for sexual, therapeutic, and magical practices. Perhaps that is why there is such a connection between mushrooms or toadstools and the Faerie realm. Extracts of Fly Agaric, when ingested properly and carefully (because remember, it is poisonous), induced wild dancing, and visions and conversations with invisible people. Many people of past times called this mushroom the "gateway to Faerieland." This mushroom isn't the only link. There are mushrooms or toadstools with names like Yellow Fairy Club, the Elfcap, Dune Pixie-Hood and Dryad's Saddle.

There is a type of mushroom which grows in circles called Fairy Rings. Many superstitions have arisen around these circles which contain very dark green grass and are edged with umbrella capped mushrooms. The talk was that these circles were charmed, and the fairies danced there on Moonlit nights, or that they grew above a subterranean fairy village. Humans were supposed to be very careful, for if one stood inside a ring on a clear moonlit night, especially May Eve or Halloween, and was in the right frame of mind, he or she could enter the Faerie realm and might be cast under the spell of the "Wee Ones." Another old story was that if you ran around one of these fairy rings nine times on the night of the Full Moon, you could hear the fairies laughing and talking below. In Northumberland, it was considered dangerous to make more than nine circles, because evil could befall you. Cattle and sheep are believed to recognize the danger of these rings and refuse to graze inside them. It was also believed that revenge would be visited upon anyone attempting to destroy the rings, and if by chance the ring was dug up or plowed, it would always reappear soon afterwards anyway, so it would be an effort made in vain. The rings themselves have often been proven by modern science to be of great antiquity, with some over 60 years old. The cause of the circles is the mycelium, which lives underground and spreads its web of threads outward. The mushrooms appearing in the grass mark the growth of the underground mycelium, and each year the ring grows larger. In some parts of the country there are fairy rings 800 feet wide. There are more than a dozen common mushrooms which form rings. Perhaps you have a fairy ring in your backyard?

There are other folktales concerning fairies and toadstools. It is said that the fairies like to adorn themselves with the caps of mushrooms, using them like tiny hats. Others say that it the mushrooms' unearthly shapes and colors, and the fact that some glow and others are poisonous, that has in times past caused humankind to think of them as spawns of the devil or bewitching fairy food.

Friendly Fungi

There are over 1,000 commonly known species and varieties of mushroom across the world—all of various colors, shapes, and sizes. Some are mysterious, and deadly, and as we have discovered, forever linked to a superstitious past. There are other more friendly fungi which we have discussed, which are edible, and fun to spice up your cooking. My two favorites, the morel, and the giant puffball, are the easiest to find and identify, and they star in the following recipes.

Many people get carried away with adding spices, tomatoes, or wine. All these ingredients do is mask the delicate taste and aroma. Simple recipes and short cooking times let the tastes shine through.

The thing to remember is that you must eat what mushrooms you find as soon as possible—within the first day or two, and no more than 4 or 5. Gently clean by running cold water briefly over the mushrooms; getting rid of sand, dirt, or insects. Pat dry with paper towels. Slice larger morels in half. Slice giant puffballs across, making 2" "steaks," and peeling off the outer skin.

Recipes

Pan-fried Mushrooms

¾   cup mushrooms

1   egg

2   tablespoons milk

¼   cup flour

   fat for frying

Beat the egg and milk together in a small bowl. Dip each mushroom in an egg/milk mixture, then roll in flour. Heat the bacon grease in a skillet, and brown mushrooms on each side in bacon grease. This makes an excellent breakfast, or serve with salads, casseroles, or fresh caught, pan-fried catfish.

Mushroom Casserole

   Mushrooms (enough to make several layers in a casserole dish)

   Bread crumbs (equal to amount of mushrooms)

2   eggs

2   cups milk

   Parmesan cheese

   Salt and pepper

   Butter

Layer mushrooms in a buttered casserole dish, topping each layer with bread crumbs. Dot with butter. Next, in a bowl combine eggs and milk, beat until mixed well. Pour this over the casserole until mushrooms are completely covered (for larger casseroles you may need more egg/milk mix). Add a little salt and pepper and sprinkle with freshly grated parmesan cheese if you wish. Bake it at 325°F until a knife inserted in this custard comes out clean.

Mushroom Balls

1   cup mushrooms
2   tablespoons butter, melted
1   cup sausage
1   cup bread crumbs
2   eggs, beaten
½   cup flour, divided
    oil for frying

For this recipe, cut the mushrooms into small cubes or pieces. Drench in melted butter; drain. Fry sausage, crumble, and add to mushrooms along with bread crumbs, eggs, and 1–2 tablespoons of the flour. Stir until well mixed. Make little balls out of this mixture and roll in remaining flour to coat the outside. Fry them in hot oil. Drain and eat.

Preserving

If you find you have far too many mushrooms to eat right away (not uncommon with the giant puffball, as one of these can feed an army sometimes), then you can dry the surplus and ensure a bounty of good eating all winter long. Clean and cut large mushrooms in thin slices. Smaller morels can be left whole. It is easiest to cube the puffballs. Lay them in a single layer on a cookie sheet in a warm oven with the door slightly ajar (do not exceed 140 degrees or they will burn and blacken). They are done when they shrink and become brittle, so check often. To reconstitute, soak in warm water 20-30 minutes, or for puffballs, just toss the dried cubes into stews, casseroles, or vegetable dishes. You can also thread morels on a fine string and hang them in a warm place to dry. These mushroom strings hanging in my kitchen seem like a magical link to the forest and woodland and I think they are quite attractive decorations—as well as being useful.

Mushroom Madness

Well, it is too late to turn back now. If you are like me, you are probably nervously pacing in front of a moonlit window, waiting for that warm rainstorm to blow up. I still haven't seen a mushroom in the making, though I've been very determined. I just have to be patient, that's all. Oh, and I'll stay away from those fairy rings when the Moon is bright and full. I don't want to tempt fate.

There are several places which sell mushroom kits and spawn, offer books and seminars and all kinds of interesting mushroom related items. Here they are:

Fungi Perfecti, P.O. Box 7634, Olympia, WA 98507, 1-800-780-9126. Send a S.A.S.E. for a free brochure, or $3.00 for an 80-page catalog.

Mushroom People, 1-800-FUNGI95. Free 300-item catalog.

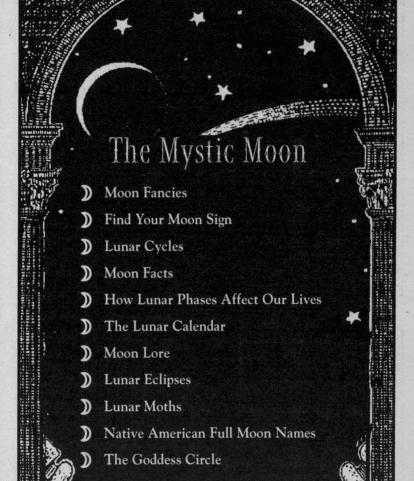

The Mystic Moon

Moon Fancies

By Emilie Jane Conroy

◑ If a woman is truly eager to bear a child, she should boil a bit of rhubarb in one cup of white wine. Then shall she place this mixture in a chalice of silver or glass, and partake of it under the light of the Full Moon. This shall make her womb ready to conceive.

◑ Two handfuls of rose petals thrown into the air at the Full Moon will bring as many joys as there are petals that fall to earth.

◑ Those people who rise when the Moon rises in the east shall be blessed with psychic gifts and second sight.

◑ Turning your back on the Moon in scorn of her influence will assure you of ill fortune.

◑ It is a good omen to spot a wild rabbit on the night of the Full Moon.

◑ To hear the hoot of an owl while bathing in the light of the Full Moon is a great boon to one's magical energies.

◑ Women should bear the image of the Moon on their person in some form to reap the greatest benefits and joys from their womanhood. Men, however, should avoid wearing a Moon image, lest their potency be damaged.

◑ It is said that a person with indentations in the skin was conceived under the Full Moon, and the mother was greatly under the lunar influence. These indentations represent the craters of the Moon.

◑ Speak your fears and troubles to the Waning Moon to have them allayed; speak your hopes and wishes to the Waxing Moon to have them realized.

◑ Sprinkle moon powder (myrrh, sandalwood, powdered roses, ginger, and orris root in equal amounts) all around the home to fill it with lunar energies.

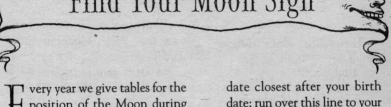

Find Your Moon Sign

Every year we give tables for the position of the Moon during that year, but it is more complicated to give tables for the Moon position in any year because of its continuous movement. However, the problem was solved long ago by Grant Lewi in *Astrology for the Millions*, a do-it-yourself manual (available from Llewellyn). Here's Lewi's system:

1. Find your birth year in the Moon Tables.

2. Run down the left-hand column and see if your date is there.

3. If your date is in the left-hand column, run over this line until you come to the column under your birth year. Here you will find a number. This is your base number. Write it down, and go directly to the direction under the heading "What to Do with Your Base Number" on the next page.

4. If your birth date is not in the left-hand column, get a pencil and paper. Your birth date falls between two numbers in the left-hand column. Look at the date closest after your birth date; run over this line to your birth year. Write down the number you find there, and label it "top number." Having done this, write directly beneath it on your piece of paper the number printed just above it in the table. Label this "bottom number." Subtract the bottom number from the top number. If the top number is smaller, add 360 to it and then subtract. The result is your difference.

5. Go back to the left-hand column and find the date before your birth date. Determine the number of days between this date and your birth date. Write this down and label it "intervening days."

6. In the table of difference below, note which group your difference (found at 4, above) falls in.

Difference	Daily Motion
80-87	12 degrees
88-94	13 degrees
95-101	14 degrees
102-106	15 degrees

Note: If you were born in a leap year and use the difference between February 26th and March 5th, use the following table:

Difference	Daily Motion
94-99	12 degrees
100-108	13 degrees
109-115	14 degrees
115-122	15 degrees

7. Write down the "daily motion" corresponding to your place in the proper table of difference above. Multiply daily motion by the number labeled "intervening days" (found at step 5).

8. Add the result of 7 to your bottom number (under step 4). This is your base number. If it is more than 360, subtract 360 from it and call the result your base number.

What to Do with Your Base Number

Turn to the Table of Base Numbers and locate your base number in it. At the top of the column you will find the sign your Moon was in. At the left you will find the degree the Moon occupied at:

7 AM of your birth date if you were born under Eastern Standard Time.

6 AM of your birth date if you were born under Central Standard Time.

5 AM of your birth date if you were born under Mountain Standard Time.

4 AM of your birth date if you were born under Pacific Standard Time.

If you don't know the hour of your birth, accept this as your Moon's sign and degree. If you do know the hour of your birth, get the exact degree as follows:

If you were born after 7 AM, Eastern Standard Time (6 am Central Standard Time, etc.), determine the number of hours after the time that you were born. Divide this by two. Add this to your base number, and the result in the table will be the exact degree and sign of the Moon on the year, month, date, and hour of your birth.

If you were born before 7 am Eastern Standard Time (6 am Central Standard Time, etc.), determine the number of hours before the time that you were born. Divide this by two. Subtract this from your base number, and the result in the table will be the exact degree and sign of the Moon on the year, month, date, and hour of your birth.

TABLE OF BASE NUMBERS

	Aries (13)	Taurus (14)	Gemini (15)	Cancer (16)	Leo (17)	Virgo (18)	Libra (19)	Scorpio (20)	Sagittarius (21)	Capricorn (22)	Aquarius (23)	Pisces (24)
0 deg.	0	30	60	90	120	150	180	210	240	270	300	330
1 deg.	1	31	61	91	121	151	181	211	241	271	301	331
2 deg.	2	32	62	92	122	152	182	212	242	272	302	332
3 deg.	3	33	63	93	123	153	183	213	243	273	303	333
4 deg.	4	34	64	94	124	154	184	214	244	274	304	334
5 deg.	5	35	65	95	125	155	185	215	245	275	305	335
6 deg.	6	36	66	96	126	156	186	216	246	276	306	336
7 deg.	7	37	67	97	127	157	187	217	247	277	307	337
8 deg.	8	38	68	98	128	158	188	218	248	278	308	338
9 deg.	9	39	69	99	129	159	189	219	249	279	309	339
10 deg.	10	40	70	100	130	160	190	220	250	280	310	340
11 deg.	11	41	71	101	131	161	191	221	251	281	311	341
12 deg.	12	42	72	102	132	162	192	222	252	282	312	342
13 deg.	13	43	73	103	133	163	193	223	253	283	313	343
14 deg.	14	44	74	104	134	164	194	224	254	284	314	344
15 deg.	15	45	75	105	135	165	195	225	255	285	315	345
16 deg.	16	46	76	106	136	166	196	226	256	286	316	346
17 deg.	17	47	77	107	137	167	197	227	257	287	317	347
18 deg.	18	48	78	108	138	168	198	228	258	288	318	248
19 deg.	19	49	79	109	139	169	199	229	259	289	319	349
20 deg.	20	50	80	110	140	170	200	230	260	290	320	350
21 deg.	21	51	81	111	141	171	201	231	261	291	321	351
22 deg.	22	52	82	112	142	172	202	232	262	292	322	352
23 deg.	23	53	83	113	143	173	203	233	263	293	323	353
24 deg.	24	54	84	114	144	174	204	234	264	294	324	354
25 deg.	25	55	85	115	145	175	205	235	265	295	325	355
26 deg.	26	56	86	116	146	176	206	236	266	296	326	356
27 deg.	27	57	87	117	147	177	207	237	267	297	327	357
28 deg.	28	58	88	118	148	178	208	238	268	298	328	358
29 deg.	29	59	89	119	149	179	209	239	269	299	329	359

		1901	1902	1903	1904	1905	1906	1907	1908	1909	1910
Jan.	1	55	188	308	76	227	358	119	246	39	168
Jan.	8	149	272	37	179	319	82	208	350	129	252
Jan.	15	234	2	141	270	43	174	311	81	213	346
Jan.	22	327	101	234	353	138	273	44	164	309	84
Jan.	29	66	196	317	84	238	6	128	255	50	175
Feb.	5	158	280	46	188	328	90	219	359	138	259
Feb.	12	241	12	149	279	51	184	319	90	221	356
Feb.	19	335	111	242	2	146	283	52	173	317	94
Feb.	26	76	204	326	92	248	13	136	264	60	184
Mar.	5	166	288	57	211	336	98	229	21	147	267
Mar.	12	249	22	157	300	60	194	328	110	230	5
Mar.	19	344	121	250	24	154	293	60	195	325	105
Mar.	26	86	212	334	116	258	22	144	288	69	192
Apr.	2	175	296	68	219	345	106	240	29	155	276
Apr.	9	258	31	167	309	69	202	338	118	240	13
Apr.	16	352	132	258	33	163	304	68	204	334	115
Apr.	23	96	220	342	127	267	31	152	299	77	201
Apr.	30	184	304	78	227	354	114	250	38	164	285
May	7	267	40	177	317	78	210	348	126	249	21
May	14	1	142	266	42	172	313	76	212	344	124
May	21	104	229	350	138	275	40	160	310	85	210
May	28	193	313	87	236	2	123	259	47	172	294
Jun.	4	277	48	187	324	88	219	358	134	258	30
Jun.	11	11	151	275	50	182	322	85	220	355	132
Jun.	18	112	238	359	149	283	48	169	320	93	218
Jun.	25	201	322	96	245	11	133	267	57	180	304
Jul.	2	286	57	197	333	97	228	8	142	267	40
Jul.	9	21	160	283	58	193	330	94	228	6	140
Jul.	16	121	247	7	159	291	57	178	330	102	226
Jul.	23	209	332	105	255	18	143	276	66	188	314
Jul.	30	295	66	206	341	105	239	17	151	275	51
Aug.	6	32	168	292	66	204	338	103	237	17	148
Aug.	13	130	255	17	168	301	65	188	339	111	234
Aug.	20	217	341	113	265	27	152	285	76	197	323
Aug.	27	303	77	215	350	113	250	25	160	283	62
Sep.	3	43	176	301	75	215	346	111	246	27	157
Sep.	10	139	263	27	176	310	73	198	347	121	242
Sep.	17	225	350	123	274	35	161	294	85	205	331
Sep.	24	311	88	223	358	122	261	33	169	292	73
Oct.	1	53	185	309	85	224	355	119	256	35	166
Oct.	8	149	271	36	185	320	81	207	356	130	250
Oct.	15	233	359	133	283	44	169	305	93	214	339
Oct.	22	319	99	231	7	130	271	42	177	301	83
Oct.	29	62	194	317	95	233	5	127	266	44	176
Nov.	5	158	279	45	193	329	89	216	5	139	259
Nov.	12	242	6	144	291	53	177	316	101	223	347
Nov.	19	328	109	239	15	140	280	50	185	311	91
Nov.	26	70	203	325	105	241	14	135	276	52	185
Dec.	3	168	288	54	203	338	98	224	15	148	268
Dec.	10	251	14	155	299	61	185	327	109	231	356
Dec.	17	338	118	248	23	150	289	59	193	322	99
Dec.	24	78	213	333	115	249	23	143	286	61	194
Dec.	31	176	296	61	213	346	107	232	26	155	277

		1911	1912	1913	1914	1915	1916	1917	1918	1919	1920
Jan.	1	289	57	211	337	100	228	23	147	270	39
Jan.	8	20	162	299	61	192	332	110	231	5	143
Jan.	15	122	251	23	158	293	61	193	329	103	231
Jan.	22	214	335	120	256	23	145	290	68	193	316
Jan.	29	298	66	221	345	108	237	32	155	278	49
Feb.	5	31	170	308	69	203	340	118	239	16	150
Feb.	12	130	260	32	167	302	70	203	338	113	239
Feb.	19	222	344	128	266	31	154	298	78	201	325
Feb.	26	306	75	231	353	116	248	41	164	286	60
Mar.	5	42	192	317	77	214	2	127	248	26	172
Mar.	12	140	280	41	176	311	89	212	346	123	259
Mar.	19	230	5	136	276	39	176	308	87	209	346
Mar.	26	314	100	239	2	124	273	49	173	294	85
Apr.	2	52	200	326	86	223	10	135	257	35	181
Apr.	9	150	288	51	184	321	97	222	355	133	267
Apr.	16	238	14	146	286	48	184	318	96	218	355
Apr.	23	322	111	247	11	132	284	57	181	303	96
Apr.	30	61	208	334	96	232	19	143	267	43	190
May.	7	160	296	60	192	331	105	231	4	142	275
May.	14	246	22	156	294	56	192	329	104	227	3
May.	21	331	122	255	20	141	294	66	190	312	105
May.	28	69	218	342	106	240	29	151	277	51	200
Jun.	4	170	304	69	202	341	114	240	14	151	284
Jun.	11	255	30	167	302	65	200	340	112	235	11
Jun.	18	340	132	264	28	151	304	74	198	322	114
Jun.	25	78	228	350	115	249	39	159	286	60	209
Jul.	2	179	312	78	212	349	122	248	25	159	293
Jul.	9	264	39	178	310	74	209	350	120	244	20
Jul.	16	349	141	273	36	161	312	84	206	332	123
Jul.	23	87	237	358	125	258	48	168	295	70	218
Jul.	30	187	321	86	223	357	131	256	36	167	302
Aug.	6	272	48	188	319	82	219	360	129	252	31
Aug.	13	359	150	282	44	171	320	93	214	342	131
Aug.	20	96	246	6	133	268	57	177	303	81	226
Aug.	27	195	330	94	234	5	140	265	46	175	310
Sep.	3	281	57	198	328	90	229	9	138	260	41
Sep.	10	9	158	292	52	180	329	102	222	351	140
Sep.	17	107	255	15	141	279	65	186	312	91	234
Sep.	24	203	339	103	244	13	149	274	56	184	319
Oct.	1	288	68	206	337	98	240	17	148	268	52
Oct.	8	18	167	301	61	189	338	111	231	360	150
Oct.	15	118	263	24	149	290	73	195	320	102	242
Oct.	22	212	347	113	254	22	157	284	65	193	326
Oct.	29	296	78	214	346	106	250	25	157	276	61
Nov.	5	26	177	309	70	197	348	119	240	7	161
Nov.	12	129	271	33	158	300	81	203	329	112	250
Nov.	19	221	355	123	262	31	164	295	73	202	334
Nov.	26	305	88	223	355	115	259	34	165	285	70
Dec.	3	34	187	317	79	205	359	127	249	16	171
Dec.	10	138	279	41	168	310	89	211	340	120	259
Dec.	17	230	3	134	270	40	172	305	81	211	343
Dec.	24	313	97	232	3	124	267	44	173	294	78
Dec.	31	42	198	325	87	214	9	135	257	25	181

		1921	1922	1923	1924	1925	1926	1927	1928	1929	1930
Jan.	1	194	317	80	211	5	127	250	23	176	297
Jan.	8	280	41	177	313	90	211	349	123	260	22
Jan.	15	4	141	275	41	175	312	86	211	346	123
Jan.	22	101	239	3	127	272	51	172	297	83	222
Jan.	29	203	325	88	222	13	135	258	34	184	306
Feb.	5	289	49	188	321	99	220	359	131	269	31
Feb.	12	14	149	284	49	185	320	95	219	356	131
Feb.	19	110	249	11	135	281	60	181	305	93	230
Feb.	26	211	334	96	233	21	144	266	45	191	314
Mar.	5	297	58	197	343	107	230	8	153	276	41
Mar.	12	23	157	294	69	194	328	105	238	6	140
Mar.	19	119	258	19	157	292	68	190	327	104	238
Mar.	26	219	343	104	258	29	153	275	70	200	323
Apr.	2	305	68	205	352	115	240	16	163	284	51
Apr.	9	33	166	304	77	204	337	114	247	14	149
Apr.	16	130	266	28	164	303	76	198	335	115	246
Apr.	23	227	351	114	268	38	161	285	79	208	331
Apr.	30	313	78	214	1	123	250	25	172	292	61
May.	7	42	176	313	85	212	348	123	256	23	160
May.	14	141	274	37	173	314	84	207	344	125	254
May.	21	236	359	123	277	47	169	295	88	217	339
May.	28	321	88	222	11	131	259	34	181	301	70
Jun.	4	50	186	321	94	220	358	131	264	31	171
Jun.	11	152	282	45	182	324	93	215	354	135	263
Jun.	18	245	7	134	285	56	177	305	96	226	347
Jun.	25	330	97	232	20	139	268	44	190	310	78
Jul.	2	58	197	329	103	229	9	139	273	40	181
Jul.	9	162	291	54	192	333	101	223	4	144	272
Jul.	16	254	15	144	294	65	185	315	104	236	355
Jul.	23	338	106	242	28	148	276	54	198	319	87
Jul.	30	67	208	337	112	238	20	147	282	49	191
Aug.	6	171	300	62	202	341	110	231	15	152	281
Aug.	13	264	24	153	302	74	194	324	114	244	4
Aug.	20	347	114	253	36	157	285	65	206	328	95
Aug.	27	76	218	346	120	248	29	156	290	59	200
Sep.	3	179	309	70	213	350	119	239	25	161	290
Sep.	10	273	32	162	312	83	203	332	124	252	13
Sep.	17	356	122	264	44	166	293	75	214	337	105
Sep.	24	86	227	354	128	258	38	165	298	70	208
Oct.	1	187	318	78	223	358	128	248	35	169	298
Oct.	8	281	41	170	322	91	212	340	134	260	23
Oct.	15	5	132	274	52	175	303	85	222	345	115
Oct.	22	97	235	3	136	269	46	174	306	81	216
Oct.	29	196	327	87	232	7	137	257	44	179	307
Nov.	5	289	50	178	332	99	221	349	144	268	31
Nov.	12	13	142	283	61	183	313	93	231	353	126
Nov.	19	107	243	12	144	279	54	183	315	91	225
Nov.	26	206	335	96	241	17	145	266	52	189	314
Dec.	3	297	59	187	343	107	230	359	154	276	39
Dec.	10	21	152	291	70	191	324	101	240	1	137
Dec.	17	117	252	21	153	289	63	191	324	99	234
Dec.	24	216	343	105	249	28	152	275	60	199	322
Dec.	31	305	67	197	352	115	237	9	162	285	47

		1931	1932	1933	1934	1935	1936	1937	1938	1939	1940
Jan.	1	60	196	346	107	231	8	156	277	41	181
Jan.	8	162	294	70	193	333	104	240	4	144	275
Jan.	15	257	20	158	294	68	190	329	104	239	360
Jan.	22	342	108	255	32	152	278	67	202	323	88
Jan.	29	68	207	353	116	239	19	163	286	49	191
Feb.	5	171	302	78	203	342	113	248	14	153	284
Feb.	12	267	28	168	302	78	198	339	113	248	8
Feb.	19	351	116	266	40	161	286	78	210	332	96
Feb.	26	77	217	1	124	248	29	171	294	59	200
Mar.	5	179	324	86	213	350	135	256	25	161	306
Mar.	12	276	48	176	311	86	218	347	123	256	29
Mar.	19	360	137	277	48	170	308	89	218	340	119
Mar.	26	86	241	10	132	258	52	180	302	69	223
Apr.	2	187	334	94	223	358	144	264	34	169	315
Apr.	9	285	57	185	321	95	227	355	133	264	38
Apr.	16	9	146	287	56	178	317	99	226	349	128
Apr.	23	96	250	18	140	268	61	189	310	80	231
Apr.	30	196	343	102	232	7	153	273	43	179	323
May.	7	293	66	193	332	103	237	4	144	272	47
May.	14	17	155	297	64	187	327	108	235	357	139
May.	21	107	258	28	148	278	69	198	318	90	239
May.	28	205	351	111	241	17	161	282	51	189	331
Jun.	4	301	75	201	343	111	245	13	154	280	55
Jun.	11	25	165	306	73	195	337	117	244	5	150
Jun.	18	117	267	37	157	288	78	207	327	99	248
Jun.	25	215	360	120	249	28	169	291	60	200	339
Jul.	2	309	84	211	353	119	254	23	164	289	64
Jul.	9	33	176	315	82	203	348	125	253	13	160
Jul.	16	126	276	46	165	297	87	216	336	108	258
Jul.	23	226	8	130	258	38	177	300	69	210	347
Jul.	30	317	92	221	2	128	262	33	173	298	72
Aug.	6	41	187	323	91	211	359	133	261	21	170
Aug.	13	135	285	54	175	305	97	224	346	116	268
Aug.	20	237	16	138	267	49	185	308	78	220	355
Aug.	27	326	100	232	10	136	270	44	181	307	80
Sep.	3	49	197	331	100	220	8	142	270	31	179
Sep.	10	143	295	62	184	314	107	232	355	125	278
Sep.	17	247	24	147	277	58	194	317	89	228	4
Sep.	24	335	108	243	18	145	278	55	189	316	88
Oct.	1	58	206	341	108	229	17	152	278	40	188
Oct.	8	151	306	70	193	322	117	240	4	134	288
Oct.	15	256	32	155	287	66	203	324	100	236	13
Oct.	22	344	116	253	27	154	287	64	198	324	98
Oct.	29	68	214	350	116	239	25	162	286	49	196
Nov.	5	161	316	78	201	332	126	248	12	145	297
Nov.	12	264	41	162	298	74	212	333	111	244	22
Nov.	19	353	125	262	36	162	296	73	207	332	108
Nov.	26	77	222	0	124	248	33	172	294	58	205
Dec.	3	171	325	87	209	343	135	257	19	156	305
Dec.	10	272	50	171	309	82	220	341	120	253	30
Dec.	17	1	135	271	45	170	306	81	217	340	118
Dec.	24	86	231	10	132	256	43	181	302	66	214
Dec.	31	182	333	95	217	354	142	265	27	167	313

		1941	1942	1943	1944	1945	1946	1947	1948	1949	1950
Jan.	1	325	88	211	353	135	258	22	165	305	68
Jan.	8	50	176	315	85	219	348	126	256	29	160
Jan.	15	141	276	50	169	312	87	220	340	123	258
Jan.	22	239	12	133	258	52	182	303	69	224	352
Jan.	29	333	96	221	2	143	266	32	174	314	75
Feb.	5	57	186	323	95	227	358	134	265	37	170
Feb.	12	150	285	58	178	320	96	228	349	131	268
Feb.	19	250	20	142	267	62	190	312	78	234	359
Feb.	26	342	104	231	11	152	274	43	182	323	83
Mar.	5	65	196	331	116	236	8	142	286	46	179
Mar.	12	158	295	66	199	328	107	236	10	139	279
Mar.	19	261	28	150	290	72	198	320	102	243	8
Mar.	26	351	112	242	34	161	281	53	204	332	91
Apr.	2	74	205	340	125	244	16	152	294	55	187
Apr.	9	166	306	74	208	337	117	244	19	148	289
Apr.	16	270	36	158	300	81	206	328	112	252	17
Apr.	23	360	120	252	42	170	290	63	212	340	100
Apr.	30	83	214	350	133	254	25	162	302	64	195
May	7	174	316	82	217	346	127	252	27	158	299
May	14	279	45	166	311	90	215	336	123	260	26
May	21	9	128	261	50	179	299	72	221	349	110
May	28	92	222	1	141	263	33	173	310	73	204
Jun.	4	184	326	91	226	356	137	261	36	168	307
Jun.	11	287	54	174	322	98	224	344	134	268	34
Jun.	18	17	137	270	60	187	308	81	231	357	119
Jun.	25	102	231	11	149	272	42	183	318	82	213
Jul.	2	194	335	99	234	7	145	269	44	179	316
Jul.	9	296	63	183	332	106	233	353	144	277	43
Jul.	16	25	147	279	70	195	318	89	241	5	129
Jul.	23	110	240	21	157	280	52	192	327	91	224
Jul.	30	205	343	108	242	18	153	278	52	190	324
Aug.	6	304	71	192	341	115	241	3	153	286	51
Aug.	13	33	156	287	80	203	327	98	251	13	138
Aug.	20	119	250	30	165	289	63	201	336	99	235
Aug.	27	216	351	117	250	28	162	287	61	200	332
Sep.	3	314	80	201	350	125	249	13	161	296	59
Sep.	10	41	165	296	90	211	336	108	260	21	146
Sep.	17	127	261	39	174	297	74	209	345	107	246
Sep.	24	226	359	126	259	38	170	295	70	209	341
Oct.	1	323	88	211	358	135	257	22	170	306	67
Oct.	8	49	174	306	99	220	344	118	269	30	154
Oct.	15	135	272	47	183	305	84	217	353	116	256
Oct.	22	236	8	134	269	47	180	303	80	217	351
Oct.	29	333	95	220	7	144	265	31	179	315	75
Nov.	5	58	181	317	107	229	352	129	277	39	162
Nov.	12	143	283	55	192	314	94	225	1	125	265
Nov.	19	244	18	141	279	55	189	311	90	225	0
Nov.	26	343	104	229	16	153	274	39	189	323	84
Dec.	3	67	189	328	115	237	360	140	284	47	171
Dec.	10	153	292	64	200	324	103	234	9	136	274
Dec.	17	252	28	149	289	63	199	319	100	234	9
Dec.	24	351	112	237	27	161	282	47	199	331	93
Dec.	31	76	198	338	123	246	9	150	293	55	180

		1951	1952	1953	1954	1955	1956	1957	1958	1959	1960
Jan.	1	194	336	115	238	6	147	285	47	178	317
Jan.	8	297	67	199	331	107	237	9	143	278	47
Jan.	15	30	150	294	70	200	320	104	242	9	131
Jan.	22	114	240	35	161	284	51	207	331	94	223
Jan.	29	204	344	124	245	17	155	294	55	189	325
Feb.	5	305	76	207	341	116	246	18	152	287	56
Feb.	12	38	159	302	80	208	330	112	252	17	140
Feb.	19	122	249	45	169	292	61	216	340	102	233
Feb.	26	215	352	133	253	27	163	303	63	199	333
Mar.	5	314	96	216	350	125	266	27	161	297	75
Mar.	12	46	180	310	91	216	351	121	262	25	161
Mar.	19	130	274	54	178	300	86	224	349	110	259
Mar.	26	225	14	142	262	37	185	312	72	208	356
Apr.	2	324	104	226	358	135	274	37	169	307	83
Apr.	9	54	189	319	100	224	360	131	271	34	170
Apr.	16	138	285	62	187	308	97	232	357	118	269
Apr.	23	235	23	150	271	46	194	320	82	217	5
Apr.	30	334	112	235	6	146	282	46	177	317	91
May	7	62	197	330	109	232	8	142	279	42	177
May	14	146	296	70	196	316	107	240	6	127	279
May	21	243	32	158	280	54	204	328	91	225	15
May	28	344	120	244	15	155	290	55	187	326	100
Jun.	4	71	205	341	117	241	16	153	288	51	186
Jun.	11	155	306	79	204	325	117	249	14	137	288
Jun.	18	252	42	166	290	63	214	336	101	234	25
Jun.	25	354	128	253	26	164	298	63	198	335	109
Jul.	2	80	214	351	125	250	24	164	296	60	195
Jul.	9	164	315	88	212	335	126	259	22	147	297
Jul.	16	260	52	174	299	72	223	344	110	243	34
Jul.	23	3	137	261	37	173	307	71	209	343	118
Jul.	30	89	222	2	134	258	33	174	304	68	205
Aug.	6	174	324	97	220	345	134	268	30	156	305
Aug.	13	270	62	182	308	82	232	353	118	254	42
Aug.	20	11	146	269	48	181	316	79	220	351	126
Aug.	27	97	232	11	143	267	43	183	314	76	215
Sep.	3	184	332	107	228	355	143	278	38	166	314
Sep.	10	280	71	191	316	92	241	2	127	265	50
Sep.	17	19	155	278	58	189	325	88	230	359	135
Sep.	24	105	242	20	152	274	54	191	323	84	225
Oct.	1	193	341	116	237	4	152	287	47	174	324
Oct.	8	291	79	200	324	103	249	11	135	276	58
Oct.	15	27	163	287	68	198	333	98	239	8	143
Oct.	22	113	252	28	162	282	64	199	332	92	235
Oct.	29	201	350	125	245	12	162	295	56	182	334
Nov.	5	302	87	209	333	114	256	19	144	286	66
Nov.	12	36	171	297	76	207	341	109	247	17	150
Nov.	19	121	262	37	171	291	73	208	341	101	244
Nov.	26	209	0	133	254	20	173	303	65	190	345
Dec.	3	312	95	217	342	124	265	27	154	295	75
Dec.	10	45	179	307	84	216	348	119	255	27	158
Dec.	17	129	271	46	180	299	82	218	350	110	252
Dec.	24	217	11	141	263	28	184	311	73	199	355
Dec.	31	321	103	225	352	132	273	35	164	303	84

		1961	1962	1963	1964	1965	1966	1967	1968	1969	1970
Jan.	1	96	217	350	128	266	27	163	298	76	197
Jan.	8	179	315	89	217	350	126	260	27	161	297
Jan.	15	275	54	179	302	86	225	349	112	257	36
Jan.	22	18	141	264	35	189	311	74	207	359	122
Jan.	29	105	225	1	136	275	35	173	306	85	206
Feb.	5	188	323	99	225	360	134	270	35	171	305
Feb.	12	284	64	187	310	95	235	357	121	267	45
Feb.	19	26	150	272	46	197	320	81	218	7	130
Feb.	26	113	234	11	144	283	45	182	315	93	216
Mar.	5	198	331	109	245	9	142	280	54	180	313
Mar.	12	293	73	195	332	105	244	5	142	277	54
Mar.	19	34	159	280	71	205	329	90	243	15	139
Mar.	26	122	243	19	167	291	54	190	338	101	226
Apr.	2	208	340	119	253	18	151	290	63	189	323
Apr.	9	303	82	204	340	116	252	14	150	288	62
Apr.	16	42	167	288	81	213	337	99	253	23	147
Apr.	23	130	253	28	176	299	64	198	347	109	235
Apr.	30	216	349	128	261	27	161	298	71	197	333
May	7	314	90	213	348	127	260	23	158	299	70
May	14	51	176	298	91	222	345	109	262	32	155
May	21	137	263	36	186	307	74	207	357	117	245
May	28	225	359	137	270	35	172	307	80	205	344
Jun.	4	325	98	222	357	137	268	31	168	309	78
Jun.	11	60	184	308	99	231	353	119	270	42	163
Jun.	18	146	272	45	195	315	82	217	6	126	253
Jun.	25	233	10	145	279	43	183	315	89	214	355
Jul.	2	336	106	230	6	147	276	40	178	318	87
Jul.	9	70	191	318	108	241	1	129	279	51	171
Jul.	16	154	281	56	204	324	91	227	14	135	261
Jul.	23	241	21	153	288	52	193	323	98	223	5
Jul.	30	345	115	238	16	156	286	47	188	327	97
Aug.	6	79	200	327	116	250	10	138	288	60	180
Aug.	13	163	289	66	212	333	99	238	22	144	270
Aug.	20	250	32	161	296	61	203	331	106	233	14
Aug.	27	353	124	246	27	164	295	55	199	335	106
Sep.	3	88	208	336	126	259	19	147	297	68	189
Sep.	10	172	297	77	220	342	108	249	30	152	279
Sep.	17	260	41	170	304	72	212	340	114	244	23
Sep.	24	1	134	254	37	172	304	64	208	344	115
Oct.	1	97	217	344	136	267	28	155	308	76	198
Oct.	8	180	306	88	228	351	117	259	38	161	289
Oct.	15	270	50	179	312	82	220	350	122	254	31
Oct.	22	10	143	262	47	182	313	73	217	353	123
Oct.	29	105	226	352	146	275	37	163	318	84	207
Nov.	5	189	315	97	237	359	127	268	47	168	299
Nov.	12	281	58	188	320	93	228	359	130	264	39
Nov.	19	19	151	271	55	191	321	82	225	3	131
Nov.	26	113	235	1	157	282	45	172	328	92	215
Dec.	3	197	326	105	245	7	138	276	55	176	310
Dec.	10	291	66	197	328	102	237	7	139	273	48
Dec.	17	30	159	280	63	202	329	91	234	13	139
Dec.	24	121	243	11	167	291	53	183	337	101	223
Dec.	31	204	336	113	254	14	149	284	64	184	320

		1971	1972	1973	1974	1975	1976	1977	1978	1979	1980
Jan.	1	335	109	246	8	147	279	56	179	318	90
Jan.	8	71	197	332	108	243	6	144	278	54	176
Jan.	15	158	283	69	207	328	93	240	18	139	263
Jan.	22	244	20	169	292	54	192	339	102	224	4
Jan.	29	344	117	255	17	156	288	64	188	327	99
Feb.	5	81	204	342	116	253	14	153	287	63	184
Feb.	12	167	291	79	216	337	101	251	26	147	271
Feb.	19	252	31	177	300	62	203	347	110	233	14
Feb.	26	353	126	263	27	164	297	72	199	334	109
Mar.	5	91	224	351	124	262	34	162	296	72	204
Mar.	12	176	312	90	224	346	122	262	34	156	293
Mar.	19	261	55	185	309	72	226	356	118	243	37
Mar.	26	1	149	270	37	172	320	80	208	343	130
Apr.	2	100	233	360	134	270	43	170	307	80	213
Apr.	9	184	320	101	232	355	131	273	42	164	302
Apr.	16	271	64	194	317	82	235	5	126	254	46
Apr.	23	9	158	278	47	181	329	88	217	352	139
Apr.	30	109	242	8	145	278	52	178	318	88	222
May	7	193	329	111	240	3	141	282	50	173	312
May	14	281	73	203	324	92	243	14	134	264	54
May	21	19	167	287	55	191	337	97	226	3	147
May	28	117	251	16	156	286	61	187	328	96	231
Jun.	4	201	339	120	249	11	151	291	59	180	323
Jun.	11	291	81	213	333	102	252	23	143	273	63
Jun.	18	29	176	296	64	201	346	106	234	13	155
Jun.	25	125	260	25	167	295	69	196	338	105	239
Jul.	2	209	349	129	258	19	162	299	68	188	334
Jul.	9	300	90	222	341	111	261	32	152	282	72
Jul.	16	40	184	305	72	212	354	115	243	24	163
Jul.	23	133	268	35	176	303	78	206	347	114	248
Jul.	30	217	0	137	267	27	172	308	77	197	344
Aug.	6	309	99	230	350	120	271	40	161	290	83
Aug.	13	51	192	314	81	223	2	124	252	34	171
Aug.	20	142	276	45	185	312	86	217	356	123	256
Aug.	27	225	10	146	276	36	182	317	86	206	353
Sep.	3	317	109	238	360	128	281	48	170	299	93
Sep.	10	61	200	322	90	232	10	132	262	43	180
Sep.	17	151	284	56	193	321	94	228	4	132	264
Sep.	24	234	20	155	284	45	191	326	94	215	2
Oct.	1	325	120	246	9	136	291	56	179	308	103
Oct.	8	70	208	330	101	241	19	140	273	51	189
Oct.	15	160	292	66	202	330	102	238	12	140	273
Oct.	22	243	28	165	292	54	199	336	102	225	10
Oct.	29	334	130	254	17	146	301	64	187	318	112
Nov.	5	79	217	338	112	249	27	148	284	59	197
Nov.	12	169	300	76	210	339	111	247	21	148	282
Nov.	19	253	36	175	300	63	207	347	110	234	18
Nov.	26	344	139	262	25	156	310	73	195	329	120
Dec.	3	87	226	346	122	257	36	157	294	67	206
Dec.	10	177	310	84	220	347	121	255	31	156	292
Dec.	17	261	45	185	308	72	216	356	118	242	28
Dec.	24	355	148	271	33	167	318	81	203	340	128
Dec.	31	95	235	355	132	265	44	166	303	76	214

		1981	1982	1983	1984	1985	1986	1987	1988	1989	1990
Jan.	1	226	350	129	260	36	162	300	71	205	333
Jan.	8	315	89	225	346	126	260	36	156	297	72
Jan.	15	53	188	309	73	225	358	119	243	37	168
Jan.	22	149	272	35	176	319	82	206	348	129	252
Jan.	29	234	0	137	270	43	172	308	81	213	343
Feb.	5	324	98	234	354	135	270	44	164	306	82
Feb.	12	64	196	317	81	236	6	128	252	48	175
Feb.	19	157	280	45	185	328	90	217	356	138	260
Feb.	26	242	10	145	279	51	182	316	90	222	353
Mar.	5	332	108	242	15	143	280	52	185	313	93
Mar.	12	74	204	326	104	246	14	136	275	57	184
Mar.	19	166	288	55	208	337	97	227	19	147	268
Mar.	26	250	20	154	300	60	191	326	111	230	1
Apr.	2	340	119	250	24	151	291	60	194	322	103
Apr.	9	84	212	334	114	255	22	144	286	66	192
Apr.	16	175	296	66	216	346	106	237	27	156	276
Apr.	23	259	28	164	309	69	199	336	119	240	9
Apr.	30	349	130	258	33	160	302	68	203	331	113
May	7	93	221	342	124	264	31	152	297	75	201
May	14	184	304	75	225	355	114	246	36	165	285
May	21	268	36	175	317	78	207	347	127	249	18
May	28	358	140	266	41	170	311	76	211	341	122
Jun.	4	102	230	350	135	272	40	160	307	83	210
Jun.	11	193	313	84	234	3	123	255	45	173	294
Jun.	18	277	45	185	325	87	216	357	135	258	27
Jun.	25	8	149	275	49	180	320	85	219	352	130
Jul.	2	110	239	359	146	281	49	169	317	92	219
Jul.	9	201	322	93	244	11	133	263	55	181	304
Jul.	16	286	54	196	333	96	225	7	143	266	37
Jul.	23	19	158	284	57	191	328	94	227	3	138
Jul.	30	119	248	7	155	290	57	178	327	101	227
Aug.	6	210	331	101	254	19	142	272	66	189	313
Aug.	13	294	64	205	341	104	236	16	152	274	48
Aug.	20	30	166	293	66	202	337	103	236	13	147
Aug.	27	128	256	17	164	299	65	187	335	111	235
Sep.	3	218	340	110	264	27	151	281	75	197	321
Sep.	10	302	75	214	350	112	247	24	160	282	59
Sep.	17	40	174	302	74	212	345	112	245	23	156
Sep.	24	138	264	26	172	309	73	197	343	121	243
Oct.	1	226	349	119	274	36	159	292	84	206	329
Oct.	8	310	86	222	359	120	258	32	169	291	70
Oct.	15	50	183	310	84	220	354	120	255	31	165
Oct.	22	148	272	35	181	319	81	206	352	130	251
Oct.	29	234	357	130	282	44	167	303	92	214	337
Nov.	5	318	96	230	8	129	268	40	178	300	79
Nov.	12	58	193	318	93	229	4	128	265	39	175
Nov.	19	158	280	44	190	329	90	214	2	139	260
Nov.	26	243	5	141	290	53	175	314	100	223	345
Dec.	3	327	106	238	16	139	277	49	185	310	88
Dec.	10	66	203	326	103	237	14	136	274	48	185
Dec.	17	167	288	52	200	337	98	222	12	147	269
Dec.	24	252	13	152	298	62	184	324	108	232	355
Dec.	31	337	114	248	24	149	285	59	193	320	96

		1991	1992	1993	1994	1995	1996	1997	1998	1999	2000
Jan.	1	111	242	15	145	281	53	185	317	92	223
Jan.	8	206	326	108	244	16	136	279	56	186	307
Jan.	15	289	54	210	337	99	225	21	147	270	37
Jan.	22	18	158	299	61	190	329	110	231	2	140
Jan.	29	119	252	23	155	290	62	193	326	101	232
Feb.	5	214	335	116	254	24	145	287	66	193	315
Feb.	12	298	63	220	345	108	235	31	155	278	47
Feb.	19	29	166	308	69	201	337	119	239	12	148
Feb.	26	128	260	32	164	299	70	202	335	111	240
Mar.	5	222	356	124	265	32	166	295	76	201	337
Mar.	12	306	87	229	354	116	259	39	164	285	72
Mar.	19	39	189	317	77	211	360	128	248	22	170
Mar.	26	138	280	41	172	310	90	212	343	121	260
Apr.	2	230	5	133	275	40	175	305	86	210	345
Apr.	9	314	98	237	3	123	270	47	173	294	83
Apr.	16	49	198	326	86	220	9	136	257	31	180
Apr.	23	148	288	50	180	320	98	221	351	132	268
Apr.	30	238	13	143	284	48	183	315	95	218	353
May	7	322	109	245	12	132	281	55	182	302	93
May	14	57	207	335	95	228	18	144	267	39	190
May	21	158	296	59	189	330	106	230	1	141	276
May	28	247	21	154	292	57	191	326	103	227	1
Jun.	4	330	119	253	21	141	291	64	190	311	102
Jun.	11	66	217	343	105	236	28	152	276	48	199
Jun.	18	168	304	68	199	340	114	238	11	150	285
Jun.	25	256	29	165	300	66	199	337	111	236	10
Jul.	2	339	129	262	29	150	300	73	198	321	111
Jul.	9	74	227	351	114	245	38	160	285	57	209
Jul.	16	177	313	76	210	348	123	246	22	158	293
Jul.	23	265	38	175	309	75	208	347	120	245	19
Jul.	30	349	137	272	37	160	308	83	206	331	119
Aug.	6	83	237	359	123	255	48	169	293	67	218
Aug.	13	186	322	84	221	356	132	254	33	166	302
Aug.	20	273	47	185	318	83	218	356	129	253	29
Aug.	27	358	146	282	45	169	317	93	214	340	128
Sep.	3	93	246	7	131	265	56	177	301	78	226
Sep.	10	194	331	92	231	4	141	263	43	174	311
Sep.	17	281	56	194	327	91	228	5	138	261	39
Sep.	24	8	154	292	53	178	326	102	223	349	137
Oct.	1	104	254	16	139	276	64	186	310	89	234
Oct.	8	202	339	101	241	13	149	273	53	183	319
Oct.	15	289	66	202	337	99	238	13	148	269	49
Oct.	22	16	164	301	61	187	336	111	231	357	148
Oct.	29	115	262	25	148	287	72	195	318	100	242
Nov.	5	211	347	111	250	22	157	283	61	193	326
Nov.	12	297	76	211	346	107	247	22	157	277	58
Nov.	19	24	174	309	70	194	346	119	240	5	159
Nov.	26	126	270	33	156	297	80	203	328	109	251
Dec.	3	220	355	121	258	31	165	293	69	202	334
Dec.	10	305	85	220	355	115	256	31	165	286	67
Dec.	17	32	185	317	79	203	357	127	249	13	169
Dec.	24	135	278	41	166	306	89	211	338	117	260
Dec.	31	230	3	131	266	41	173	303	78	211	343

Lunar Cycles

Your **lunar high** occurs when the Moon is in the same sign as your natal Sun. If you are a Sagittarius, for example, your lunar high will occur when the Moon is in Sagittarius. The result would be a time of inspiration, when new ventures could be successfully implemented. It is a day when you are most emotionally like your Sun sign. It is a day when your thinking is most sound.

Your **lunar low** occurs when the Moon is in the sign opposite your natal Sun. If you are a Taurus, your lunar low would occur when the Moon is in Scorpio. Since you are least sure of your decisions on this day, try to postpone major decisions. You will run into opposition in whatever you may start. This is, however, a good day to exchange ideas since you are much more aware of other people. You may feel restless and will want to keep busy. Plan constructive (but not demanding) projects.

If you know the sign and degree of the Moon at the time of your birth, you can determine your **lunar birthday**—when the transiting Moon is conjunct (in the same sign as your natal Moon). If your natal Moon is in Gemini, your lunar birthday is when the Moon is in Gemini. This is a time when you respond rather than initiate. You might be absorbed in feelings and sensations. You will often want to be in the company of women on this day.

If you know the positions of your natal planets, you can plot the Moon's passage over these points.

Mercury: A good day for ideas and communications.

Venus: Go out and have a good time.

Mars: Work hard. You may be irritating or irritated.

Jupiter: Don't overindulge. You feel optimistic and self-confident.

Saturn: Look into yourself. You are realistic and feeling serious today.

Uranus: Surprises and excitement. A good day to explore and experiment.

Neptune: You are very emotional. You may forget things and feel lost.

Pluto: You want to be alone.

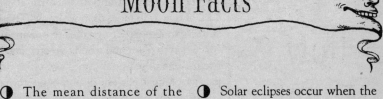

Moon Facts

- The mean distance of the Moon from Earth is 238,857 miles.

- The mean orbital speed of the Moon is 2,287 miles per hour.

- The Moon rotates at approximately 10 miles per hour.

- The circumference of the Moon is 6,790 miles.

- The diameter of the Moon is 2,160 miles.

- The Full Moon occurs when the Moon is exactly opposite the Sun.

- The Moon's gravity works together with the centrifugal force from the earth's revolution and with the Sun's gravity to create the tides.

- It is believed that the center of the Moon is molten. Disruptions from this molten center cause Moon quakes.

- Lunar eclipses occur when the earth moves between the Sun and the Moon.

- Lunar eclipses can only happen at a Full Moon.

- Solar eclipses happen between 2 and 5 times per year.

- Solar eclipses occur when the Moon moves between the earth and the Sun.

- Solar eclipses can only happen at a New Moon.

- There are never more than 3 lunar eclipses in one year.

- Lunar eclipses always happen within 14 days of a solar eclipse. They can occur either before or after the solar eclipse.

- There are usually 13 Full Moons in one year. The second Full Moon in a month is called the Blue Moon.

- The apogee is the point where the Moon's orbit takes it farthest from the Sun. The perigee is the point where the Moon is closest to the sun.

- During the time between the first quarter Moon and the Full Moon, the Moon is said to be in its gibbous phase.

- The lunar nodes are the points at which the orbital path of the Moon crosses the ecliptic. The ecliptic is the plane of the earth's orbit around the Sun.

How Moon Phases Affect Our Lives

By Jackie Slevin

The shining disk in the night sky that has held human attention since the dawn of time tells more than we know. Those shifting shadows that signalled to our ancestors when to plant and when to reap marked the passage of seasonal cycles as well as the passage of life itself. The display of nocturnal celestial phenomenon held a myriad of visual delights; planets "wandered," stars twinkled, and meteors darted about in showers of light. Many star patterns remained constant for the navigation of nomadic tribes. One thing was certain; the Great White Circle was always changing its appearance. It mysteriously monitored the growth patterns of the mineral, vegetable, and animal kingdoms, and these kingdoms were in a continual state of change, for change is the only evidence of life.

To observe the Moon's phases was to partake in the ritual of reflection, which is indeed the Moon's favorite pastime. This distant disk symbolized the patterns of development from life to death, as virtually all living things have a beginning, a middle, and an end. We're all familiar with the biblical quote from Ecclesiastes that became a credo for the sixties: "To everything there is a season and a time for every purpose under heaven.[1]"

The Moon pulls the trigger on timing the events that define the experiences of our lives. It can only be observed through the reflection of the Sun and, since it is the nature of the Sun to shine with a fierce light, we can only too easily become blinded by it. Being too bright to comfortably observe, the best way to view cosmic light was from reflection of the Moon. Although the Sun is 400 times larger than the Moon, the Moon is 400 times closer to the Earth. All the better for earthly observation on a clear night. Early peoples knew it was a powerful mirror of their earthly experience and behavior, and thus began to record the occurrences of the changes, or phases, which happened eight times during each cycle. Some of the most primitive etchings on rocks discovered on archaeological sites worldwide are the recordings of the Moon phases, and these rough etchings were humankind's first calendars. As the phases repeated themselves without fail over time, the lunar calendar was formulated.

What better way to streamline your life than to plan your schedule according to Nature's timekeeper? The Great White Circle and Her measured movements determine the rhythm of the tides, shellfish activity and marine life, and the surface tension of all fluids on the planet; not to mention the moods of the public. "It has been shown that at the time of the Full Moon, and especially during a lunar eclipse, the surface tension of all fluids is increased (the molecular cohesive forces of the surface of any fluid). Because our bodies consist largely of water, this increase in molecular tension is bound to produce a biochemical effect upon our bodies. Furthermore, our bodies tend to take on and hold larger quantities of water during the Full Moon phase each month. The skull, being the only area of the body that cannot readily expand with increased fluid pressure,

> *We shall never learn to feel and respect our real calling and destiny, unless we have taught ouselves to consider everything as moonshine, compared with the education of the heart*
>
> —Sir Walter Scott

therefore exerts greater pressure upon the brain cells, which ultimately effect our behavior patterns.'" Is it any wonder that the root word for lunatic is *luna*, which is Latin for Moon?

Since the Moon rules the Mother principle and Mother Nature in general, let's take a look at how She intended the population to perform in their daily lives. It's Her prerogative to change Her mind, only She calls it a phase. She always comes through on schedule and would like you to follow Her example. Your Mother should know.

The first phase is the New Moon, the Dark Night of the Moon, when darkness reigns. No lunar reflection is visible; living organisms are left to their own devices with no magnetic field to guide them. All life forms stem from chaos and void. The New Moon symbolizes life at its most basic form, the seed. In order for a seed to sprout, survival tactics come front and center. It is a pure, masculine energy, the primitive warrior who lives on impulse and thrives on spontaneous action, requiring no direction whatsoever. Instinct is its only guide. Mental awareness is acute, yet full consciousness is not present. During this wholly subjective time it is best to plant seeds in all forms, whether you plant a garden, devise a new method of strate-

gy or undertake a new project, the New Moon is the starting point. Not every seed is expected to sprout, as any gardener will tell you. Nor will every project reach the finish line, yet this is the time for laying the foundation for your desired goal. One never knows where their beginnings will lead them. You're at the starting line and the shot is being fired. Go for it! Great oaks from little acorns grow.

The following phase is the Crescent Moon, the time of manifestation, when the seeds sprout. The wise gardener now examines his bed of seeds and thins out those that never sprouted; they are cast aside for the scavenging birds. The promises, vows, and plans that were established during the New Moon are now revised, as new developments have come into play. Some prospects, like the discarded seeds, have also been completely forgotten. Those visible green shoots, however, represent the first stage of development of your new desire. They struggled through the metamorphosis from tiny speck to organic growth and, needless to say, not everybody else made it through. Your projected thoughts have taken form, and it is in this Crescent phase that we are most vulnerable. There is much unconscious resistance in public attitude during this period and the phrase "yeah, but..." is the order of the day. Like toddlers in the playground, we're up and running, but our definitive outcomes remain to be seen. Just as all promises are not delivered, not all sprouts take root. Those that do move on to the next stage of development—seedlings.

The first quarter Moon, also known as the Half Moon, is the phase of the seedling. Our goals have now taken root in our consciousness and sprouted leaves; future growth is assured as there is no turning back. We're now bound and determined to deliver the promises we made at the New Moon, revised or otherwise. Literally or figuratively, we roll up our sleeves and seize an opportunity to do something—anything—to see our projects through. We become walking combustible missiles in action; we'll find a crisis or make one happen, but we just can't keep still. The outer world steps in with its own agenda and requires us to conform to some degree. Who does it think it is, anyway? Whether this agenda rewards our efforts or throws a monkey wrench at us, we're ready for it. We're in the emotional state of the teenager and we need action, whether it's a challenge to our abilities or a rebellion to launch. If we're confused and don't know which way to turn, this is the time to seek guidance and/or direction. Move over, Superman, we're coming through.

While undergoing baptism by fire, we are faced with the fact that moving forward with a burning tenacity can lead to problems. Flies in the ointment become inevitable, but they are met with anger and frustration. We're now in the phase of the Gibbous Moon, where we find ourselves up against a rock and a hard place. After such a good start with the greatest enthusiasm, why do we meet up with such obstacles at this point? This phase can bring disillusionment in its wake as we're so close, yet so far. The plant is now ready to bloom, but it can't bloom fast enough. Something has to give. It's time to rehash, rewrite, and clarify, because nobody told you there'd be days like these. Analyze your options and put yourself in a survivor mode. Pull out all the stops on patience and let go and let God.

The Moon is now at the end of Her waxing phase; she will no longer increase in light as She's reached Her fullest point of illumination. The Full Moon is the Moon in full bloom. She's all lit up doing her balancing act with the Earth, as She's exactly opposite the Earth during this time. The mood of the population is now blazing at a high pitch and it's open season on human behavior. The Full Moon uses Her magnetic field to influence the water levels in our bodies to harness all our capabilities and bring our actions to fruition. The results of this polarity send a push me-pull you message to earth dwellers to stand in the spotlight of your own particular achievement, because it's ready to harvest. You've reached your goal; you can't shine any brighter than you do right now and if you're not feeling particularly fulfilled during this time, discontent and frustration may take root and flourish and you may shine in a dark light. All that increased illumination and heightened magnetic energy field has to get channeled somewhere, and if you haven't planned your schedule according the Moon's phases, Mother Nature's orchestrations become distorted. Agitation becomes blown out of proportion and thus we encounter Full Moon madness; the negative manifestations of which are legendary. Bask in the light of achievement or howl uncontrollably; the choice is yours. We also become obsessed with relationships during this time, as the Moon is exactly opposite the Earth. It's as if the two Lights are pitted against each other in a cosmic game of ping pong and heightened sensations are the ball. The Full Moon marks the end of the waxing phase; She has increased Her light to her full capacity and now begins Her journey home.

After the emotional feeding frenzy of the Full Moon comes the Disseminating Moon, or what this writer refers to as the "Morning After Moon." The party's over; all that high anxiety has passed. Depending on how we reacted during the heightened awareness of the Full Moon, we either cry in our coffee or delight in our results. As the Full Moon represented the plant in full bloom, the Disseminating Moon symbolizes the fruit on the vine. This is the time when we review where we've been, where we are now, and decide our next move. If this process requires deep introspection and painful realization, then so be it. Now is the time to re-hone our skills and demonstrate and distribute. The profit-minded gardener or farmer now harvests his or her crop and promptly heads for the marketplace. The fruit must be picked, or else it will die on the vine. The rest of the population wisely holds their current projects up to the light and troubleshoots for any flaws. This is the sum total of our work and, whether we're satisfied or not, we must put our name on it and accept it in its final form. Our growing season has ended and we'll reap what we've sown. This is also the time to reach out and lend a hand to your neighbor who is having trouble harvesting their crop, or bringing their projects into their final phase. In so doing, you might just get first pick before it all goes to the market. To disseminate means to scatter or disperse widely and, in biblical terms, we must now cast our bread upon the waters and it will return to us a hundredfold.

The Last Quarter Moon represents pay day in terms of consciousness. Our tally sheets are on the cosmic payroll desk and this phase of the Moon will determine our commission and ultimate income. If we completed our tasks and followed through on schedule, we can honestly and humbly expect our just desserts. Are we pleased with our harvest or final result? If so, we can pass "Go," collect $200 and remain a player. If not, gnawing feelings of inadequacy rise to the surface and we must come to terms with the reality that, in order to remedy our output, then we have to change on the inside in order to improve on the outside. This can result in private disappointment coupled with internal crisis as slowly we turn and head back to the drawing board. Just as the plant that grew from the seed at the New Moon has withered and now died a natural death, so our inner structure may wither to make room for the new season of growth. The lunar cycle is winding down and coming in for the home stretch.

Draw the veil. The Dark Night of the Moon is upon us. This last and final phase is known as Balsamic, an Old English noun with several definitions. One of which is an "aromatic ointment for ceremonial or medicinal use.[3]", another is "any

agency that heals, soothes and restores[4]".This is the perfect description of this Dark Night, as this is the time to retreat, restore, and rejuvenate. It's the time to let go of the Moon's magnetic tie on us and be cast adrift in the void so that the soothing energy can filter through and the healing can take place. The field must be weeded and the desk cleared. It's the time to withdraw and meditate. Psychic energy is at its peak as we let our intuition guide us through the shoals in darkness, by tuning in, inner navigation is successful. By shutting out, we may encounter fog and chaos. Here in the Dark Night we contemplate our higher purpose and clear the path for Destiny to take over. In this midnight of the psyche, Mother Nature tucks us in for a good night's sleep. She's come full circle back to the beginning, and She wants us to be well rested for the forthcoming New Moon. We'll need all our energy for the new growing season. Mom always did know best.

Bibliography

1 Ecclesiastes, Chapter 3.

2 Jansky, Robert Carl. *Interpreting the Eclipses*. Astro Computing Services, 1977. P. 24.

3 *Webster's Unabriged New World Dictionary*. Barnes and Noble Books, 1989. P. 115.

4 Ibid.

The Lunar Calendar

By K. D. Spitzer

The double-faced god Janus guards the turning of the year and calls for contemplation regarding the passing of the old year and the advent of the new. This is an arbitrary benchmark, however, and is part of a solar-based calendar. We adopted the solar-based calendar in this country in 1752, although its origin goes back to Pope Gregory, who dictated the January 1st to December 31st span in 1582 to reconcile a 10-day discrepancy in the old calendar first established by Julius Caesar.

This is, in fact, only one of the calendars in our lives, and it is civil. Others are astrological, religious, ritual, social, fiscal, and natural.

The Great Goddess Moon was the first reassuring presence used to mark the passage of time. There was, of course, the movement from daylight to night and then to daylight again, but that just required a simple one/two counting procedure using the Sun by day and Moon by night. On the other hand, the Moon as shapeshifter offered a slow and changing passage through the night skies so that its very journey presented a record that could be counted.

Calendars based on lunar cycles reckon time as beginning and ending at sunset. In nomadic or agricultural societies, the lunar year originally was only 10 months long with a period about 2 - 3 months in the winter called the dark time. Work in the fields, gardens, and woods ceased and this period was used for social activities and rest.

It is interesting to note that the English word of measurement comes from an old English word for the Moon, and its origins are even older than that. Clearly the Moon was an important constant in the natural rhythm of life that later required the ability to count and measure.

The first noticeable occurrence of the Moon divides the night sky into its two largest components: a period of time when the Moon punctuates the dark and an equal period when it does not. Each of those periods can be divided in half again. The English word "fortnight" refers to 14 nights, and that word is derived from a word meaning "the span of time from the New Moon to the Full Moon, which of course is 14 nights. A "sennight" is the seven nights of each quarter of the Moon. So many cultures have used the span of 7 nights as a ritual measure that 7 has become a sacred number.

A remnant of the Coligny Calendar of the Celts, which residesign a museum in France, divides the Lunar cycle in half and, as is common with this method, groups most of the "good" days in the first half of the cycle and clusters the "bad" days at the end. It shows a 62 "Moons" cycle of 5 years plus a couple of "months" of catch-up to keep the whole in time with the seasons.

This was undoubtedly part of a larger 19-year cycle which was worked out at calendar sites like Stonehenge and others on the Continent.

People around the world have used the Moon to measure time. Some counted from Full Moon to Full Moon; others counted

The Moon as shapeshifter offered a slow and changing passage through the night skies so that its very journey presented a record that could be counted

from the New Moon. Some cultures needed to name just the phases and others, like the Chinese and Hawaiians, had a need to name each night of the cycle.

Full Moons were named for the activities that took place under their light, or described conditions at the time of their occurrence. The January Full Moon has been known as the Snow Moon, the Wolf Moon, the Frost on the Inside of the Lodge Moon, and most descriptive of all in the northern latitudes, the Hunger Moon.

The Arab world still uses a Moon-based calendar, and the fact that until this century they were largely a nomadic people may explain it. It was only when tribes moved from hunting and gathering and settled in permanent locations that they needed a more reliable system to mark the seasons and meet their needs.

The Babylonians kept track of lunar cycles by watching the Moon move through certain constellations. This type of measurement marked the beginning of lunar astrology, and also the lunar calendar. Partially because of their Sun worship, the Egyptians developed a purely solar calendar of 12 months, each equally of 30 days, plus another five that were inserted to keep it aligned with the Nile inundation.

Using just the Moon for counting throws off the whole system within the first year; the seasons which are dominated by the Sun do not line up with the Moon cycles. A lunar year of 12 months is 354 days, which is 11.25 days short of a solar year. To add another month to make 13 is 383 days, or 17.34 days too many.

Counting by the Sun offers a longer cycle, and when the Babylonians figured out how to quarter it with the Solstices and Equinoxes, the solar calendar year began to blend quite nicely with the agricultural seasons. However, this did not provide for festival times, and so the next problem for astronomers and mathematicians was blending the lunar and solar cycles.

The Greek myth about Atalante is probably a calendar tale. Atalante, who represents the Moon, can outrun anybody. In the myth, she offers her virtue to anyone who can best her in a foot race. The entrance fee was high; to lose the race is to lose one's life.

Atalante is unbeatable for many years until finally the Goddess Aphrodite gets tired of Atalante's eternal virginity. To even the odds, she offers three golden apples to Hippomenes, who throws them down during the race. As Atalante stops to pick up each apple, Hippomenes is able to pass her and win the race. The three apples represent the three extra months the Greeks needed to add to their calendar so the Sun and Moon would arrive at the same point.

Eclipses and the need to predict their arrival with pinpoint accuracy also fueled the drive for an exact calendar. For many cultures, the ability to predict an eclipse had serious dynastic consequences.

The Egyptians in particular needed timed cycles that coincided with the Nile flooding. Their system was a little more complicated as it also required reliance upon the Dog Star Sirius in combination with the Sun and Moon. Indeed it was the Egyptian astronomers who first managed to marry the cycles of the Sun and Moon into a civil calendar for Julius Caesar.

This calendar was the Julian Calendar, and 1500 years later was only 10 days off. When you consider all the problems involved in making a satisfactory marriage of solar and lunar cycles, this was a relatively small margin for error. It was beginning to be a problem, however, when Pope Gregory advocated, not only adding these 10 days, but also an extra day every fourth year. With some other minor tinkering, it is still the calendar we use today.

So when you settle in for your new year ruminations, remember the sage advice of Sargon, the old Babylonian who said that if the Moon can be seen the first night of the year, the country will be peaceful; the heart of the country will rejoice. 1996 commences with the Moon in the first quarter in Taurus. Pour a one quarter glass of white wine to toast the Queen of the Night Skies and offer a batch of the following in tribute. Most of the ingredients are ruled by the Moon.

Crab and Shrimp Toasts

- 1 cup flaked white crabmeat
- ¾ cup cleaned cooked shrimp
- 2 teaspoons lemon juice
- 2 Tablespoons butter
- ¼ cup flour
- 1¼ cup 2% milk
- 2 Tablespoons marsala or sherry
- 1 Tablespoons minced parsley
- 2 Tablespoons whipping cream
  Salt and pepper
- 4 toasted baguette slices

Mix crab, shrimp, and lemon juice and set aside. Melt butter in a saucepan, stir in flour, and cook one minute. Remove from heat and gradually stir in milk. Return to heat and bring to boil, stirring constantly. Reduce heat and simmer 5 minutes. Stir in the wine; remove from heat and add parsley, cream, and seafood. Season to taste with salt and pepper. Spread on toasts and garnish with parsley. Serves 4.

Lunar Eclipses

By K.D. Spitzer

Everyone knows that eclipses are an evil omen. At most, they are viewed with uncertainty; at the very worst, they can portend bad luck for an individual, a tribe, or even a nation. They can foretell war, famine, destruction, or death!

Assigning this kind of power to heavenly bodies invites serious study of them. Investigation is necessary to ascertain the possibilities of predicting eclipses. The easiest way to begin is with simple observation. This, of course, is a mysterious concept to those of us who can't recognize a phase of the Moon without resorting to an almanac!

Briefly, solar eclipses occur at the dark of the Moon or the New Moon. Both Sun and Moon are conjunct at this time; that is they are both in the same line of observation from the Earth. Ordinarily, because of their proximity, the New Moon cannot reflect any light from the Sun, but about every six months it also partially or totally blocks the Sun light to the observers on Earth.

A lunar eclipse occurs when the Moon is full, and reflecting sunlight across the entire surface visible to earthlings. The astronomical lineup for this has the Earth sandwiched between the opposing Sun and Moon. It doesn't happen with every Full Moon, but about every six months the Moon travels through the shadow cast by the Earth standing in the Sun's light.

Civilizations all over the world used observation to set up simple calendars and in turn begin to predict eclipses and other planetary activity. Quite often astronomers were put on the public payroll in order to protect the state against unseen and mysterious forces. This could backfire on these soothsayers.

For example, in ancient Athens a lunar eclipse was predicted to occur on the eve of a major war with Syracuse. The Athenian king was advised by his astrologers to keep the fleet safe in the harbor; the omens suggested the ships would be destroyed, most likely in the coming battle.

The lunar eclipse occurred as predicted and naturally a storm blew up. (It was a full Moon, comprehende? It brings increased storms and rain...) After bypassing the Syracuse fleet and leaving it safely at sea, the ferocious storm swept to shore and sunk almost every ship in the harbor. Surviving written reports do not mention it, but the Athenians probably killed the astrologers.

Many ancient civilizations used a lunar-based calendar. In some ways, this required more scientific skill to produce than a solar-based calendar. Although it does not appear so, the Moon follows a regular sweep through the sky. The Sun is a little easier to track as it takes six months to reach its outside limits on the horizon: at midsummer on the northern horizon and midwinter on the southern. The Moon reaches its limits in only two weeks.

However, there is an additional and very subtle movement of the Moon. Those northern and southern boundaries change very slowly through the course of an 18.61 year cycle. The Moon sweeps out an a broad elliptic for nine years and then narrows down for another nine.

Everyone knows that eclipses are an evil omen. At most, they are viewed with uncertainty; at the very worst, they can portend bad luck for an individual, a tribe, or even a nation

The Moon's orbit does not parallel the Earth's orbit, although it passes through it twice a year. These points where it passes are called the Moon's nodes. When the Moon passes through the Earth's ecliptic from below, this point is called the ascending node, north node, or dragon's head. The way back is the descending node, south node or dragon's tail. It is the 18.61 year cycle that marks its repeat to the original point on the ecliptic.

To add to the confusion, it takes 346.62 days or one eclipse year for the Sun to "travel" from the north node to the south node and then back again. This eclipse year is 20 days shorter than the tropical year because of the declination of the moon's orbit. In practical terms, this mean that we have an eclipse every 173.31 days or about 20 days earlier than the year before.

We should not casually underestimate the difficulty of first discovering and then measuring the 18.61 year cycle. First of all, sometimes the Moon reaches its outside limits during the day and thus is invisible. The Moon's phases do not follow a regular pattern with these limits and therefore, one might actually observe a Full Moon, but a New Moon or thin crescent Moon might be missed. Also, eclipses may not be apparent in the part of the world where astrologers are sitting and waiting for it.

It would take a couple of generations to mark the 18.61 year cycle, test it, and then anticipate it. Also, this cycle is more easily observed in the northern latitudes than in the southern; so it is altogether remarkable that the Babylonian and Mayan astronomers not only noted it, but built remarkably accurate calendars that incorporated the cycle.

The Mayan and Babylonian astronomers favored a mathematical approach, based on the phases of the Moon and the eclipses themselves. It is in direct contrast to the Greek approach and that of the megalithic builders who measured the orbital swings of the Sun and Moon along the horizon.

A salient characteristic of stone circles like Stonehenge in England or even the one found in Wyoming, are the stone markers to observe the northern and southern lunar standstills as well as the 18.61 year cycle. The Aubrey holes at Stonehenge, according to some astroarcheologists, were established to help make eclipse predictions.

Eclipses are serious business in agricultural societies, especially ones that venerate or fear heavenly objects. In what is called the Dresden Codex, the Mayans kept such accurate count of Lunar and Solar cycles that their eclipse table is off by only one day in 4500 years. (Of course, as the Athenian astrologers could attest, it is one thing to accurately predict an eclipse and an entirely different matter altogether to discern its meaning!)

Then there is the case in ancient China. Eclipses were not evil omens there, but an actual dragon eating the Moon. Fortunately the all-powerful emperor could slay the dragon and save the Moon for the continuing prosperity of the farmers. In order to remain prepared for this ahead of time, he secretly kept astrologers on the public payroll.

Chinese astrologers in general were fond of wine, women, and Moon watching; and as part of the contract, all were provided by the state. One eclipse season, the astrologers were so busy enjoying the first two that they forgot about the last one. The emperor did not get his early warning and thus could not commence the ritual to slay the dragon. Consequently, the public went into a panic and there was a crisis of confidence in the government. You can bet the rent that the astrologers were the first to go in and clean up.

Lunar Eclipses

October 8, 1995 at 14°54

This is a penumbral lunar eclipse and will be visible in the Northwestern US. The Penumbra is an area which is partially illuminated but is outside the actual deep shadow cast by the Earth. It is sort of like a halo.

April 4, 1996 at 14°31

This is a total lunar eclipse which will be visible in the Eastern US when the Moon is rising.

September 27, 1996 at 4°17

This a total lunar eclipse which will be visible in most of North America.

Note the move this year from a Taurus/Scorpio axis to an Aries/Libra one.

Moon Lore

When the Sun takes to its bed of gold, a silver light rises to light the Earth. A gentle creature, much shyer than her garish brother, the Moon rules with a gossamer hand. For all of her tender ways, her tug is strong, just like the soft hand of a willful mother. She rules the tides of sea and sailor, pulling us all into her mysterious realm. For some, her secret ways are welcome; for others, frightening. For all, they are fascinating. Here are some of the ways our ancestors viewed and relied on the Moon and her powers.

Precautions

Anyone who works in a hospital will be able to tell you the origins of the word "lunacy." It's proven that many more disturbances of violence or mental imbalance occur during the Full Moon. As Shakespeare said in Othello, "It is the very error of the Moon, She comes more nearer Earth than she was wont, and makes men mad." To avoid the Moon's effect on your personality, you have to plan ahead. First, pick buttercups when the Moon is in the sign of the bull or the scorpion. Then press them to your neck in the wane of the Moon. Hold them steadily there for at least 9 minutes, more if you suspect you may have serious problems like becoming a werewolf or other severe symptoms. This accomplished, you will be free of lunacy.

You must watch out, though; sleeping in the Moonlight can still bring tragic results, whatever the precautions. No decent

By Verna Gates

mother would allow a child to sleep in the Moonlight for fear of poor math skills, and in severe cases, Moon-blindness. Sailors never sleep on deck when the Moon is out. They dread color blindness, a real handicap when it can already be difficult to decipher sky from sea. To point at the Moon seven times also risks instant loss of sight.

In general, if you are concerned about Moonlit nights, use this simple Irish charm: "I see the Moon and the Moon sees me. God bless the priest who christened me." If you don't happen to be Catholic, you can substitute the words "God bless the sailors on the sea" (who always need a little extra protection) or "God bless the Moon and God bless me." Any of these variations should do the trick.

In these days of sunscreens and dire warnings of sunburns, you may be more worried about the Sun's effect than the Moon's. To avoid the damage of Sun-exposed skin, you can protect yourself for several summers by taking precautions during an eclipse. The secret is to burn a palm leaf as a sacrifice. This activity will give the added benefit of preventing sunstroke.

> *It is the very error of the Moon, She comes more nearer Earth than she was wont, and makes men mad*
>
> —Shakespeare

Marriage

Determining whom you will marry is an important aspect of life, even in these liberated days. However, in the time when a woman's entire future was based on whom she met at the end of the aisle, it was impera-

tive to make the right choice. Naturally, the mystical abilities of the Moon were brought in to give her assistance. An old charm advises maidens to take a new black handkerchief out during the first new Moon of the new year. Hold the handkerchief up so that it hangs between you and the Moon. (If you can't afford a black silk hanky, you can cross your hands in front of your eyes three times and peer through your fingers.) Then say:

New Moon, New Moon, I greet thee!

Grant me this night my true love to see,

Not in Sunday best nor worst array,

But in his clothes for everyday;

That tomorrow I may know him,

From among all other men.

Now, walk backwards until you are inside and in your bed. Speak to know one and get straight under the covers. Go to sleep as fast as you can and you will dream of your future husband.

Once you find your mate, always marry during a growing Moon. Many cultures believe the Full Moon will bless you. On Mangaia Island, the Full Moon is a woman named Ina, a noble wife. She spins all the day, crafting a cloth of pure white clouds. When she was younger, she took a husband of the Earth to live with her on the Moon.

As his days grew short, she sent him home on a rainbow, as her kingdom could not be witness to death. As Earth's women marry beneath her shining full face, she grants the union years of happiness.

Others say the woman in the Moon is Mary Magdalene, who lives there to atone for her sins in life. The spots are formed from the many tears she sheds over past misdeeds. She, too, will shine down with grace on maidens marrying their beloved under a Full Moon.

As the old folks say, never use an old Moon to lead home a wife, or you'll never be happy in life. If you want lots of children, marry under a Full Moon. This fat, round orb will fill your life with fertility.

Childbearing

Forget the new technology to determine a child's sex. Just think back to conception. If you conceived during the light of the Moon (New Moon to Full), the baby is a boy. If you conceived during the dark of the Moon (Full Moon to New Moon), the baby is a girl. This technique also works if you want to predetermine the sex of your child. Just be alert to the Moon through the bedroom window, especially since in Greenland the women believe they can get pregnant just by lying in the Moonlight!

A pregnant woman should never issue forth in the Full Moon. Unless, of course, she ties a set of keys around her waist, covering the baby. Otherwise, the child will be born with a harelip or other wolfish features.

For ease of delivery, try to plan for a Moon on the increase. The baby tends to be in charge of its birth time, so pray for a child willing to be born on a waxing Moon, and not a waning. The hardest labors of all occur during the New Moon, the time when old folks say, it's as dark as the inside of a cow.

As for the child, contradictions abound. Some say no Moon, no man. In *The Return of the Native* Thomas Hardy records that a child born at the New Moon never comes to anything. Others say if you are born when the Moon is one day old, you will live a long life with plenty of wealth. A child who is smart enough to give his mother ease and be born in the light of the Moon will surely be intelligent.

Children

To discipline children, especially around the holidays, it's only necessary to remind them of the man on the Moon. He's there for his lack of self-control. He suffered from an unusual attraction to cabbages, not a serious problem in adolescents of today, but perhaps in olden times. At any rate, his cravings became so powerful that he resolved to steal a few heads for his supper. That in itself isn't so bad, but his timing was terrible. He stole on Christmas Eve. As soon as the deed was accomplished, a child in white, riding a white horse, galloped straight up to him and said, "You who would thieve on a holy night, get thee and thy sack to the Moon!" There he sits with no cabbages, to serve as an example to the young.

Enterprises

First of all, check where the New Moon rises. For good luck all month, at whatever you undertake to do, be sure the New Moon rises over your right shoulder. The people of many lands have sworn by the ability of the Waxing Moon to help increase everything from crops to coins. Few of our ancestors would recommend any activity meant to bring prosperity or happiness to be commenced during a waning Moon. Only one activity was aided by the darker side of the Moon—war. The Romans record the Druids' dread of fighting during the Waxing or Full Moon. Once the Full Moon was past, however, they were ready to face the enemy.

Medical Moon

One reason the Druids declined to fight during the waxing Moon was the tendency for wounds to bleed more profusely during this time.

Anyone (who's observant and honest) in a hospital will tell you wounds bleed more in surgery during the Waxing Moon. So, it is probably wise to plan surgery, especially elective procedures, during a waning Moon, preferably, the New Moon. A New Moon incurred incision can use the waxing increase to heal faster.

The Moon can also be a helpful force in dental treatments. If you suffer from the toothache, simply place the tooth of a murdered man (it's really best if you can find one from an executed criminal) on your on aching dentifrice. However, to be effective, this action must take place in a graveyard, at midnight, under a Full Moon. This treatment will also cure hiccups and all manner of fear-oriented ills.

Planting and Weather

If planting, take note of when the New Moon is in the sign of the fish, for wet weather is coming your way. However, should the Moon lie on her back, resting on the crescent, look for dry weather ahead. The nearer the Moon comes to changing at midnight, the better the weather will be during the coming week. A Moon lying high in the horizon means bundle up for a cold spell and cover the crops. Watch for the first snow. If it happens during the New Moon, you're in for a hard, cold winter.

The Moon also predicts snow once winter commences. Look for the Moon dog—who runs around the Moon in circles chasing its tail. It creates the halo look—shining as a saintly reminder that there may be sledding tomorrow.

Clear Moon—frost soon.

Large halo around winter's Moon—look for snow very soon.

Jack and Jill—Weatherlore

Long before Jack and Jill made their way up the infamous hill, they occupied an important place in serious adult literature: weather lore.

At one time, Jack and Jill lived as real children, picking wildflowers, running through the woods, and helping their mother draw water. Only then their names were Hjuki and Bil, very Scandinavian. One day, they were kidnapped by the Moon. We can only assume the Moon was very thirsty to descend to Earth to snatch two youngsters and the bucket of water they were hauling between them. Or lonely. In any case, the Norse names gradually Anglicized into Jack and Jill and an allegory for the Moon.

Another story tells that Jack and Jill served a grumpy old man who always called for more water. They drew bucket after bucket of water for his persistent voice—a fact well noted by the watchful Moon. One day, they awoke and didn't hear the old man calling, but they went to draw water anyway. When they got back to the hill, they heard the Moon speaking to them. She explained they had been carrying water to keep a stream atop the hill filled. She invited the children to rest their labors and join her on the Moon. They did, and now the clouds water the stream.

"Jack and Jill went up the hill"—as they climb the crescent, you can see more and more Moon. "To fetch a pail of water"—you can see the two children, complete with pail, at Full Moon. "Jack fell down"—just how much water spills during Jack's fall was a sure-fire rain predictor of the Middle Ages. "And broke his crown"—Jack's head breaks the edge of the Full Moon and the cracks begin to tear it down to the crescent. "And Jill came tumbling after"—as Jill rolls across the Moon, one Moon spot after another disappears and the Moon wanes.

As most nursery rhymes, Jack and Jill transcend simple words and images to delve into deeper meaning of the world around us.

Just how the weather casters of the Middle Ages determined how much water Jack spilled from the bucket, however, remains somewhat of a modern mystery.

Moon Thoughts

As Grandmother rests full and fat in the sky, ask her for the secrets she doth hide. Look upon the beauty of her face and see reflected Earth's majesty. Send her a wish and she'll grant what you want. Or simply sit quietly below this, our most wondrous nighttime apparition, and revel in her mysteries. The Moon pulls on the 80% of our bodies that is water. She also dances with our minds, dallies with our emotions, and pulls us upward, to see our own higher selves.

Lunar Moths:

The Beautiful, Useful, and Forgotten Creatures of the Night

By Carly Wall

If you've ever turned on a porch light on a warm summer's evening, or chanced to cosy up to a good book late at night as your lamp cast a glow against the window, you've seen and met one of the most beautiful, and ignored creatures of the night—the moth! And yes, though most of us ignore them as pests that flutter and bat against the porch lights or brightened windows, these night creatures have influenced and shaped our lives in more ways than one.

About Moths

Moths are members of an order *Lepidoptera*, to which the moth's daylight cousins, the butterflies belong. It includes over 11,000 species. Unlike butterflies, moths rest with wings flattened. They also often have beautiful feathery antennae like elaborate headdresses (males of the species have more elaborate and feathery antennae, since these feathers are the "noses" of the moths, used to find nectar and in the case of males, mates). Most are drab colored because they are night creatures, although moths are slowly evolving to suit our present polluted environment and becoming dark-colored to camoulflage themselves on pollution-blackened trees.

Butterflies do not have a sense of smell. They go by sight, and the flowers they visit, most of which stay open during the day and night, are marked with bright colors, stripes, dots, or marks like targets. Moth flowers are usually white or faintly tinted. They are highly fragrant, however, opening only at night for the moths to suck at the nectar. Such perfume can be detected over great distances on the evening breeze, and so these flowers announce to the moth population that there's some good eating nearby.

The moths serve a purpose by keeping the world populated with the most fragrant of the fragrant flowers. How we would miss the sweet perfume of them; the evening primrose, sweet-scented heliotrope, lilies, and jasmine or mexican orange.

I like to think of moths as "keepers of the scent," for theirs is a sophisticated sense of smell, since this is what guides them through the long Moonlit nights. Of all the creatures of the night, the moths have a beauty and grace all their own; although there are some moths who do fly by day. The nocturnal moths' single natural purpose is to pollinate nightblooming flowers or to mate and perpetuate their species. Moths number around 8000 species of Lepidoptera in North America, so you get an idea of the variety of the night-life. It is much more varied than the daytimers, which makes me wonder if the silvery night has more significance than the golden daylight? It is hard to say. I can tell you that there are as many "night-owls" (humans who love the night) as there are "early-birds" (those of us who love the day). Variety is the spice of life, right? But this isn't the moths' only contribution to our lives. There is another fascinating side. One with a rich and glorious history, and one still in use today, because of its value to humans. It is from a certain species of moths that we get our silk.

Of all the creatures of the night, the moths have a beauty and grace all their own

The Silk Worms

There is an extended family of silk moths, which includes the Saturniidae and the

Bombycidae (true silk moths), producing silk in different proportions. The 1,200 species of true silk moths are grouped into seven moth families spread across the New and Old Worlds. Eighty per cent of the saturnids live in the tropics. Here are highlighted a few of the more interesting creatures:

Actias luna

The luna moth (*Actias luna*) is one of the giant silkworm moths—the most beautiful of the bunch. It was named after the Roman goddess of the Moon, Luna, or Selene (the Greek Moon goddess). She was said to be the sister or daughter of the Sun, and perhaps the moths' beauty inspired its name. Wings of the Luna span over 4 inches wide, are pastel green, and it has large owl-like eye markings on the wings, with the hindwings having a long tail. They are common throughout the East, ranging from Canada to Florida, and westward toward Texas. The caterpillar feeds on beeches, hazelnuts, willows, and cherries.

Bombyx mori

The true silkworm, which is to say the one used to produce our silk today, the Bombyx mori or "Mulberry silkworm," is not native to North America, but came from Asia, where over 5000 years ago the Chinese first learned to unravel the silk and use it in making cloth. The legend is that around 2640 BC, the Chinese Empress Hsi Ling-Shi, was drinking hot tea when a coccon fell into her drink. She fished it out, only to have it unravel into a silken thread. It wasn't long before the spinning and weaving potential was realized and soon silken robes were made. Most all moth and butterfly caterpillars produce silk cocoons, but most make threads of silk too short for us to use easily, except the Bombyx, which spins threads up to 3,900 feet long.

This talent made the catepillar a very valuable commodity—for from it we produce fine garments, lingerie and silk stockings, wall hangings, bed clothing, tapestries, carpets, banners, and can produce beautiful paintings on silk canvases as well a printing from silk-screening, gloves, parachutes and more. In ancient China, it was common practice to wrap corpses in silk. Carpets of silk, made by pressing with wool, were made in China in the T'ang Dynasty from AD 618, and pieces still exist today. Silk is also a great insulator and has been used for insulating electric wires. It is noted that Ben Franklin made use of silk in the manufacture of his kites. The ancient Romans used silk threads for tying up blood vessels, and in Britain today, it is still in use for surgery. Fishing nets and ropes were also made from silk, as well as silk string for musical instruments.

Bombyx mori is a very accomodating caterpillar which is not found in the wild any longer. It is creamy white with a few brown lines in its 2-inch wings.

Tusseh

The Tusseh silk moth is the second major source of silk. It is a large Indian moth with a wingspan of almost 6 inches. Their coccoons are at least twice as large as the Bombyx and greyish-brown. The only problem is that these moths cannot be domesticated. In India, guarding of the wild caterpilars is done in the jungle and continues today. Such wild silk is rougher than the "homegrown" kind.

Atlas

The Atlas moth (*Attacus atlas*), is the largest moth species in the world. It produces a silken cocoon from which "fagara" silk comes, used by natives of India for thousands of ears. It is not made on a large scale and in fact, India is he only place where Tusseh and Fagara silk are made from wild silk.

Other Interesting Moths

The Io is a member of the giant silkworm moth family, but its silk is almost unusable. The moth is quite unusual in that is has red-purple wings, and eye-spots on the wings. However, the caterpillar, which is green with brown or reddish bands, bordered with white running down each side and very hairy, is one of the few caterpillars whose hairs are poisonous.

The Gypsy moth (*Porthetria dispar*), is a beautiful moth whose caterpillars do great damage by feeding on the leaves of shade and forest trees. It was brought over from Europe to Massachusetts in 1866 by a man who unsuccessfully tried to raise it for silk production. A few escaped to multiply, and without natural enemies here, it became a pest. When enough hatch in one place, they can strip a whole forest bare of its leaves.

Another interesting fellow is the Isabella Tiger moth (*Pyrrharctia isabella*). The moth is less than an inch long and dark orange in color, but it is the caterpillar most of us are familiar with. He's called the wooly bear, seen in fall. He has a furry coat of reddish brown, capped black on each end. Wolly bears eat perennials and trees, corn, sunflowers, birches, elms, and maples. There's a folkloric belief that you can tell what kind of a winter is coming up by noticing the black bands on this caterpillar. If the black bands are larger than the red, a harsh winter is foretold; smaller black bands tell of a mild winter to come.

The Making of Silk

Raising silkworms commercially involves feeding them a diet of chopped up mulberry leaves, later whole leaves as they grow. The noise of thousands of caterpillars eating has been described as like the sound of a pounding rain. They have to be fed every three or four hours, day and night.

From China, silk production spread to England. Italy took the moths to heart, but it was the fifteenth century before silk was also being produced in France. In the beginning, family-owned silk raising farms had a hard time harvesting all the mulberry leaves necessary. It was common in the nineteenth century in southern France and the Piedmont region of Italy for cooperatives to distribute batches of eggs to peasant families. The silk worms were then raised in dark cellars and outhouses. One ounce of eggs produced young caterpillars requiring 3 feet of space, increasing 3 times that in each stage of growth. Each household in the Cevennes asked for a specified weight of eggs from the local cooperative. The weight could indicate the number of silkworms each household could support from its available mulberry trees.

Shortly after Easter, the lady of the house was give charge of the eggs. Sometimes she would place them in a pouch to be carried between her breasts to keep them warm, other would wrap them in handkerchiefs and place them behind stoves, others tried using the warmth of the manure beds. Today, moths are induced to lay eggs on cards, and special incubation rooms with steady temperatures make raising much easier. In earlier times, the eggs had to be watched over day and night. Incubation took 10 days, with the normal cycle being that the eggs hatch 6-12 weeks after being laid, after the critical cold spell (i.e. winter, whether natural or induced by lowering the thermostat in the room).

Before modern convieniences, there was always the problem of the worms hatching before the mulberry leaves were out, so the guessing game was to keep the eggs cool until the time was right, and then in 10 days eggs would hatch. The caterpillars, once large enough, could be transferred to small boxes with adequate ventillation. They are non-stop eating machines for about one month. There was always the fear of running out of leaves to feed them. Five thousand caterpillars would need 10 sacks of mulberry leaves a day. 500 pounds of leaves makes a little over 2 pounds of silk.

Another fear was disease. At the beginning of the nineteenth century, French silk-raisers found their caterpillars turning black, smelling, and dying the next day. It was such a terrible problem that they gathered between them enough money to pay Louis Pasteur, the leading expert on microscopic disease at the time, to travel to Paris and help them. He declared the disease a virus, and prescribed more sanitary conditions in selecting and raising the caterpillars.

The "Golden Age" of silk production was the end of the nineteenth century in Cevennes, when many French country folk added a "silk raising" room calleda "magnanary," to their homes. It had to be well-ventillated, with fireplaces in each corner to keep temperatures "just right." Many superstitions arose around them, one being that the caterpillars were disturbed by any violent noise, including storms, and steps were taken to protect them thusly. It was noticed that they stopped feeding at these times (perhaps due to the atmospheric pressure changes). If a thunderstorm passed, a live coal had to be carried around the magnanarie to drive away the evil spirits and calm the caterpillars. Iron was also thought to be lucky for the silkworm. The room also had to smell sweet, and the floor was sprinkled daily with vinegar, and herbs strewn around, such as lavender, rosemary, thyme, or pennyroyal.

Once well-fed and matured, the fat caterpillars of the Bombyx are pale blue/white. Sometimes brown ones pop up, indicating wild ancestry. These moths have been cultivated so much that they are not found in the wild. The Bombyx has wings but almost never uses them anymore because of its domestication. They have also been bred to be quite calm, and have no interest in straying off like the other caterpillars. We cannot really know how the true wild Bombyx moth looked or exactly where they originated because we have raised them for over 5,000 years. Most probably they originated in the East and from the slight resemblance, entymologists guess that they stem from the B. mandarina species.

Once caterpillars are matured, they can then be encouraged to make coccoons from which the silk comes. The traditional way to do it in France was to take branches of broom and stand it in the silkworm beds. The coccoons serve as protection from predators because of the toughness of it. It takes 2-3 days to spin it. Inside, the caterpillar goes through an amazing change, forming new hormonal, nervous, and respiratory systems to become the moth.

The silk is secreted from two pairs of silk glands which secrete a liquid that hardens on contact with air. The colors of coccoons vary among moth types and families, but some of the finest are a rich yellow-orange, others are beige or brown. These are the natural colors of raw silk. Of course, for the silk farmer, next came the other chores once the coccoons were spun.

Some of the coccoons are allowed to hatch so that the moths can produce the eggs to replenish the supply of coccoons once more. Most of the coccoons, however, are dropped into boiling water to kill the pupa inside, and to dissolve the glue which binds the thread together. Immersed in hot water for only a few seconds, the coccoons can then be unraveled into delicate threads. The single strand of silk making up each coccoon may be 500-1,300 yards long. They are then combined to make a thread that cannot be duplicated by any synthetic fibers. It takes 25,000 coccoons to make 1 pound of silk. That's a great deal of work for the caterpillars and silk farmers!

All of this work depended so much upon luck and fate, that the French, during the early years of silk raising, used the old folkloric custom of timing their chores to coincide with the phases of the Moon. It was a custom in rural France, that the best time to cut mulberry leaves was during the increasing Moon, when they were offered to the hungry caterpillars at the increasing Moon. They knew back then that certain plants were far more potent at certain times of the month and it is interesting to see that insects too are affected by the Moon's curious influences. In Cevennes, farmers always gathered and sold their coccoons on June 23rd, holding a celebration day at the completion of the difficult tasks of silk-raising. The old broom branches were burned in a bonfire, there was much dancing and eating, and after that, the cycle would begin all over again.

Today, the annual world silk production is around 60,000 million tons, with China maintaining its lead in the production of silk each year. We've come quite a long way from a coccoon in a hot cup of tea. So on one of those warm nights when you switch on the porch light, and the moths come round to flutter and bat, you'll know they aren't just pests after all. But I'll bet you'll still be wondering why they are attracted to bright lights—yet ignore the Moon, only to be influenced in other ways by the various phases of the silvery ball. It's one of life's little mysteries, I guess, and until the moths talk, we'll have to keep on wondering.

Native American Full Moon Names

Ojibwa

January: Great Spirit Moon

February: Sucker Spawning Moon

March: Moon of the Crust on the Snow

April: Sap Running Moon

May: Budding Moon

June: Strawberry Moon

July: Middle of the Summer Moon

August: Rice-Making Moon

September: Leaves Turning Moon

October: Falling Leaves Moon

November: Ice Flowing Moon

December: Little Spirit Moon

Algonquin

January: Wolf Moon

February: Snow Moon

March: Sap Moon

April: Seed Moon

May: Flower Moon

June: Strawberry Moon

July: Buck Moon

August: Sturgeon Moon

September: Corn Moon

October: Raven Moon

November: Hunter's Moon

December: Cold Moon

The Goddess Circle:

A Lunar Portrait of Feminine Spirituality

By Karin E. Weiss

My concept of a circle, or wheel of the archetypal powers of women's sexual and spiritual and creative emergence has grown from a synthesis of three areas of personal and professional interest that have been evolving in my life since I was too young to know it. These are sexuality, astrology, and women's ancient goddess religions. I cannot say exactly when "conception" occured, but at some point around ten years ago I became pregnant with the idea of a cycle of feminine archetypes, and I've been giving birth ever since: writing a book, conducting workshops, and sharing the ideas with other women.

Feminine spirituality is about becoming whole. It's about containing, connecting, uniting, and bonding. It's about affirming and celebrating our bodies, the Earth, the animals, and all living things. It's about harmonizing and balancing the masculine and feminine principles in all of our lives. In the first lesson we learn that divinity exists in everything, that everything is sacred, that every life has unique purpose and meaning while at the same time being part of all else. The Mother-god's lessons are contained in circles, cycles, spirals, webs, and wheels; the great symbols of rounding, turning, and connecting that are metaphors for life in the feminine way.

We find the feminine spiritual message revealed by the turning of the seasons, depicted in the constellations of the Zodiac, and demonstrated with the Native American Medicine Wheel, the Sacred Stone Circles of ages past, and traditional ethnic round dances from many cultures. Sacred traditions celebrate the mystery of the cycle of death and rebirth. Everywhere in nature we find webs and networks creating patterns and making connections between multiple and varied points of creation. In dream and meditation we learn of our deep spiritual connections in the maze of the Labyrinth and down the spiraling paths which lead to a sacred center, the womb of Mother Earth.

Above all, we find our feminine spiritual experience of cycles reflected in the monthly dance of the Sun and Moon. The lunation cycle symbolizes a Sacred Union of the masculine and feminine principles within each of us. This monthly pattern of the Moon's increase, fullness, and decrease has been a guide in the human quest for meaning throughout time. Our search for wholeness can be described metaphorically in its eight phases, depicted as "faces" of feminine archetypes, based on lunar goddess traditions combined with astrology and psychology.

We find our feminine spiritual experience of cycles reflected in the monthly dance of the Sun and Moon

The Basic Lunar Cycle and Corresponding Archetypes

There is a universal cycle of "emergence-growth-dispersion-withdrawal" that describes every creative process and is reflected in eight phases of the Moon: New, crescent, first quarter, gibbous, Full, disseminating, last quarter, and balsamic. Each of the eight archetypal figures in our goddess pantheon reflects a specific phase/face in this cycle, briefly defined as follows:

☽ **New Moon**-Mother-Containment-Nurturance.

☽ **Crescent Moon**-Maiden-Assertion-Innocence.

☽ **First Quarter Moon**-Wild-woman-Action-Freedom.

☽ **Gibbous Moon**-Muse-Expression-Creativity.

☽ **Full Moon**-Lover-Fulfillment-Romance.

☽ **Disseminating Moon**-Companion-Synthesis-Mutuality.

☽ **Last Quarter Moon**-Warrior-Reaction-Passion.

☽ **Balsamic Moon**-Wisewoman-Release-Mystery.

What the Archetypes Mean in Our Lives

Mother clarifies our essential body-knowledge of rhythms and cycles, the quality of nurturance, and the elemental powers of fertility, pregnancy, and birthing new life. She teaches about our connections with the Earth, and the acts of conception, creation, and sustenance of life. Her lessons coincide with traditional meanings of beginnings and gestation during the New Moon. Winter Solstice is her Holy Day, a time of rebirth and renewal.

Maiden weaves themes of innocence, playfulness, and curiosity in women's developing sexual-spiritual identity. She teaches about emergence and initiation into the mysteries of puberty. Her lessons coincide with the Crescent Moon, which traditionally prefigures the "coming out" of our individuality as the lunar form breaks out, fresh

and vulnerable. Candlemas is her Holy Day, a time of initiation and introduction.

Wildwoman identifies an uninhibited form of raw sexual energy that manifests when, at any age, we are moved to let our passionate emotions and erotic power be known. She teaches us freedom to be physically and emotionally uninhibited by the artificial restraints of civilization. Her lunar correlate is the First Quarter Moon, which traditionally symbolizes a time of struggle to break free of inhibitions from the past. Spring Equinox is her Holy Day, a time of rejuvenation and return.

Muse calls forth women's creative imagination and encourages our unique self-development independent from that of others. Her lessons concern communication and giving voice to individual vision. These coincide with the Gibbous Moon, which represents a cyclic point of mastering self-expression. Beltane is her Holy Day, a time of blossoming and exclaiming the beauty of life.

Lover embodies the most explicitly erotic, lusty, and sensual aspects of women's sexuality. She teaches lessons about attraction and desire, helping us recognize the distinctions between sexual attraction, affection, attachment, and love. Her correlate is the romantic Full Moon, with its associated meanings of beauty, fullness, and magnetic enchantment. Summer Solstice is her Holy Day, a time of high romance at midsummer.

Companion has the most direct affiliations with the patriarchally defined role for women as partners who support men's identity ambitions. She oversees our relationships and is concerned about the impact we have on others. Her lessons focus on other-awareness, trust, and equality. Her lunar correlate, the Disseminating Moon, traditionally implies a time of sharing our personal gifts, interests, and energy with others. Lammas is her Holy Day, a time of abundance and thanksgiving.

Warrior brings forward more autonomous qualities that allow women to stand up for our rights and protect ourselves from invasion. She rules passionate, courageous sexual, spiritual, and creative energy. In the Warrior's classroom, we learn lessons of strategy, defense, and self-motivation. These coincide with the Last Quarter Moon, which represents a time of clarifying one's own boundaries and mastering the responsibilities of self-authority and ownership. Autumn Equinox is her Holy Day, a time of dedication and liberation.

Wisewoman is the mysterious aspect of Woman. She brings to conscious light hidden meanings of our sexual-spiritual power that re-veals the "dark," or Shadow, side of life and teaches lessons about overcoming our fear of the unknown. She enjoins us to transcend mundane limits of our self-image and claim the higher powers of mystical vision, passionate faith, and sacred ecstasy. She is related to the Balsamic Moon, or "dark of the Moon," which traditionally is a time of deep mystery and prophecy. Samhain is her Holy Day, a time of casting out, letting go, and healing.

How the Archetypes Interact on the Wheel

Just as divine energy can't be contained in any one part of our lives, the archetypes on the wheel overlap in their meanings and areas of influence. Nothing in feminine spirituality is rigidly defined or set apart, for the overlying assumption is that everything is related, that each part contains something of the others. This intricate interweaving of symbols creates a harmonious synthesis, an ultimate blending of mysteries, that gives a natural flow and vital meaning to our lives far above and beyond the obvious mundane issues with which we all struggle daily. All aspects of our lives interact, forming networks that support each other when we remain open to their messages and are willing to go with the flow of continual growth and change. The ancient wisdom provides us with many tools to do this. Among those tools are the mysteries of the Moon and her cycles, and the venerable art of astrology.

Circles have no beginning or end. We may enter a circle-teaching at any point. This is a core lesson of feminine spirituality: that life itself is an ongoing, neverending process and what we perceive to be beginnings and endings are only so because of our limited understanding. Yet, because we perceive life from the perspective of our limited self, we must orient ourselves with recognizable symbols so as to avoid becoming lost in a chaos of choices. One nearly universal system of orientation, recognized by most ancient wisdom traditions, entails a fixing of four directions and their elemental symbols—Earth, Air, Fire, and Water. Although different traditions vary slightly in their interpretations of the directions, general agreement as to their meanings is remarkable. The traditions I've chosen to embrace teach that East (the rising position) is represented by the element of Air and brings the experience of illumination; South (high noon position in our Northern hemisphere) is represented by the element of Fire and brings the experience of faith; West (the setting position) is represented by the element of Water and brings the experience of a

quest or seeking; and North (the midnight position in our Northern hemisphere) is represented by the element of Earth and brings the experience of wisdom. In modern psychological terms, East is mental energy, South is spiritual energy, West is emotional energy, and North is physical energy.

Complementary Pairs

The Goddess Wheel, as I've envisioned it, places the 8th and 1st archetypes, the Wise Woman and the Mother, at the top of the circle, holding the North point between them. These two share the knowledge of sacred life mysteries. They unite through our wisdom about the intimate connections between life and death, between birth and regeneration, between body and soul. Through our inner Wise Woman and our inner Mother, we learn to join the healing of nurture with the wisdom of detachment.

At the right is the East point, standing between the 2nd and 3rd archetypes, Maiden and Wildwoman. These two share a knowledge of innocence and spontaneity. They unite through our illumination in the exuberance of newfound delights and the passion of uninhibited, untamed curiosity. They also work together to help us face the fear of our unexplored limits, test our boundaries, and help us recognize our need for guidance

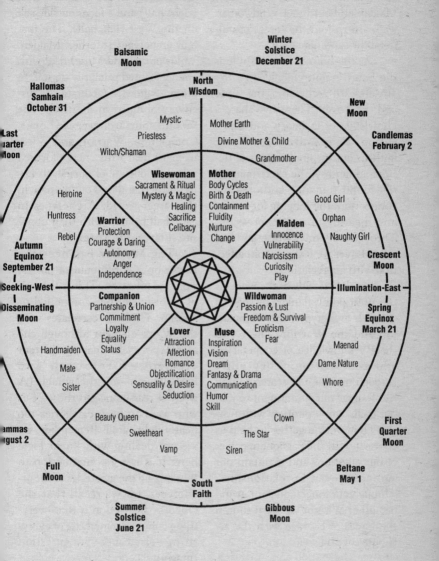

A Goddess Circle

and guarding. Through our inner Maiden and our inner Wildwoman we learn to join the forces of vulnerability and fierceness.

At the bottom of the circle is the South point, embraced by the 4th and 5th archetypes, the Muse and the Lover. These two share a knowledge of intimacy and captivation. They unite through our faith in our inspired visions of desire and fantasy, the excitement of newfound romance and creative connection, the longing for beauty and meaningful self-expression. Through our inner Muse and our inner Lover we learn to join affection with appreciation.

On the left side of the wheel is the West point, flanked by the 6th and 7th archetypes, the Companion and the Warrior. These two share a knowledge of cooperation and competition. They unite through our quest or search to find the courage of commitment to join our goals and aspiration with others. They work together to help us connect with the passionate power of our emotions and maintain our autonomy even in relationships. Through our inner Companion and our inner Warrior we learn to join the forces of courage with the attributes of pride.

Balanced Pairs

The wheel divides into two hemispheres, which can be seen to separate into a self-focus on the East (right half) and a focus outside self on the West (left half). The first four archetypes (Mother, Maiden, Wildwoman, and Muse) deal with energy focused primarily on self, to promote growth, facilitate the discovery of our own meaning. The second four archetypes (Lover, Companion, Warrior, and Wisewoman) deal with energy focused primarily outside of ourself, to impact others and find our purpose in the larger world. Archetypes in each half balance with their opposite sister on the wheel.

The **Mother** balances the **Lover** on a continuum of possession and affection. This is the axis of emotion, either compelled or chosen. This axis correlates with the Water element although the archetypes each occupy a different element—Fire/South and Earth/North—on the wheel. (A word of reassurance to those of us who want to keep categories too neatly delineated: Remember, we are not dealing with linear logic here. It is not a contradiction to thus mix up the meanings of the archetypes, for we recall that the Goddess' first lesson is that everything contains something of everything else. Let go of rigid categories!)

The **Maiden** balances the **Companion** on a continuum of playfulness and responsibility. This is the axis of relation, with self or other. It correlates with the Earth element, although the archetypes occupy Air/East and Water/West on the wheel.

The **Wildwoman** balances the **Warrior** on a continuum of passion and courage. This is the axis of action, free or directed. It correlates with the element of Fire, although the archetypes occupy air/East and water/West on the wheel.

Finally, the **Muse** balances the **Wise Woman** on a continuum of idealism and knowledge. This is the axis of vision, personal or universal. This axis correlates with the element of Air, even though the archetypes occupy positions of fire/South and Earth/North on the wheel.

In our lives these opposite pairs of energies can seem to be in conflict, yet they ultimately work to help us balance different needs. The Mother and the Lover both bring up issues of attachment; both engage our emotions at a deeply compelling level where we struggle with the agony and ecstacy of holding, of bonding, and of letting go. Our need to give nurture balances our need to attract loving relationships. The Maiden and the Companion both bring up issues of dependence, both engage us physically to interact with the world in order to experience ourselves in relation to others. The

need to learn cooperation balances the need to know ourselves better. The Wildwoman and the Warrior both bring up issues of autonomy, both engage our intuitive spirit to assert our desires, beliefs, and rights. Our need for personal survival balances our need for dedication to a larger purpose. The Muse and the Wise Woman both bring up issues of awareness, both engage us intellectually and imaginatively to explore ideas and ideals. The need for creative self-expression balances the need for universal understanding.

The Process of Growth Around the Wheel

To wrap it up, we now return to the original concept of the circle, walking the round of archetypes as they lead us through a natural creative process that applies to every living thing, and is exemplified by the evolution of a plant. In the first phase (Mother), the seed germinates and roots are established. In the second phase (Maiden), the first vulnerable green shoots push themselves above ground. In the third phase (Wildwoman), the plant's stems, roots, and leaves gain strength and resilience. In the fourth phase (Muse), buds form, encapsulating and drawing forth the promised creative product of the plant. In the fifth phase (Lover), beautiful flowers bloom, attracting pollinating birds and insects to the plant. In the sixth phase (Companion), the flowers give way to produce the ripe fruit of the plant which hold the seeds for its future generations. In the seventh phase (Warrior), the plant gives up some of its fruit to be harvested and used strategically in the creation of other products for the world. In the eighth phase (Wise Woman), the plant goes back to seed and lies dormant in the ground as it stores energy for the rebirth of a new cycle to come. Our own growth and development can be seen to evolve in a similar pattern at many levels of our lives, from our daily and monthly hormonal cycles that describe moods and energy output, to the larger patterns of development in our relationships, careers, creative endeavors, and family lives.

As I reflect on the many levels of meaning revealed by this circle of archetypes, I'm convinced I'm being shown an essential and long-neglected truth: that our feminine sexual energy is a sacred source of vital creativity that has the power to heal and cleanse the world of its great imbalances: violence, greed, and domination. As women and men learn to accept and integrate the various aspects of ourselves, we heal not only our own lives and relationships, but through them we create models that help re-vision entire global systems of interaction between peoples of all nations and the Earth on which we all live. Not every woman will hear, and women need not carry responsibility alone, but good women in equal partnership with good men can save the world from destruction, can reclaim health, happiness, and love for the Earth and all its creatures. If we don't do it now, then when?

From the **Mother** and **Child**
springs the **Maiden** who
evokes the **Wildwoman** who
releases the **Muse** who
inspires the **Lover** who
becomes the **Companion** who
arouses the **Warrior** who
discovers the **Wisewoman** who
heals the **Mother** and **Child** from whom again
springs the **Maiden**

Personal Lunar
Forecasts

By Gloria Star

About the Author

G loria Star is the author of this year's new lunar forecasts. She also wrote the Sun Sign descriptions and yearly and monthly horoscopes for *Llewellyn's 1996 Sun Sign Book*. An internationally renowned astrologer, author, and teacher, Gloria has been a professional astrologer for more than 20 years. In addition to writing *Llewellyn's Sun Sign Book* forecasts since 1990, she is the author of *Optimum Child: Developing Your Child's Fullest Potential through Astrology* (Llewellyn 1987) and a contributing author to the 1995 and 1996 versions of *Llewellyn's Moon Sign Book*; *Houses: Power Places in the Horoscope* (Llewellyn 1990); and *How to Manage the Astrology of Crisis* (Llewellyn 1993). She is currently acting as editor for a forthcoming astrological anthology series for Llewellyn.

Gloria is active within the astrological community, has served on the faculty of the United Astrology Congress (UAC) since its inception in 1986, and has lectured for groups and conferences throughout North America. She is a member of the Advisory Board of the National Council for Geocosmic Research (NCGR), has served on the Steering Committee for the Association for Astrological Networking (AFAN), and has edited the AFAN newsletter since 1992.

Gloria makes her home in the shoreline township of Clinton, Connecticut, with her husband Richard and son Chris.

Understanding Your Personal Moon Sign

By Gloria Star

Your personal astrological chart contains many different factors. Astrologers chart the positions of the Sun, Moon, and planets at the time of your birth. These positions indicate specific information about your personality, needs, and self-expression. Your Sun describes the expression of your ego self, and your expression of solar energy is usually easy to observe. But your Moon is another story. The Moon's energy is internalized, subconscious, and more intimate than the Sun.

To determine your personal Moon sign, you can use the tables beginning on page 201 of this book. This will allow you to make an approximation of your Moon sign. But if you want to know the exact degree of your Moon, a competent astrologer can provide that information after calculating your personal astrological chart. You can also order a copy of your chart calculations from Llewellyn Chart Services by using the order form in the back of this book.

The qualities of the Moon are expressed through your habits, the types of expressions and responses which operate below the surface. The Moon represents that part of you which collects and assimilates everything you experience and is the energy of your "feeling" self. This energy shapes the qualities of your thoughts, and as the repository of your emotions, the Moon stimulates your basic emotional nature. You use the energy of the Moon when you tune into your basic feelings about anything. The Moon is working when your "habit" self takes over. You might want to think of your Moon as your internal recording device. Some of those recorded messages operate on a regular basis, but you can add more information at any time, and you can change or alter them as well. Unfortunately, some of the messages recorded in the subconscious are difficult to erase, even when you're ready to change them.

Your Moon also indicates the needs you have for basic security, and suggests the experience of "home." Home can be both a place and a feeling, and when you feel "at home," you are experiencing the energy of your Moon. As you mature and have the opportunity to make choices about where and how you live, an understanding of the lunar energy in your psyche will help you determine a home environment which supports your needs for comfort, safety, and emotional stability.

The astrological sign of your natal Moon gives you insights into the filter through which you absorb your impressions and life experiences. Because the Moon indicates information about your impressionability, your Moon sign will tell you about your vulnerability as well as your inner strength. Lunar energy is the energy of nurturance and support, with your Moon sign showing the manner in which you express these qualities toward others and toward yourself. And the Moon tells a story about your relationship with and feelings about your mother, as well as the way you nurture or mother others (even if you are a man!). It's one of the primary features of your feminine inner self, just as the Sun is a feature of your masculine inner self.

Moon is the soul. It is the part of yourself which shines forth from deep within your eyes. It is the quality of yourself which soars to the heights of ecstasy or plummets onto the rocky cliffs of despair. Spiritually, the Moon is the repository of all that you have been, and therefore influences all that you can become. And emotionally, your Moon contains everything you need to feel safe and secure, once you learn how to find out what that is. Your Moon equals your moods. And more importantly, your Moon determines your capacity for true joy.

This section of *The Moon Sign Book* is designed to help you understand the basic cycles which will effect you at an emotional level throughout this year. The transits to the Moon provide different forms of stimulation and influence, and some of these cycles may be quite important in helping you reshape your life. But always remember that you are the one responding to these energies, and that you have a wide range of choices about the ways you can use these influences to bring alterations into your life. The planets provide stimulation, it is through your free will that you determine your responses.

Aries Moon

Independence it not just an idea for you: it's a necessity. You feel a strong desire to be free to experience life on your own terms if you have your Moon in Aries. That doesn't mean that you are comfortable with the idea of spending your life alone, because you do love the company of others and may feel most inspired when you have a chance to do something which has a strong influence in the lives of others. But your attitude is definitely "Me first," even if you try not to admit it.

You thrive on excitement, and need plenty of room for spontaneity. You may feel that your best strengths arise when you're on the spot and have to let the best of yourself shine through. Challenges get your energy moving. Your courage can be immense, and you rise to the occasion while the faint of heart shy away. But you sometimes feel impatient when life becomes predictable, or when you feel that you've fallen into a rut. Then, that part of you which just loves a crisis goes to work. After all, if there's not a crisis happening around you, you can probably create one within the hour!

Knowing that you sometimes need crisis for stimulation, it's a good idea to find life situations which allow you to channel this energy. Something like emergency medicine, crisis intervention counseling, or military service can be just the ticket to keep you out of trouble while you get right into the thick of things. Your spirit of adventure keeps you alive, and you may feel most happy when you have plenty of time and room to play. Yet you're capable of rising to any occasion, and when the world needs someone to fight for what is right, there's no stopping you. You can be the champion.

The Year at a Glance for Aries Moon

Saturn moves into Aries, where it will remain through 1997, so you need to prepare for a period of emotional reckoning. During the next two years, you'll feel more keenly aware of your needs. This is your time to determine your highest emotional priorities, and to find a way to satisfy them. Even if you're basically happy with your life choices you may become more critical of yourself or others, just as a test (sort of like a personal audit of your emotional bank book). But many times over the course of this cycle, you may find that your old security blankets are becoming pretty worn. You may feel that others are simply not there for you when you need them most, especially since Jupiter's influence stimulates high expectations on your part.

Before you give up, look at yourself. Have you been holding back, sending mixed messages, or failing to uphold your emotional commitments? If so, then this period can be extremely difficult, especially since the Solar and Lunar Eclipses can escalate emotional crisis this year. Relationships can be especially important, and your approach toward others may need to undergo revision. The difficulty arises if you're attempting to avoid your real needs, or if you're trying to carry emotional burdens for others. Some of those burdens simply have to go, whether or not you want to release them. In fact, if you're hanging onto a person, situation, or emotional response pattern which is no longer supporting your needs, then this period can be downright painful. It's amazing that the pain stops when you decide to release your grip on what you no longer need! Pluto's transit over the next few years will help you do just that, and will also aid the healing process. Additionally, the influence of Uranus can stimulate you to take a fresh approach toward fulfilling your needs. If you've fallen into a rut, this energy will help to propel you into a more exciting form of self-expression.

Overall, you are challenged to establish clear emotional priorities. You must become more supportive of yourself and your needs, and you must take responsibility for your emotional commitments. You may feel more ready now to uphold your promises, and to take a serious stand at making sure that your highest needs are your highest priority.

Affirmation for the Year

**I easily release negative attitudes as I move forward
toward changing my reality.**

January

Your eagerness to express your feelings can open new doors. That restless energy to try something new and different escalates, and you may jump into a situation before you know much about it. Romantically, this period can be full of delightful surprises, but you can also run into problems if you get into vulnerable territory with your partner. You might forget that just because you want something, it does not necessarily mean that someone else wants it too! However, you're in a great position to communicate your intentions, and if you make an effort to consider the effects of your actions and words, your spontaneity may be right on target. Find positive ways to express your ingenuity, and allow yourself more freedom to express the way you honestly feel. Try to be aware of the part you play when conflicts escalate, since unnecessary tension can be too divisive.

February

Even though you may feel somewhat frustrated by tracing over territory you thought you had already covered, a little patience can go a long way. It's easy to feel victimized, especially if you've been misunderstood and nobody seems to want to clarify the situation. Rough waters grow calmer once Venus enters your Moon sign on the 9th. Whether you're in the mood for tender caressing or passionate lovemaking, sharing affection stabilizes your emotions and helps to dissolve the pressures from the outside world. Try to keep things in perspective, since you may have unrealistic, but emotionally charged, expectations of yourself or others. Be kind to yourself, and plan some harmless self-indulgence. Self-acceptance is the key to your happiness this month. And taking a more open-ended approach to all your relationships allows you to extend that acceptance to others, too.

March

You may sense that you're out of step with the rest of the world, especially if you're caught up in an infatuation or if you've been the victim of another's deceit. Even though you may be in denial, it's critical that you deal with your feelings and needs as realistically as possible. Focus your desires in a way which will allow you to adjust your demands or expectations, and try to be flexible in your attitudes toward yourself and others. Get in touch with your hopes and dreams. Reach back into your past and forgive yourself so that you can open to the possibility of having what you want instead of compromising your needs. Clarity emerges after the 25th, with Mercury and Mars providing the energy you need to go after your desires. But watch your aggressiveness, since you can be abrasive or too abrupt, unless you make an effort to be more sensitive to the people around you.

April

Although you may know what you want, you can easily send mixed messages unless you become more attentive to the way you direct your emotional energy. However, your impetuous approach to others can be endearing, and you may feel more content, since you're more certain of yourself. Relations with women are important, and may improve significantly over this cycle. Your emotions are softened, but you're still eager to assert yourself, and are unlikely to take no for an answer if you sense the smallest glimmer of hope. Your courage is strong, and if you need to make some changes, you'll feel more confident about taking the necessary steps. Breaking bad habits is also easier near the Solar Eclipse in Aries on the 17th, since you're less likely to give away your power in any situation, including power lost through detrimental habits or attitudes.

May

You may be reconsidering a commitment, especially if you feel it would stand in the way of your progress. Before you take rash steps, give the situation a chance to change. You may be able to walk away, but you must first determine the price. If your obligation is complete, then it may be time to move on. But if you're just running out because the pressure is on, then think again, because guilt can be a heavy burden! You need to feel whole, alive, and free, and you may only need to make a few modifications to effectively change your life circumstances. Improve your health now by making a few dietary adjustments which are designed to help you lighten up and experience more consistent energy. Look for other areas which could stand some improvement, since this is a great time to get things just the way you want them — after expending some effort in the process!

June

Your determination to have your needs fulfilled intensifies, and you have the right energy to achieve the realization of your hopes. Making improvements at home can be enjoyable, especially if you're adding the color, comfort, and flair which reflect your true nature. Surprising changes mid-month may bring renewed hope, and your ability to express your feelings is encouraged by improved receptivity from others. Modifications in your intimate relationships encourage the alchemy you've longed to experience. Nourishing yourself may be more easily accomplished by allowing the love which fills your heart to overflow onto everyone around you. Basking in the joy of content-ment may not be enough unless you're also experiencing some challenges. Just keep things in perspective, and take advantage of the opportunities which allow you to openly express your ideas and intimate thoughts.

July

Persistent worry drains your emotional vitality, since you may be re-acting to imagined circumstances or overreacting to the situation at hand. Caution may be important, especially in new circumstances, but jumping to conclusions before you have the facts can make you feel overly anxious. Greater understanding arises through opening the channels to communication (which includes listening!). Your convictions may be strong, but if you're confused or if you doubt your abilities, then you may miss a tremendous chance to get what you re-ally want. Listen to your inner voice, but be alert to the responses from others in your personal environment. Feeling more centered and confident after the 15th, you may have reason to celebrate suc-cess with someone you love. Trust your creative instincts: they add a spark which is difficult for anyone to resist!

August

You're more sensitive to criticism, and may even feel that you're un-der attack when the pressure is on. Turmoil at home may seem to be continual, especially if you're making changes, moving, or remodel-ing. Your personal desires can be at odds with the wishes of others around you, and you can easily jump to conclusions and lunge into a defensive posture as a response. You can also be more impulsive than usual, and may actually stir up controversy with others, who can become irritated if your behavior or attitudes seem to be too abrasive. After much leaping from frying pan to fire, you may finally figure out a way to stay out of the conflict unless you must absolutely be involved. Allow yourself to forgive and release your hostilities through constructive channels. Convey your need to win into positive ventures, but leave it out of emotional disagreements, where reaching a consensus may be much more productive!

September

After a brief period of confusing feelings, your life seems to get back on track from the 10th onward. But watch for a tendency to be in the midst of deceptive emotional circumstances, or in denial about the reality of a situation early in the month. Take your time before you make emotional commitments, since you may need to feel more certain. Any doubts are signals that you need to slow down and clarify the nature of your own feelings. Give yourself room and time for spontaneous enjoyment of the things, people, or situations which make your heart sing. Loving energy and pleasurable experiences can be highly self-confirming, especially if you have ample opportunities to let someone know how you really feel. Even though you may have stumbled, you can easily get back into the swing of things. Just be sure that you promise only what you can deliver, because there will be a price to pay later on if you get in over your head. Use the energy of the Aries Lunar Eclipse on the 27th to help you clarify and deal with any emotional crises which emerge.

October

New situations arise which challenge you to get rid of attitudes or habits you've long outgrown. Your personal courage can be stronger, allowing you to take the steps necessary to initiate changes or move into new directions. Emotional intensity increases, stimulating you to take strong action in regard to expressing your deeper feelings. But you may feel somewhat uncertain about your self-worth, especially if you're trying to gain validation from others, instead of following your own convictions. The real courage you feel now comes from the courage of your own convictions. This is one of those periods when your ability to lead is called into action, even if you are as unfamiliar as everyone else with the territory you're exploring. You possess the strength, vision, and inventiveness to move ahead, and may be delighted with the results of taking the challenge. After all, what is life without a crisis or two?

November

Your quest to improve your life circumstances escalates, and you may be tempted to throw everything away just to get rid of the clutter. Before you call the garbage collector, take another look at what you're discarding. Your emotional clearing can be the result of shifting your focus, and you may discover that it's time to tie up those loose ends instead of running away from them. It's easier to talk about your inner thoughts and to share your feelings after the 14th, and an understanding friend may offer just the support you need to move forward. A new attitude toward personal responsibility is emerging. In the process of cleaning out some physical and emotional closets you may recover an aspect of yourself which has been needing some extra attention. The healing promised by these cycles allows you to experience greater unity between your inner self and the outside world. But remember: you can orchestrate the changes.

December

Although people can strongly influence your moods, their power is only as strong as you allow it to be. Your psychological filters may be clogged with negative thoughts which sap your power. So before you think you have to get out of a situation which seems to be caused by someone else, become more conscious of your own responses or attitudes. A successful battle which results in subconscious change is never easy, because your old habits can come back to haunt you and test your resolve. This is one of those periods in which your old fears or desires raise their heads. However, if you're convinced that the changes you've made are more harmonious, then this is only a test. If you have your doubts, perhaps you'll have a chance now to honor a part of yourself which you abandoned in haste. Love is your answer, but it begins deep within, where your power sustains it, making you capable of achieving more than you ever dreamed possible.

Taurus Moon

The Moon in Taurus generates a powerful need to feel stable, safe, and secure. You are especially connected to the qualities we define as Mother Earth, and you may have a powerful craving to feel and express the shelter and nurturance promised by this archetypal character. You seek peace, and love quiet moments which allow you to forget the hubbub of life and just enjoy the beauty and serenity. Your inner domain is filled with sensual delights, and you are happiest when your world reflects that same solid sensuality. Most satisfied by things you can touch and hold close to your heart, you are less likely to be drawn to the abstract.

Although you may think you're driven to accumulate a strong material or financial footing because it makes you feel more secure, you can easily become lost in the trappings of materiality unless you stay in touch with your inner desires. Subsequently, your need to maintain, conserve, and build a sturdy foundation may leave little room to make changes. The idea of change is okay if you have plenty of time to accommodate, and if you orchestrate the experience. But when it comes from outside and seems beyond your control, your stubborn attitude can be like a landslide. And sometimes, you may feel that you're trapped beneath the rubble wrought by your own inflexibility. Yet when there is crisis, and everyone else needs a shelter from the storm, you are there, like the Rock of Gibraltar, providing a safe haven. It's just that maintaining the balance is not always easy.

Your feelings are not likely to waver, once you've set your mind on something. And that steadfastness can help you become a supportive and reliable parent, friend, or partner. When it counts, you have the patience to wait or to persevere. You understand that growth takes time and nurturance. Now, if you could just be comfortable using those pruning shears....

The Year at a Glance for Taurus Moon

There are ample reasons to feel confident about this year, although you may experience a bit of anxiety, sensing that change is blowing in the wind. With Jupiter traveling in the earth sign of Capricorn, your inner self is experiencing a deep sense of optimism and even protection. You may feel like expanding your understanding of others, or at least opening your mind to a broader sense of reality. But you're also experiencing the influence of Uranus, which can seem to create a short in your emotional circuitry. The changes stimulated by this cycle can actually be quite benign, even though some of them do seem to come about in rather unexpected ways.

And depending upon the actual zodiac degree of your Moon, you may have a couple of years before you experience the impact of Uranus squaring your Moon.

It sounds rather ominous, but all you have to remember is that you're ready to remove the barriers in your life which have prevented you from asserting your needs. Luckily, you don't have to change overnight, but when you look back, it may seem that things happened rather quickly. The big shifts are occurring within your habitself. No longer are you content to just run on automatic pilot. You're more personally engaged in breaking free and feeling alive. Other planetary influences are also part of your evolutionary change, and you may need to take the first steps instead of waiting for a windfall. It's time to open the windows and let some fresh air into your inner sanctum.

Saturn's influence over the next two years encourages you to build on the foundations you've already created. Making the best use of your resources is important, but you may also discover that your priorities are shifting, and that some of your old requirements for security now seem to get in your way. It is okay to acknowledge these differences — it's called maturity!

To fully enjoy the benefits of Jupiter's transit, find ways to experience life to its fullest. Find healthy forms of indulgence, and become aware of the things which provide a feeling of joy. Look for ways to share joy with others, since generosity of spirit feeds your soul most effectively now. But negative forms of self-indulgence, selfish acquisitiveness, or overextending your resources for the momentary thrill can have a destructive impact on your stability. Moderation might be the best path after all.

Affirmation for the Year
I have abundance enough to share!

January

After a period of easy expressiveness, there may be an abrupt change in your emotional climate by the 12th. If you feel angry but don't do anything about it, you may just carry around an undercurrent of agitation. But you're likely to blow a fuse if someone tries to force you to change your mind or your feelings. This is a great time to let off steam, whether through exercise or creative expression. If you've finally lost your patience with a situation which works against your best interests, you'll feel ready to walk away and forget about it. Talking about your feelings after the 17th helps you recover your momentum, and you may even be able to clarify a situation which has deteriorated due to poor communication. Reaffirm for yourself where you stand. Let those elements in your life which are working serve as your platform in the midst of any difficulties. Do savor the good parts, because there are some juicy moments.

February

Just because someone tries to challenge you doesn't mean you have to get into the middle of their conflict. You may feel like you're watching Don Quixote jousting at windmills. Deep within, you're experiencing the conviction of your values and ideals, and you may feel your own sense of direction is guiding you more strongly than ever. A more constructive use of your anger emerges, allowing you to apply this energy toward breaking away from things which prevent your own growth. By the 15th, you're feeling more courageous about letting others know how you feel, instead of hiding behind your own insecurities. Let your imagination guide you, and combine visualization with external action. Instead of just hoping you can have what you want, go about asserting yourself to create situations which allow you to manifest those dreams. Affirm to yourself that your needs count, and know that you can create a place to fulfill them.

March

With Venus transiting over your Moon this month, you'll be feeling much more like yourself. The other planetary cycles also provide positive stimulation, and you may feel more openly expressive, since you seem to be on a more solid footing emotionally. By taking time to drink in the beauty and joy around you, and sharing these things with those you love, your sensibilities are altered. You may perceive your life, choices, and situations in a more positive light. Your tenderness and steadfastness provide the right energy to stabilize your close relationships, and you are more willing to assert yourself in ways which allow others to know where you stand. Your pleasure receptors are on high sensitivity, so allow yourself to experience those things which nurture your heart and soul. Fill yourself with love and hope, and open your heart so that this light shines forth onto everyone.

April

Less leisurely activity may not be as much fun, but you can still enjoy this period. You may be more worried about your finances, which can take some of the spring out of your step, but if you simply take the time to examine the facts, you may feel more light on your feet. You might relish curling up with a good book during your off hours. If you have a sweetie, enjoy some quite time together away from everyday pressures. But watch for your own anxieties, because they can literally absorb your positive energy. Your frustrations may arise from unfulfilled expectations, so try to remain realistic whenever possible. Envision what you want, mentally creating the alterations you desire. Look within yourself for the blocks which prevent the changes, and make the best possible use of all your resources, including time and energy. Your contentment level improves later. Now all you have to do is take it one day at a time.

May

Well, you thought your pace might slow to a more comfortable and graceful speed, and there are ample periods of respite. But watch out for the unexpected interruptions or irritating situations which emerge from the 2nd to 10th. You may wish to maintain an inner calm, but can actually feel more bitter than sweet. Explore your anger or resentment, if it arises, because it may be time to let go of the situation which created it. In fact, if you've let something smolder for a long time, then this is the perfect time to get your feelings out and rectify the situation once and for all. Let your family and close friends know that you may be a bit short-fused, but use this energy to courageously stand up for your needs. And if you've been waiting for the right time to break away from old habits or to get out of a situation which is no longer healthy, it has arrived. The New Moon in Taurus on the 17th is just the right stimulation to be certain.

June

Your momentum continues to keep you on track, and if you're going after something you want, then there's little that can stop you. Your actions can be highly deliberate, and an assertive attitude overshadows your usual placidity. But a power play can uncover some complex issues which you had not anticipated. You're challenged to step into a new position and to find more direct methods for expressing your emotional needs by mid-month, and may even be more satisfied with your straightforward approach. Although you may have to spend a lot of time dealing with family obligations, you can emerge from your experience with a strong sense of self- accomplishment. Part of the test arises from knowing when to take on a burden, and when to allow someone else to be responsible. Your energy and resources are better served by applying your strengths and acknowledging your limitations.

July

Your sense of compassion needs a healthy outlet, and you feel stimulated to share your resources more readily — as long as the other person really appreciates what you have to offer. Merely wasting time, energy, or money will result in your feeling used or depressed, so try to be deliberate in your choices and realistic with your promises. You need solid commitments, both from yourself and from others, but may, instead, feel like there's a lot of hot air blown around and very little substance to touch. The distractions around you can make you feel out of step, but by keeping that connection with your soul, your innermost self, you will connect with your own rhythm. Then, you may feel more as though you can glide through the dance with much greater ease. Let your creativity flow, and listen to your dreams this month. The quiet voices within have a lot to tell you about your secret desires.

August

An easygoing pace arises from your sense of feeling more synchronized with the natural flow of things. You're more focused, and can enjoy ample opportunities to satisfy your needs without expending such great effort. But if there is something you want, you'll also find it easier to coordinate your desires with your actions in order to manifest those wishes. Your emotions are positively intensified, and you're hungry to taste the richness of passion, and to allow your sensual side to indulge in a few pleasures. Conventional attitudes have to be respected, however, and you'll be most comfortable in situations which honor a sense of decorum. Things loosen up a bit later in the month, and you may find that you're completely enthralled with a person, creative project, or an idea because of the way your needs are satisfied. You're discovering some of your own secrets. It's amazing how we can even hide from ourselves, isn't it?

September

Early on you're in a tremendous cycle for personal expressivity, and may feel much more content. After the 7th you may become more easily agitated as a result of situations which interrupt your plans. Your patience diminishes to a fine thread for a while, especially if things are not going as you planned. Try to open to the possibilities of something new, and look at the differences which have emerged in your life. Perhaps you do need to make a few alterations and bring yourself up to date, instead of allowing yourself to stay safe, but unfulfilled. If you feel that something is wrong, it may be because you've allowed the demands of others to overtake your own priorities. And you may also be feeling some jealousy because someone else has what they want, but you are walking away with the consolation prize. Dismantle your own internal barriers, and find a way to talk about your feelings. A journal might be a good tool for objectivity.

October

More at ease with yourself, your confidence is increasing. But this month does have its challenges, and some of them are a result of unresolved circumstances. Repressed feelings from the past are easily triggered now, and you may sometimes feel that you're dealing with the straw that broke the camel's back. So before you collapse under the weight of unnecessary guilt, anger, or negativity — let it go. Concentrate on filling your heart with love, and allow the love to fill the empty spaces left by the release of what you no longer need. Deal with anger or hurt directly, and address your feelings for what they are. Everything cannot always be beautiful, but you can touch the beautiful part of yourself. If you feel like lashing out, call on your inner strength first. You may discover that your enemy has suddenly shrunk to an insignificant size.

November

You're entering a period of strong personal power, and can feel a greater harmony between your inner and outer self. You can also use the energy of this time to deal with some deep issues, and may discover some fascinating elements of your shadowy inner self. Confronting your shadow is not entirely comfortable, since you can easily project these feelings onto others in your personal environment. It's always easier to blame the other guy, but you're not really interested in pointing fingers. You want to be whole, and you'll find that honest communication and pure attempts to cope with situations and address the issues will help you achieve your aims more effectively. Evasiveness or deception may be more difficult to pinpoint, especially if you're just allowing yourself to see what you want to see, instead of accepting things as they are.

December

Centered. It's been a while since you knew the feeling — when you're really in the flow. But now, that feeling returns, and you can be so much more at home with yourself, your relationships and every element of your life. The future seems tangible, not just an illusory butterfly tantalizing your hopes, and the present is extremely palpable. Your dreams of stability, security, and safety can be more easily fulfilled. Home is becoming a true comfort. You are embracing yourself, your needs, and your desires as fully as possible. But there is a challenge, and you can sense it in the distance, maybe not too far away. It's the challenge to have more, but with less weight and less misuse. It's the challenge to stand firmly, knowing that with a grain of corn, you have all you need. Taurus Moon Zen: More is Sometimes Less.

Gemini Moon

The Moon is Gemini is ravenous. But the hunger is not physical — it arises from an insatiable curiosity about absolutely everything. Heaven forbid that Gemini Moon should miss anything. That is, after all, the greatest fear: that something absolutely spectacular and enthralling would be out there and not experienced. You need to know. Your mind needs stimulation. And you need variety in other forms, too. Multiple variations in friends, lovers, partners, creative opportunities, career choices, places. Settling down is difficult. Getting distracted is all too easy.

You are challenged to learn to remain-open minded as a way to develop true understanding. It sounds easy, but becomes difficult. With so much going on in your head, you sometimes find it difficult to listen to anyone else, or to truly see what you observe! Just as you find one truly fascinating situation, you glimpse another possibility and, before you know it, you're complaining about having too much to do. You may wonder why some people are so slow, but may not realize that they did not see you blow by. Your laughter rings through the air, but your quick wit is sometimes not enough to cope with the truly painful moments. Yet, you can put them in perspective and move on (one of your gifts).

You are the eternal child, filled with wonder and seeking as many chances as possible to find more. At the center of your being dances a lighthearted, ever-youthful soul. However, you can also be the wise teacher, and may secretly desire to be revered for your intelligence and wisdom. Oh, but to find that wisdom, when there is so little time, and so much to experience. Your frequent flyer miles and rail pass are continually used. But your favorite chair may need a little more wear.

The Year at a Glance for Gemini Moon

After a couple of years of slow developments, the pace of change begins to feel more reasonable as you move through this year. Your intuitive sensibilities are strongly enhanced, and you'll find more ways to blend those flashes of insight with all the "rational" data you're accumulating. If your Moon is in early degrees of Gemini, you may actually feel like you've just been launched into orbit. Even though you may not be experiencing this cycle yet, you can hear the countdown. So, you know that you need to lighten up and release unnecessary emotional attachments in order to fully enjoy the experience of letting your wings unfurl.

Saturn's influence from April of this year through the end of next year provides positive self-confirmation, and you may finally be willing to release some destructive habits. Your ability to see things more realistically also brings a sense of self-restraint, which may help you ignore some of those distractions and concentrate on the important issues. In addition, the eclipses of the Sun and Moon this year help you get things in their proper perspective.

But you're also aware of some very deep changes, and may feel that you are confronting the unresolved emotional issues which have been buried in your subconscious mind. It's time to clear out the cobwebs and bring new life into your soul. Your relationship with your inner self can become quite significant, and as old issues emerge, you have a chance to release feelings of shame, guilt, or fear which serve no purpose except to stifle your sense of joy. Venus transits in Gemini from April through July, bringing you in touch with a clear realization of your values, and stimulating you to examine your self worth, and to take a closer look at your relationships.

You're eager to feel the winds of change, and can be highly instrumental in creating those changes yourself. Some of those new experiences may seem to arrive on your doorstep by surprise, but you're ready to deal with them, and to find a way to incorporate them into your life. You're also feeling more keenly aware of your environment, and may want to make some changes in your personal space which reflect your needs more effectively. Your feeling of "home" is undergoing a transformation. You'll be happiest when you have the space, and when you've given yourself permission, to be fully expressive of your needs. It's not likely that you'll resist such an opportunity, but you could miss it if you keep all your windows closed.

Affirmation for the Year
I am confident about fulfilling my true needs.

January

Social interaction provides enjoyable moments with friends or family, and you may play a significant role in bringing others together. Your objectivity is more noticeable early in the month, when your feelings of worth are enhanced by the support of others. Your emotional sensitivity can get in the way of your rational decisions after the 15th, when you'll have trouble separating your values and feelings about things from the facts. In matters of the heart, it's a good idea to give yourself time to decide how you really feel before you commit, but pressures from others may make it difficult to stay detached. You may be reaping the harvest of your own lack of emotional responsibility. If you're honest with yourself about your needs, then you have nothing to fear. Independence is frequently a state of mind and being, not a permission slip obtained from your homeroom teacher.

February

Your self-confidence improves, along with your ability to pursue the fulfillment of your desires. Although you may feel that communication is sadly lacking, you must make an effort to stay clear, and an even greater effort to ascertain the feelings, needs, and opinions of others. Look for ways to nurture your inner self during the Full Moon on the 4th, and remember to take the requests of others seriously. Yet you also must allow yourself to say no instead of just placating. Because over-commitments made now will not be an acceptable excuse when you can't show up to meet your obligations. You're not interested in spending your time alone, and need interaction to maintain your emotional buoyancy. Even a phone call can lift your spirits, and it may be just what someone else needs from you, too! Feelings of vulnerability emerge after the 15th, but you just need to know when to step out of the way, instead of getting caught in another's emotional backwash.

March

You may feel that you're continually under pressure from others, and may have grown tired of their demands. Even though you may want to leave, most emotionally charged situations require you to stay involved and face the music. After all, you're wanting and needing clarification, and you've been complaining about feeling misunderstood. So take a stand and share your feelings and concerns. Talk about your needs, too. Fight for what you want; but be alert to the possibility that you might lash out in ways which can damage a relationship, so fight fairly! Sometimes an argument helps to clear the air. But if you're just building more resentment or if you deliberately create a setup (even for yourself), then you'll run into big trouble. What do you really want? If you don't know, then some honest introspection might help you decide. Calmer, clearer days and nights emerge after the 23rd.

April

A sense of emotional satisfaction emerges near the time of the Moon's Eclipse on the 4th, and with Venus moving into Gemini, you're also craving more of the sweet things life has to offer. Seek out healthy forms of self-indulgence, like spending time doing the things that make your heart flutter with joy. Love is your driving motivation, and becomes the key to your personal fulfillment. But you may not find it where you had thought. There's a mystery, and you're eager to uncover the precious jewels which have lain hidden and locked away beneath the surface. The key is in your hands, and unlocks your own heart. The courage to pursue your desires grows. Your intuitive and visionary insights inspire you to move beyond your current limitations. The blocks in your path are easier to see near the time of the Sun's Eclipse on the 17th, so pay attention!

May

Just as you're cruising down the highway of life, a detour arises.... Maybe it's more like a wake-up call, but the barricades still slow you down. Obstinate attitudes from others make your job more complicated. You had a plan, good ideas, and they still might work. You need to take a second look before you decide for sure that you want to invest your emotional energy and time. Selfish attitudes are not working very well, either, now — whether they're coming from you or someone else. Developing a more profound sense of gratitude is part of this new quality of love emerging. Show gratitude to yourself by honoring your limitations and supporting your self-worth. Give

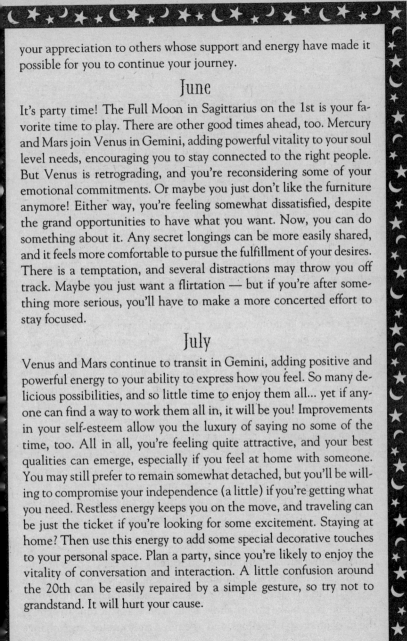

your appreciation to others whose support and energy have made it possible for you to continue your journey.

June

It's party time! The Full Moon in Sagittarius on the 1st is your favorite time to play. There are other good times ahead, too. Mercury and Mars join Venus in Gemini, adding powerful vitality to your soul level needs, encouraging you to stay connected to the right people. But Venus is retrograding, and you're reconsidering some of your emotional commitments. Or maybe you just don't like the furniture anymore! Either way, you're feeling somewhat dissatisfied, despite the grand opportunities to have what you want. Now, you can do something about it. Any secret longings can be more easily shared, and it feels more comfortable to pursue the fulfillment of your desires. There is a temptation, and several distractions may throw you off track. Maybe you just want a flirtation — but if you're after something more serious, you'll have to make a more concerted effort to stay focused.

July

Venus and Mars continue to transit in Gemini, adding positive and powerful energy to your ability to express how you feel. So many delicious possibilities, and so little time to enjoy them all... yet if anyone can find a way to work them all in, it will be you! Improvements in your self-esteem allow you the luxury of saying no some of the time, too. All in all, you're feeling quite attractive, and your best qualities can emerge, especially if you feel at home with someone. You may still prefer to remain somewhat detached, but you'll be willing to compromise your independence (a little) if you're getting what you need. Restless energy keeps you on the move, and traveling can be just the ticket if you're looking for some excitement. Staying at home? Then use this energy to add some special decorative touches to your personal space. Plan a party, since you're likely to enjoy the vitality of conversation and interaction. A little confusion around the 20th can be easily repaired by a simple gesture, so try not to grandstand. It will hurt your cause.

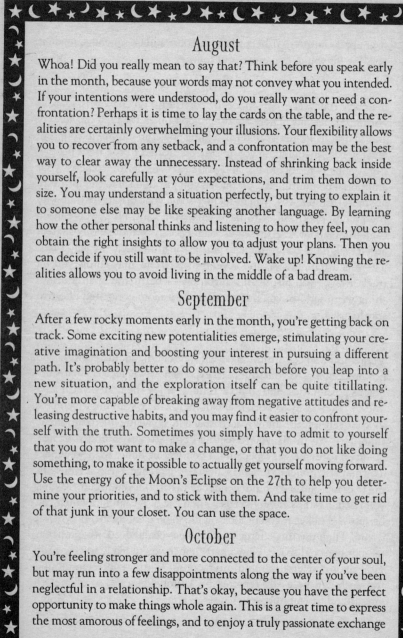

August

Whoa! Did you really mean to say that? Think before you speak early in the month, because your words may not convey what you intended. If your intentions were understood, do you really want or need a confrontation? Perhaps it is time to lay the cards on the table, and the realities are certainly overwhelming your illusions. Your flexibility allows you to recover from any setback, and a confrontation may be the best way to clear away the unnecessary. Instead of shrinking back inside yourself, look carefully at your expectations, and trim them down to size. You may understand a situation perfectly, but trying to explain it to someone else may be like speaking another language. By learning how the other personal thinks and listening to how they feel, you can obtain the right insights to allow you to adjust your plans. Then you can decide if you still want to be involved. Wake up! Knowing the realities allows you to avoid living in the middle of a bad dream.

September

After a few rocky moments early in the month, you're getting back on track. Some exciting new potentialities emerge, stimulating your creative imagination and boosting your interest in pursuing a different path. It's probably better to do some research before you leap into a new situation, and the exploration itself can be quite titillating. You're more capable of breaking away from negative attitudes and releasing destructive habits, and you may find it easier to confront yourself with the truth. Sometimes you simply have to admit to yourself that you do not want to make a change, or that you do not like doing something, to make it possible to actually get yourself moving forward. Use the energy of the Moon's Eclipse on the 27th to help you determine your priorities, and to stick with them. And take time to get rid of that junk in your closet. You can use the space.

October

You're feeling stronger and more connected to the center of your soul, but may run into a few disappointments along the way if you've been neglectful in a relationship. That's okay, because you have the perfect opportunity to make things whole again. This is a great time to express the most amorous of feelings, and to enjoy a truly passionate exchange with a lover or partner. Making everyday situations special is easier, and your flirtatious manner and witty remarks can enliven the most dull circumstance. The Sun's Eclipse on the 12th emphasizes a particularly open emotional period for you, and you're not likely to shy away from pursuing the fulfillment of your needs or desires. Your need to confirm your real feelings allows you to take a strong position in romantic situations, instead of just falling victim to the illusions. Find creative ways to express your thoughts and feelings.

November

You're more emotionally sensitive, especially in situations where your vulnerabilities are exposed or abused. If you've acted too soon, you may pull away. You can run into argumentative circumstances or strife, and may feel that you've become the victim of another's attack. But you can also be more insensitive to others, and may have your eyes set on achieving your own personal ambitions or desires, and unwittingly say or do things which create contests with others. Conflict does not have to be destructive, but it can easily escalate. Try to deal with any conflicts as they arise, or the inner turmoil will drive you nuts. Without stooping to a level which is beneath your dignity, you can be direct, articulate, and project an intelligent option to what may be a ridiculous situation.

December

You may feel a little out of place, especially if you're pulled into situations where you feel smothered by others. A few positive distractions allow you to maintain your sanity. The most pressing experience this month arises from your need for personal space, and your actions or words can become alienating if someone pushes you too far. Stay aware of your sense of internal limitations, and let off steam a little at a time to avoid feeling excessive anger or frustration. Find time to fully experience situations which allow you to feel free, alive, and inspired. Much of the heaviness lifts following the New Moon on the 10th, but you may not feel that you're home free until after the 22nd. Mercury's retrograde from the 23rd to 31st adds an extra stress factor, especially if you're in a hurry. Maybe the lesson is learning to slow down, or perhaps you just need to take the time to listen closely.

Cancer Moon

The quintessential mother resides deep within your being. That need to provide tender, nurturing energy to everything and everyone drives your psyche. You adore watching things grow. In fact, you have a knack for the perfect recipe when someone or something is dwindling — like a magical potion disguised as chicken soup. Your energy flows easily with the tides of time, and you understand the meaning of cycles and change. Your soul needs to feel at one with the sanctity of life. Home is more than a place for you. It is a feeling you can create wherever you are. That's why others gravitate toward you. They love the comfort.

Even though you have a powerful emotional sensibility, your appetite for closeness may never be satisfied. You can hold onto the past with tremendous tenacity, and although you're happy when your brood grows up, you may not be too happy when they leave the nest. You can fear abandonment, but when you're in the comfort zone in the center of yourself, you know that a part of you will continue forever. Yet it's still difficult to let go, and sometimes very hard to know when to back away. If someone pleads for space, you may think they no longer care. But the truth is, you can go too far, when your intention was only to secure their safety.

Try focusing a little of that nurturance on yourself. It may seem strange at first, because, after all, you wouldn't want to be selfish. Think in terms of "self-full." Once you learn the healthiest ways to nourish yourself, you will have more to offer to the world around you without depleting your own emotional vitality. And after you've dried your tears after a good-bye, remember the joy and feel the love. Learn to celebrate life stages and revel in the delight of your own connection with the Eternal Divine Mother. It might be just as easy as settling back into your favorite easy chair and watching the sun set.

The Year at a Glance for Cancer Moon

Although you may want to be completely confident and optimistic about this year, and even though you see many signs of progress around you — you may not trust that all is well. In truth, this is a year of emotional contrasts. In many respects, you feel that you deserve a

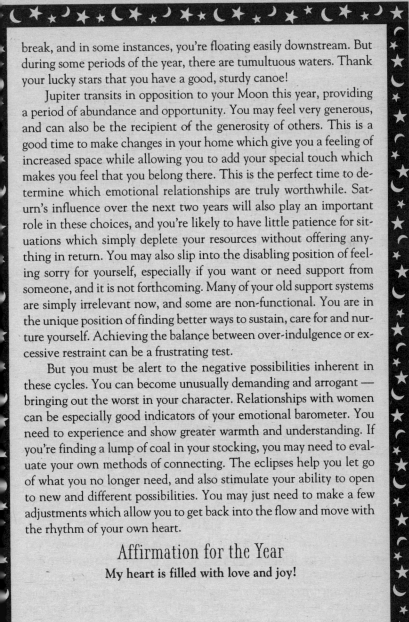

break, and in some instances, you're floating easily downstream. But during some periods of the year, there are tumultuous waters. Thank your lucky stars that you have a good, sturdy canoe!

Jupiter transits in opposition to your Moon this year, providing a period of abundance and opportunity. You may feel very generous, and can also be the recipient of the generosity of others. This is a good time to make changes in your home which give you a feeling of increased space while allowing you to add your special touch which makes you feel that you belong there. This is the perfect time to determine which emotional relationships are truly worthwhile. Saturn's influence over the next two years will also play an important role in these choices, and you're likely to have little patience for situations which simply deplete your resources without offering anything in return. You may also slip into the disabling position of feeling sorry for yourself, especially if you want or need support from someone, and it is not forthcoming. Many of your old support systems are simply irrelevant now, and some are non-functional. You are in the unique position of finding better ways to sustain, care for and nurture yourself. Achieving the balance between over-indulgence or excessive restraint can be a frustrating test.

But you must be alert to the negative possibilities inherent in these cycles. You can become unusually demanding and arrogant — bringing out the worst in your character. Relationships with women can be especially good indicators of your emotional barometer. You need to experience and show greater warmth and understanding. If you're finding a lump of coal in your stocking, you may need to evaluate your own methods of connecting. The eclipses help you let go of what you no longer need, and also stimulate your ability to open to new and different possibilities. You may just need to make a few adjustments which allow you to get back into the flow and move with the rhythm of your own heart.

Affirmation for the Year
My heart is filled with love and joy!

January

Confusing situations make it difficult to stay emotionally centered, especially if things are changing too quickly. Your usual approach to staying centered may not work very effectively, and making the adjustments can leave you feeling exhausted and frustrated. Before you become despondent, be attentive to the differences between what you can and cannot control. You may discover that you can actually be quite effective in making accommodations for your own feelings and needs. Others may be surprised by what seems to be a rebellious attitude on your part, but you're really just ready to speak your mind. Your increased emotional sensitivity may not allow much room for you to deal with additional crises, and you may just have to allow someone to take care of their own needs and demands. Maybe that's why they invented a microwave oven and an answering machine!

February

More certain about your priorities, you are beginning to feel more stabilized. But be on the alert for the occasional red herring. You may feel a bit more compulsive about the details of your domestic situation, but at the same time, your attitude toward maintaining order is much more relaxed. After all, life is sometimes a messy experience. It's not likely that differences in taste will stand in your way of doing things as you prefer. A little emotional blackmail can occur mid-month, when you are more vulnerable to such manipulations by others, and you may be tempted to try the passive-aggressive approach if you're not getting what you want. A more honest approach might feel better in the long run, and you'll do yourself a favor by not giving into those pressures brought to bear by others, either. Life flows more gently after the 19th, and the turmoil is replaced by considerable calm.

March

A feeling of certainty arises over the course of this month, allowing you to take a more definitive approach toward pursuing the fulfillment of your needs and desires. A strong emotional commitment seems natural, and you can confirm for yourself the true value of any relationship. Questions about life choices are more easily answered, since you can process the choices by getting in touch with your inner sense of har-

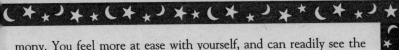

mony. You feel more at ease with yourself, and can readily see the truth of others, which helps you determine the extent of your involvement with them. Talking and becoming more direct in expressing love and tenderness satisfies both your own questions and the concerns of others. You don't have to sneak in the side door. Instead, you can walk right through the front threshold and declare your feelings. Later on you may wonder where the courage came from, but for now, take advantage of it and make some of your dreams a reality.

April

Your patience seems to evaporate, but you may have little choice other than to deal with things as they are and make room for any delays or blocks in your plans. Although you may know intellectually that you need to slow down, you may be reluctant to do so. However, pushing too hard will result in little progress. Conserve your emotional strength by finding healthy outlets for expressing your anger or frustration. Your expectations can become quickly overblown, and you may be left with the string dangling from your hand while your beautiful balloon floats off into space. By determining a reasonable outcome which fits with the reality of a situation, you can avoid feeling crestfallen. You definitely need to concentrate on the present moment and the development of your future, because getting stuck in the past will only hamper your progress. Achieving the balance is a true challenge, especially near the eclipses on the 4th and the 17th.

May

Now that the storms are subsiding, you may be feeling more confident about your choices. Your passion for life grows, and you may even have reason to celebrate. It's easier to talk about your needs, and you may be able to re-evaluate your feelings or thoughts about something which happened in the past. This is a great time to clear the air, and deal with conflict or emotional trauma which has been blocking your ability to move forward in your current life situation. Your courage and conviction can be intensely powerful, and through showing your own strength, you will help to strengthen others, too. You'll find that open expression adds a positive definition to many aspects of your life, and that following your heart makes just as much sense as trying to analyze all the data. The bottom line may come down to whether or not you can live with your choices, not whether they make sense to everybody else.

June

Good communication continues to give you a strong foothold in most situations, although you may feel a bit like withdrawing for a brief period just to recover your strength. A period of reassessment of your needs can be just the right choice, and you might even want to take a look at your your physical/emotional link to determine if some attitude adjustments might lead to better health. There may also be a physical component if you're feeling emotionally out of sorts, so try to be holistic in your approach. Undercurrents of agitation can arise by the 14th, especially if your feelings have been hurt by insensitive remarks. Pressure from family may be the last straw, so give yourself a break by acknowledging what you really want, instead of trying to act like the nice guy. Make a clear assessment of your situation, and begin to devise a plan which will allow you to make positive modifications.

July

Unless you stay alert, you may feel that you've been emotionally ambushed. Your old patterns of response may come back to haunt you, even if you have been trying to make deliberate changes. The same things still trigger your anger or remind you of your pain. Once again, it's back to the drawing board. That means you'll need to have some good dialogues with yourself, perhaps using a journal to help you objectify your thoughts and feelings. A talk with your best friend can also give you the insights you need to get out of your rut. The desire is there, but creating the new path is not always easy. Listen to your dreams. Pay attention to the things that bring your photographic memory of an old situation into play. Use what you've learned to give you a stronger foundation, but try not to stand still too long, or the fresh concrete may solidify your position!

August

After a slow and deliberate start, things finally get moving. A highly spirited period of emotional intensity develops, allowing you ample opportunity to indulge your passions. You're still plagued by the need to keep your expectations in check, since projecting too much onto someone or a situation can lead to trouble. This is your time to revel in pleasurable experiences, and to enjoy sharing your hopes and fulfilling some of your fantasies. You're open to experimentation, as long as you feel safe. You have some great insights into the origins of those guilt feelings that sometimes get in the way of enjoying the beautiful side of life. Use visualization combined with action to help you break away from these old patterns, and allow yourself to feel free, alive, and full of joy. Life definitely seems worthwhile, and your relationships can blossom. Your attitudes toward experiencing love are becoming more accepting, and you'll find that allowing this pure energy to fill your heart and soul brings renewal.

September

Even the practical, everyday focus which overtakes your life cannot squash your enthusiasm. A powerful feeling of ecstasy can engulf you early in the month, and the inspiration you experience can be the source of new hope for the future. But you'll not feel like staying in the dream for too long, since you're eager to get things moving. Your reconsideration of a plan during the New Moon on the 12th allows you to formulate a different approach which feels much more on target. As the time of the Moon's Eclipse on the 27th grows closer, you may begin to feel a bit nervous and overly anxious. Some of that anxiety is due to your fears of the unknown. However, some of it is the result of your experience, which tells you that there may be reason to be more cautious. Move carefully in emotionally-charged situations, and try to maintain as much objectivity as possible when dealing with mundane or financial matters. Keep an open mind.

October

Relationships can be a strong source of turmoil, or you may face a crisis in your personal relationships near the time of the Sun's Eclipse on the 12th. This does not imply that things are in bad shape, but that energy is released which stimulates significant awareness which can lead to change. You can no longer ignore any difficulties, but you also have a powerful window of opportunity which allows you to determine a different direction. Accepting your changing needs and embracing the alterations and growth which others are experiencing can lead to a feeling of rebirth. You're getting rid of emotional clutter. Your sense of discrimination is improving, allowing you to make choices which are more comfortable and less compromising. Troubles arise this month from poor communication. So be clear, direct, and make sure you reach an understanding.

November

Smoother sailing—finally—and you're feeling more confident about making sure that your needs are met. Your affections grow stronger, and you'll be more confident expressing your thoughts and feelings from the 1st to 14th. Differences in taste can account for much of the conflict between you and your partner, and you may also have divergent ideas about the best ways to use your resources. If the hassles overwhelm the good side, you may determine that staying involved is not worthwhile, but it's more likely that you'll make an effort to clear up misunderstandings and accept your differences. After all, variety can be intriguing, and you may feel more excited by a challenge than by a passive partner! Your emotional integrity is definitely strengthened, and you're more interested in reinforcing your relationships than destroying them.

December

You're feeling restless and may need some positive distractions to stimulate your creativity and passion for life. You're high-spirited and may feel quite playful. At home, activity levels are on the increase, and entertaining or inviting others to share in festivities can be highly enjoyable. But expect to run into some bullheaded differences in opinion if you bring up issues which have always been trouble. Know when to sidestep, or better yet, decide to provide a more pleasant diversion. Even though you may crave some family closeness during the Full Moon on the 24th, you may run into conflicts because everything is not perfect. Drop the illusion. Nothing is ever perfect, but sometimes, for the moment, it does get pretty good. Delight in that part. Let the rest go.

Leo Moon

Driven by the need for recognition, you crave attention and may dream about standing in the spotlight. Even though your heart pounds intensely enough that you're certain the people in the back row can hear it, once you're on stage, you shine like the Sun.

But most of all, you just want to enjoy yourself: to laugh, play, and be a kid again. If you could avoid it, you probably wouldn't grow up. No matter what your age, your playful manner draws others to you. Your warm hugs soothe the most devastating hurt, and your protective loyalty can be as reliable as the passage of time.

Sometimes, your need to be the center of attention works to your advantage, but you can also become unbelievably demanding. Although you can be extremely generous, if you're feeling insecure, you can also be totally selfish and highly possessive. You prefer living in a peaceful kingdom, and may not appreciate disruptions when you're enjoying things as you like them. Should you feel that your reputation or security are threatened, your willful nature emerges. You can hold onto feelings, attitudes, or situations for too long, yet you love changes when you can orchestrate them in your grand manner. Your head knows the difference between being loyal or being locked in, but sometimes your heart has a different feeling.

Creativity is not an option for you, but is, instead, a way of life. And to keep your creative fire burning brightly, you've learned that it is necessary to allow love to grow in your heart. As you experience a positive feeling of love for yourself and develop your link with the true power residing within your soul, you find it easier to be less self-absorbed and more self-expressive. After all, the world is your stage, and you are the ultimate performer. Just remember that you are still loved even if there is no audience and you cannot hear the applause.

The Year at a Glance for Leo Moon

A sense of emotional stability emerges this year, although you can sense that significant changes are occurring deep within your soul. Your habitual responses may seem to have become dull routine, and you're ready to ignite the spark of life. The slow-moving planetary transits combined with the influence of the Solar and Lunar Eclipses provide the perfect backdrop for a re-evaluation of your attitudes toward nurturing yourself and fulfilling your higher needs. You may welcome the variations and modifications as an opportunity to move forward and experience more from life.

Over the next several years, the planets Uranus and Pluto will transit in strong aspect to your Moon. These are the types of cycles which prompt tremendous alterations in your sense of home, family, and emotional satisfaction. Things beyond your control may result in your need to deal with different circumstances or unexpected situations, which cause you look at your life and your needs from another perspective. If you feel the beginnings of major transformations stirring deep within and take the time to listen to your feelings, you can be the engineer of significant changes instead of feeling like a puppet in the game of life. Your needs are definitely different, and it may be necessary to take another look at your choices of career, partners, or environments to determine if they still fit your new profile.

It is unlikely that you will burn all your bridges, since you are keenly aware of the need to maintain a strong foundation. In fact, building that foundation through constructive focus allows you the luxury of standing on a stable platform while you let go of what you no longer need. Jupiter's cycle stimulates a period of adjustment, and helps you keep your mind open to new and different ideas. Even though a spirit of rebellion can prompt you to close off nonproductive pathways, your desire to become more freely expressive will open many new doors. This can be an exciting year for relationships, since you are taking a more unconditional approach toward yourself and others.

Once Saturn enters its two year cycle in Aries in April of this year, you may find it easier to take on emotional responsibilities and keep your promises. This transit marks a period of personal maturation, and you may also experience a desire to build a more defined sense of home and family. It can seem natural to shoulder more of the burden, but it also feels good to allow for the transitions which occur when you enjoy lending emotional support to others who are learning to stand on their own.

Affirmation for the Year
I embrace my evolving needs.

January

You can feel at odds with others, and may have little patience in tolerating their eccentricities—especially if they get in your way. Although you may feel a bit withdrawn the first few days of the month, you can be plagued with situations which are filled with misunderstandings. Vague innuendo can lead to outright conflict by mid-month. Jumping to conclusions is just as provocative as leaping into action too soon, so try to think before you respond. If you determine that a situation calls for you to take a stand, you're in a great cycle to take a firm position, or to fight for your needs and rights. The most frustrating circumstances are likely to arise when you attempt to be direct, because you may be accused of being too aggressive. Instead of adopting a belligerent attitude because nobody seems to understand you, channel some of that energy toward clearing away the obstacles in your path.

February

Relationships continue to be a thorn in your side when they're not working out, but you're also becoming more creative in your approach to resolving difficulties. The Leo Full Moon on the 4th adds intensity, but also stimulates your free expression of your desires. Your connections with women improve as the month progresses, and even though your passions still drive you, your manner is tempered by a stronger sense of loving care. Your thoughts may also be less polarized, although your particular prejudices do emerge in conversation with close friends. This is a month of paradox and confrontation with strong emotional impact. After trying the direct technique, you may feel more comfortable with a "wait and see" attitude. Inaction on your part can be misinterpreted as weakness by your competitors or detractors, so keep your awareness at a high level of receptivity.

March

Just when you thought you had settled on something, you may step on the wrong toes or put your foot in your mouth. It's okay for you to have your preferences, but your differences in taste can provoke a strange impasse in an intimate relationship. To avoid the alienation, agree to disagree and allow for the complexities of diversity. Trying to force another to conform to your wishes simply will not work right now, and the other person will not have much more luck trying the same with you! A freer flow of affection emerges after the Equinox on the 20th, and you can work a little of your special magic in romance after the 24th. Your charming elegance works to your benefit, although the shy or reserved types may still complain that you're just "too much." But you know what you have to do to be satisfied with your own performance, and after a while, even the most conservative people will have to agree that you were right.

April

Now you're more comfortable with yourself, and if you need to be on the spot or in a circumstance which calls for higher levels of performance, your confidence in yourself will carry you through any presentation. Your thoughts are less compulsive during these cycles, and the energy of the eclipses inspires greater confidence in your convictions. Discerning the needs of others may also be easier, although you may not be especially satisfied with the outcome of some of your conversations. Try to listen more carefully, because your own concepts or ideas are likely to override another's ability to get through to you. Once you've opened the doors of your mind, you may uncover some delightful surprises, especially in matters of the heart. Determine how you really feel and take the chance that letting someone else know where you stand will work to your advantage.

May

Emotional intensity mushrooms, and your natural tendency toward over-dramatizing your feelings can be blown out of proportion. Rash actions or stubborn attitudes can be carried to the extreme, leading to a destructive conclusion. Your sensitivity to criticism or confrontation is easily triggered. Some situations may seem to change overnight, while those which you want to alter seem to be carved in stone. Even though you may want to dynamite something just to get it out of your way, you're not likely to achieve the results you're after if you are too impulsive. The emotional fireworks can be quite a show, and you can easily lash out at others in your family or close environment just because you are in conflict with yourself. Yet these energies can be quite helpful if you're needing motivation to make changes.

June

A nagging tendency to push things until you've achieved satisfaction can be highly irritating to others, but you may not like it, either. Your motivation is likely to arise from an high level of impatience with the status quo, and you may be particularly frustrated if you're lacking the support of a significant individual. You may also be taking a stubborn stance just because you're feeling indignant. Most of the conflicts are likely to escalate until the 13th, when an emerging attitude of tolerance allows you to accept your situation. From this position, you can begin the task of creating a more effective form of communication which allows you to express both your ideas and feelings. Intimate relationships improve significantly following the New Moon on the 16th, and your ability to cooperate with change is also more marked. The contrast from a month ago can be amazing!

July

Now that you're back on track, you're eager to keep the momentum going and can be highly expressive without overwhelming others in the process. You might even enjoy sitting back part of the time and allowing yourself to be entertained and coddled. The nice thing is that this pampering can emerge naturally. You're more open about your feelings and needs, and have a remarkable ability to influence others. This is an extremely playful period, and spending time with or around children can be amusing and gratifying. Since you're also taking stock of your close relationships, you may need to vent some old hurts just to clear the air in addition to talking about your hopes for the future. Your need to create a stable foundation extends from your personal life into your expression in the outside world, and you may have just the right support from your good friends and close family members to help you get your dreams off the ground.

August

Although you may hope to continue with the progress you've made on the personal front over the last few weeks, the momentum does slow.

There are a few pot shots from left field you had not anticipated, and these can quickly drain your good humor if you endup having to cover for too many mistakes—particularly if you're not responsible for them in the first place! Maneuvering between your hopes and the expectations of others can be quite treacherous, particularly if you get your signals crossed. Try to anticipate problems through more effective listening. Instead of just going for window dressing in the romance department, make a decided effort to build on your past successes by continuing to offer support instead of just demanding attention. Allow yourself to take some time to reflect on your deeper needs, and give love time to grow. Concentrate just as much on releasing the past, so you can be more appreciative of what you have now.

September

After a few days of what feels like sleepwalking, things finally get moving once Venus and Mars enter Leo by the 9th. For the remainder of the month, you may feel on top of the world, especially if you have an experience which opens your heart to new or renewed love. By allowing yourself to try an experimental or different approach to expressing your feelings or showing your creativity, you can attract positive attention and excitement, and may even experience the spark of a new romance or friendship. Your confidence in yourself adds courage to your convictions and direction to your efforts, and you are in a superb position to create things just as you need them to be. Before you have this success, you must first determine what you want, or at least be open to finding some answers to your desires. Just standing in the doorway waiting for something to happen will not work, but with direct action and adequate preparation you can bowl them over with your charismatic charm.

October

Still eager to express your feelings, you also benefit from a period of improving communication. There's a tendency to feel that you have to overemphasize your strengths, and you can also fool yourself by seeing only the best side of someone else, instead of also accepting their limitations. To avoid becoming caught in the trap of expectations, try to determine the level of commitment you're making. How much time and energy will a situation really require? You may want to have it all tomorrow, but the potential for delays does exist, and you may also have other obligations which must be answered first. However, your drive and persistence can help you overcome most obstacles in your path, and your desire to keep everything on a straightforward level can assure more self-confidence while inspiring greater trust from others.

November

By concentrating on attaining a greater sense of inner harmony, you can quell even the most tumultuous storms. Your warmth gives impetus to your personal relationships, and by extending your support to another, you may also rekindle a flame which has been waning. You can demonstrate the type of support and tenderness which endears you to the heart of another. Most importantly, you can address your own inner conflicts by embracing the aspect of yourself which shines as pure love. Since you're not likely to feel that you have to push so intensely to attain the realization of your desires, you may be more successful in reaching your goals. Be aware of verbal disagreements which cause you to question your involvement. The problem may just be one of semantics, but you can run into different viewpoints which could fundamentally weaken the situation. Avoid shutting the door unless you really want to keep it closed.

December

You may feel that you're required to give up too much in order to get what you want, but you may just be confronting some old selfish or possessive attitudes which are overdue for revision. To decide the best approach, take a personal inventory. If you've just been hanging in there because your pride will not allow you to let go, then maybe it's time to say good-bye. In the depth of your soul, you may want nothing more than to be free to express your needs, hopes, and desires. Where those wishes have been altered by greed, fear, or guilt, the results can become very dissatisfying. Now you can eliminate those elements which pollute the purity of your dreams and surrender once again to new hope for the future. During the New Moon on the 10th, strike a bargain with yourself to avoid compromising your needs, while truly acknowledging the needs of those who share your life.

Virgo Moon

A sense of striving to be ever more competent keeps you feeling that you are constantly on your toes. Deep within your soul resides a keen-eyed observer who never misses anything. Your focus is drawn to the minute detail, which can sometimes fascinate you so completely that you are transported into ecstasy. Your ideals are tethered to the highest stars. Continually prodded to become better at whatever you are doing, you not only understand the concept of self-improvement, you probably invented it. And on top of that, you even like to work! Producing something from your efforts and abilities makes you feel alive.

Because your mind is constantly analyzing everything, doing nothing is difficult. Learning to let go of those thoughts which keep your mind spinning in circles takes patience and deliberate focus on your part, but once you've mastered those "filtering" techniques, you experience greater peace with yourself. Drawn to situations which allow you to give of yourself, you shine when you serve. Yet you have to be careful to avoid becoming the victim or the martyr—a position you can either attract or create for yourself, especially if you feel inadequate or imperfect. Embracing real self-acceptance can be the key to gaining a real sense of personal power.

Although you may feel compelled to meet an unwritten set of expectations, it is important to occasionally strike a few requirements from your list in order to retain your sanity. Very little escapes your critical sensibilities—so you may as well find a reasonable outlet for them. Learning to train your sharp awareness so that you open to greater tolerance can be just as exciting as uncovering the problems you see so clearly. Making a few mistakes might help you remember that you are, after all, still human.

The Year at a Glance for Virgo Moon

After feeling overextended for the last year, you'll appreciate some of the balancing elements which arise throughout 1996. A little self-indulgence can be a positive way to heal some of the bumps and bruises left from Saturn's opposition and Jupiter's square transits to your Moon which are now ending. Now that you've cleared out some of the unnecessary things from your life, you have room to let in a more profound feeling of self-confidence and optimism, along with an occasional treat.

Pluto and Uranus are also stimulating a lengthy period of change, and bring significant alterations in your needs. If your Moon is in early degrees of Virgo, you'll feel the strongest effect of these cycles during the next two to three years. Otherwise, you'll see some evidence of these transformational changes on a more gradual scale over the next several years. In either case, the basis of your needs is shifting. You may be thinking about making profound revisions in your place of residence, your intimate relationships, or your work. One thing becomes perfectly clear: if you no longer need it, you'll now be able to let it go. To make the best use of these energies, determine the attitudes or response patterns which you'd like to modify in some way, and start there.

You're also challenged this year to take a more careful look at your intimate relationships and your level of satisfaction. Before you jump to the conclusion that something must be wrong, you might instead discover the things that are very right with your circumstances. If you're wanting more, you can use these cycles to help you uncover the mystery of what's missing or the best way to go about making the most out of your existing resources.

The eclipses bring your focus to the inner workings of your psyche and emphasize the relationship between soul, mind, and body. To create an optimum level of health, you may first have to open your mind to a different way of viewing what you can and cannot have. Better yet, look at what you do or do not allow yourself to experience. Maybe it's time to stop withholding and to learn to laugh and play more often.

Affirmation for the Year
My life is filled with happiness and comfort.

January

You may feel like you're taking two steps forward and one step back. But if you maintain a good sense of judgment in your decisions, you will realize that you're making progress. The emotional frustration you're feeling probably arises from the situations which crop up unexpectedly, particularly from the 7th to 16th. You can lash out in anger at someone who may simply be in the way of your wrath, but can mend any hurts by taking the time to express your real intentions. It's more likely that you are simply feeling agitated because of the interruptions to your careful plans. It's crucial that you use this time to find out about problems or difficulties, because you have the right energy to tie up those loose ends, release the past, and prepare to move forward. Your creative imagination is working overtime after the 15th, and can provide you with a fresh perspective on your needs and desires.

February

Fine-tuning is natural for you, but some of the adjustments you're making now may require a bit of soul-searching. Your emotional attachments need to be examined to determine if you're allowing yourself to meet your real needs, or if you're holding back out of fear. By addressing the origins of these fears, you can free yourself of the inhibitions which prevent you from realizing the fulfillment of your needs. You're likely to be confronted with an emotional power play mid-month which may test your resolve to honor your higher needs. Caving into the pressure can be counterproductive. Your vulnerabilities seem to be more easily triggered, and talking about your situation with a good friend may help you get back in control. Be careful about your projections this month, because you may be aiming your emotional fears or anger at a partner who has little to do with the problem. Allow yourself to own and accept your feelings. Then if a situation with another person needs to be addressed, you will be better prepared to reach a workable agreement.

March

Your attitude can be highly confrontational, and you may even be unreasonably argumentative. But should you need to defend yourself, your needs, or your position, you will feel the courage to accomplish your aims. Relationships are primed for growth under these influences. Personal reflection during the Full Moon in Virgo on the 5th can be illuminating, but you are more vulnerable to criticism and may overreact, so try to maintain your focus. If you've reached your limits with an intolerable situation, you may also decide to break away from it or face the problems directly. By the time of the New Moon on the 19th, you're ready to move ahead, but old obligations can hold you back. If you've been taking responsibility for your needs, then this cycle can be somewhat stabilizing. If you've been ignoring the reality of your situation, then consider this a wake-up call.

April

Many of the pressures which have kept you from putting yourself or your needs in their proper priority are subsiding. You're eager to move ahead. Your feelings about your work are also changing, and if you've been unhappy with the type of support (or lack of it) you're receiving, then you may decide to use this period to document your case. Sound thinking accompanies the cycles this month, and considering the practicalities is just as important as making room for innovation and creativity. Even though everything may not be in "perfect" condition near the time of the Sun's Eclipse on the 17th, your confidence is high, and you are in an excellent period to generate support and enthusiasm from others. Your intelligent presentation can be very appealing, and your conscientious attitudes work to your advantage.

May

You're feeling much more confident, and approach your work and relationships with stability and good ideas for future growth. This is a period of strengthening and rebuilding, and can result in establishing the kind of security you've needed. During Mercury's retrograde from the 4th to 27th, you can release or review situations from the past and eliminate those unfinished emotional issues. Your approach to conflict can become more soothing than irritating, and you may even discover a positive way to use crisis or conflict to promote growth or change. But one thing is changing: your values are undergoing a shift. Things you once held dear or desires which once motivated you may seem unimportant or inconsequential. In your intimate relationship, you may discover that the real value arises more from the commonality and support you offer one another than any of the externals which originally drew you together.

June

A few distractions can get in your way this month, especially if you feel that you've gotten into a rut. Before you start on several different things at once, try to control yourself! All your fastidious plans can be blown away rather quickly, and you need to have some room for emotional flexibility without losing sight of your priorities. Developing an idea or concept, or continuing the momentum in an existing relationship feels most consistent through the 12th. You may run into an old emotional block or experience the rumblings of unresolved anger from the 12th to 15th, when even your usual calm demeanor transforms to indignation. Your vulnerability arises due to your memories of injustice, or feelings of shame or guilt which can be easily triggered by a circumstance which seems to repeat that same old pain. But you can be more objective now, and break out of this repetitive pattern which seems to awaken without your consent. Changing is not easy, but if you can experience the freedom you deserve, isn't it worth the effort?

July

Although you may feel more open about communicating your ideas or feelings, you may also be more critical and less tolerant than you have been in the past. You can feel a sharp contrast between what you want and what you have, and if you direct your energy toward rectifying this situation, you can make significant progress. Turmoil at home is likely. The real discord resides within. If you've been the victim of your own destructive habits or negative attitudes, you have probably reached your limits, and may be ready to do whatever is necessary to begin the process of change. You can also break away from situations which limit your ability to satisfy your needs, and you may just as easily burn bridges which you do not intend to torch. Use your sense of discrimination to determine your actions, instead of just responding on impulse. Directed cutting away can be productive. Impulsive lashing out only creates damage.

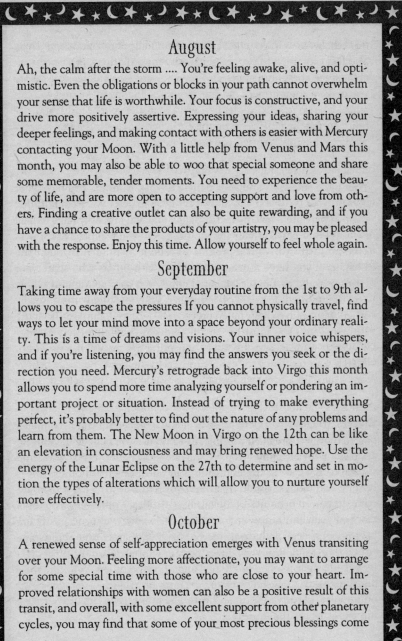

August

Ah, the calm after the storm .... You're feeling awake, alive, and optimistic. Even the obligations or blocks in your path cannot overwhelm your sense that life is worthwhile. Your focus is constructive, and your drive more positively assertive. Expressing your ideas, sharing your deeper feelings, and making contact with others is easier with Mercury contacting your Moon. With a little help from Venus and Mars this month, you may also be able to woo that special someone and share some memorable, tender moments. You need to experience the beauty of life, and are more open to accepting support and love from others. Finding a creative outlet can also be quite rewarding, and if you have a chance to share the products of your artistry, you may be pleased with the response. Enjoy this time. Allow yourself to feel whole again.

September

Taking time away from your everyday routine from the 1st to 9th allows you to escape the pressures If you cannot physically travel, find ways to let your mind move into a space beyond your ordinary reality. This is a time of dreams and visions. Your inner voice whispers, and if you're listening, you may find the answers you seek or the direction you need. Mercury's retrograde back into Virgo this month allows you to spend more time analyzing yourself or pondering an important project or situation. Instead of trying to make everything perfect, it's probably better to find out the nature of any problems and learn from them. The New Moon in Virgo on the 12th can be like an elevation in consciousness and may bring renewed hope. Use the energy of the Lunar Eclipse on the 27th to determine and set in motion the types of alterations which will allow you to nurture yourself more effectively.

October

A renewed sense of self-appreciation emerges with Venus transiting over your Moon. Feeling more affectionate, you may want to arrange for some special time with those who are close to your heart. Improved relationships with women can also be a positive result of this transit, and overall, with some excellent support from other planetary cycles, you may find that some of your most precious blessings come from the women in your life. During the middle of the month, you may also feel prompted to express generosity toward others, but be reasonable, since these influences also tend toward overindulgence. Before you make a commitment of time, money or energy, make sure you can afford it! You're seeking the best ways to assure your security and stability during the Full Moon on the 26th, and exhausting your resources or overindulging in things you do not need will have a negative effect.

November

Your pace quickens, and your patience grows thinner. You have your eyes on your goals and will allow very little to deter you from fulfilling them. There are a few distractions, and you will probably have to deal with a power play early in the month before you feel firmly on track. Like-minded individuals provide excellent assistance through the 14th, so if you have a need to associate with others who share your views or to be part of a communal effort, you can feel right at home. You'll run into differences of opinion and can feel highly frustrated by others who seem to have fallen prey to self-deceptive thinking from the 16th to 23rd. You must be careful to avoid becoming the victim of what you want to see, instead of accepting the reality of a situation. Watch your tendency to "enable" others in their own negative behaviors. Maintain a firm stand which is self-supporting, not self-effacing.

December

You're driven by a superb sense of self assurance and can accomplish more than you dreamed possible, just because you believe in yourself. A passion for life guides your feelings and may direct your actions, and if you've been weak in expressing your affections for another, this is your time to make certain that that person hows you feel. The courage of your convictions works to your benefit. Eager to break out of stale routine, you can engineer things just the way you want them. There is a possible trap: you can be too controlling, thereby alienating some of your best supporters. By directing your efforts toward the things you can actually influence or change and allowing others to follow their own paths, you may have a more genuine experience of achievement. Your enthusiasm sparkles, and your laughter heals. This is your time to shine. Make the most of it.

Libra Moon

Somewhere in life there resides a true serenity, a sense of calm, harmony, and beauty which is like Shangrila. You not only dream about it, you need to create it. That same dream contains the perfect lover and the relationship which provides support without overriding your autonomy. But can you ever find it in life? If anyone is willing to give it a try, it's you. If anyone needs to find that place inside your soul, it is you. For the brief moments when you discover a fragment of this hope, your eyes reflect those colors and, like a magnet, can attract what could be the answers. But in your heart of hearts, you know it's only temporary, until the balance changes again.

Yet it is maintaining that inner balance which is your gift. Others look to you for objectivity because you can somehow see both sides. You do understand that sometimes the paradox is what makes the complete picture beautiful. In the midst of the conflict, you pray for a place of solace. You saw the potential for the conflict and weighed it against the other side—the thrill— and decided to go for it anyway.

You have the reputation of never knowing for sure what you want until you've completed a complex set of deliberations. Then, once you do decide, you may have regrets for what you did not choose. What a curse. To have the dream, you have to pay for it. When you have to stand up and fight for what you want or need, you can do it. The price you pay is the pain of shattering the peace, and you walk away feeling very fragile. In the end, you have to become your own partner. Isn't it amazing that you cannot have the "other" partner until you've found one inside yourself?

The Year at a Glance for Libra Moon

This year may be filled with more temptations than you can count. And you have every reason to be skeptical, because some of them may be tests designed to challenge your resolve to honestly satisfy your higher needs. Underneath it all, you can feel an excitement, knowing that you're moving toward the tip of the iceberg. You just need to be sure that your raft works.

The Solar and Lunar Eclipses are specifically influential, since they fall in the Aries/Libra axis. Emotional crises can reach a boiling point, and resolutions which have needed to occur may finally be forthcoming. The only problem is that there are endings associated with these changes, and you may feel reluctant to let go, especially if you cannot see exactly where you're going next.

If you cannot decide which way to go, then somebody else may decide for you. Your alternative is simple: you must become more aware of your feelings and needs, and you must determine the best ways to make sure that these needs are met.

With Saturn entering Aries, where it will transit through 1998, you may also feel some pressure to take on responsibilities which inhibit your freedom of movement. You are not required to carry more than you can support, and if you try, then you'll feel even more inhibition. Your best approach is to find ways to become stronger, and to learn how to say no when necessary. In the final analysis, you will have to deal with the necessities, and you cannot ignore your obligations during these next two years. If you try, they appear like huge rock slides on your path. You need a firm foundation now, and you have the ability to create a platform which will support you for years to come.

The long-lasting cycles of Uranus and Pluto are also important. Whether you're experiencing their influence in its most powerful sense this year, or sometime within the next seven years, you can feel the surging of these energies in your life. You are awakening to a renewed sense of yourself, and you're capable of making significant breakthroughs in your psychological development. Your awareness grows at an exponential level, and you are likely to decide that what once felt safe and secure, now seems like a yoke around your neck. Your personal revolution can be a constructive one, but first, you have to incorporate a sense of the things you need to retain.

Affirmation for the Year

Change is safe.

January

Strong magnetism is one thing, but you're not relying on your charisma to set things in motion. You're eager to move ahead, and by combining your charm with a positive sense of assertiveness, you can accomplish your objectives. But there are a few snags early in the month which are the result of double messages, and you may have to clarify your intent before someone will cooperate with you. You may be the victim of false assumption, so getting the message straight benefits you as well. Feelings of passion can overwhelm your sense of logic, and you may get caught in your own illusions before you wake up, so give yourself time to pull away and regroup. You are open to deception later in the month, more because you're not hearing clearly than because someone intends you harm. Find out exactly what has been agreed upon before your make your commitment.

February

Although there are still a few vague messages out there, you've learned not to count on something until you have reason to trust. Fortunately, you're still willing to put forth the effort to go after what you want, but you may run out of steam toward the end of the month, especially if you've been following the wrong lead. Or you may simply grow tired of being the pursuer. Highly charged sexual energy sparks an intimate relationship, and you may find that body language is much easier to understand than verbal messages. Communication does improve near the time of the New Moon on the 18th. You're also experiencing differences in taste, and can be appalled by the lack of refinement you see around you. It's probably not a good idea to try to change it, yet you can create situations which are comfortable for you, and refuse to support those which are offensive.

March

Your experience has taught you that certain things are appropriate, but you might be surprised by the number of unwritten rules you're tempted to break this month. You do have your standards, and are unlikely to violate them unless you are forced to do so. You're caught in a vise between your expectations and disappointment during different periods, mostly due to the selfishness you encounter from others. Before you point fingers, make sure that you have not been the primary "enabler" of such selfish behavior, and promise yourself that you'll stand up and speak out for your own needs. You may even feel the stirrings of a competitive quality within yourself near the end of the month, and if you're feeling insecure, you may have to deal with feelings of jealousy. Remind yourself of your strengths and project your best qualities, instead of comparing yourself to an inaccurate yardstick.

April

The Moon's Eclipse in Libra on the 4th can usher in a stimulation of strong feelings of emotional instability, but there is an alternative. To strengthen your position, make an honest assessment of your feelings. Relationships are especially critical, and if you've been unhappy about your situation, you may finally be willing to speak up and do something about it. Repressing your emotions can be extremely self-destructive now, and you must allow yourself the opportunity to release what you feel. Anger can be a constructive force, and you have a chance now to use that energy to initiate positive changes and renew your vitality. Because your artistic sensibilities are also enhanced now, you may find that coupling the fiery impatience you're feeling with your creativity, you can achieve a strong sense of emotional harmony, and the resulting form of expression can be extremely satisfying.

May

Frustrated by stubborn outside resistance, you can still maintain your inner peace by allowing time to enjoy those things you find beautiful. You're still likely to fight against the odds, but once you get a feeling for the situation, you can make the proper adjustments. Consider this a good time to complete the things you've procrastinated about for one reason or another. By removing the obstacles from your path now, you'll have more room for spontaneity later. It's like you're behind the slowest truck on the interstate, but it's the only lane that will take you to your exit. Your feelings of love grow now, and you may also be more confident in social situations. Although you may begin to question your relationships, you can use this period of analysis to determine whether or not you want to stay involved. You may just need a change of attitude.

June

Much deliberate effort to keep things running smoothly early in the month finally pays off. You're ready for clear sailing after the 12th, and may even feel capable of trying a totally different approach toward fulfilling your emotional needs. Communication improves, and sudden breakthroughs from the 12th through the 16th can bring a real excitement. In your eagerness to celebrate your good fortune, you may become forgetful about your obligations. If you ignore them, you'll definitely get a sharp reminder beforethe end of the month. But you can also incorporate your commitments into your new freedom and allow everyone to share the joy which boosts your spirit. Your passion gains momentum, and any creative project or artistic expression can be especially fulfilling. Reconsiderations about emotional attachments may prompt you to get back into a situation which had become difficult. You are finally making a breakthrough.

July

There's very little that can stop you if you have your mind set on something now, and the highly charged emotional energy which accompanies this time is more supportive than overwhelming. Your sense of artistic refinement needs an outlet, and whether you're spending more time in creative pursuits or social situations, others are very likely to offer their endorsement of your efforts. Double messages can create a setback mid-month, and trying to step out of the way until the dust settles may just get you into trouble. You need to listen, observe, and then clarify, or you may be branded with something which does not fit your intentions. Placating will not be as effective as dealing directly with the problems at hand. For the greater part, you can redirect the flow or focus to be assured a more harmonious result. Avoid over obligating your time or energy near the end of the month, and listen to your intuition to help you decide.

August

Your patience is shorter now, especially if you had your mind on a certain outcome and you're being forced to wait, or if you're running into resistance from someone else. You are also likely to run head-long into your own fears, since some of the things happening now can easily trigger old memories of disappointment or hurt. You can fall victim to extreme levels of emotional vulnerability if you've extended your expectations beyond realistic proportions. In your frustration, you can lash out against those who share your life, just because they are there. Maintaining your emotional center is difficult, but not impossible. You just have to work at it more, and with your increasing awareness, you may experience a fresh perspective. In many respects, this cycle provides just the right impetus to break away from your old responses while you courageously move into new territory.

September

Although the first week seems like one confusing situation after another, you can also use this time to take it easy and slow your routine. Pushing against the flow just wears you down. Inner conflicts haunt your dreams, and during the day, you may feel that you're just not in touch with reality. The danger of this time arises if you allow your illusions to overtake your good sense. After the 10th, you can feel that the crisis has subsided and that you are back on track. Your passion for life returns, and you may feel that you have transformed in some way. In your love relationship, you're unlikely to sit back and wait for something to happen. If you want something, you'll be comfortable taking action to assure that you are satisfied. The energy of the Moon's Eclipse on the 27th encourages you to harmonize your obligations with a more free expression of your needs and feelings.

October

Adding substance to your life involves focusing on a broad range. At home you may want to add a special touch to your environment, change the colors, or bring something into your home which makes you feel more comfortable. Your critical eye can also uncover the imbalances in your love relationship, and you may also be interested in making sure that your friendships are producing mutual support. Anything which has been smoldering beneath the surface emotionally reaches a crisis point near the time of the Sun's Eclipse in Libra on the 12th, especially if you failed to take an honest look at the situation in April. This escalation allows you to determine the best approach to dealing with your relationships, but you'll also feel more in touch with your inner self. That microscopic enhancement of your internal make-up gives you a chance to understand what is really at the core of your soul.

November

Cooperation and harmony are your hope, and you can set the example for the best ways to achieve this, whether at work or at home. But your efforts can be thwarted if you've promised more than you can deliver, so try to be realistic before you agree to participate in a time-consuming situation or before you decide to chair that committee. You're drawn to fill your heart with love, which begins by using this cycle to support and appreciate yourself— without comparing. An inspirational period begins on the 14th, helping you unleash pent-up emotion by directing it into productive arenas. Your illusions about yourself, or false impressions of another, can cause difficulties during the week of the 17th if you jump into something with little knowledge or inadequate preparation. The awakening may feel like a bucket of ice water— but at least you'll get the point.

December

Demands from others can leave you feeling that there is little time or opportunity to take care of your own needs. Just remind yourself that you do have control over the things which influence your stability, and funnel your "outreach" into situations which nourish you, too. Strengthening your emotional foundation may also mean that you need to reach back into your past and rectify unfinished issues before you can move forward. Contrast between the way you see yourself now and the way you used to be can be just what you need to abandon those old hopes, or to release the pain or guilt which has driven you toward insane levels of expectation. You're no longer content just to be sure that everyone else is happy while you go back into the corner and observe. The change starts by putting yourself back into the picture as an important element. After all, the reason you're alive is to enhance your soul growth— and that does not mean that you have to take the leftovers.

Scorpio Moon

Without a doubt, if anyone feels the depths of emotion, it is you. You have the most keen sense of what happens on an inner level, and your penetrating gaze conveys that awareness to anyone who looks into your eyes. While others ignore their shadows, you know that you must embrace yours, and may, since you were a child, have been fascinated by concepts which society considers taboo. You have curiosity about birth, death, sex, pain—all the things "polite" society has swept under the carpet. You know that life is a transformational experience, and you accept these realities, because when you do not, they haunt your dreams.

In many ways, you are the natural psychologist, ever probing into the depths of human consciousness, ever curious about what lies beneath the surface. You are never satisfied with a shallow relationship —whether with a friend, family member, or lover—because you can sense the unspoken and would just as soon deal with it. When your feelings grow too intense, you can stuff your them better than anyone else. You will know that there is a storm brewing deep within, but your cool manner would never give it away. Because you fear that someone might find out, you can erect barriers which keep everyone out of that inner sanctum. Then, when you want to let someone inside, when you need the intimacy, your frustration with your old defense mechanism can be monumental. But you possess a secret weapon. If you're willing, you can be reborn.

Before it's all said and done, you'll realize that rebirths have occurred over and over again; because you are intent on getting to the core. Much like the caterpillar's metamorphosis, your life is filled with phenomenal changes. You know all the emotions, from despair to ecstasy. Yet you'll probably always want to be sure you have that cocoon handy—just in case.

The Year at a Glance for Scorpio Moon

Over the last twelve years, Pluto has been transiting in Scorpio, and at some point during this time, you confronted the depths of your soul. In many ways, this cycle gave you the insight that you can survive anything, if you're willing. And now, with Pluto moving into its next

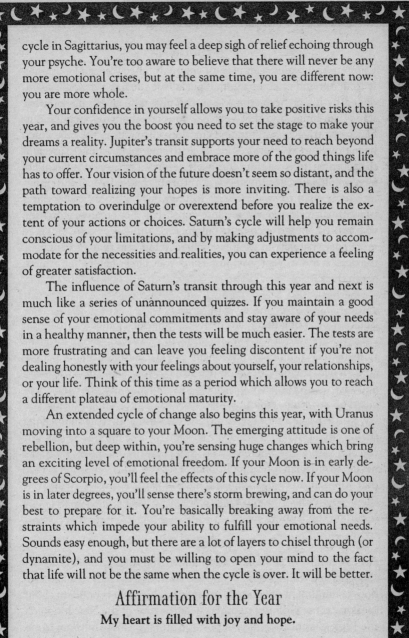

cycle in Sagittarius, you may feel a deep sigh of relief echoing through your psyche. You're too aware to believe that there will never be any more emotional crises, but at the same time, you are different now: you are more whole.

Your confidence in yourself allows you to take positive risks this year, and gives you the boost you need to set the stage to make your dreams a reality. Jupiter's transit supports your need to reach beyond your current circumstances and embrace more of the good things life has to offer. Your vision of the future doesn't seem so distant, and the path toward realizing your hopes is more inviting. There is also a temptation to overindulge or overextend before you realize the extent of your actions or choices. Saturn's cycle will help you remain conscious of your limitations, and by making adjustments to accommodate for the necessities and realities, you can experience a feeling of greater satisfaction.

The influence of Saturn's transit through this year and next is much like a series of unannounced quizzes. If you maintain a good sense of your emotional commitments and stay aware of your needs in a healthy manner, then the tests will be much easier. The tests are more frustrating and can leave you feeling discontent if you're not dealing honestly with your feelings about yourself, your relationships, or your life. Think of this time as a period which allows you to reach a different plateau of emotional maturity.

An extended cycle of change also begins this year, with Uranus moving into a square to your Moon. The emerging attitude is one of rebellion, but deep within, you're sensing huge changes which bring an exciting level of emotional freedom. If your Moon is in early degrees of Scorpio, you'll feel the effects of this cycle now. If your Moon is in later degrees, you'll sense there's storm brewing, and can do your best to prepare for it. You're basically breaking away from the restraints which impede your ability to fulfill your emotional needs. Sounds easy enough, but there are a lot of layers to chisel through (or dynamite), and you must be willing to open your mind to the fact that life will not be the same when the cycle is over. It will be better.

Affirmation for the Year
My heart is filled with joy and hope.

January

Differences in values can prompt you to distance yourself emotionally from a friend or companion, especially if you feel personally abandoned by his or her actions. You can also take an uncharacteristic stance, and may find that your opinions are changing. Sudden outbursts can trigger conflicts, and emotional issues from the past which have been buried or ignored are likely to emerge. Learning to use conflict constructively during this cycle confers a tremendous feeling of freedom. If you're feeling angry, it's probably better to deal with it immediately than to swallow your feelings until a more "appropriate" time. By directing your anger into constructive or creative activities, you may be able to accomplish more. One thing is certain, you'll be more passionate about whatever you're doing, and there is very little that can stand in your way. Just know your target before you launch your attack.

February

You may be acting like you have a chip on your shoulder, so make an effort to be aware of what you're projecting to avoid getting into battles which do not need to be fought. An ego conflict can flare out of control near the Full Moon on the 4th, but you can address the issues and move beyond petty disagreements which waste your time. Focused on reaching resolution instead of adding to your problems, you have little patience for immature attitudes from others. You're seeing the futility of trying to influence someone whose mind is closed. But you can also realize where your attitudes may need some revision. It's never easy to abandon a conditioned response, and even if you decide that you want to change, you still have to battle against your old routines. Your desire to forgive opens a door to resolution after the New Moon on the 18th.

March

An easier flow of communication allows you to express your deeper thoughts and feelings to someone you trust. You're ready to make a serious commitment to yourself, and may be able to feel confident about speaking those promises to others near the time of the New Moon on the 19th. Clarification of your position gives you more freedom to express yourself, and by openly discussing expectations, you'll be able to establish a firm foundation for long-term growth. Any work which needs to be done at home, or signing contracts which pertain to purchase or home improvement, can be highly successful during the week of the 17th, when your realistic thinking is coupled with positive support from others. Opportunities to stabilize a partnership or serious love relationship emerge, and you may be more willing to address your mutual needs. Remember that you don't have to fix everything. Resolution works best when it's shared.

April

Even though you may have a clear idea about what you want, you can still run into periods of self-sabotage when your fears crop up at the most inconvenient times. In your attempts to alter your attitudes, you're likely to run into those old messages which whisper quietly about your failings. During the Lunar Eclipse on the 4th, you may feel the stirrings of vague discomfort which is difficult to pinpoint. By the time of the Sun's Eclipse on the 17th, you have a clear concept of what you're up against. Even if your outside situations show little change, your inner self is more optimistic about the future. The quiet alterations you make behind the scenes will ultimately have their effect on outside impressions. Deceptive attitudes and actions from others do not escape your keen awareness, but you may not want to show your hand until you're sure you've won the bet.

May

If you feel threatened by another's confrontation, you're not likely to just roll over and play dead. It takes very little to awaken your wrath, and if you need to fight a battle now, you should warn your opponent that they could be in for heavy losses. You are also at risk, and before you take on a challenge, determine what you're willing to risk. Sudden or impulsive reactions early in the month can be costly, especially near the time of the Scorpio Full Moon on the 3rd. For the next several days, it may not take much to push you over the edge. Maintain your center, and deal with your own internal issues. By recognizing the source of your inner conflict, you can avoid unnecessary strife, and you may be less prone to project your negative feelings onto someone who is undeserving of your anger. If difficulties do exist, they will be apparent enough without creating new ones due to unresolved feelings from the past.

June

A more mindful attitude allows you to attain greater objectivity about your needs. Your manner can be too abrasive through the 12th, when saying what's on your mind can stir up quite a bit of controversy. A few minor alterations may be all that are necessary to rectify the problems which occur. But you can also alienate others if you fail to redress any misunderstandings. In some circumstances, you may be glad to be rid of the hassle, but if you really want to maintain a connection, you may have to open up and make the first-move. Your work obligations can seem to get in the way of your emotional needs late in the month, but if you make the effort to add a little extra "comfort time" to your schedule, it can take the edge off the stress you're feeling. Shallow attitudes from others can be quite irritating this month. Do your best to know when to speak and when to keep your ideas to yourself.

July

Some circumstances get a bit complicated. You may have to deal with a number of distractions, which makes it difficult to feel that you're really getting what you want. Although it's easier to get your ideas across from the 1st to 15th, all your efforts may seem to have been in vain when new directions emerge mid-month. Yet making the connections is important, and some of the shifting focus may give you a chance to try an altogether different approach. One thing is sure: you can certainly see past the facade. If someone else wants to get caught in an illusion, you don't have to jump off the cliff too. You might be better off waiting for a more auspicious time to speak your mind if you cannot see any value in challenging or addressing a situation. That undercurrent of nervous energy stems from wanting to act, but knowing that you don't have everything together yet.

August

You may be ready to move ahead, but there are some obligations you must address before you are free to do as you please. You're also running headlong into your own unrealistic expectations, and may have to trim your sails a bit in order to accommodate the realistic view of your situation. New options emerge after the 10th, when you're more productive and when you're likely to feel that you can handle things. A conservative attitude colors even your boldest plans, so you don't have to worry about getting in over your head emotionally. Give yourself time to enjoy your personal environment, and to add a few creature comforts which support your need to feel safe and secure. You might even enjoy entertaining at home, or at least inviting your intimate friend, lover or partner to share a bit of physical, emotional, and spiritual sustenance.

September

Stepping out of the high level of activity and enjoying an escape from the everyday can be extremely rejuvenating from the 1st to 8th. And if you must continue with your daily routine, do allow time for reflection, contemplation and creative expression. Your dreams can be visionary, and you may have a strong sense of your future path from the images and messages your receive during your dreams or periods of reverie. You can also trust your impressions of others, but need to be skeptical of anyone who offers an unrealistic promise. In many ways, you may feel that this month ushers in a time of emotional purging. Doing some external clearing, along with inner housekeeping, can get rid of the clutter you find so distracting. But watch a tendency toward compulsiveness, and think again before you burn old those old diaries or give away something you hold dear. Good-byes can be pretty final now.

October

An easygoing attitude puts a damper on some of your frustrations, but you're still not likely to want to stay around a situation which just doesn't fit your needs any longer. However, you can take a more practical approach to addressing any emotional issues which arise, and you may find it easier to explain your feelings and needs and work out solutions to your personal problems. An undercurrent of agitation still stirs beneath the surface, and your patience wears thin near the time of the Solar Eclipse on the 12th. But as the month draws to a close, you may have a different viewpoint on a relation-

ship or a circumstance in which you have a strong emotional investment. An alluring attraction can be fascinating, and may tempt you
to stray from your commitments. Even if you're free to pursue it, you
may be disappointed in the final outcome unless you walk in with your
eyes open.

November

A quiet confidence inspires you to pursue the attainment of an important hope or goal. Deliberate and persistent effort work to your advantage. Your ability to keep a secret allows you to follow your inner hopes
without letting the cat out of the bag. If you've been waiting to launch
a pet project, or to approach your partner with your feelings about
something important, the energy of the Scorpio New Moon on the
11th gives you just the right impetus to get things moving. Still plagued
with a few unrealistic expectations, you may have to alter your plans
in order to achieve your desired results, but you have a better chance
of getting what you want now. If there's been any confusion about your
wants or desires, they should be pretty clear now, and there's no time
like the present to make certain that they are fulfilled.

December

Your experience of a deep and abiding love can be a reality. You're realizing the importance of doing things which support your own worth,
and by increasing your self-acceptance, you also increase your ability
to attract others who can see your strengths and support your needs.
Yet you may not feel particularly "needy" now, and can be more comfortable reaching out and giving to others. Relationships with men
and women improve. Your confidence allows you to be positively self-
assertive. Your imagination and sensitivity are working overtime after the 12th, and special efforts pay off with supportive gestures from
others. It's even easier to request help when you need it instead of
waiting until you're about to collapse under the weight of your obligations. Remember how you accomplish this for future reference.

Sagittarius Moon

You need to feel free. Free to follow whatever inspires you, free to move, to travel, to explore ... but most of all, you need to feel free to express and experience the broadest possible range of concepts and ideas. Your hunger is for truth, and the longer you live, the more you may realize that there is a profound difference between truth and facts. Your ideals reach beyond the stars, and your hope for the future is boundless. When you observe injustice, you may feel personally assaulted. In your zeal to find the answers or to step into another adventure, you can forget that others may not be so tempted to find the next horizon.

Home for you may not be a place, but can instead be more like a quest. You're at home when you're growing, learning, and when you feel the connection between your spirit and your heart. You can embrace other cultures, and may be fascinated by the language and philosophy of different peoples. Your preference is to see things from the perspective of the mountain top, instead of getting caught in the maze of the forest.

In relationships, you need someone who will understand the importance of independence, and you're not likely to stick around if you feel smothered or inhibited. Although the ideal of a companion to share the journey of life does exist for you, you may discover that finding someone of strong vision, playful heart, and courageous spirit is quite a challenge. If you do find that person, you may be able to keep a commitment. Staying on the move does not necessarily mean that you have to physically go anywhere. In your mind, your heart, and your soul, you will always been journeying, questioning, and wondering about all the vast possibilities and reasons, and will continue to search for the Grail of Truth.

The Year at a Glance for Sagittarius Moon

Your sense of emotional stability grows much stronger. You're ready to fill in some of the vacant spaces in your personal foundation. Although much of your optimism of last year was tempered by the need to meet your responsibilities, you'll find a more efficient way to answer your obligations while moving forward during 1996. A deep sense of personal power is ready to emerge. Before you can embrace it, you may have to let go of some old attitudes.

After April, when Saturn moves into Aries, you'll feel much less confined and may also sense that the pace of your life is more comfortable. You're also experiencing some profound changes at a deep level due to the influences of Uranus and Pluto. The two outer planets move very slowly, and their influences are more gradual. However, during the year either planet aspects your Moon, you will feel a definitive change in the way you address and relate to your own inner needs. If your Moon is in early degrees of Sagittarius, then you'll feel this influence during the next two years. But if your Moon is in mid to late degrees, then the most profound changes in consciousness influenced by these cycles will occur later, within three years and into the early part of the next century. Regardless of the exact degree of your Moon, you'll be able to use the lessons learned and wisdom gained from these cycles for many years.

Your ability to tune into the "collective consciousness" is enhanced, and you may sense that you are involved in things which reach far beyond your own personal needs. But it is in answering your personal needs that you will make the choices, direct your thoughts, and take the actions which change the resonating energy which affects life around you. Your awareness of this connection becomes extremely marked now. Instead of sensing that this is a burden, you may experience this time as a tremendous challenge which quickens your heart, mind, and spirit.

The Solar and Lunar Eclipse cycles draw your attention to your relationships and stimulate your need to become a more effective communicator. You will certainly see the shortfalls in this area, and can also grow through developing your strengths in linking your thoughts and ideas with others. You may also find that just as quickly as you learn, you will be returning that knowledge or experience through teaching or guiding others. This experience may bring the greatest wisdom, like manna from heaven.

Affirmation for the Year

I am open to wisdom in all its forms.

January

You're feeling highly creative, and may want to get involved in a project or situation which allows you to use your talents to their fullest. The feelings which take root in your heart may seem more like a dream, but over the next few weeks, you may feel more courageous about taking action to make sure that your desires are fulfilled. However, there can be a few inhibitions, and most of them may seem to come from another's unwillingness to listen to your point of view. The question of appropriate action and workable timing also arises, and even though you may feel ready to pursue something (or someone), the time to do so may not materialize. The inspiration you're feeling is genuine, and if you can avoid becoming too distracted by the obstacles in your path, you may actually be awakening a new aspect of your consciousness.

February

You can feel blocked by either your own emotional attachments, or by someone else. If you've left unfinished emotional business, it's quite likely that you'll have to face the music and contend with your real feelings. If you regret an action or a choice, admitting your regrets can begin the healing process. To resolve problems, try to determine how much of the issue revolves around what is currently going on, and how much is based on held-over pain. The Full Moon on the 4th brings a positive time to acknowledge your feelings. Should you want to begin anew, an easier flow of emotional energy emerges on the 9th which stimulates a deeper sense of trust of your own feelings. Be aware of your own impatience, which may prompt you to give up just before the fruit is ripe. Try to avoid acting on impulse from the 15th to 21st, when some cutbacks can be productive, but prematurely breaking away can cause unnecessary damage.

March

You've heard of the concept of instant karma? Well, you may think it is all directed at you this month! If you pay attention, you'll realize that the lessons you're learning are all about getting in touch with the effects of your words and actions. Unlike some periods, you can't just deliver a farewell address and ride away into the sunset. It may seem that you're having to fight your battles alone, yet you know that feeling sorry for yourself accomplishes nothing. Determine your choices, find ways to stand up for your needs by doing things which provide positive nurturance. Even though you're frustrated, try to hang in there until you accomplish your goals. If a commitment has become a burden, perhaps you need to review your approach and attitudes toward it. You may not be able to walk away, but you can lighten your load.

April

As a reward for surviving the tests of the last several months, the cosmos has decided to give you a short break. Sketchy though it may be, you can see a workable plan forming, and you're eager to get back into the action. You can be somewhat self-absorbed, but your interest in accomplishing your aims can prompt you to pay attention to the demands you must meet. You may also feel more ready to consider a commitment, at least short term, which will add some structure to your life. However, your heart is easily distracted, and you may be tempted to chase after a few rainbows, only to discover that what you left behind was more beautiful and rewarding. A more deliberate pace coupled with definitive goals suits you best during this cycle. You can still have your adventures. Do be wary of the allurements occurring near the time of the Sun's Eclipse on the 17th and through the end of the month. They may be mere illusions with little substance.

May

Relationships can be rather sticky, and you might wish that you were less involved and free to give into your playful urges. But face it. The challenge now can actually be rather juicy, and might be more interesting than just sitting on top of a mountain. Your questions about the way you feel arise from a re-evaluation of your own sense of love, and you may find little comfort in the advice of poets or sages. You need to know deep within your heart where love resides, and how to make it grow. Although you may think you live just within the moment, you're realizing how all those moments are somehow connected to a whole. You're seeing the big picture. If you don't like it, now is the time to determine how you want to change it. Much of the clutter in your mind and heart is the result of the things you never got around to doing. It's like reviewing all your old journals, realizing that there is meaty material in there, but that there are also a lot of rambling thoughts. Pull out those gems and get busy.

June

Contrasts abound. After you've managed to navigate around the blocks in your path, an extremely restless energy drives you to increase your explorations. A power struggle from the 11th to 17th can leave you feeling exhausted if you burn out all your energy at once. You may feel that you're always on the defensive instead of having a chance to pursue your desires. By considering the effects of your words and actions you'll avoid alienating those you hope to endear. Emotional conflicts can be the order of the day, and others may think you've lost your objectivity. Undercurrents of anger or frustration add an edge to your demeanor, and you may even have trouble communicating clearly. Watch for the possibility of projecting your own inner conflicts or unconscious drives onto others. By finding an effective way to deal with turmoil or difficulty, you will learn a lot about yourself and may even come to terms with a long-standing problem in a relationship.

July

Relationship disputes reach a peak, although learning to use your differences in a constructive manner can prove to be quite invigorating. You may discover that you want different things, and because of that might decide that you're ready to move on to something else. Other alternatives do exist, and you're in a great position to create a situation which allows you to accept your own needs for personal expression while encouraging the same thing from your partner or family. If you're the only one who seems to be in conflict, stop to determine where the problem really resides. Avoid troublesome double-talk after the 19th, and take the time to listen to what others are really saying before you jump to a conclusion. Achieving a different perspective on yourself and your goals creates a feeling of renewed hope. You're ready to prove your worth to the world, but may have to start by first accepting it for yourself.

August

Clarifying your position over and over again can be exhausting. You may feel like handing out a brochure just to avoid having to repeat yourself. The difficulty is likely to reside in the way you present yourself and the manner in which you express your emotions. Instead of allowing others to deal with their responses and then returning once the dust clears, you'll be better off trying to work through a crisis or deal with the issues when they emerge. Just because others seem to overreact does not mean that they are wrong and you are right. You also have an obligation to let others know what you really want and need from them. This is an emotionally strained period, but not necessarily a time filled with confrontation or new problems. You are experiencing triggers which leave you feeling insecure, and need to find a way to alter the picture.

September

During the first week you may encounter some bizarre images in your dreams, or may feel like you're just out of touch with yourself or with the others who share your life. Things change quite dramatically after the 7th, when unexpected surprises or events cause you to develop a different outlook. A highly inspiring period ensues, and you may feel the return of an enthusiasm you thought lost. Balancing your expenditure of creative energy within the framework of your commitments is almost automatic. By the time of the Moon's Eclipse on the 27th, you can be riding high. Even the changes which are occurring can seem to be like gates opening to a wider horizon. Using the energy of this time to become more fully aware and self-expressive helps you to build a powerful foundation for future growth. Your generosity of spirit is contagious and can encourage others to open their hearts, too.

October

To avoid running into minor altercations over preferences, try to make an effort to listen or observe before you leap into action and make changes. Most of the emotional conflicts which occur this month are likely to be the result of petty differences, but if carried too far, even those situations can damage your trust for one another. If you're making improvements or changes at home, strive to create a situation which provides a feelings of increased mobility and openness. Territorial disputes can put a damper on an otherwise tranquil environment. These can escalate near the time of the Full Moon on the 26th, but may not occur at all if you're been making an extra effort to assure that open communication and clear understanding has been the order of the day. If you've been unaware, you can feel that you're slapped in the face by a harsh reality.

November

You have very little patience, and may seem to be more angry than cooperative when things are not going your way. Passions run high, and you can channel this energy toward making huge improvements in your love life. You're eager to enjoy some fun-loving and playful alternatives, and may also be ready to get out of a rut in your communication. Any creative writing or speaking can help you feel more emotionally open, and you may also be more flexible in situations which had previously seemed unapproachable. You can also become more loving and attentive, and will certainly be willing to take the time to enjoy tender expressions from others. You may need to escape from the pressures or from the stale routine of your "ordinary" life from the 17th to 22nd, but still need to maintain objectivity to avoid falling victim to your own illusions.

December

Others may seem less flexible, but before you point fingers, determine for yourself if you've become too judgmental or rigid. You'll run into confrontations if you try to force your beliefs or ideals onto others, even though you may think you have "pure" intentions. Take time to evaluate your underlying motivations near the time of the Sagittarius New Moon on the 10th, because you can easily shift positions and be more accommodating. If you're basically aware of your emotions, you may realize that some old issues are still percolating to the surface, and may add a more abrasive quality to your attitudes. Your deeper needs soften under the influence of Venus' transit in Sagittarius from the 17th to 31st. But you're still feeling a bit impatient, so try to remember that everyone may not move at your lightning speed.

Capricorn Moon

For you, life is a long series of campaigns to succeed. You're driven more powerfully than many others to attain your aims, and may seem to be too structured by those who would prefer to spend their time in idle pursuits. You need these challenges, you thrive on them. Even as a small child, you loved the accolades from your parents when you accomplished standing, walking, speaking, reading ... and it continues throughout your life. Once your eye is set on your objective, your determined, persistent efforts are always directed to achieve that aim.

Because you've had a chance to see the reality of the puzzle of life, you frequently laugh to yourself about certain acts of futility. Even when you are in ridiculous positions, you see the humor, but sometimes don't let on to the rest of the world, who assume you've always worn a suit and tie. You can seem too disciplined, too cautious, and are all too familiar with the unwritten set of rules shaping your decisions and actions. But deep within your soul, you know that you must master certain tasks and achieve certain goals in order to feel peace with yourself. Your work is more than a job— it is an integral part of the expression of your soul.

In relationships, you may have little time for frivolous choices. You can be tender and loving, and may value acts of romance which help you solidify your commitments. You run into trouble when issues of control emerge; you don't like the idea of someone else telling you what to do. Your partner needs to appreciate your practical needs, and must also understand your priorities. Excessive emotion is a waste of energy for you, but learning to express your feelings can bring you a stronger sense of personal growth. If it's important, you will open your heart. After all, if you want something, you are not likely to stop until you get it!

The Year at a Glance for Capricorn Moon

What a powerful and positive period you're experiencing, with Jupiter transiting over your Moon this year! This cycle provides an undercurrent of inner confidence which radiates through all your actions and choices. You may feel more optimistic, and feel as though you can finally risk reaching beyond your current boundaries and explore new options or territory. This period is linked to a cycle which occurred in 1972 and 1984, and you may find that you are building on some of the choices and opportunities which presented themselves during those periods.

During the early part of this year, you may see more measured progress in achieving the realization of your hopes and wishes. By April, a period of testing or crisis is likely to cause you to re-evaluate your choices. If you've been aware of the changes and challenges over the last few years, then you may find that the tests of this spring and fall are more like a personal audit. But if you've been ignoring your emotional needs, this time is a wake-up call. You can no longer rely on the old standby responses or supports. Some of those supports may not exist anymore, and many you will have outgrown. Saturn's cycle tests your resolve, and you may feel that you have to face many of your challenges alone. In some instances, it's better that way. If you feel that just once, you'd like to have somebody there for encouragement or comfort, you may want to take a look at the way you've nourished relationships. Perhaps it is time to let somebody in, after all.

The Eclipses also emphasize your needs in relationships and your participation in relationships with others. A conscious awareness of your unconscious drives can make a big difference between your satisfaction with your partner or family situation. You may actually be able to turn things around and develop the kind of association which presents a truly unified platform of support. If you are standing alone, you may decide you can finally invite the support and participation of others. This is very much a period of seeing the working of the Law of Karma: what you sow, you also reap. If you want to change the outcome of the harvest of your emotional needs, then this is the time to become a better farmer.

Affirmation for the Year
I accept and nourish my emotional needs.

January

Even though you may not openly admit it, you're likely to feel emotionally vulnerable during the Full Moon on the 5th, but if you stay in touch with your inner feelings before you make a decision, you'll be happier with the outcome of a decision. By blending your inventive ideas with affirmative action you can accomplish an exciting result, and may even inspire some exceptional support from others. After the 8th, you may spend more time in pursuit of your outside obligations, but you may still want to allow ample time to enjoy the fruits of your labors. If you sense that your life has gotten out of balance with your needs, you can envision and activate a new plan for yourself during the Capricorn New Moon on the 20th. Taking care of yourself needs to become a more comprehensive experience. After all, they won't be reading your resume at your funeral!

February

Your ability to bring even the most complex concepts into practical terms works to your advantage this month. Expressing your needs, thoughts, and feelings is easier, especially if you're establishing a strong sense of trust with your partner. Personal commitments can be stabilizing and their success is more assured if you define your position from the the 1st through the 11th, and you can be strongly realistic in your approach. However, you'll enjoy a break in your routine from the 10th to 12th, and may even want to plan a time to enjoy your favorite recreation after the 14th. Even though you may not put escape high on your priority list, you will enjoy a break in the action after the 20th, when you may be feeling quite playful. Give yourself time to reflect, and allow your imagination and sense of vision to work to your benefit. It's time to create the foundation which will support your dreams and fulfill your hopes.

March

Feeling more sure of yourself and your worth, you can use this period to satisfy many of your needs. Your creative talents blend beautifully with your practical sensibilities, allowing you to produce something which is highly viable. At home, you may want to make some improvements which allow you to express your personal preferences.

You're also looking for more effective ways to safeguard your valuables, and may become more security conscious. You're not driven by fear as much as by purely realistic concerns. A sense of sophistication may also accompany your manner, drawing a more positive response from others who are impressed by your confidence and good taste. A loving energy fills your heart now, and you may be more inclined to show tenderness and appreciation, endearing those who care about you. Most of all, you find it easier to love yourself.

April

Impatient with the slow progress, you can feel extremely frustrated if things are not going the way you planned. Even in the midst of setbacks or difficulties, you can be highly effective in communicating and making the right connections, which can facilitate some forward progress. If you feel that everything is stalled, concentrate on the things which are right in front of you. You may have to overcome a few obstacles before you reach the objectives you've targeted. Most of the problems should emerge by the time of the Moon's Eclipse on the 4th, giving you ample time to devise a new plan which you can put into action after the Sun's Eclipse on the 17th. You'll feel much more confident about your options late in the month, although confusing interruptions to your careful preparations can undermine your sense of self-reliance. If you can, wait for a while to take any risks, and use this time to regroup.

May

You may be sitting back watching everyone else scramble while their foundations crack, and after you've had a chance to carefully evaluate the situation, you may be the one who arrives at the most workable solution. Although you might prefer to have a better sense of self-control during a period of surprises from the 2nd to 10th, some of the unexpected changes may actually prompt you to step onto paths you would never have considered. A tendency to withhold information can work to your detriment, since through disclosing some of your emotional secrets you may actually get free of their grip on your psyche. Time spent with a good friend can be self-confirming and may also give you a chance to repay their support with your encouragement and help. This is a time to establish strong mutually beneficial associations, and to reaffirm your commitments.

June

You may feel more stable from the 1st to 12th, but after that time many of the distractions and diversified interruptions can play havoc with your ability to focus on the task at hand. This can be irritating, and you may feel an increasing sense of hostility toward circumstances which keep requiring you to move with the times. You have your own pace, and will not appreciate being pushed, prodded, or probed. If you can assess the situation by asking questions and gathering facts, you may be better prepared to cope with the outside changes. The inner changes are another question. Maybe you do feel a need to shift your priorities, but choosing the best way to do it can drive you nuts. Take advantage of the insights others can offer, and allow your own consciousness to open to a different point of view. You don't have to adopt an alien philosophy, but you may have to adjust your attitudes. Lip service will not suffice. You want to see and feel worthwhile results.

July

You're better at initiating action than adapting to situations which others create, but you may have to adopt a temporary position in order to get to the point where you can assert your own ideas. Part of the challenge this month revolves around your needs to listen to others, particularly those who are emotionally tied to you. If someone expresses feelings that you are not as supportive as they want you to be, try to hear them without falling into your own sense of guilt. You may think to yourself, "If they only knew." But the problem may be that they don't! It is possible to alter the way you communicate your feelings so that someone else can really feel that they are as important to you as you are to them. Even though it's a bit irritating to make the modifications, you may eventually like things better after the change, but the period of adjustment can be a pain in the neck.

August

You're more direct about expressing yourself, and may even be abrasive in situations which try your patience. Maintaining the proper perspective between your expectations and the possibilities is not easy this month. You can feel especially mistrustful of your own judgment if problems keep repeating themselves. This is an exceptional time to make headway, because you're seeing the strengths and the weaknesses of your life circumstances. After identifying the weak link in a structure, all you have to do is replace it or fortify it in some way. It's like knowing which part to order, but discovering that the parts department is closed for the weekend. Alternatives do emerge, and you are the one who can create most of the most workable solutions. Family turmoil can also abound, and you may run into issues you thought were settled long ago. Maybe this is just a test.

September

Watch for illusory traps from the 1st to 8th, when your viewpoints can be misguided by a false impression or by self-deceptive denial. This is a good time to get in touch with your inner self, but it may not be such an easy time to have to deal with the practical side of life. During Mercury's retrograde from the 4th to 26th, you have a chance to review your previous choices or actions, and may actually determine a better way to synthesize the demands of the outside world with your personal needs. Interruptions to your routine or schedule can be the result of your need to be more attentive to family or relationship demands, but you may also run into difficulties at work which cause you to take another look at the way you're approaching your career. There's little time to simply ruminate over the possibilities. You feel the pressure of having to carry out your deliberations while in the midst of accomplishing your everyday tasks.

October

All your diligent effort begins to pay off. But there is a hitch. When you need support, you may have to ask for it—and when you do, it should be forthcoming. A crisis in personal relationships may escalate during the time of the Sun's Eclipse on the 12th. You're feeling less emotionally scattered and better integrated. It's still easy to be irritated by circumstances which just seem to serve as interference, but you're better equipped now to determine the best ways to attend to your priorities. However, if you're unhappy with your relationship, your work, or your personal habits, this is an excellent time to break out of old routines and to experiment with different possibilities. Remind yourself that you're only experimenting, and that you can make alterations at any time. After a while, the adjustments will seem more "normal," and in the end, you may have what you want!

November

Although you and your significant other may have a different opinion about your favorite decor or what to include on the menu, the fundamental integrity of your relationship is stronger now. The petty disparities matter very little in the long run, and you have better things to do than to concentrate on the silly arguments. You're feeling quite courageous about accomplishing the fulfillment of your desires, and that courage is very attractive. Even a stale relationship can be brought back to life, and your persistence works to your benefit whether you are in pursuit of a person or a goal. Your emotional juices are flowing, and where you may have blocked your own happiness, now you are eager to express and experience joy. This is a healing time, and that healing works on every level of your life. By addressing your needs for stability, security, and accomplishment, and integrating with your higher spiritual needs for unity with the essence of divine power, you are becoming whole.

December

An increasing passion for life awakens a deeper emotional sensibility, and can help you change your focus from external to internal. Then, integrating the inner and outer self makes sense: it's more efficient. You operate more effectively, and your life brings greater reward. It sounds so simple, you may wonder why you were ignoring it before, but you were just distracted by all those details and demands. Although you may be a person of few words, you'll discover that sharing your thoughts and ideas opens many doors. If you've ever hoped to create the manifestation of your dreams, this is the time when you may seem to be witness to the real magic of life. None of that illusory stuff, you're seeing results. No longer afraid to dream, this is your time to let the images and feelings flow through, while you direct them through your own self-expression. Ancient knowledge, timeless truth, real progress—you'll smile with satisfaction.

Aquarius Moon

D aring to be different is not just a choice for you: it is a necessity for your soul's survival. You thrive on those things which support your uniqueness, and are inspired by experiences which allow you to break out of the rut of convention and create your own path. You feel a strong kinship with the lot of humanity, but have little patience for ignorance or prejudice. You are drawn to unusual circumstances, ideas, and people, but may feel uncomfortable if you're forced to link your identity with theirs. After all, you would prefer a higher level of individuality, like being the trendsetter.

Your intuitive powers have been a strong ally since your childhood, and even when you strive to be purely logical, you always hear that small voice of truth whispering and urging you to explore and include other possibilities. You can develop a quality of genius: an exciting, but frequently lonely, place. Your friends and family may adore you, because you always possess an ability to accept them unconditionally. But you're difficult to tether. You abhor restraint, especially restraint of your mind, and will resent anyone who tries to force you to act against your own principles.

To protect your exceptional need for personal space, you frequently keep others out of your walls. Once someone gets inside, you may still hide away or escape to provinces undetected or unreachable when you need your freedom. When you do take one of your journeys into the realm of possibilities, you're difficult to reach, projecting a detachment which can feel cold to someone who wants your embrace. You don't intend to break their hearts, but sometimes do—just because you must follow that eternal urging to be, feel, and experience something beyond ordinary reality.

The Year at a Glance for Aquarius Moon

The underlying currents influenced by the slower moving outer planets provide an exceptional backdrop this year. You're entering a period of new-found freedom, punctuated most especially by the planet Uranus entering Aquarius, where it will remain for the next seven years. The influence of this transit upon your emotions and needs will remain throughout this time, although it will be more intense during specific periods, depending upon the exact degree of your Moon. This energy stimulates a period of personal revolution unlike any other. Old habitual responses which undermine or interfere with the fulfillment of your higher needs will be altogether too confining, and you'll be ready to release those attitudes or habits in favor of greater personal freedom. You may discover old enemies, like fear or guilt, as you make the effort to be free. But the light of truth shrinks their power, allowing you to break away.

The influence of the Solar and Lunar Eclipses adds emphasis to your needs to change, and may also stimulate your choice of a different approach to your personal relationships. The eclipse cycles work more like a gentle awareness prodding you to evaluate your feelings and discover the truth. The real impact of the eclipses will be felt in the fall, when Saturn's influence underscores theirs. Saturn's transit during 1996 begins a two-year cycle of emotional clarity. You may feel more aware of yourself, your life situation, and your longings than ever before. The contrasts drawn during this time will allow you to determine which elements of your life are supportive and which serve only to inhibit your progress.

If your Moon is in early degrees of Aquarius, you will experience profound changes this year which can range from moving, to pursuit of a different career path, to alterations in your family and personal relationships. At the core of these shifts is your need to become fully expressive. If your Moon is in later degrees of Aquarius, you'll begin to make more of those changes during the next few years. But the urging is there. You can feel that you are at the tip of the iceberg. That question, "If not now, when?" seems to drive many of your decisions.

Despite many of these modifications, you may feel quite stable from within your inner sanctum. If you've been unaware of your needs, your true yearnings, and your sense of purpose, this time can be quite disconcerting. However, if you have been developing that connection to your inner self, then you may feel that you're better prepared to stage your personal reformation. One thing is certain: you're definitely awakening!

Affirmation for the Year
My spirit soars on the wings of discovery!

January

Inspired to express your creativity as freely as possible, you may take more emotional risks just because they carry very little threat. Acting too quickly from the 8th to 13th can bring surprising results. It's important to be aware of the reasons for your need to change, since change for its own sake can be too costly in the long run. If you've been waiting for the right time to finally make a break, to complete something which had once been important to your growth, or to move into a new direction, then you may feel ready to take the leap. If you still need a little time to make preparations, you still have a strong window of opportunity next month, but you may find it easier to gain outside support by starting now. Confusing communication from the 20th to 26th can give you reason to re-evaluate before you act.

February

Despite a few snafus, you're still moving forward, although your sense of confidence may be diminished if you cannot seem to get your point across. More abstract forms of communication may say it best— like art or music, since words can be charged with emotional semantics or may be easily misunderstood early in the month. Your restless energy allows you very little time to just sit back and contemplate your options, because you may prefer to be in the midst of the whirlwind. But you are more sure of your values and priorities, and others may show their appreciation for what you have to offer after the 9th, adding their endorsement to your ideas or actions. Clarity in communication emerges after the 15th, when you'll also feel more like taking a fresh approach to any existing problems can lead to a positive conclusion. Avoid the pitfalls and delays of power struggles by listening and becoming more sensitive to the responses of others.

March

The pace of change slows considerably, and you may have to deal with or satisfy the conservative elements to continue your progress. Unfinished projects and the weight of lacking completion can inhibit your proficiency. Rather than feeling totally frustrated, you'll have a better experience if you acknowledge the limitations and find the best way to deal with them. Satisfying these requirements may assure that you'll be able to move ahead without these unnecessary burdens or concerns. Study the results of your previous actions and determine where the problems or difficulties reside. You may uncover some of your own resistance to change. After all, even though you may think of yourself as a mover and a shaker, you have your issues, too! Damage control accomplished, you'll be ready to initiate different choices and may be quite confident about pursuing a new direction after the 24th.

April

While others may be concerned about doing everything in the most proper manner, you're looking for the best avenue to accomplish the realization of your dreams during the Lunar Eclipse on the 4th. Friends and cohorts who share your enthusiasm help to further your aims, and you may also be more willing to add your blessing to a community effort or political endeavor which is close to your heart. Getting involved with others of like mind can be positively self-affirming now, and your special genius can also be used to great advantage in situations which need to change. Your relationships are more stabilized, but you can give the wrong impression if you make promises before you've had a chance to consider the nature of the obligation. Check into the details prior to making commitments, or you may have a real mess to untangle. Try to be more tolerant of those who cannot move with your speed.

May

Your futuristic thinking may seem out of place, and you may feel rather like an alien in some situations. To avoid sticking out like a sore thumb (unless that's your intention), try to temper your reactions, words, and manner from the 1st to 10th, since those who tend to respond from emotion rather than from thinking may completely misunderstand, and can be the source of unnecessary turmoil. You might be more comfortable in situations which allow you to observe, or if you're doing something others cannot understand, you may be safer in a circumstance which is private and more self-contained. Your own internal turmoil can also be more intense than you had realized, and if you've not been paying attention to your feelings, you may be surprised at the number of people who seem to be angry or upset with you. If that's the case, you could be dealing with strong projections of unresolved feelings on your part. Confront your own issues as honestly as possible.

June

You're still facing some of those same stubborn attitudes, whether your own or another's, through the 11th. But during the Full Moon on the 1st, you may gain a little objectivity about them, and may be willing to reconsider your position in order to achieve a better understanding. You're eager to make progress, and if you will put the efforts into achieving a peaceful solution, you'll be surprised at the results. The overall atmosphere around you changes by the 12th, when a profound sense of relief can emerge due to your awareness of the significance of your actions over the last few weeks. Even though you may feel more like gliding along, you're in an exceptional cycle to make headway in resolving personal crisis or in beginning a new relationship after the 12th. Your creative energy is growing at an exponential level, and you might prefer to funnel your power into something which has a more personal sense of satisfaction, than into something which requires the approval or support of others.

July

Relationships with others improve, particularly your relationships with the women in your life. If you've wanted to make romantic overtures, but haven't allowed yourself the luxury, you can experience some success in this arena, too. The most significant shifts occurring are those which happen within yourself now. A renewal of your values and your sense of self-worth prompts you to feel both an increase in confidence in yourself and a desire to experience even greater joy. The momentum of your actions and choices made now can carry you through some less harmonious periods which lie ahead. Be on the alert after the 15th for head to head conflicts with others whose opinions may be very different from your own, or those whose ideas do not include room to accommodate your unique style. You may feel like doing something shocking just for the heck of it. Just be sure you can afford to pay the price.

August

What you're dealing with now is more like the backlash of situations which you had thought were already settled. This does not have to be an extreme problem. In fact, some of the issues which arise may allow you to see your strengths and vulnerabilities more clearly. There are some adjustments required, and these need to be reached with an honest consensus rather than a resentful compromise. You may feel like you're doing more repair work than innovative development, yet your work may illuminate future possibilities. You're also experiencing some difficulty accepting emotional sensitivity and its influence on your thinking. You may be shocked to discover that you do have an emotional investment in something you thought you had chosen out of pure logical analysis. Even though you realize that you just "feel" what you feel, you have always liked to think you had your emotions reasonably contained.

September

After a rather soggy start, things get moving by the 7th, and you're on the path of exciting new discovery. But the object of your desire, however tantalizing, may be out of reach due to circumstances beyond your control. If your frustrations get the better of you, you can become too aggressive or painfully direct, creating alienation where you had hoped for conquest. Although the excitement and the ecstasy of the moment are sometimes worth any resulting pain, you're likely to decide that you're willing to go the distance because the payoff is just too delicious. Since you don't like to be confrontational and you may feel competitive, you can become rather defensive if your weaknesses get in your way. But you're more capable now of calling on your strengths to support you in your time of need.

October

You're still driven to accomplish your aims, but may have a different viewpoint on the best way to succeed. Social situations can provide an interesting backdrop to your sense of emotional wholeness, and you can be more open to allowing others to be a significant part of your life. You're pretty discriminating about your choices, though, and even if you have a great time at the party, you may still go home alone. Inspirational and creative ideas provide a great impetus from the 9th to 26th. This period also marks an improvement in communication, and may be a good time to investigate a concept by talking over your opinions and questions with others. The period near the Solar Eclipse on the 12th can encourage a resolution to conflicts. Even though you may have been confronting some unresolved turmoil from the past, another situation can become quite sticky near the Full Moon on the 26th.

November

You have the best of intentions, can be generous in your actions and attitudes, and still run into close-minded obstruction from others from the 1st to 13th. You must remember that you have choices about the way you respond. You can feel defeated, or you can step away from the situation and gain a different perspective before you try a different approach. You are likely to pursue a different focus after the 13th, anyway. However, if someone is holding a grudge, you may discover that you're the victim of their undermining attempts to damage your position. You may not want to make adjustments, and may have to do some fine-tuning in order to have the peace of mind you require. Family hassles may also need your direct involvement, so try to address the concerns which arise and deal with them as immediately as possible.

December

You can be accused of being too self-involved, especially if someone expects you to know what they want or to have an understanding of their preferences. Your choice may not be their cup of tea, so do a bit of investigating first. If you have specific desires, it's also a good idea for you to speak up and state your own favorites. You might just prefer to go off on your own and avoid the possibility of confrontation altogether, but you're likely to discover that if someone expects your presence, that it would be a problematic choice. Maintaining your personal space while accommodating for the others who share your life can work out. Your spontaneity works to your advantage from the New Moon on the 10th through the 18th. Quiet moments from the 22nd through 31st provide an excellent support for your creative needs, so design a few.

Pisces Moon

Your thirst, a seemingly unrelenting thirst, is for the nectar of the transcendent unity with the Source. You experience realms of consciousness which allow you to float beyond ordinary reality into the world of imagination, a place where all time and space are meaningless. Your sensibilities are highly charged, allowing you to feel things which are unnoticeable by most. You understand what the mystics say about life, eternity, and the power of mind. You fight an eternal battle between knowing when to let go and when to hold on.

Your sense of compassion allows you to forgive what others cannot tolerate. Life is a grand symphony, and you appreciate all the qualities of every instrument, although you prefer to hear the transcendent chords of harmony among all living things. When discord or the cries of suffering permeate the atmosphere, you may feel them deep within your soul. Learning to develop an emotional and spiritual filter is necessary, and maintaining your emotional boundaries is critical. Your imagination is immense, and like the artist who sees a landscape from another realm, you can respond emotionally to what you imagine just as powerfully as you respond to what your senses tell you.

When the pressures or pain of life grow too immense for you to handle, you are the master of escape. You need a home space which provides you with an ability to escape and rejuvenate before you face the harsh light of day again. You need to feel free and safe during your dream time, and function better if you have a quiet beginning to your day. Sometimes, that need to escape can drive you more intensely than the need to be in touch with the experience of reality. You are vulnerable to being drawn into illusions or can go too far inside yourself, where it is safe, warm, and where your reality is much more palatable and enchanting than that of the outside world. It is that thirst for unity driving you again. As you grow more aware, you are realizing that you are never truly separated from the Source. That separation, too, is an illusion.

The Year at a Glance for Pisces Moon

Self-confidence is easier to access now, with Jupiter's supportive transit to your Moon. And you may feel much more capable of creating life on your own terms and providing the qualities in your home environment which reflect your needs for beauty. In your dealings with the outside world, you can feel much safer. Saturn's transit through Pisces over the last two years, and continuing until April of this year, has taught you about your emotional strengths and limitations. If you've been paying attention, you've also learned the best ways to feel more stabilized. You've eliminated (or lost) many of the things you no longer need, and now it's time to fill the cornucopia with a new quality of abundance and joy.

Although Pluto's cycle in Sagittarius is just beginning, you're also aware of some deep changes which will be occurring over the next twelve years. This is such a long period that you may not feel that you must be in a hurry to deal with it—and you do not. The impact of Pluto's influence will be felt most intensely when it conjuncts your Moon, and that depends upon the degree of your Moon. If your Moon is from zero to five degrees of Pisces, you're feeling this influence now. Otherwise, it will occur later. This is not a comfortable cycle, because you have an undercurrent of discontent operating no matter what else is going on. The discontent arises because of your need to undergo a deep transformation in the way you fulfill your needs. You can make the changes, and you will reach the level of awareness you hope to achieve, because this energy provides a desire to get to the core of your inner self and become whole.

Your image of future possibilities is brighter during this year, although you might prefer to wait a while longer before springing it on the rest of the world. The Eclipse cycles help you get in touch with your inner self more clearly. If there is a crisis precipitated by the Eclipses, it is more than likely to occur in your need to release some of your illusions in favor of real possibilities. You're directing your dreams by making the adjustments which will allow you to accept what you can and cannot change, and focusing your vision in the direction of what you can achieve.

Affirmation for the Year
My heart is filled with joy and laughter!

January

Although you may feel a little out of step due to the influence of Mercury's retrograde, as long as you keep an open mind, this can be a reasonably creative period. Your methods of dealing with any crises or conflicts which arise may involve less confrontation and more acceptance, which does, after all, feel better to you anyway. You may find it difficult to tolerate outright disruption, and will definitely not enjoy situations where others are so self-absorbed that they create problems for everybody else. Once Venus enters Pisces on the 15th, you may feel much more comfortable enjoying your own preferences, although you can experience a situation which puts you face to face with something you just do not like from the 16th to 20th. Taking a direct approach may be the quickest way out. After the 20th, you are in a great position to draw things into your life which are more to your liking.

February

Experiencing a stronger sense of emotional stability, you may be willing to take on an important commitment or to reaffirm an existing one. At the very least, you're more aware of your deeper feelings, and can be more self-assured in your determinations of what you do or do not want and need. Relationships which are supportive of your needs grow stronger under these influences, while those which have outlived their usefulness may end. Your feelings about other life choices are also more marked, although you may be more comfortable making any changes concerning work or career after the 18th. If you run into a power struggle mid-month, you may have to defend your position, but you have all the ammunition necessary to be highly effective. If you're ready to break out of a situation, you're also be more likely to walk away than to stick around and wait for a miracle. You've reached your limit.

March

Stronger convictions accompanied by self-confidence allow you to make the changes or pursue directions which lead to the accomplishment of your dreams and the fulfillment of your desires. If there are blocks in your path, you're at the point of being able to deal with them on very real terms and can even move beyond them. Fears or anxieties are more easily addressed now. If you're faced with completing something important, you can reach your goal, but only if you stay focused on the task at hand. Distractions work to your disadvantage, and you're not likely to allow many of them. If family members or others try to project their fears onto you, you can either stand up to them, or know deep within yourself that you are right to fulfill your needs, and that their fears have more to do with their issues than with you.

April

There's a lot of juggling going on. You may be dealing with situations which seem to be a bit foreign, and there can be a number of possibilities which capture your interest. Keeping things in perspective is tricky, but will be necessary if you are to avoid undermining your own stability. You may also be challenged to accept or tolerate some things or situations which are not necessarily to your liking. Rather than feeling like a martyr, try to limit your exposure. If differences in values or taste create a dispute or a break in a relationship, you are more likely to allow the other person their preferences. If you also hold a resentment for the situation, you're not doing anybody any good. If you choose to postpone your own gratification, then accept that choice without mucking it up with all those complex emotions. You'll feel happier, and everybody else will be relieved, too.

May

Your patience is now paying off, and you may be much more satisfied with a firm decision or definitive position. If you want something, it's likely that you'll go after it. Although you may have been a quiet observer before, now you can be a formidable force! There's only one hitch—you may be very interested in the beginning, but after a while, you may decide that you're not so intrigued. So, if you're just exploring, say so. Admit it to yourself. Then everybody, including yourself, will be much happier if you decide to try another path. Maybe you are ready to make a commitment, and if so, you'll follow through. You have to give yourself room to grow, knowing that you are always evolving. That's keeping a commitment to yourself. And you, after all, are the one you live with all your life.

June

You're feeling like clearing a few things out of your closets, especially if they no longer suit your needs. Emotionally, you're doing the same thing. Although you may be more gentle in your approach early in the month, your thrust now is to prune away what is spent and open the way for continued growth. After the 12th, you may feel that you're the one being pruned, and though you can be flexible, you will not appreciate painful altercations. You can be quite vulnerable near the time of the New Moon on the 16th, and by respecting your vulnerabilities, you help to maintain your strength and emotional integrity. It may take a very direct confrontation to convince you that you need to make a few changes or to get away from a relationship or situation which is no longer working. Sometimes, the major break arises from confronting your own attitudes about the way you nourish yourself. You may have to eliminate a few of the things you consider "goodies" in order to experience the true richness you deserve.

July

You're ready for something different, and may enjoy the idea of an exotic situation better than the reality. It's like going to a tropical island, only to discover that there is no indoor plumbing. But you've always been one to make the best out of something, and if you do get yourself in a jam, you will be okay. If you're involved in creative pursuits, much of this energy will be felt with some dissatisfaction with your endeavors. And in relationships, you may feel that you're basically happy, but may wonder why you seem to be discontent. Paradox abounds, and you can feel squeezed in the middle. What may continue to emerge is a confrontation with so many of the limitations which put a damper on your enthusiasm. This is the time to find out what really triggers your anxieties, feelings of inadequacy, or fears of failure. Then, by making a direct effort to address these things, you will see your options in a different light.

August

Passions grow, and your longing to experience the consummation of your desires can drive you to be more positively assertive. Your actions and efforts make a significant impact on your experience of inner satisfaction, and instead of waiting for someone else to make the right move, you're more confident about taking the initiative. It's time to be comfortable with self-assertiveness, and to discover the sense of personal strength which accompanies it. Relationships are especially emphasized during the next two months, and now you are in the enviable position of being able to call most of the shots! There's a lot of power there, and you may find that you really like it. Your version of power has a kind face and a gentle touch. If you've dreamed of ecstasy but have never experienced it, perhaps it's time to see if it's really possible. Allow the intensity of your passions to work their magic during the Pisces Full Moon on the 28th.

September

The flow of emotional energy is more stirring from the 1st to 8th. After that time, you may feel that the demands or concerns of everyone else overwhelm your own needs or inclinations. At first, making the adjustments may be okay, but you may lose your patience if you feel ignored. You may have to make the effort to assure that you have time to satisfy your real needs and to enjoy your life. Pushing your concerns out of the way works to your disadvantage, because it leaves you feeling spent with less energy to share or give to others. You also need to examine your feelings about your work, and to make sure that you're in a situation which allows you to use your best talents and to feel that you are gaining acceptable rewards. If you are dissatisfied with either work or relationships, your first actions now need to be to determine any changes you may need to make in your own attitudes. Then you can address the outside influences.

October

Although this can be a period of warmth and nurturance, there may be some traps associated with these cycles. It is easy to do things to excess, especially if you are drawn to a relationship which is not really right for you. Even if your fascination involves a friendship, you may still be experiencing something which feels good at a certain level, but your sense of discretion can be impaired. The difficulty arises from the fact that you really need to be consumed by the sweetness, and because of that, you can ignore the problems. You'll have an underlying feeling of agitation with yourself, and you can be irritable at strong times. Use any emerging irritability as a sign that something may be wrong, and that you're just not seeing it very clearly. Then, once you determine the problem, you can make the necessary adjustments in your attitudes or attachments and experience a more satisfying result.

November

If you've been waiting patiently for something to happen, and it's just not been forthcoming, then you will probably feel that your patience has been exhausted. You're eager to get things moving, and a restless energy keeps you from falling into complacency. You can be more direct about expressing your feelings and pursuing your goals, but you may also be less sensitive to the needs of others and can jump into a situation prematurely. If you are insecure in a relationship, it will take very little to awaken your feelings of jealousy if someone or something arrives on the scene to tempt your partner. Before you decide that the jealousy is useless, use it to dig into your own feelings of dissatisfaction. Perhaps you have not been making the most of your personal resources, or you've been ignoring what you really want. This is the right time to get everything out on the table and deal with it directly in a responsible manner.

December

Loving relationships improve, and your ability to express your feelings is strengthened. You can still seem to be confrontational, and may be short-fused, but you have a better sense of what you want. Communication is easier after the 4th, and even during Mercury's retrograde cycle from the 23rd to 31st you're likely to have a good ability to reach out to others. You're experiencing a period of positive self confirmation, and may be able to use your expanded awareness of the bigger picture to help someone else understand his or her own possibilities or options. Even though it's important to take care of your personal needs, you are more focused on those around you, and you can keep a good balance between the two. Inviting others to share in your good fortune feels great, since you're experiencing a true joy which is most complete when it is shared with those you love.

Directory
of
Products
&
Services

THE PRAYER SYSTEM THAT NEVER FAILS

Almost all of us at some time or another have prayed to God when in need – only to later feel disappointed that our prayers were unanswered. Either God isn't there or He is simply too busy to attend to our needs – this is the impression we are left with. Only desperation drives us to prayer: when all else has failed and we are at the end of our tether – only then do most of us turn to prayer: and then we pray with that sinking feeling that our supplication will not be heard.

Also at the back of our minds is the lingering impression that prayers were only answered in Jesus' time, a time when miracles were commonplace. All the great miraculous events recorded in the Bible happened so long ago – in a time when man seemed closer to God, life was far simpler, and God's prophets walked amongst us.

BUT THE REAL REASON WHY OUR PRAYERS ARE NOT ANSWERED IS THAT WE DO NOT KNOW HO TO PRAY. THE PLAIN FACT IS THAT *OUR PRAYERS NEVER REACHED GOD IN THE FIRST PLACE.*

What you should know is that THE SAME GOD WHO MADE MIRACLES HAPPEN 2000 YEARS AGO CAN – AND DOES – MAKE MIRACLES HAPPEN TODAY: BUT *ONLY IN RESPONSE TO THOSE WHO KNOW HOW TO CONTACT HIM.*

Now – for the very first time, in absolutely simple and plain English – the mysteries of the Gospels have been unveiled to reveal *JESUS' OWN SYSTEM OF ANSWERED PRAYER.*

THE PLAIN FACT IS THAT ONCE YOU KNOW THE RIGHT WAY OF PRAYING YOU WILL ALWAYS *RECEIVE A GUARANTEED ANSWER FROM GOD.*

All this is revealed in the new book 'THE PRAYER SYSTEM THAT NEVER FAILS' – a book which itself is the result of prayer! Having discovered the hidden secrets of Successful Prayer, the author Dr. D.J. Lightfoot prayed to be directed to a publisher who would publish his findings. We are happy he was guided to us because we were struck by the power and simplicity of what he wrote, and feel privileged to be the ones to make it public.

THIS IS NO ORDINARY BOOK ABOUT PRAYER. Unlike other books it shows how to acquire that rarest quality which most of us lack: FAITH – the faith to know that our prayers will be answered.

This remarkable book reveals how the PUREST AND DEEPEST FAITH can be yours – effortlessly! – as a gift from God!

Lack of faith is the greatest single stumbling block to the answering of prayer – this book provides you with the immediate removal of that obstacle. You will feel blessed and renewed as you read this book – not because of any air of heavenliness about it, but BECAUSE OF THE SHEER COMPELLING LOGIC OF THE AUTHOR'S REVELATIONS.

YOU WILL FEEL DEEP IN YOUR HEART ONCE YOU READ THIS BOOK THAT FOR THE FIRST TIME IN YOUR LIFE YOU *KNOW* THAT YOUR PRAYERS WILL BE HEARD AND ANSWERED!

This book is called 'THE PRAYER SYSTEM THAT NEVER FAILS' precisely because it contains that. WITHIN ITS PAGES ARE THE SECRETS OF A LIFE FILLED WITH BLESSEDNESS AND GOOD FORTUNE ... A LIFE FREE OF SORROW AND SUFFERING!

Nor is this a book of rituals or impossible-to-follow instructions. It shows how to pray anywhere and any time: and most importantly of all: HOW YOU CAN BE TOTALLY ASSURED OF AN ANSWER TO YOUR PRAYERS.

This book can be used by persons of all faiths. The principles in it are universal and apply just as readily to Muslims, Hindus and Jews as they do to Christians.

And neither is it necessary to be a church-goer or a religious person in order to get your prayers answered. *ANYONE CAN RECEIVE AN ANSWER TO THEIR PRAYERS ONCE THEY APPLY THE SECRETS IN THIS BOOK.*

But why should anyone turn to prayer at all, especially if they are not religious? It is important to distinguish between the prayer of the religious and the prayer of the average person who seeks the solution to a pressing problem. It is ironic that the religious person can pray all his life and never receive an answer to his prayers. The fact is that he is praying the wrong way, that is the 'usual' way. But the person who hasn't seen the inside of a church or mosque for ten years will obtain a definite, positive result if he prays in the manner described in this book.

And what can one pray for? WHATEVER YOUR NEED YOU CAN PRAY FOR IT – AND WITH THIS BOOK'S SYSTEM YOU CAN FEEL ABSOLUTELY CERTAIN OF A POSITIVE ANSWER FORM GOD! Because God responds to only one kind of prayer – as Dr. Lightfoot demonstrates from the Bible and his own and the personal experiences of others – and *THAT KIND OF PRAYER HE ALWAYS ANSWERS!*

God wants you to be financially secure and happy – and will give abundantly ONCE YOU KNOW THE GUARANTEED FORMULA FOR REACHING HIS HEART!

He can give you true love and friendship ... and will give abundantly. ONCE YOU KNOW THE GUARANTEED FORMULA FOR REACHING HIS HEART!

He can give you true love and friendship ... an adoring mate ... a successful marriage ... an end to bitterness between yourself and another. If your partner has deserted you for another God can reconcile you– once you know the right way to pray!

God can help you in a difficult legal situation – THE SAME MIRACLES THAT GOD MADE HAPPEN 2000 YEARS AGO CAN BE MADE TO HAPPEN (FOR YOU) AGAIN *RIGHT NOW!*

God can protect you from physical danger. He can immobilize your enemies and tormenters. He can make those of evil intent towards you soften their hearts.

If you are in financial difficulty turn to God with a prayer., follow this book's simple formula, and you will experience not only immediate peace but RECEIVE DIVINE HELP in solving your problems!

But the most miraculous of all are the modern duplications of what Jesus made happen 2000 years ago: the walking of the lame, sight restored to the blind, etc.

THERE IS VIRTUALLY NO ILLNESS OR DISABILITY THAT CAN NOT RESPOND TO THE SCIENTIFIC PRAYER SYSTEM OF JESUS. In some cases where there is no hope only prayer can effect relief ... and sometimes a TOTAL CURE. Advertising restrictions prevent us from describing prayer's efficacy in this way., but the book explains all. NOBODY WITH A SERIOUS HEALTH PROBLEM SHOULD IN OUR VIEW, OVERLOOK THE POSSIBILITIES OFFERED BY PRAYER, as revealed in this book.

So we urge you to reconsider the value of prayer – in the light of this book's revelations. Prayer, as originally revealed in the Bible, DOES work, but only for those who understand the mystery behind Jesus' parables. The mystery is de-mystified in plain, direct English in this book. The secrets disguised by Jesus' sayings are revealed to unfold the greatest spiritual and material potential for every man, woman and child. NOTHING IS UNATTAINABLE THROUGH THE MIGHTY POWER OF THIS PRAYER SYSTEM.

This book explains step by step the vital ingredients required for successful prayer, showing when and how to pray: how to receive faith: and the ways in which God will answer you. The book's instructions culminate in one page of Nine Master Secrets which reveal at a glance everything you need to know in order to always get your prayers answered. But there is more: In addition to 'THE PRAYER SYSTEM THAT NEVER FAILS' this book also contains the entire text of Dr. Lightfoot's first work "THE POWER STRUGGLE' which is a striking account of the age-old conflict between good and evil, and how this cosmic struggle is manifesting itself on planet Earth today.

The dream of most people is to have God on their side. Now at last this can be so for you. To order your copy of this important book send just $14.95.

Send money order or personal check made payable to Finbarr for £14.95 to: **Finbarr International, 16 Turketel Rd., Folkestone CT20 2PA, England.** Price includes express air mail: delivery guaranteed within 14 days. We have been shipping books worldwide since 1946: for our complete catalogue of books add $1. Readers in England send £6.

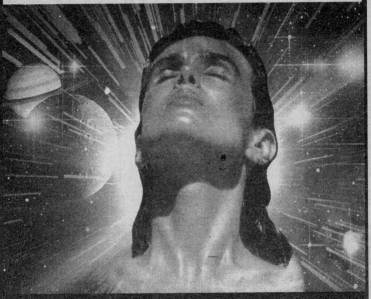

WALTER MERCADO
"THE MOST POWERFUL PSYCHIC IN THE WORLD"
Talk to one of Walter's exclusive psychics!
As celebrity host of "Walter and The Stars", seen by millions of people on worldwide Hispanic television, Walter Mercado is now reaching out to find new friends. Well known for his astrological and psychic forecasts and for helping many thousands of people see the "road ahead" his exclusive astrologers and psychics are now available to help answer questions about your life and your future. Walter has always felt that nobody should fear not having enough Health, Love, Money or Friends and vowed to help everyone achieve their goal of finding a rich fulfilling life. Find out about your future and help resolve your personal problems now!
25 years of experience!
CALL NOW!
1-900-740-1343
$3.99 per minute
Entertainment for adults over 18
JSA CORP. MIAMI, FL

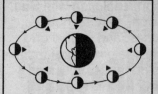

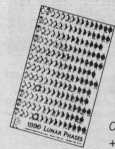

Classifieds

Llewellyn's Computerized Astrological Services

Llewellyn has been a leading authority in astrological chart readings for more than 30 years. We feature a wide variety of readings with the intent to satisfy the needs of any astrological enthusiast. Our goal is to give you the best possible service so that you can achieve your goals and live your life successfully. **Be sure to give accurate and complete birth data on the order form. This includes exact time (A.M. or P.M.), date, year, city, county and country of birth. Note: Noon will be used as your birthtime if you don't provide an exact time. Check your birth certificate for this information! Llewellyn will not be responsible for mistakes made by you.** An order form follows these listings.

SIMPLE NATAL CHART
Learn the locations of your midpoints and aspects, elements, and more. Discover your planets and house cusps, retrogrades, and other valuable data necessary to make a complete interpretation. Matrix Software programs and designs The Simple Natal Chart printout.
APS03-119 . . . . $5.00

PERSONALITY PROFILE
Our most popular reading also makes the perfect gift! This 10-part profile depicts your "natal imprint" and how the planets mark your destiny. Examine emotional needs and inner feelings. Explore your imagination and read about your general characteristics and life patterns.
APS03-503 . . . . $20.00

LIFE PROGRESSION
Progressions are a special system astrologers use to map how the "natal you" develops through specified periods of your present and future life. With this report you can discover the "now you!" This incredible reading covers a year's time and is designed to complement the Personality Profile Reading. **Specify present residence.**
APS03-507 . . . .$20.00

COMPATIBILITY PROFILE
Are you compatible with your lover, spouse, friend, or business partner? Find out with this in-depth look at each person's approach to the relationship. Evaluate goals, values, potential conflicts. This service includes planetary placements for both individuals, so send birth data for both. **Indicate each person's gender and the type of relationship involved** (romance, business, etc.).
APS03-504 . . . . .30.00

PERSONAL RELATIONSHIP INTERPRETATION

If you've just called it quits on one relationship and know you need to understand more about yourself before testing the waters again, then this is the report for you! This reading will tell you how you approach relationships in general, what kind of people you look for and what kind of people might rub you the wrong way. Important for anyone!

APS03-506 . . . .$20.00

TRANSIT REPORT

Keep abreast of positive trends and challenging periods in your life. Transits are the relationships between the planets today and their positions at your birth. They are an invaluable timing and decision-making aid. This report starts on the first day of the month, devotes a paragraph to each of your transit aspects and their effective dates. *Be sure to specify present residence for all getting this report!*

APS03-500 – 3-month report $12.00
APS03-501 – 6-month report $20.00
APS03-502 – 1-year report $30.00

BIORHYTHM REPORT

Some days you have unlimited energy, then the next day you feel sluggish and awkward. These cycles are called biorhythms. This individual report accurately maps your daily biorhythms and thoroughly discusses each day. Now you can plan your days to the fullest!

APS03-515 – 3-month report $12.00
APS03-516 – 6-month report $18.00
APS03-517 – 1-year report $25.00

TAROT READING

Find out what the cards have in store for you with this 12-page report that features a 10-card "Celtic Cross" spread shuffled and selected especially for you. For every card that turns up there is a detailed corresponding explanation of what each means for you. Order this tarot reading today! *Indicate the number of shuffles you want.*

APS03-120 . . . .$10.00

LUCKY LOTTO REPORT (State Lottery Report)

Do you play the state lotteries? This report will determine your luckiest sequence of numbers for each day based on specific planets, degrees, and other indicators in your own chart. Give your full birth data and middle name. *Tell us how many numbers your state lottery requires in sequence, and the highest possible numeral. Indicate the month you want to start.*

APS03-512 – 3-month report $10.00
APS03-513 – 6-month report $15.00
APS03-514 – 1-year report $25.00

NUMEROLOGY REPORT

Find out which numbers are right for you with this insightful report. This report uses an ancient form of numerology invented by Pythagoras to determine the significant numbers in your life. Using both your name and date of birth, this report will calculate those numbers that stand out as yours. With these numbers, you can tell when the important periods of your life will occur. *Please indicate your full birth name.*

APS03-508 – 3-month report $12.00
APS03-509 – 6-month report $18.00
APS03-510 – 1-year report $25.00

ULTIMATE ASTRO-PROFILE

More than 40 pages of insightful descriptions of your qualities and talents. Read about your burn rate (thirst for change). Explore your personal patterns (inside and outside). The Astro-Profile doesn't repeat what you've already learned from other personality profiles, but considers the natal influence of the lunar nodes, plus much more.
APS03-505 ....$40.00

ASTROLOGICAL SERVICES ORDER FORM

SERVICE NAME & NUMBER_____

_____

Provide the following data on all persons receiving a service:

1ST PERSON'S FULL NAME, including current middle & last name(s)

_____

Birthplace (city, county, state, country) _____

_____

Birthtime _____ ☐ A.M. ☐ P.M. Month _____ Day _____ Year _____

2ND PERSON'S FULL NAME (if ordering for more than one person)

_____

Birthplace (city, county, state, country) _____

_____

Birthtime _____ ☐ A.M. ☐ P.M. Month _____ Day _____ Year _____

BILLING INFORMATION

Name _____

Address _____

_____

City _____ State _____ Zip _____

Country _____ Day phone: _____

Make check or money order payable to Llewellyn Publications, or charge it!
Check one: ☐ Visa ☐ MasterCard ☐ American Express

Acct. No. _____ Exp. Date _____

Cardholder Signature _____

Mail this form and payment to:

LLEWELLYN'S PERSONAL SERVICES
P.O. BOX 64383-K912 • ST. PAUL, MN 55164-0383

Allow 4-6 weeks for delivery.

SUPER DISCOUNTS ON
LLEWELLYN DATEBOOKS AND CALENDARS!

Llewellyn offers several ways to save money on our almanacs and calendars. With a four-year subscription you receive your books as soon as they are published. The price remains the same for four years even if there is a price increase! Llewellyn pays postage and handling. *Buy any 2 subscriptions and take $2 off! Buy 3 and take $3 off! Buy 4 and take an additional $5 off the cost!*

Subscriptions (4 years, 1997-2000) Available on these annuals only:

❐ Astrological Calendar	$48.00
❐ Sun Sign Book	$27.80
❐ Moon Sign Book	$27.80
❐ Daily Planetary Guide	$39.80
❐ Organic Gardening Almanac	$27.80

Dozen Orders: 40% Off

Order *by the dozen* and save 40%! Sell them to your friends or give them as gifts. Llewellyn pays all postage and handling on dozen orders.

1996	1997		
❐	❐	Astrological Calendar	$86.40
❐	❐	Sun Sign Book	$50.04
❐	❐	Moon Sign Book	$50.04
❐	❐	Daily Planetary Guide	$71.64
❐	❐	Magical Almanac	$50.04
❐	❐	Organic Gardening Almanac	$50.04
❐		Myths of the Gods & Goddesses Calendar	$86.40
❐		Pocket Planner: Daily Ephemeris & Aspectarian	$57.24

Individual Copies of Llewellyn Almanacs and Calendars

When ordering individual copies, include $4 postage for orders $15 & under and $5 for orders over $15. Llewellyn pays postage for all orders over $100.

1996	1997		
❐	❐	Astrological Calendar	$12.00
❐	❐	Sun Sign Book	$6.95
❐	❐	Moon Sign Book	$6.95
❐	❐	Daily Planetary Guide	$9.95
❐	❐	Magical Almanac	$6.95
❐	❐	Organic Gardening Almanac	$6.95
❐		Myths of the Gods & Goddesses Calendar	$12.00
❐		Pocket Planner: Daily Ephemeris & Aspectarian	$7.95

PLEASE USE ORDER FORM ON LAST PAGE.

LLEWELLYN ORDER FORM

Llewellyn Publications
P.O. Box 64383-K912, St. Paul, MN 55164-0383

You may use this form to order any of the Llewellyn books or services listed in this publication.

GIVE TITLE OF BOOK, AUTHOR OF BOOK, ORDER NUMBER AND PRICE.

_____

_____

_____

_____

_____

Shipping and Handling: Include $4 for orders $15 & under; $5 for orders over $15. Llewellyn pays postage for all orders over $100. We ship UPS when possible. Please give street address (UPS cannot deliver to P.O. Boxes). **Now Available — Second Day Air! Cost is $8/one book; add $1 for each additional book.**

Credit Card Orders: In the U.S. and Canada call 1-800-THE-MOON. In Minnesota call 612-291-1970. Or, send credit card order by mail. Any questions can be directed to customer service 612-291-1970.

❏ VISA ❏ MasterCard ❏ American Express ❏ Check/M.O.

Account No. _____

Expiration Date _____ Phone _____

Cardholder Signature _____

Name_____

Address_____

City _____

State _____ Zip _____

MN residents add 7% sales tax to cost of book(s)